KOREN SHADMI
THE ABADDON

Z2 Comics
Publisher: Josh Frankel

Copyright: Koren Shadmi
This edition copyright Z2 Comics Inc
All Rights Reserved

First Edition / November 2015

Z2 Comics
336 East 61st Suite AB New York, New York 10065

PART ONE

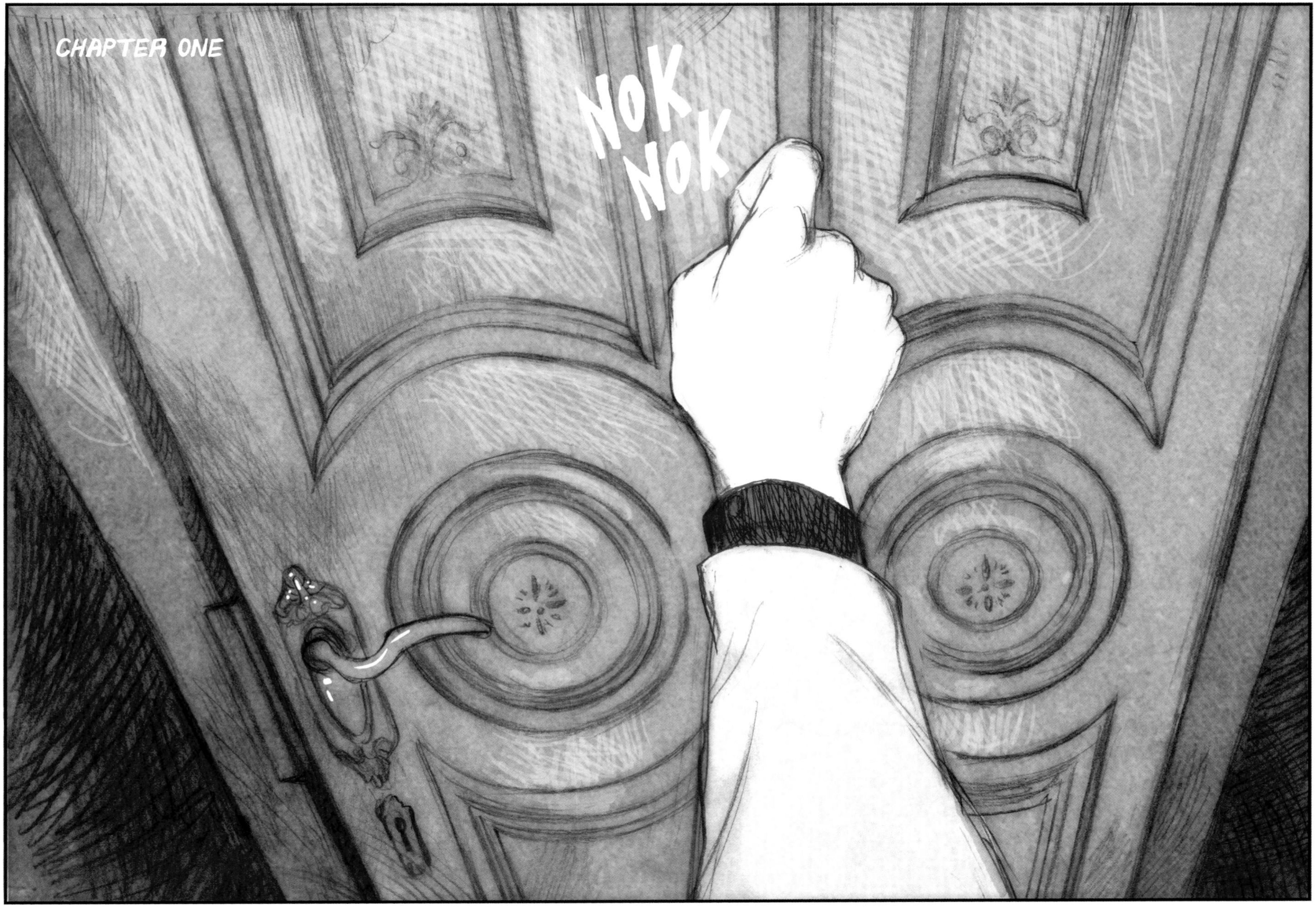
CHAPTER ONE
NOK NOK

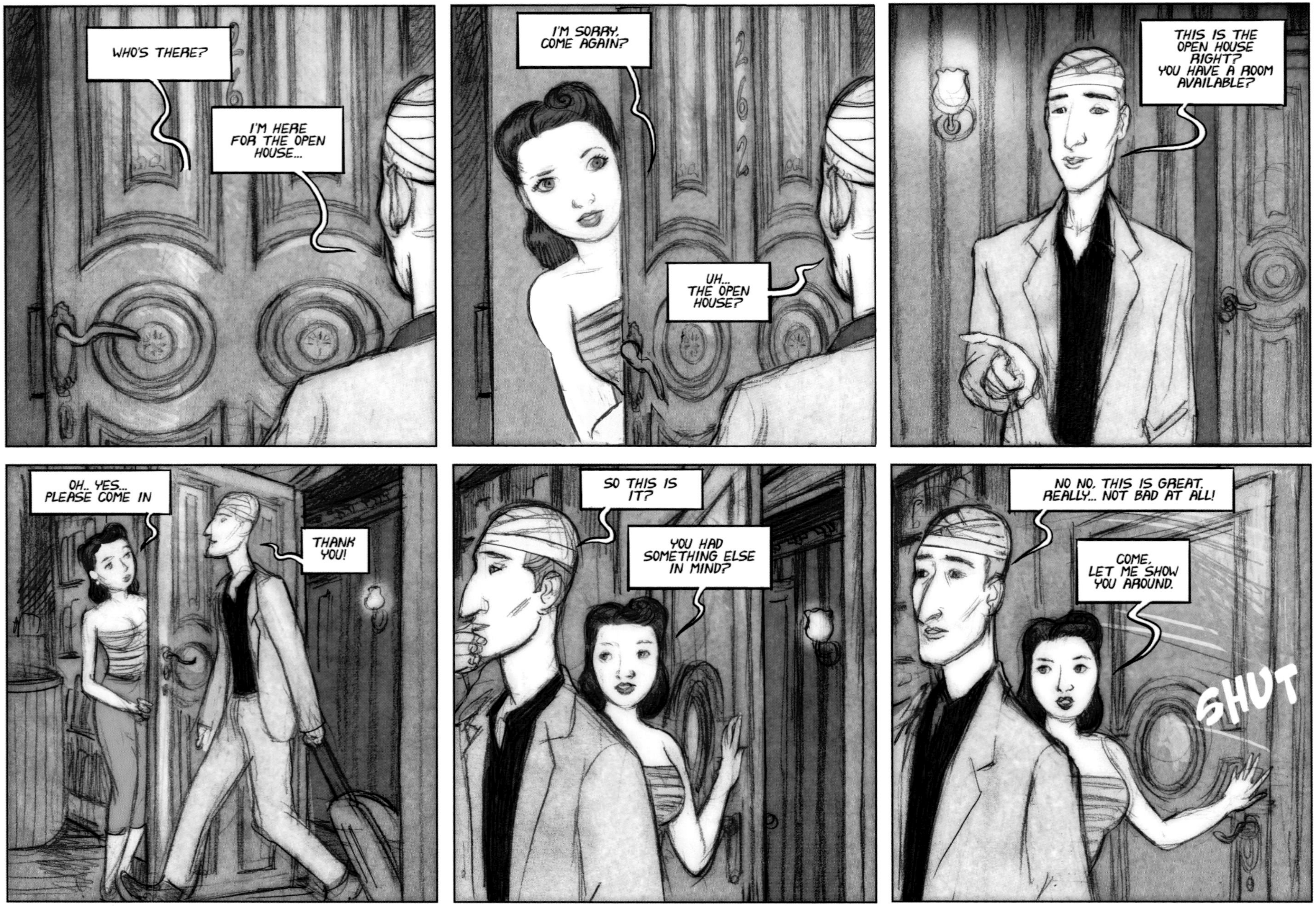
WHO'S THERE?
I'M HERE FOR THE OPEN HOUSE...
I'M SORRY, COME AGAIN?
UH... THE OPEN HOUSE?
THIS IS THE OPEN HOUSE RIGHT? YOU HAVE A ROOM AVAILABLE?
OH.. YES... PLEASE COME IN
THANK YOU!
SO THIS IS IT?
YOU HAD SOMETHING ELSE IN MIND?
NO NO. THIS IS GREAT. REALLY... NOT BAD AT ALL!
COME, LET ME SHOW YOU AROUND.
SHUT

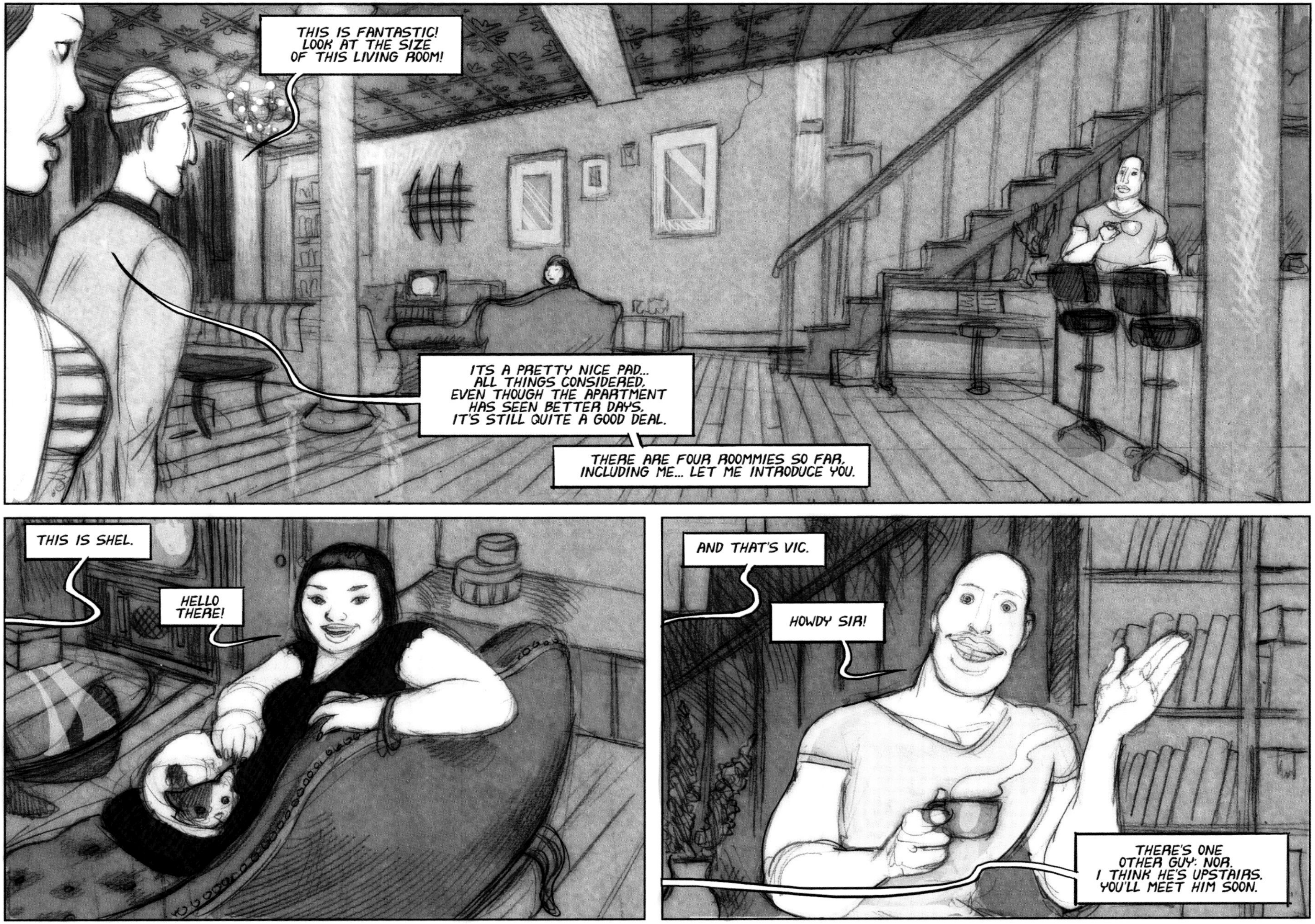
THIS IS FANTASTIC! LOOK AT THE SIZE OF THIS LIVING ROOM!
ITS A PRETTY NICE PAD... ALL THINGS CONSIDERED. EVEN THOUGH THE APARTMENT HAS SEEN BETTER DAYS, IT'S STILL QUITE A GOOD DEAL.
THERE ARE FOUR ROOMMIES SO FAR, INCLUDING ME... LET ME INTRODUCE YOU.
THIS IS SHEL.
HELLO THERE!
AND THAT'S VIC.
HOWDY SIR!
THERE'S ONE OTHER GUY: NOR. I THINK HE'S UPSTAIRS. YOU'LL MEET HIM SOON.

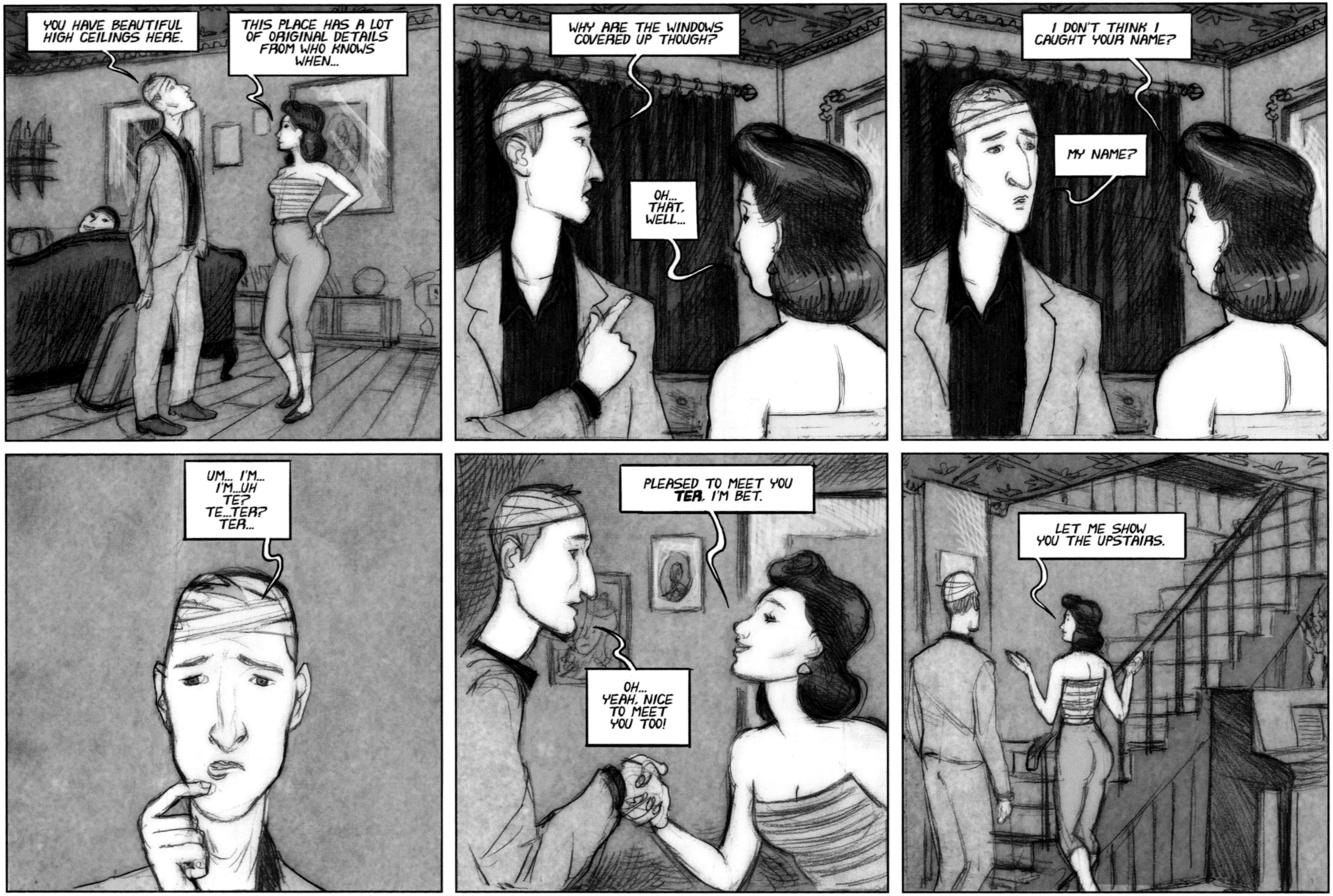
YOU HAVE BEAUTIFUL HIGH CEILINGS HERE.
THIS PLACE HAS A LOT OF ORIGINAL DETAILS FROM WHO KNOWS WHEN...
WHY ARE THE WINDOWS COVERED UP THOUGH?
OH... THAT, WELL...
I DON'T THINK I CAUGHT YOUR NAME?
MY NAME?
UM... I'M... I'M...UH TE? TE...TER? TER...
PLEASED TO MEET YOU **TER**, I'M BET.
OH... YEAH, NICE TO MEET YOU TOO!
LET ME SHOW YOU THE UPSTAIRS.

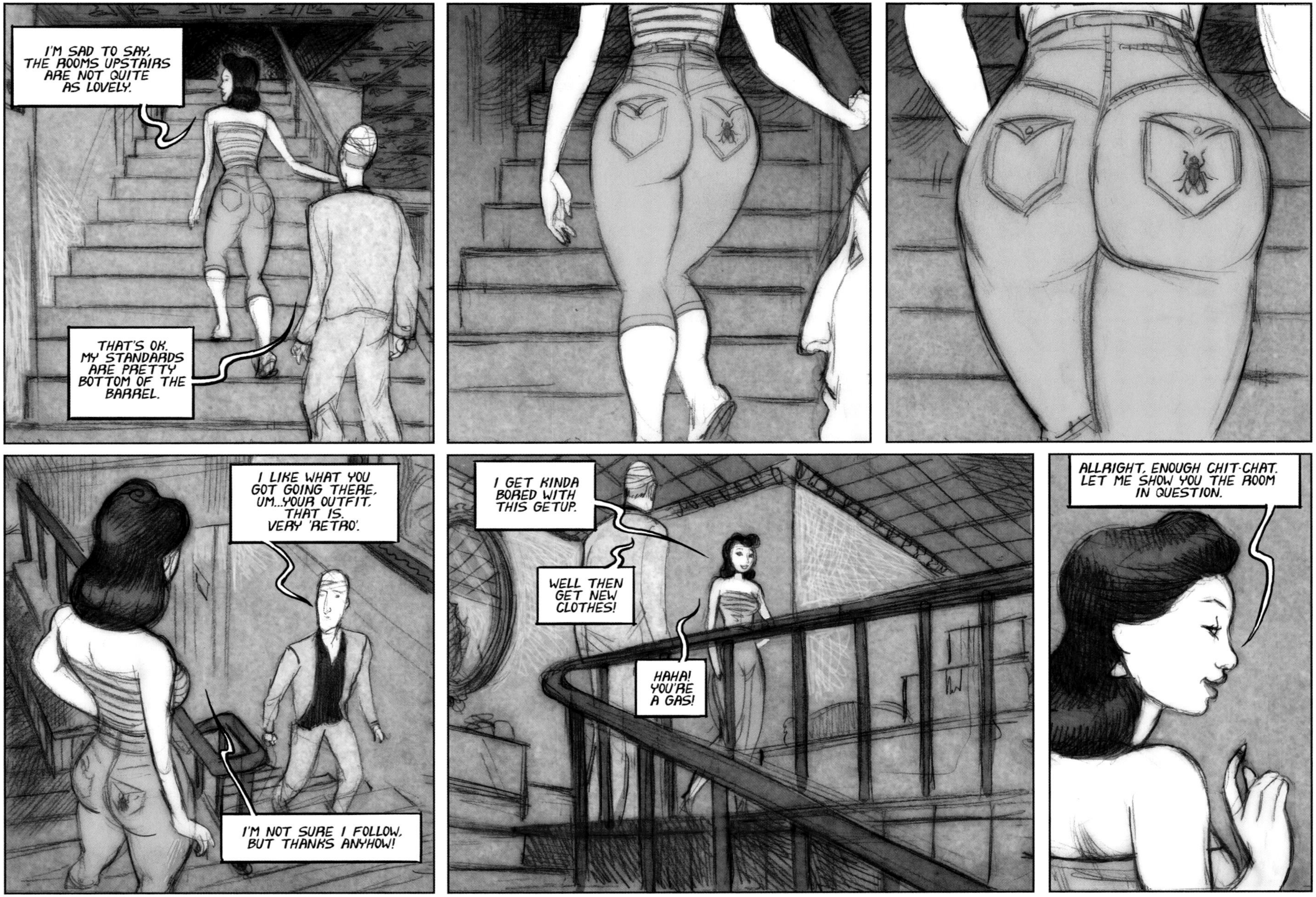
I'M SAD TO SAY, THE ROOMS UPSTAIRS ARE NOT QUITE AS LOVELY.
THAT'S OK. MY STANDARDS ARE PRETTY BOTTOM OF THE BARREL.
I LIKE WHAT YOU GOT GOING THERE, UM...YOUR OUTFIT, THAT IS. VERY 'RETRO'.
I'M NOT SURE I FOLLOW, BUT THANKS ANYHOW!
I GET KINDA BORED WITH THIS GETUP.
WELL THEN GET NEW CLOTHES!
HAHA! YOU'RE A GAS!
ALLRIGHT, ENOUGH CHIT-CHAT. LET ME SHOW YOU THE ROOM IN QUESTION.

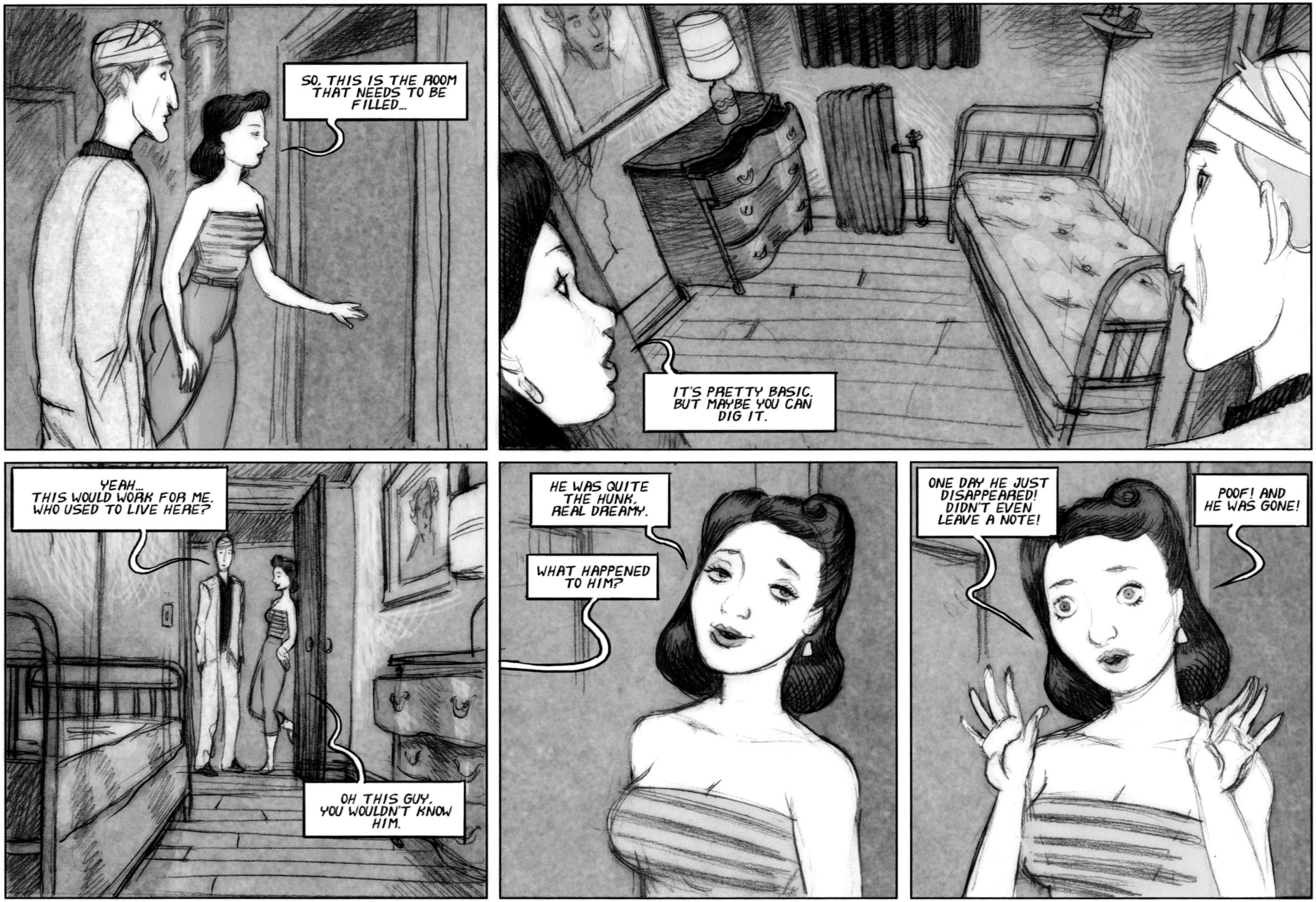
SO, THIS IS THE ROOM THAT NEEDS TO BE FILLED...
IT'S PRETTY BASIC. BUT MAYBE YOU CAN DIG IT.
YEAH... THIS WOULD WORK FOR ME. WHO USED TO LIVE HERE?
OH THIS GUY. YOU WOULDN'T KNOW HIM.
HE WAS QUITE THE HUNK. REAL DREAMY.
WHAT HAPPENED TO HIM?
ONE DAY HE JUST DISAPPEARED! DIDN'T EVEN LEAVE A NOTE!
POOF! AND HE WAS GONE!

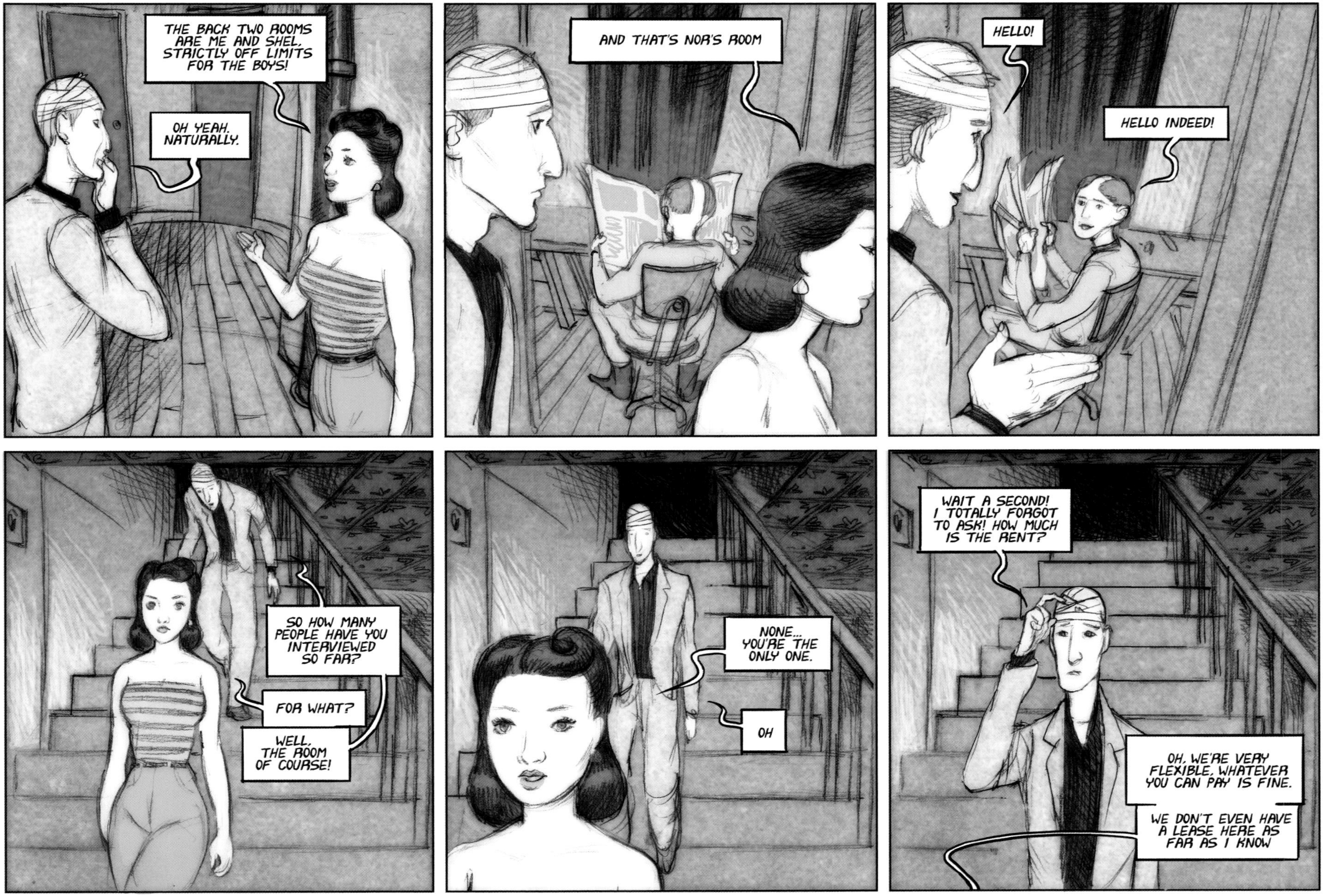

THE BACK TWO ROOMS ARE ME AND SHEL. STRICTLY OFF LIMITS FOR THE BOYS!
OH YEAH. NATURALLY.
AND THAT'S NOR'S ROOM
HELLO!
HELLO INDEED!
SO HOW MANY PEOPLE HAVE YOU INTERVIEWED SO FAR?
FOR WHAT?
WELL, THE ROOM OF COURSE!
NONE... YOU'RE THE ONLY ONE.
OH
WAIT A SECOND! I TOTALLY FORGOT TO ASK! HOW MUCH IS THE RENT?
OH, WE'RE VERY FLEXIBLE. WHATEVER YOU CAN PAY IS FINE.
WE DON'T EVEN HAVE A LEASE HERE AS FAR AS I KNOW

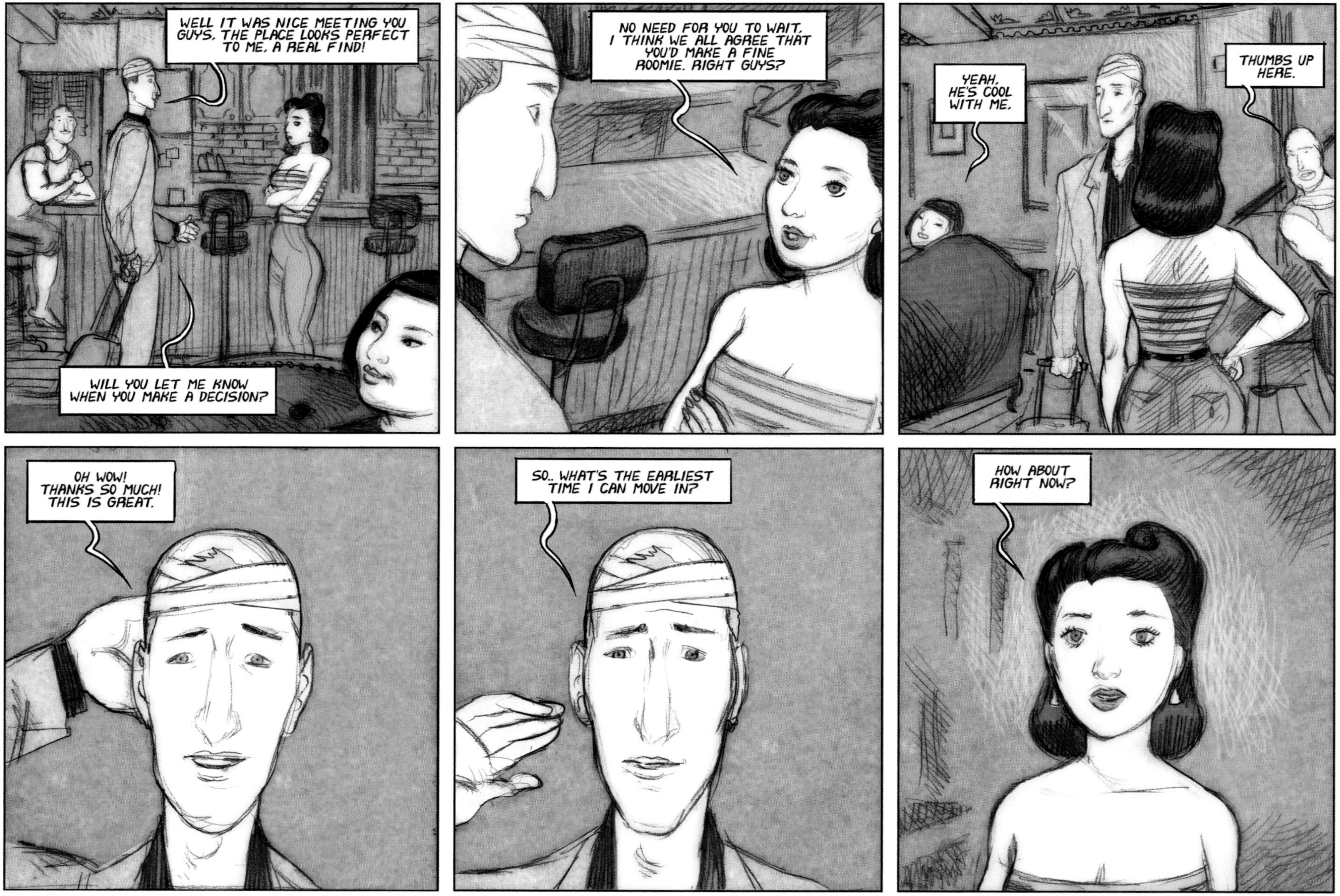
WELL IT WAS NICE MEETING YOU GUYS, THE PLACE LOOKS PERFECT TO ME, A REAL FIND!
WILL YOU LET ME KNOW WHEN YOU MAKE A DECISION?
NO NEED FOR YOU TO WAIT, I THINK WE ALL AGREE THAT YOU'D MAKE A FINE ROOMIE. RIGHT GUYS?
YEAH, HE'S COOL WITH ME.
THUMBS UP HERE.
OH WOW! THANKS SO MUCH! THIS IS GREAT.
SO.. WHAT'S THE EARLIEST TIME I CAN MOVE IN?
HOW ABOUT RIGHT NOW?

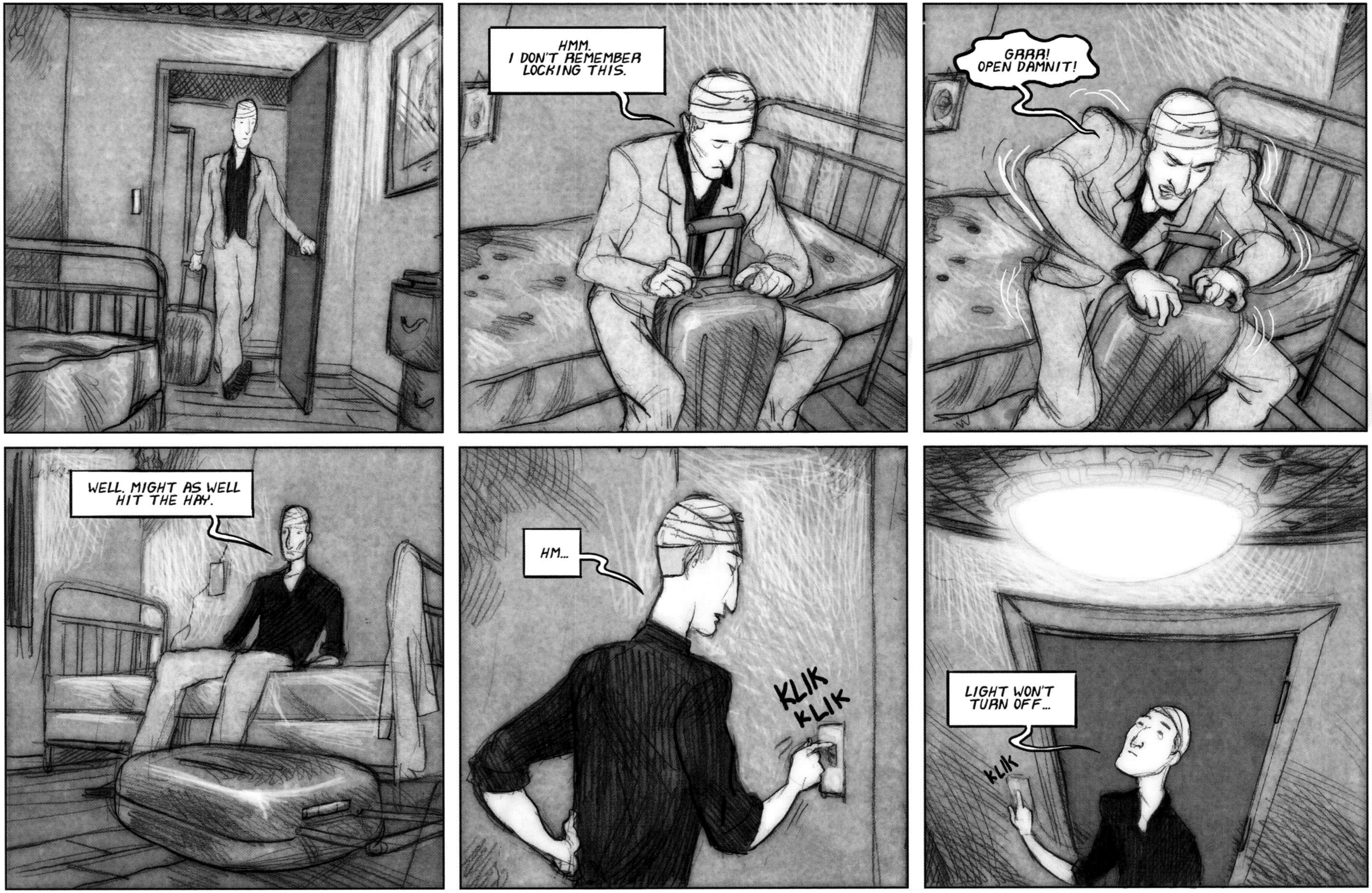
HMM.
I DON'T REMEMBER
LOCKING THIS.
GRRR!
OPEN DAMNIT!
WELL. MIGHT AS WELL
HIT THE HAY.
HM...
KLIK
KLIK
LIGHT WON'T
TURN OFF...
KLIK

ALLRIGHT MAGGOTS!
COCK YOUR WEAPONS!

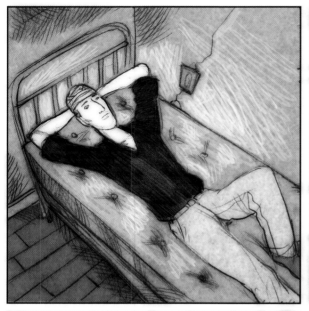

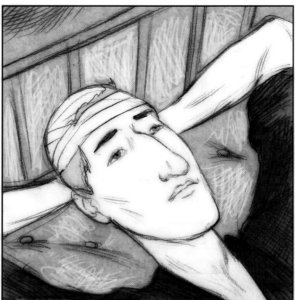

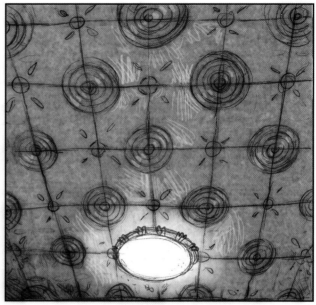

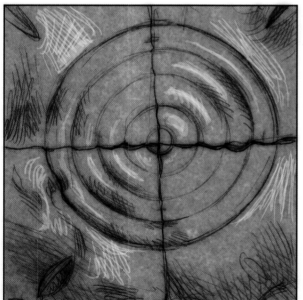

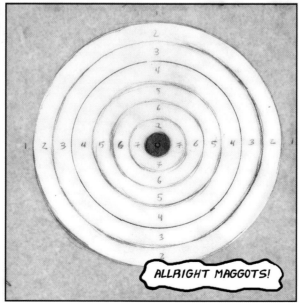

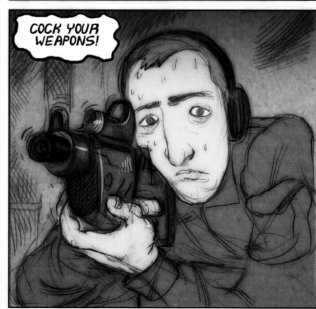

NOW HOLD IT THERE... LOOK AT YOUR TARGETS! FOCUS!
PRIVATE! WHAT THE HELL DO YOU THINK YOU'RE DOING?
AIMING?
IS THAT HOW WE TAUGHT YOU TO SHOOT? LAYING THERE LIKE A PRINCESS?
SPREAD YOUR LEGS PRIVATE!
...NOW LOOK STRAIGHT AT THAT TARGET. LOOK AT IT LIKE YOUR LIFE DEPENDS ON IT!
HOLD YOUR GUN STEADY PRIVATE.
NOW...
SHOOT.

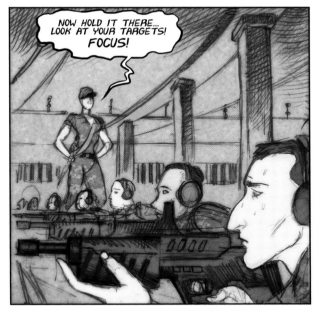

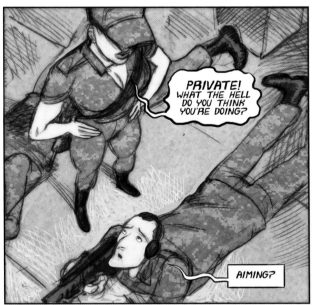

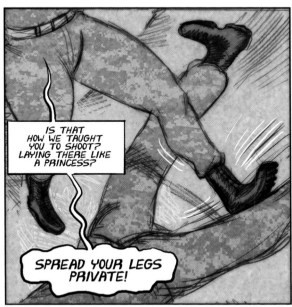

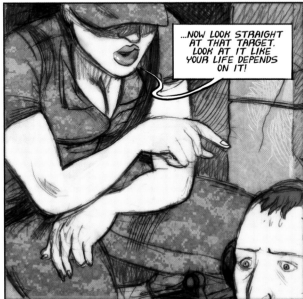

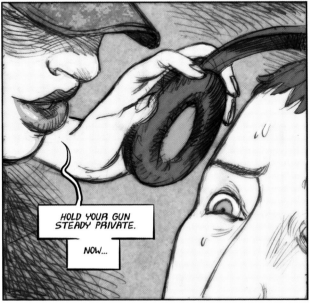

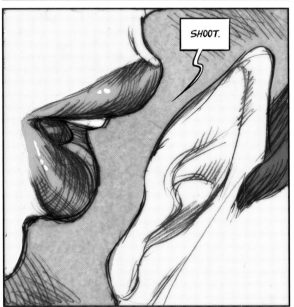

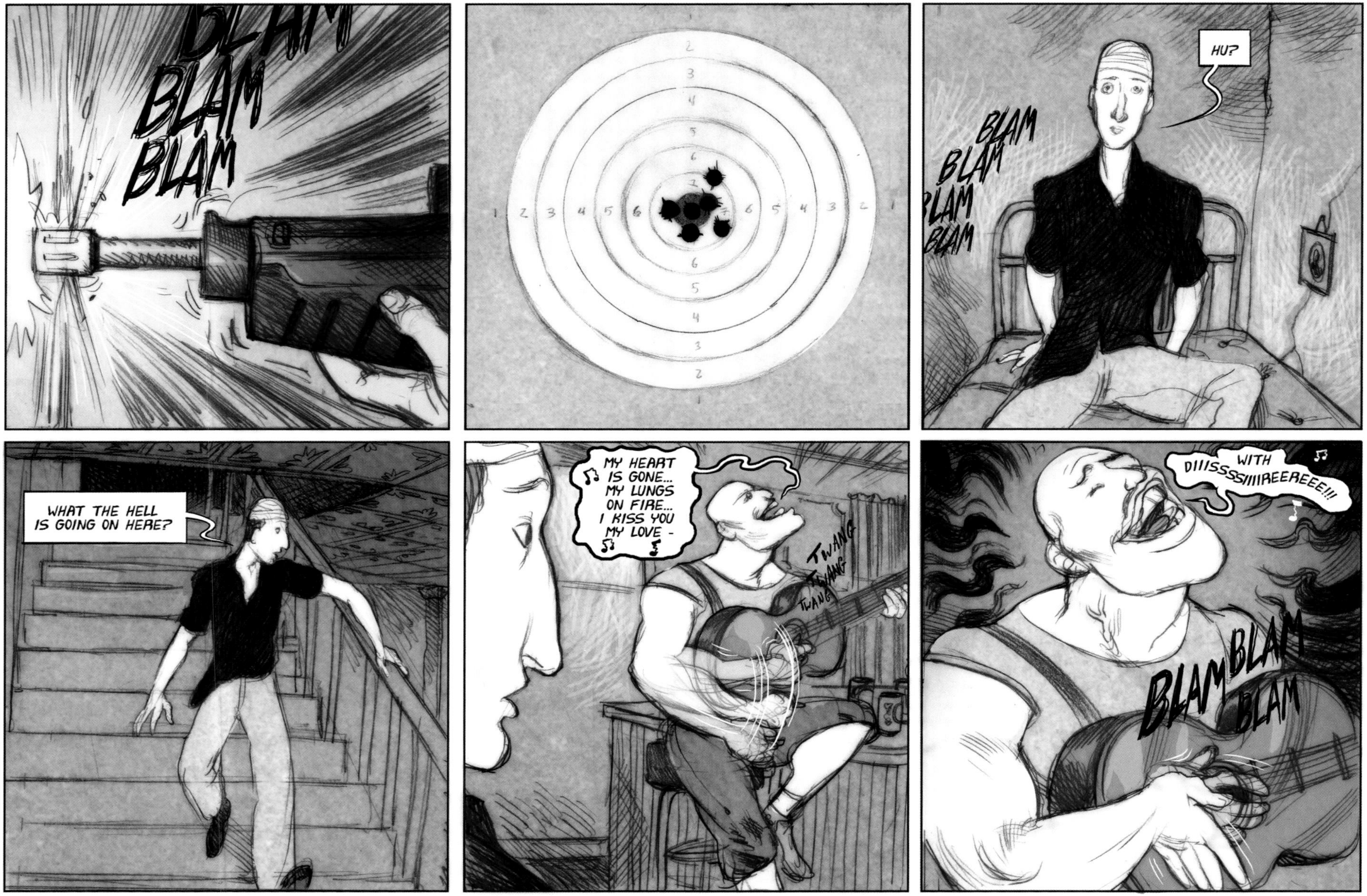
BLAM
BLAM
BLAM
HU?
BLAM
BLAM
BLAM
BLAM
WHAT THE HELL IS GOING ON HERE?
MY HEART IS GONE... MY LUNGS ON FIRE... I KISS YOU MY LOVE -
TWANG
TWANG
TWANG
WITH DIIISSSSIIIIREEREEE!!!
BLAM
BLAM
BLAM

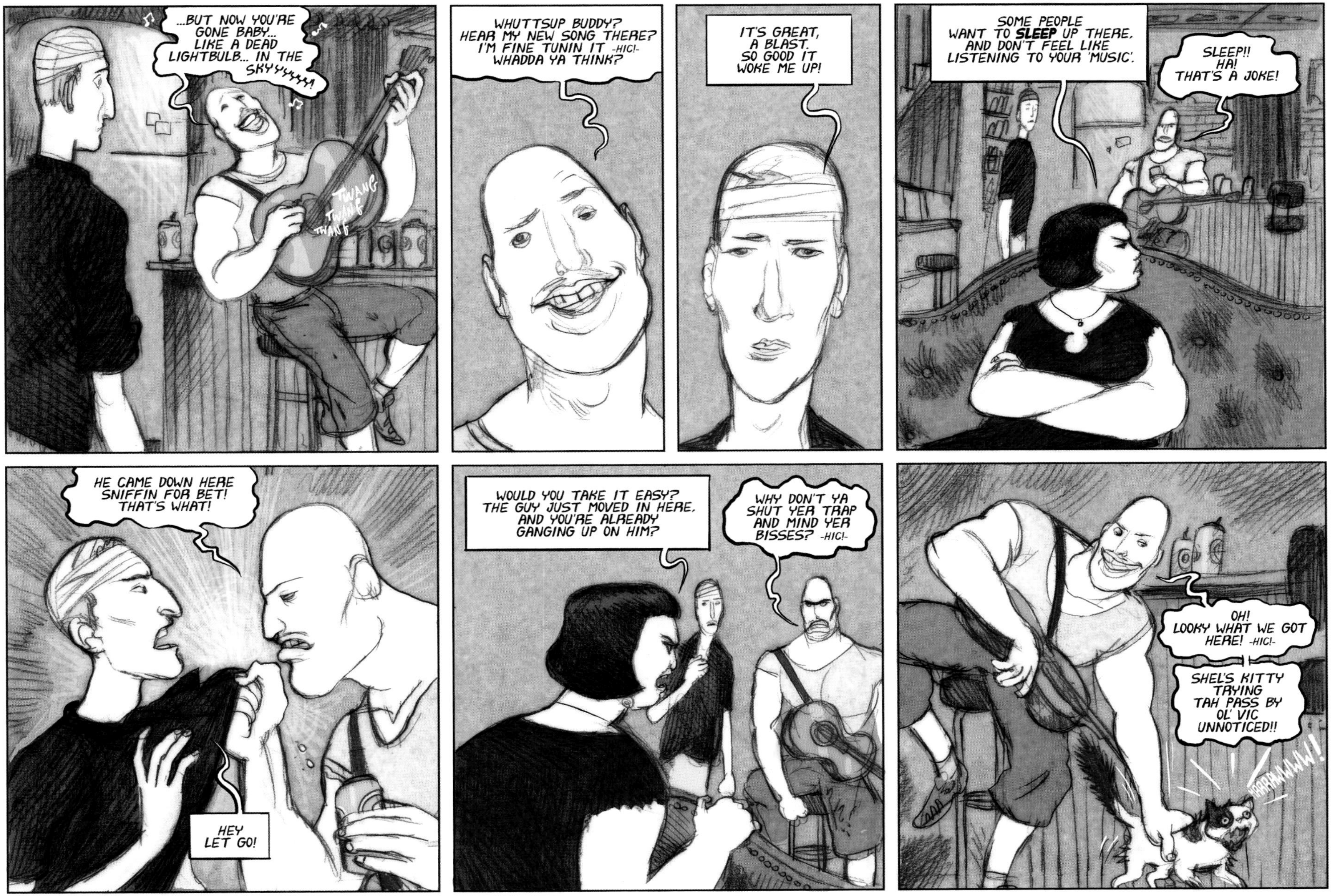
...BUT NOW YOU'RE GONE BABY... LIKE A DEAD LIGHTBULB... IN THE SKYYYYYYY!
TWANG TWANG TWANG
WHUTTSUP BUDDY? HEAR MY NEW SONG THERE? I'M FINE TUNIN IT -HIC!- WHADDA YA THINK?
IT'S GREAT, A BLAST. SO GOOD IT WOKE ME UP!
SOME PEOPLE WANT TO **SLEEP** UP THERE, AND DON'T FEEL LIKE LISTENING TO YOUR 'MUSIC'.
SLEEP!! HA! THAT'S A JOKE!
HE CAME DOWN HERE SNIFFIN FOR BET! THAT'S WHAT!
HEY LET GO!
WOULD YOU TAKE IT EASY? THE GUY JUST MOVED IN HERE, AND YOU'RE ALREADY GANGING UP ON HIM?
WHY DON'T YA SHUT YER TRAP AND MIND YER BISSES? -HIC!-
OH! LOOKY WHAT WE GOT HERE! -HIC!-
SHEL'S KITTY TRYING TAH PASS BY OL' VIC UNNOTICED!!

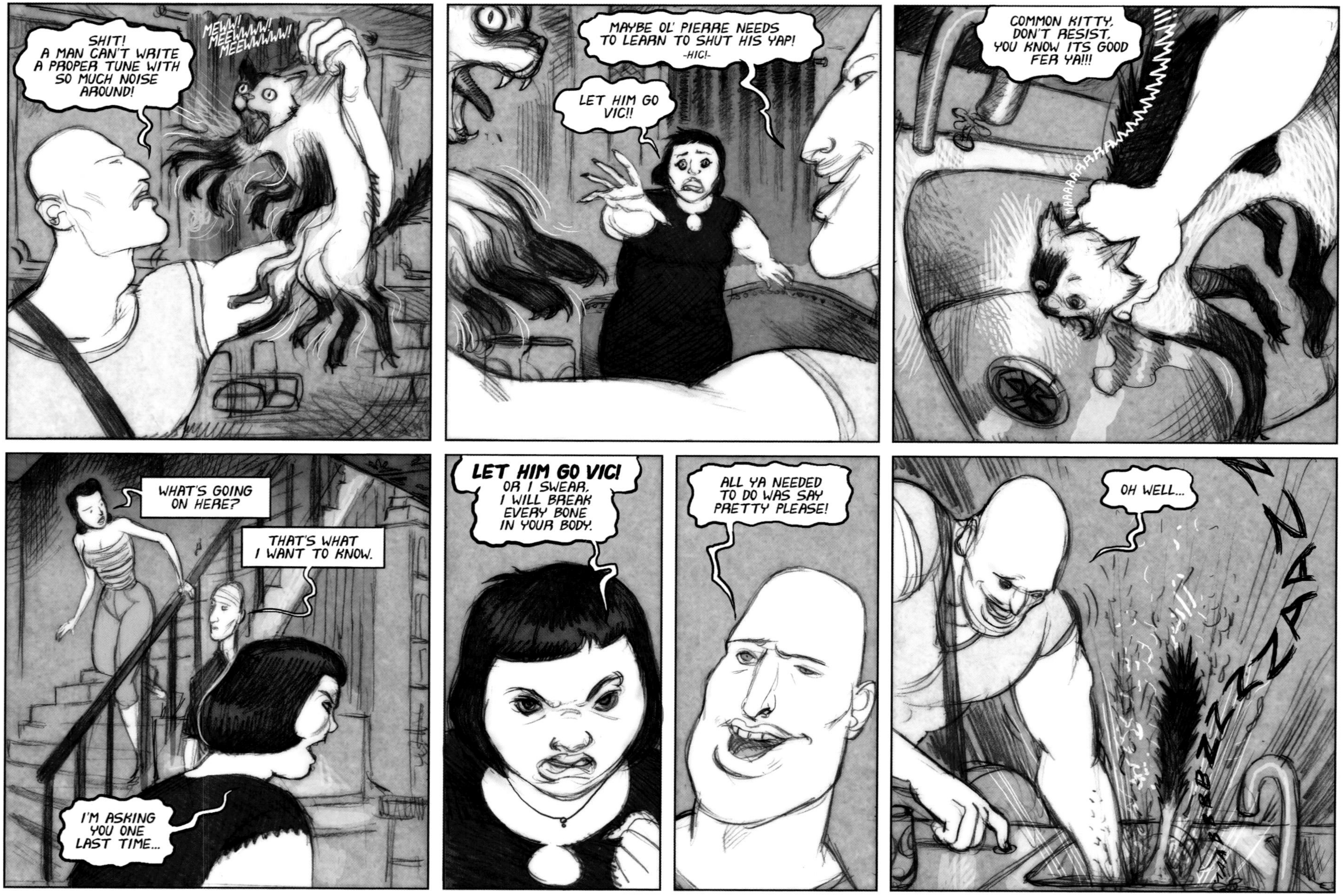
SHIT! A MAN CAN'T WRITE A PROPER TUNE WITH SO MUCH NOISE AROUND!
MEWW!! MEEWWWW! MEEWWWWW!
MAYBE OL' PIERRE NEEDS TO LEARN TO SHUT HIS YAP! -HIC!-
LET HIM GO VIC!!
COMMON KITTY, DON'T RESIST, YOU KNOW ITS GOOD FER YA!!!
WHAT'S GOING ON HERE?
THAT'S WHAT I WANT TO KNOW.
I'M ASKING YOU ONE LAST TIME...
LET HIM GO VIC! OR I SWEAR, I WILL BREAK EVERY BONE IN YOUR BODY.
ALL YA NEEDED TO DO WAS SAY PRETTY PLEASE!
OH WELL...

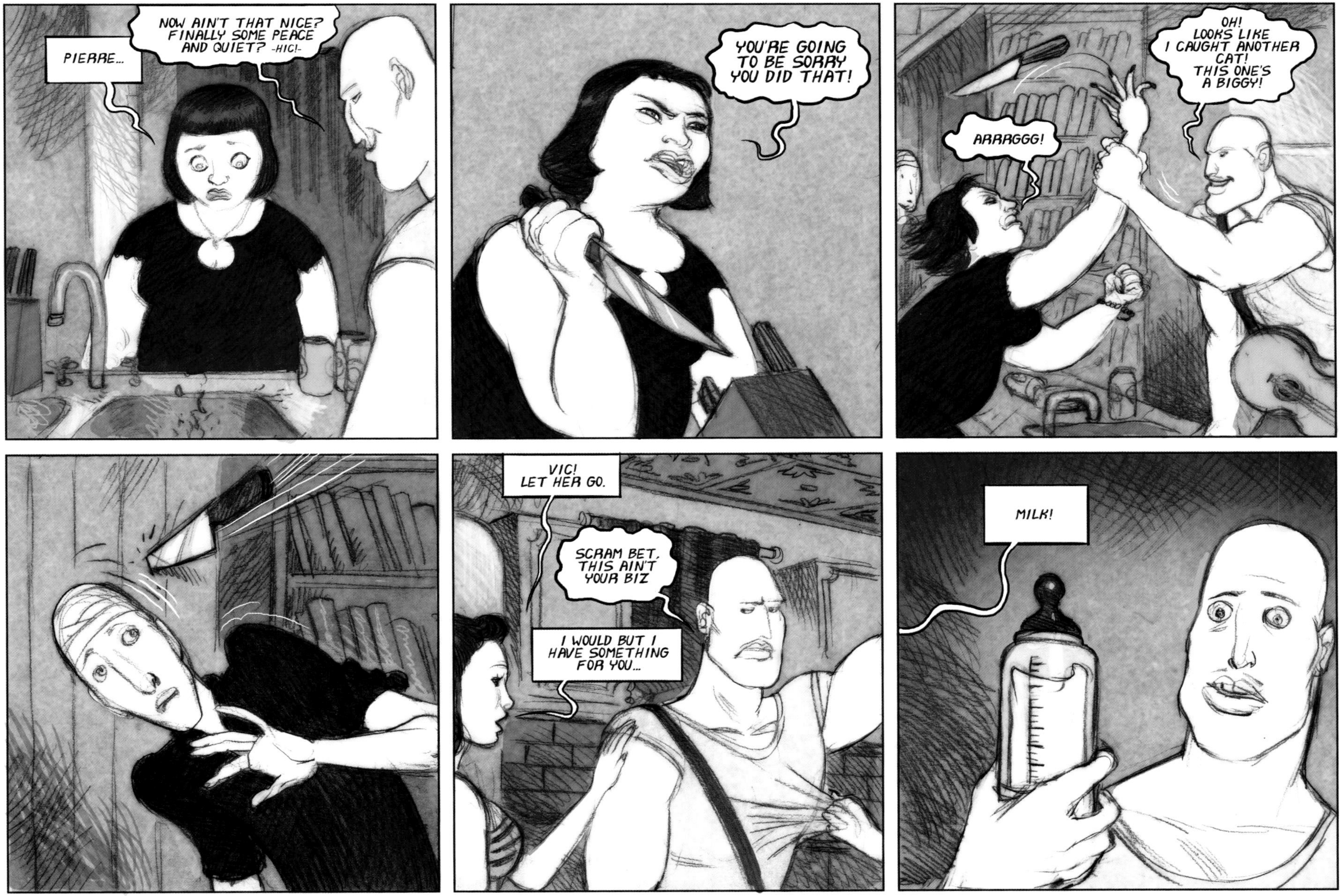
PIERRE...
NOW AIN'T THAT NICE? FINALLY SOME PEACE AND QUIET? -HIC!-
YOU'RE GOING TO BE SORRY YOU DID THAT!
OH! LOOKS LIKE I CAUGHT ANOTHER CAT! THIS ONE'S A BIGGY!
ARRRGGG!
VIC! LET HER GO.
SCRAM BET. THIS AIN'T YOUR BIZ
I WOULD BUT I HAVE SOMETHING FOR YOU...
MILK!

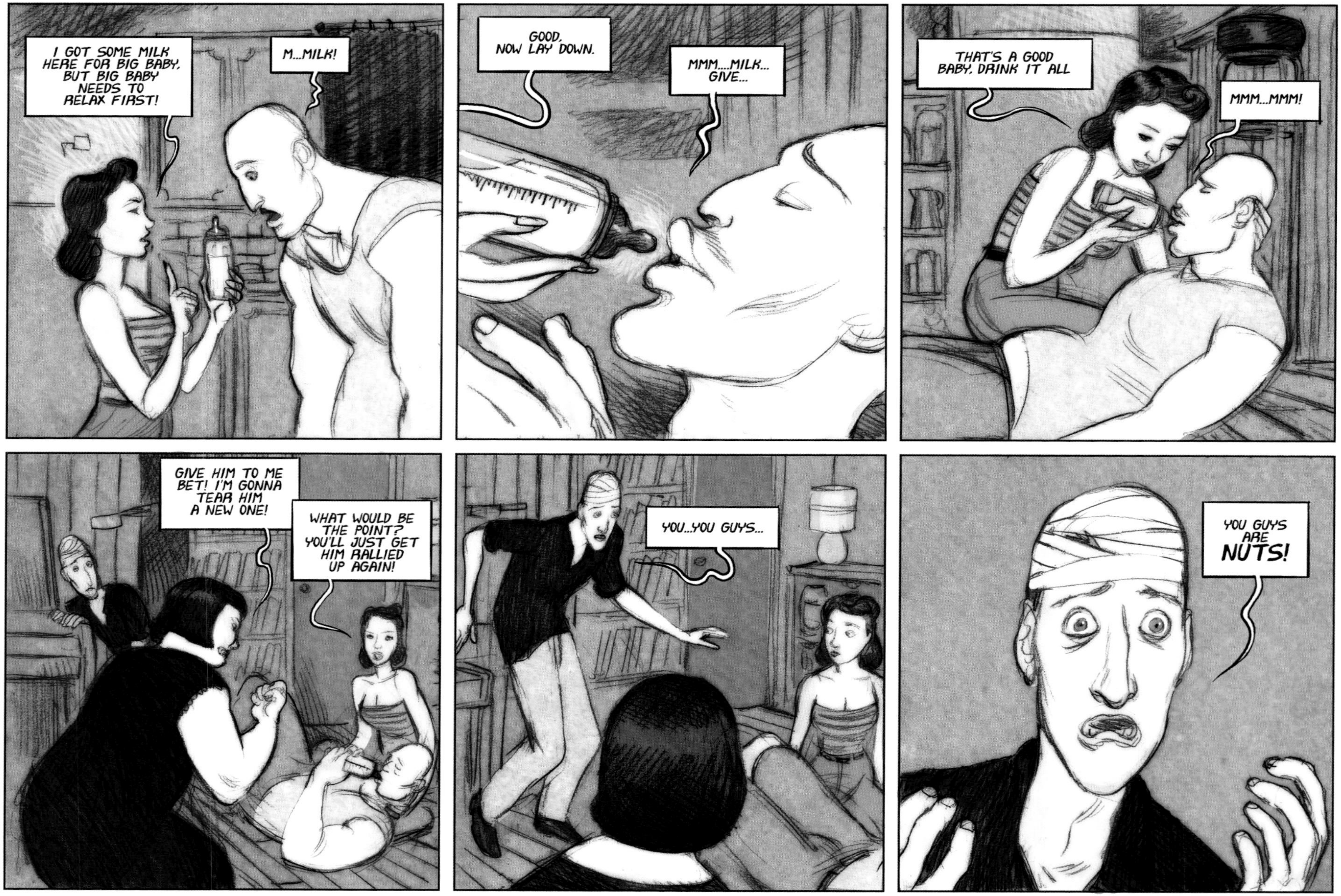
I GOT SOME MILK HERE FOR BIG BABY, BUT BIG BABY NEEDS TO RELAX FIRST!
M...MILK!
GOOD, NOW LAY DOWN.
MMM....MILK... GIVE...
THAT'S A GOOD BABY, DRINK IT ALL
MMM...MMM!
GIVE HIM TO ME BET! I'M GONNA TEAR HIM A NEW ONE!
WHAT WOULD BE THE POINT? YOU'LL JUST GET HIM RILLED UP AGAIN!
YOU...YOU GUYS...
YOU GUYS ARE NUTS!

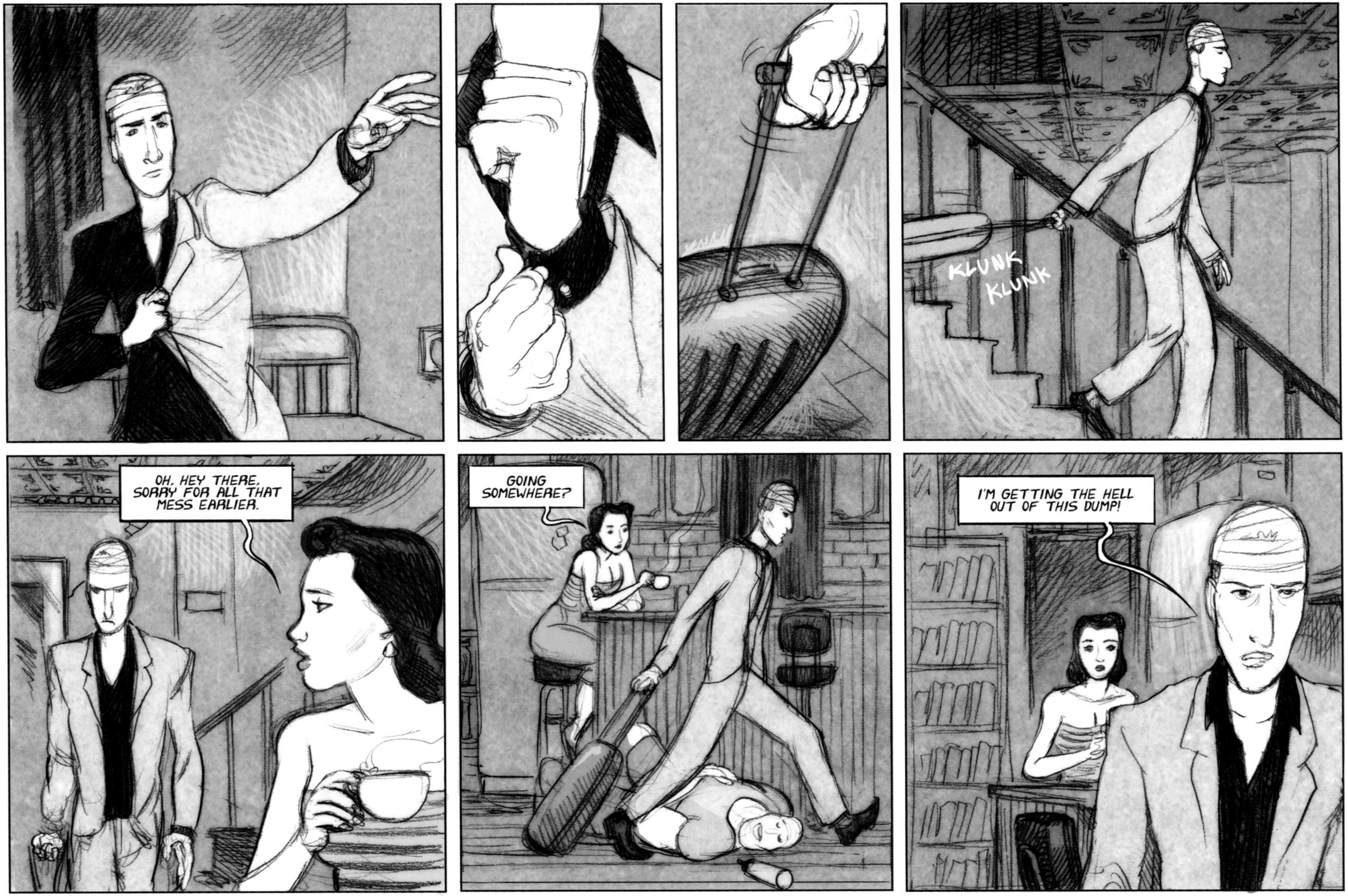
KLUNK
KLUNK
OH, HEY THERE. SORRY FOR ALL THAT MESS EARLIER.
GOING SOMEWHERE?
I'M GETTING THE HELL OUT OF THIS DUMP!

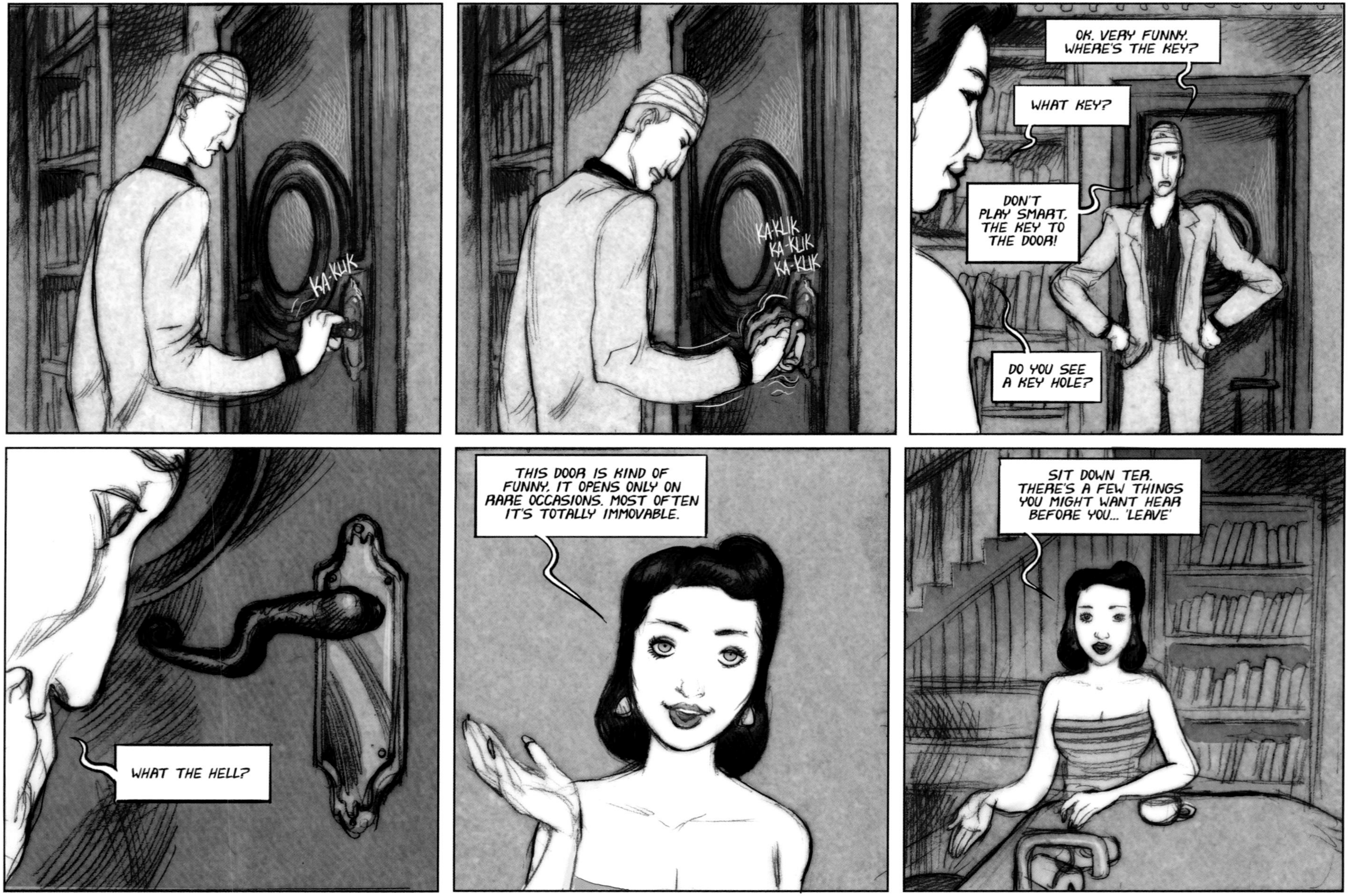
KA-KLIK
KA-KLIK
KA-KLIK
KA-KLIK
OK. VERY FUNNY. WHERE'S THE KEY?
WHAT KEY?
DON'T PLAY SMART, THE KEY TO THE DOOR!
DO YOU SEE A KEY HOLE?
WHAT THE HELL?
THIS DOOR IS KIND OF FUNNY. IT OPENS ONLY ON RARE OCCASIONS. MOST OFTEN IT'S TOTALLY IMMOVABLE.
SIT DOWN TER. THERE'S A FEW THINGS YOU MIGHT WANT HEAR BEFORE YOU... 'LEAVE'

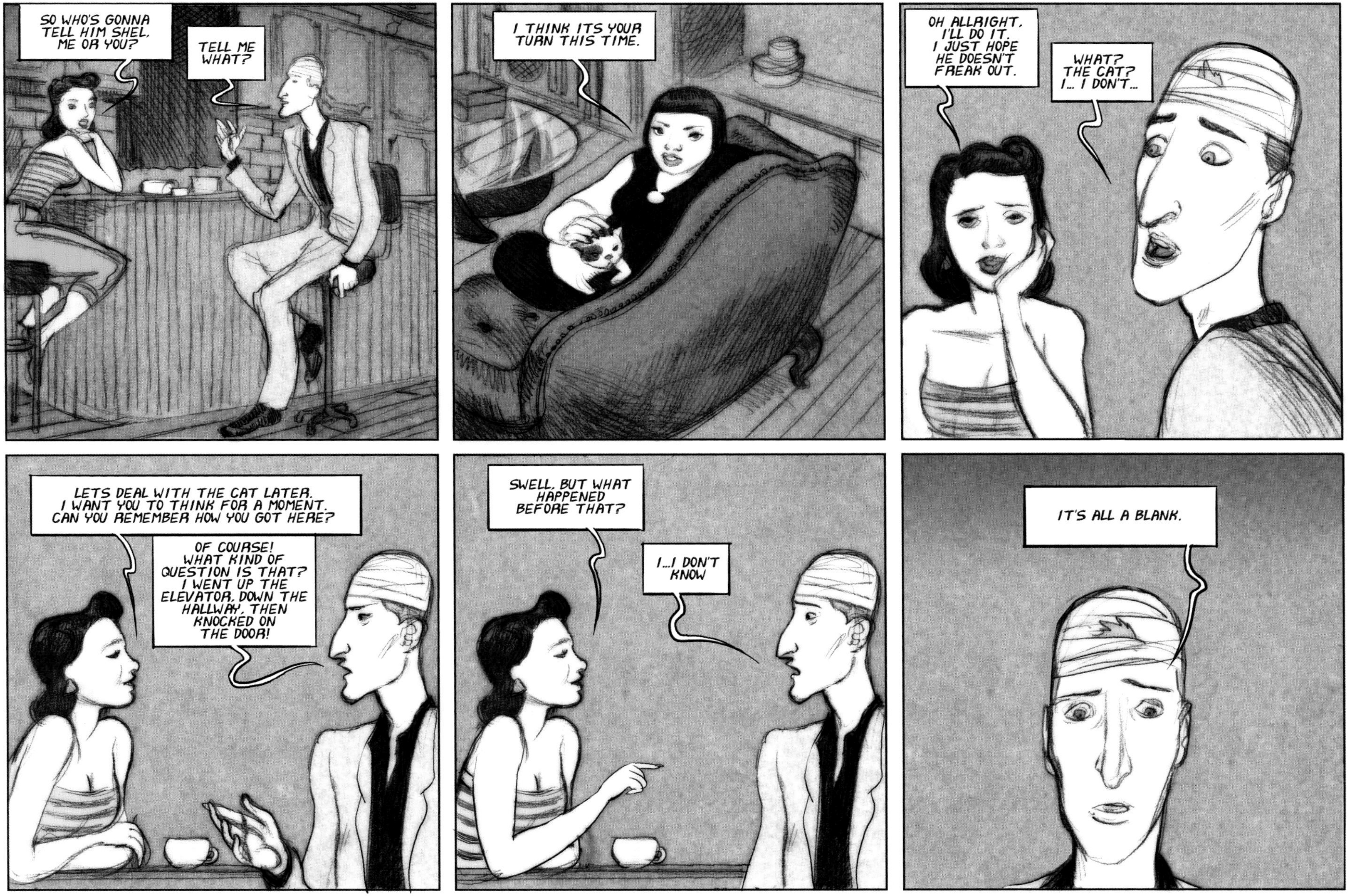
SO WHO'S GONNA TELL HIM SHEL, ME OR YOU?
TELL ME WHAT?
I THINK ITS YOUR TURN THIS TIME.
OH ALLRIGHT, I'LL DO IT. I JUST HOPE HE DOESN'T FREAK OUT.
WHAT? THE CAT? I... I DON'T...
LETS DEAL WITH THE CAT LATER. I WANT YOU TO THINK FOR A MOMENT. CAN YOU REMEMBER HOW YOU GOT HERE?
OF COURSE! WHAT KIND OF QUESTION IS THAT? I WENT UP THE ELEVATOR, DOWN THE HALLWAY, THEN KNOCKED ON THE DOOR!
SWELL, BUT WHAT HAPPENED BEFORE THAT?
I...I DON'T KNOW
IT'S ALL A BLANK.

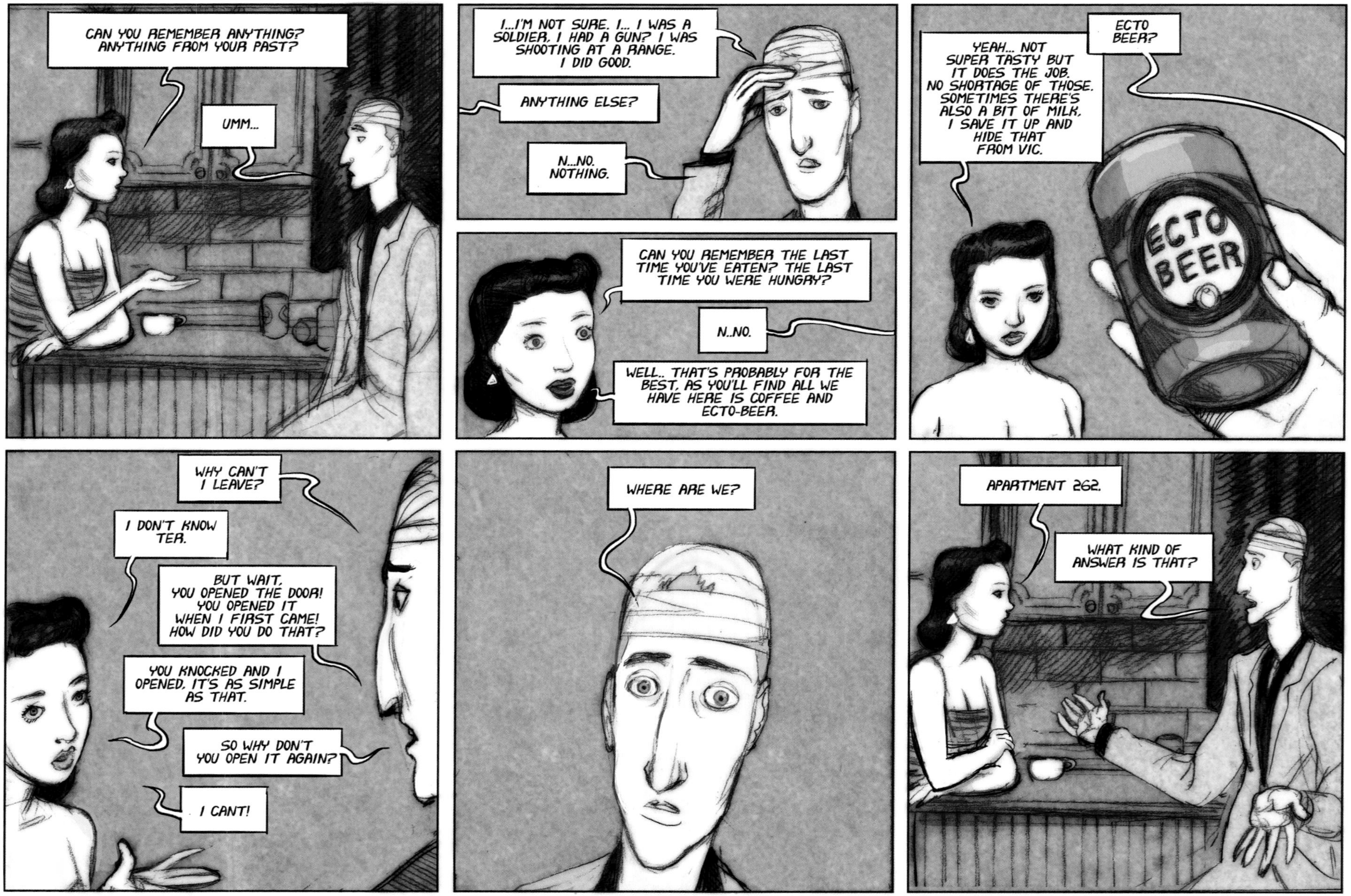
CAN YOU REMEMBER ANYTHING? ANYTHING FROM YOUR PAST?
UMM...
I...I'M NOT SURE. I... I WAS A SOLDIER, I HAD A GUN? I WAS SHOOTING AT A RANGE. I DID GOOD.
ANYTHING ELSE?
N...NO. NOTHING.
CAN YOU REMEMBER THE LAST TIME YOU'VE EATEN? THE LAST TIME YOU WERE HUNGRY?
N..NO.
WELL.. THAT'S PROBABLY FOR THE BEST, AS YOU'LL FIND ALL WE HAVE HERE IS COFFEE AND ECTO-BEER.
ECTO BEER?
YEAH... NOT SUPER TASTY BUT IT DOES THE JOB. NO SHORTAGE OF THOSE. SOMETIMES THERE'S ALSO A BIT OF MILK, I SAVE IT UP AND HIDE THAT FROM VIC.
ECTO BEER
WHY CAN'T I LEAVE?
I DON'T KNOW TER.
BUT WAIT, YOU OPENED THE DOOR! YOU OPENED IT WHEN I FIRST CAME! HOW DID YOU DO THAT?
YOU KNOCKED AND I OPENED. IT'S AS SIMPLE AS THAT.
SO WHY DON'T YOU OPEN IT AGAIN?
I CANT!
WHERE ARE WE?
APARTMENT 262.
WHAT KIND OF ANSWER IS THAT?

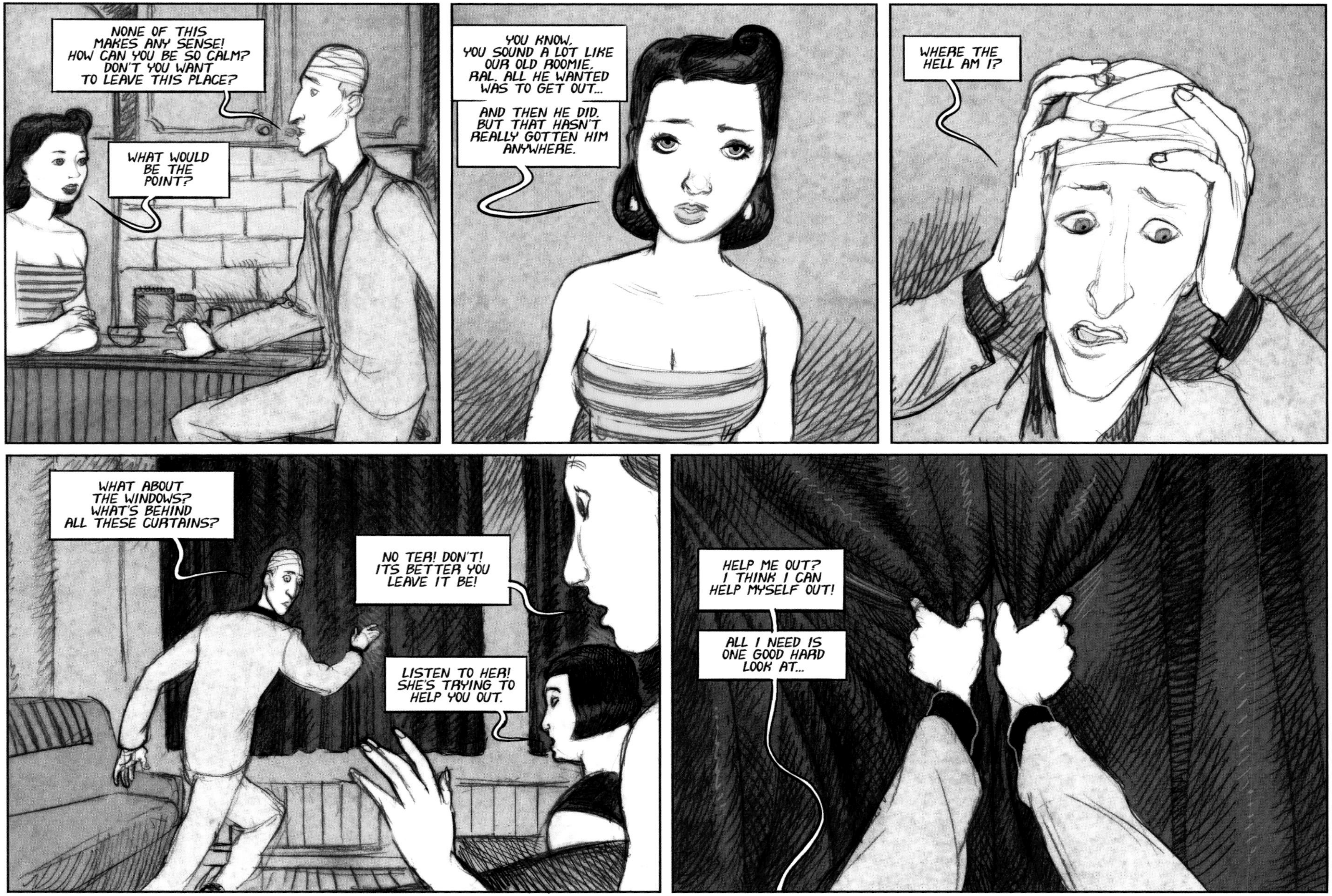
NONE OF THIS MAKES ANY SENSE! HOW CAN YOU BE SO CALM? DON'T YOU WANT TO LEAVE THIS PLACE?
WHAT WOULD BE THE POINT?
YOU KNOW, YOU SOUND A LOT LIKE OUR OLD ROOMIE, RAL. ALL HE WANTED WAS TO GET OUT...
AND THEN HE DID. BUT THAT HASN'T REALLY GOTTEN HIM ANYWHERE.
WHERE THE HELL AM I?
WHAT ABOUT THE WINDOWS? WHAT'S BEHIND ALL THESE CURTAINS?
NO TER! DON'T! ITS BETTER YOU LEAVE IT BE!
LISTEN TO HER! SHE'S TRYING TO HELP YOU OUT.
HELP ME OUT? I THINK I CAN HELP MYSELF OUT!
ALL I NEED IS ONE GOOD HARD LOOK AT...

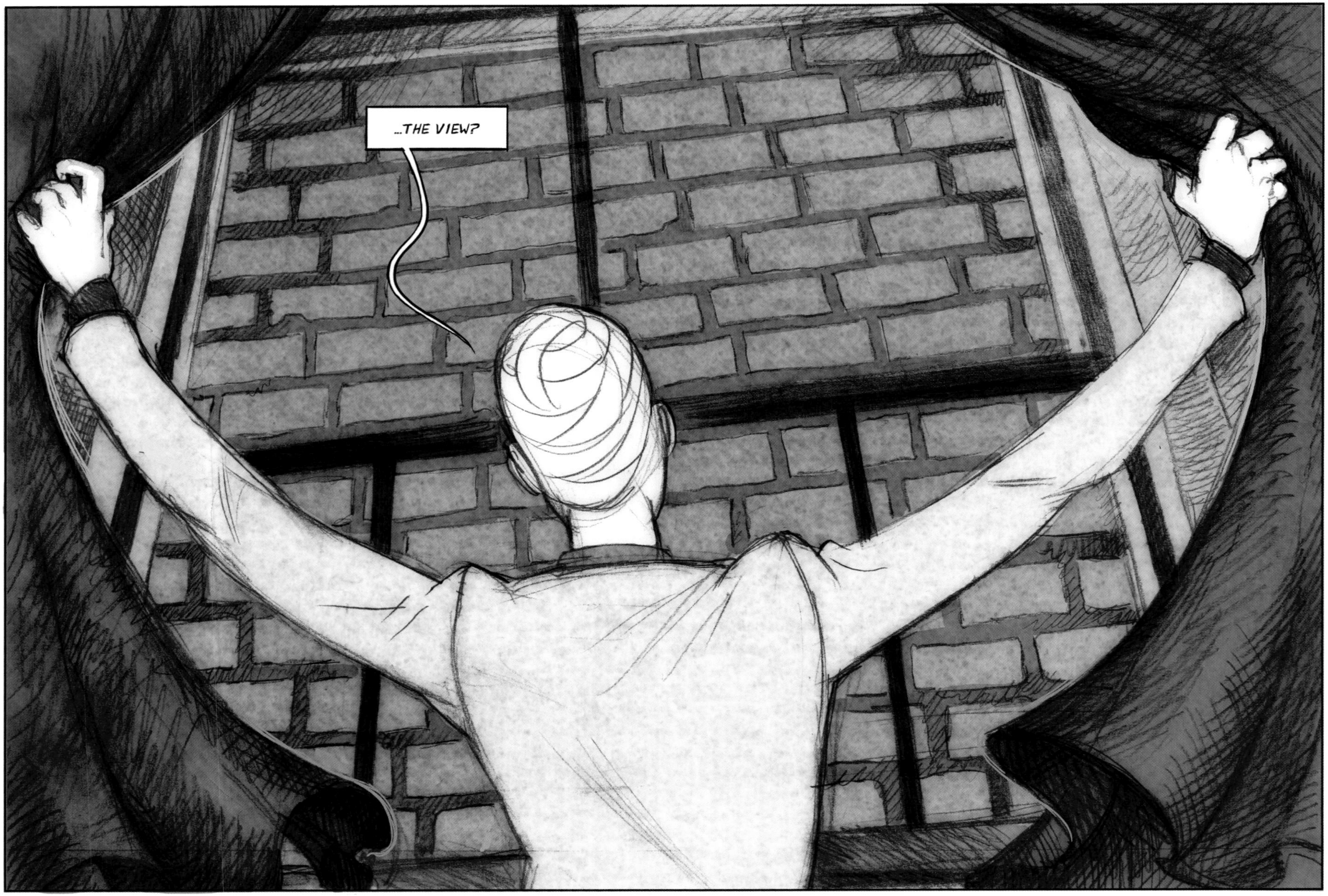
...THE VIEW?

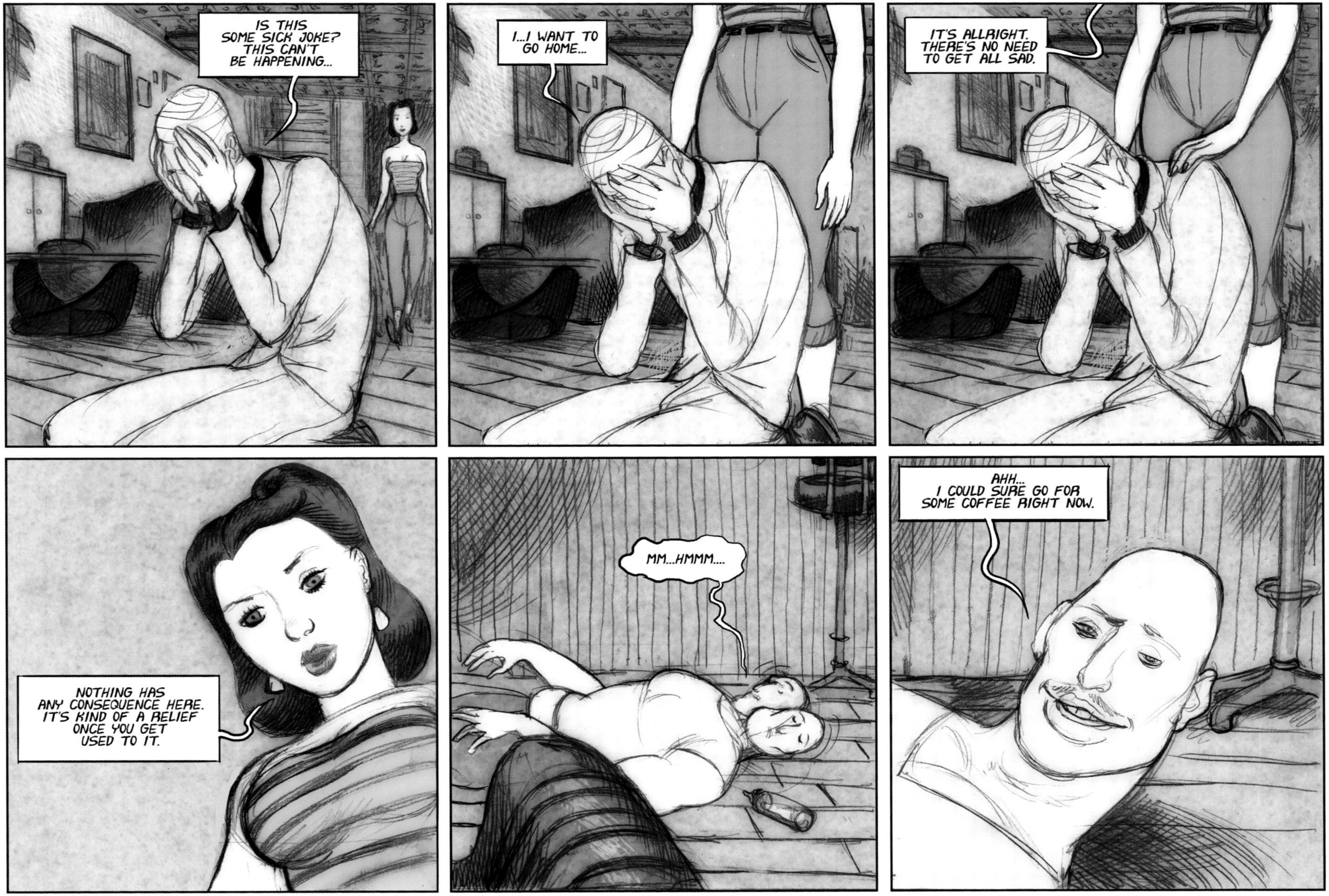
IS THIS SOME SICK JOKE? THIS CAN'T BE HAPPENING...
I...I WANT TO GO HOME...
IT'S ALLRIGHT. THERE'S NO NEED TO GET ALL SAD.
NOTHING HAS ANY CONSEQUENCE HERE. IT'S KIND OF A RELIEF ONCE YOU GET USED TO IT.
MM...HMMM....
AHH... I COULD SURE GO FOR SOME COFFEE RIGHT NOW.

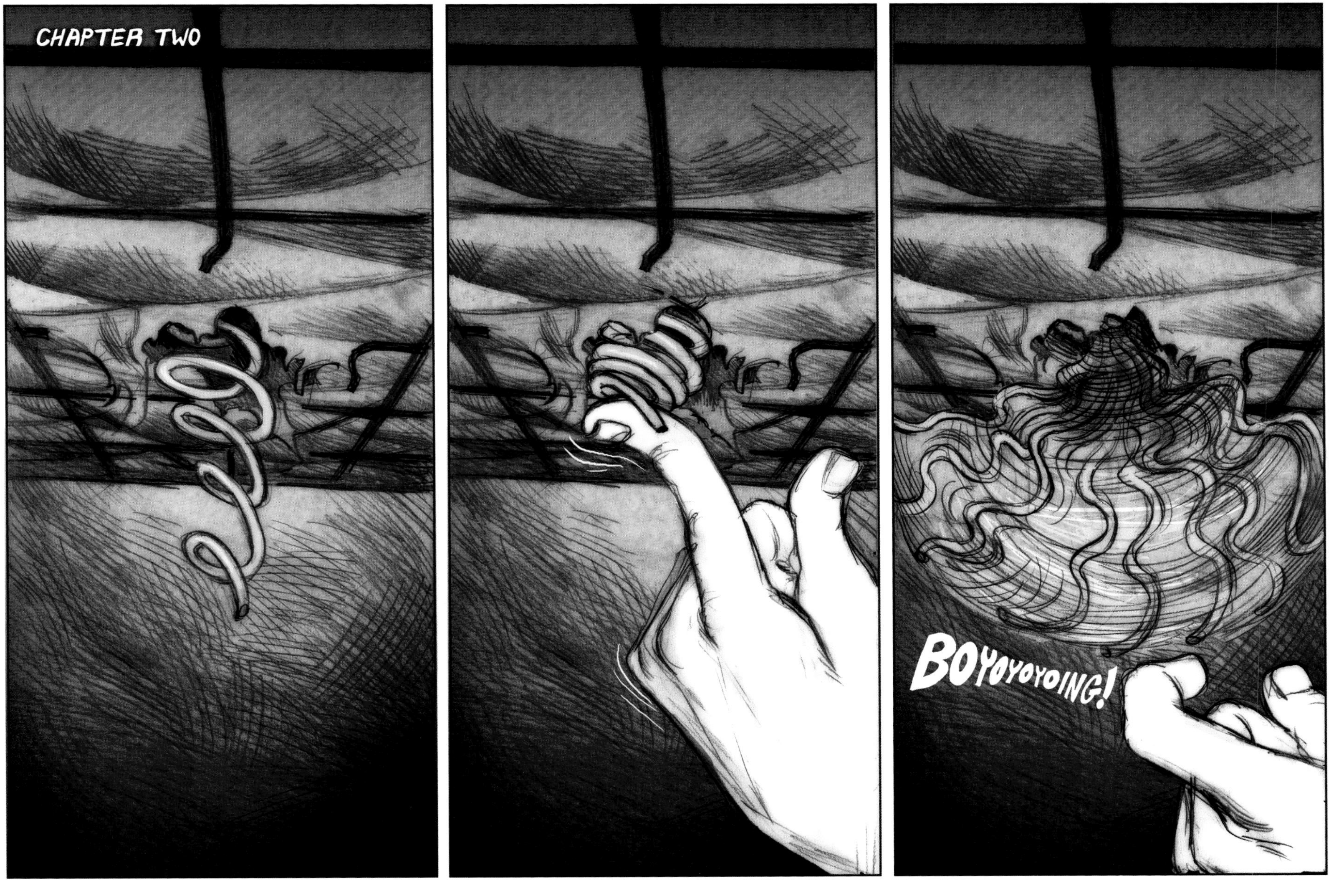
CHAPTER TWO
BOYOYOYOING!

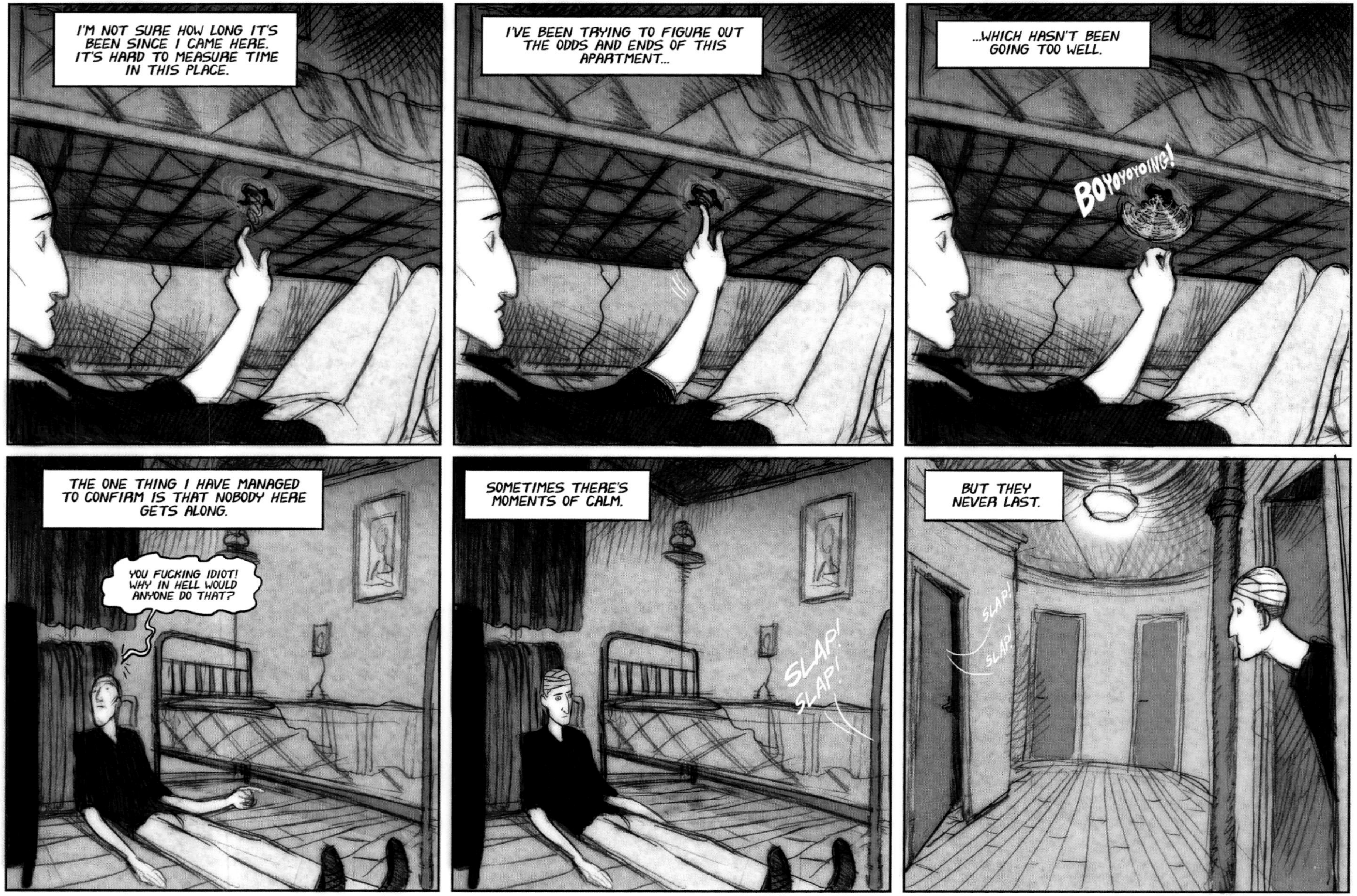
I'M NOT SURE HOW LONG IT'S BEEN SINCE I CAME HERE. IT'S HARD TO MEASURE TIME IN THIS PLACE.
I'VE BEEN TRYING TO FIGURE OUT THE ODDS AND ENDS OF THIS APARTMENT...
...WHICH HASN'T BEEN GOING TOO WELL.
BOYOYOYOING!
THE ONE THING I HAVE MANAGED TO CONFIRM IS THAT NOBODY HERE GETS ALONG.
YOU FUCKING IDIOT! WHY IN HELL WOULD ANYONE DO THAT?
SOMETIMES THERE'S MOMENTS OF CALM.
SLAP! SLAP!
BUT THEY NEVER LAST.
SLAP! SLAP!

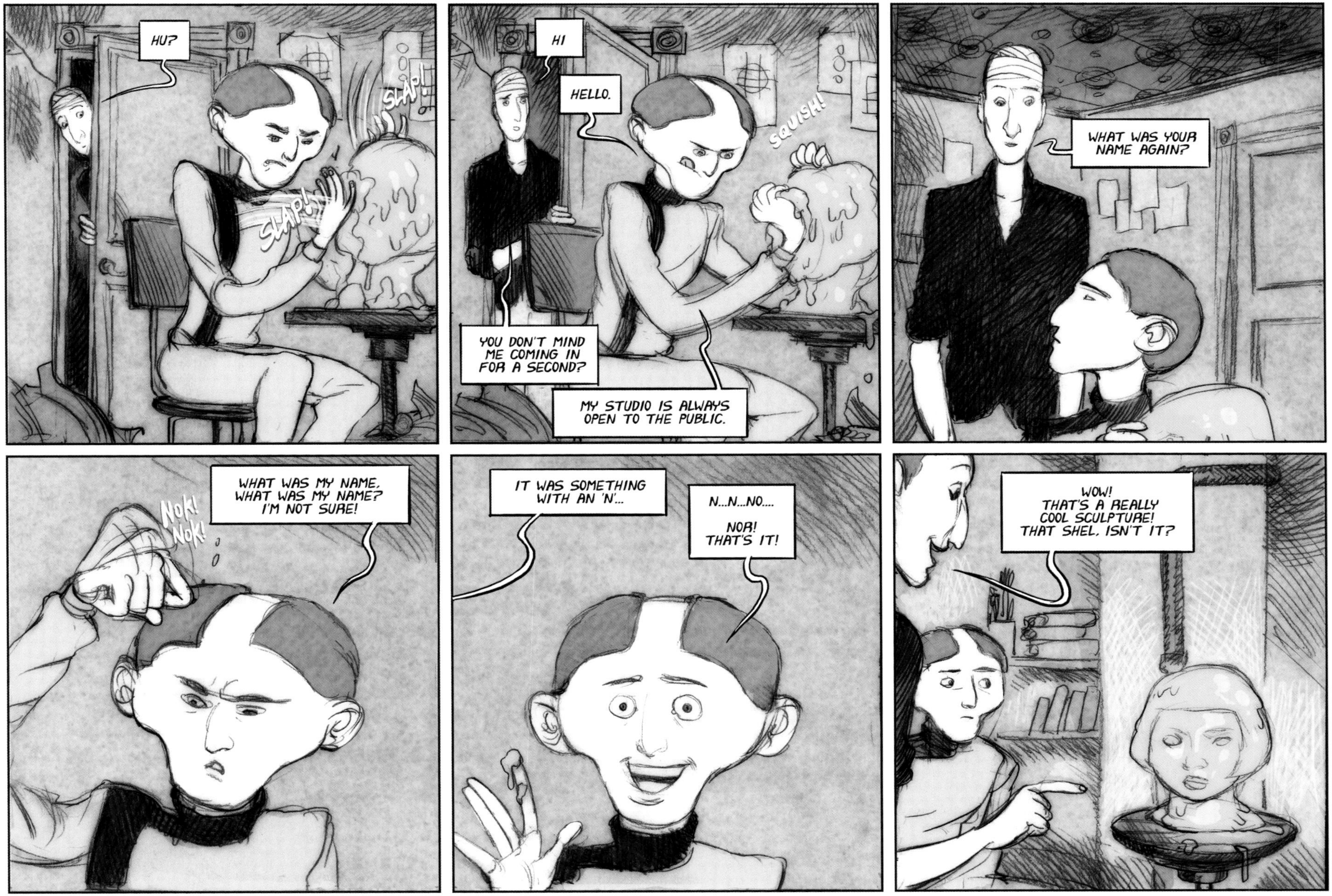
HU?
SLAP!
SLAP!
HI
HELLO.
SQUISH!
YOU DON'T MIND ME COMING IN FOR A SECOND?
MY STUDIO IS ALWAYS OPEN TO THE PUBLIC.
WHAT WAS YOUR NAME AGAIN?
NOK! NOK!
WHAT WAS MY NAME, WHAT WAS MY NAME? I'M NOT SURE!
IT WAS SOMETHING WITH AN 'N'...
N...N...NO....
NOR! THAT'S IT!
WOW! THAT'S A REALLY COOL SCULPTURE! THAT SHEL, ISN'T IT?

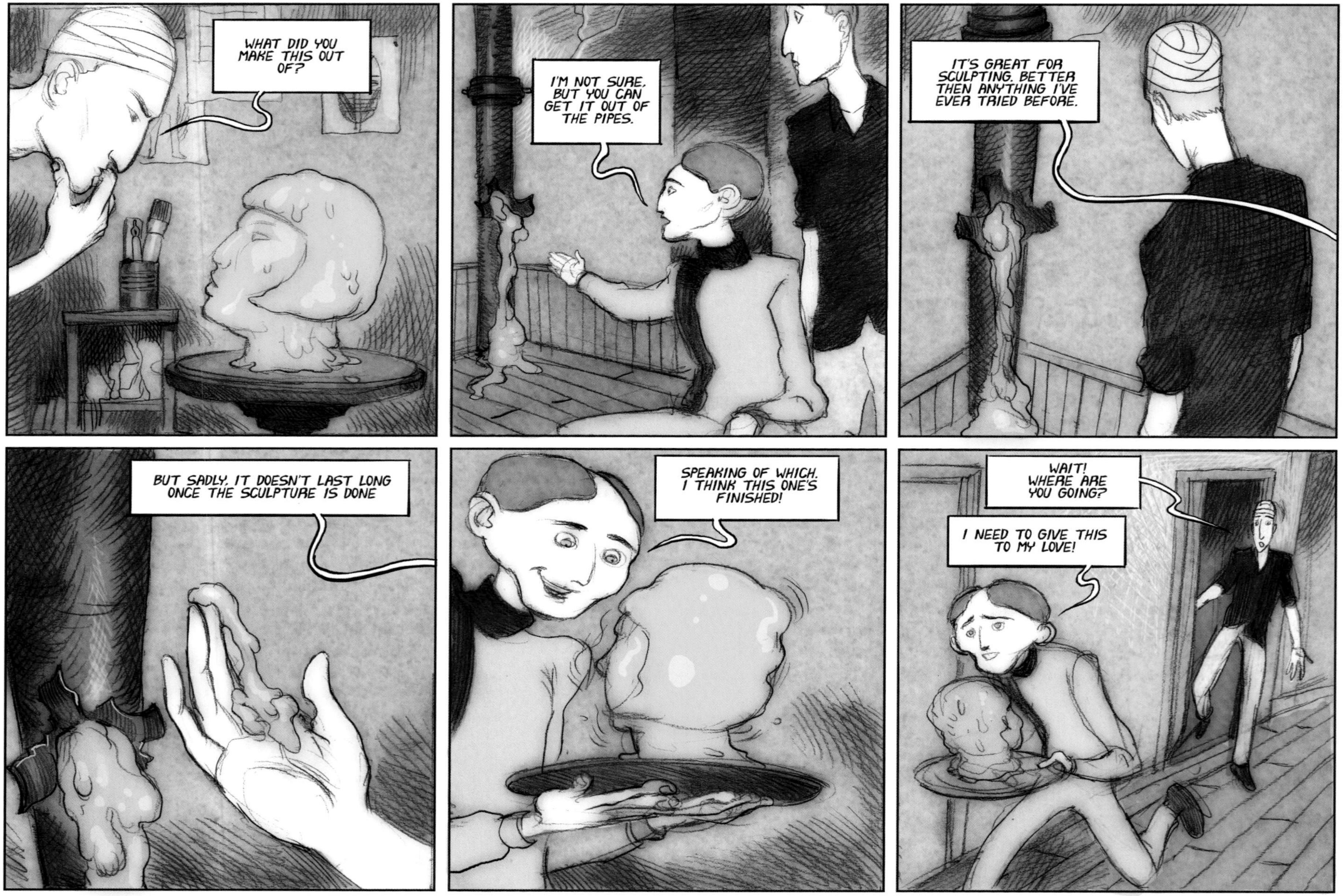
WHAT DID YOU MAKE THIS OUT OF?
I'M NOT SURE. BUT YOU CAN GET IT OUT OF THE PIPES.
IT'S GREAT FOR SCULPTING. BETTER THEN ANYTHING I'VE EVER TRIED BEFORE.
BUT SADLY, IT DOESN'T LAST LONG ONCE THE SCULPTURE IS DONE
SPEAKING OF WHICH. I THINK THIS ONE'S FINISHED!
WAIT! WHERE ARE YOU GOING?
I NEED TO GIVE THIS TO MY LOVE!

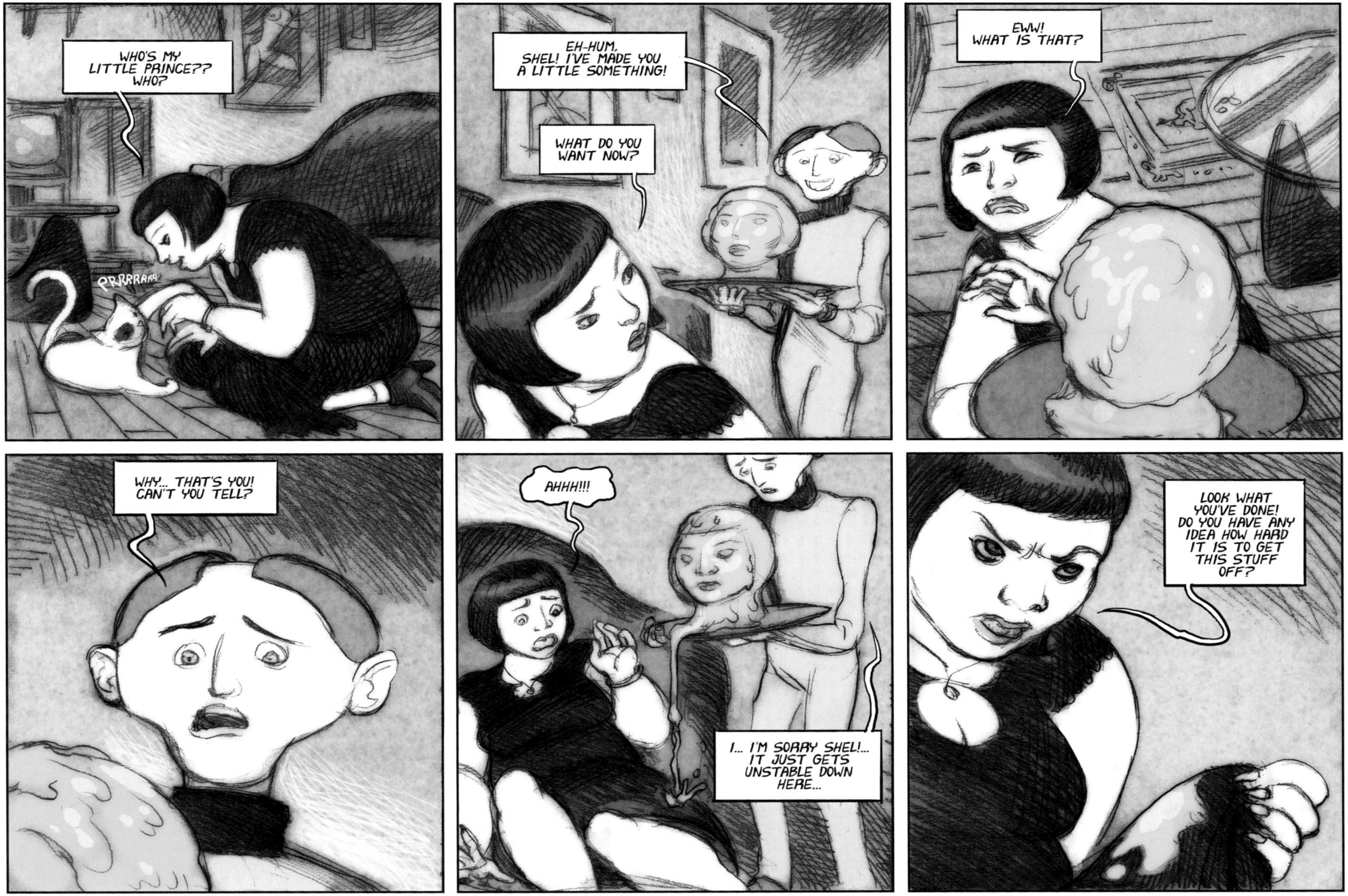
WHO'S MY LITTLE PRINCE?? WHO?
PRRRRRRR
EH-HUM, SHEL! I'VE MADE YOU A LITTLE SOMETHING!
WHAT DO YOU WANT NOW?
EWW! WHAT IS THAT?
WHY... THAT'S YOU! CAN'T YOU TELL?
AHHH!!!
I... I'M SORRY SHEL!... IT JUST GETS UNSTABLE DOWN HERE...
LOOK WHAT YOU'VE DONE! DO YOU HAVE ANY IDEA HOW HARD IT IS TO GET THIS STUFF OFF?

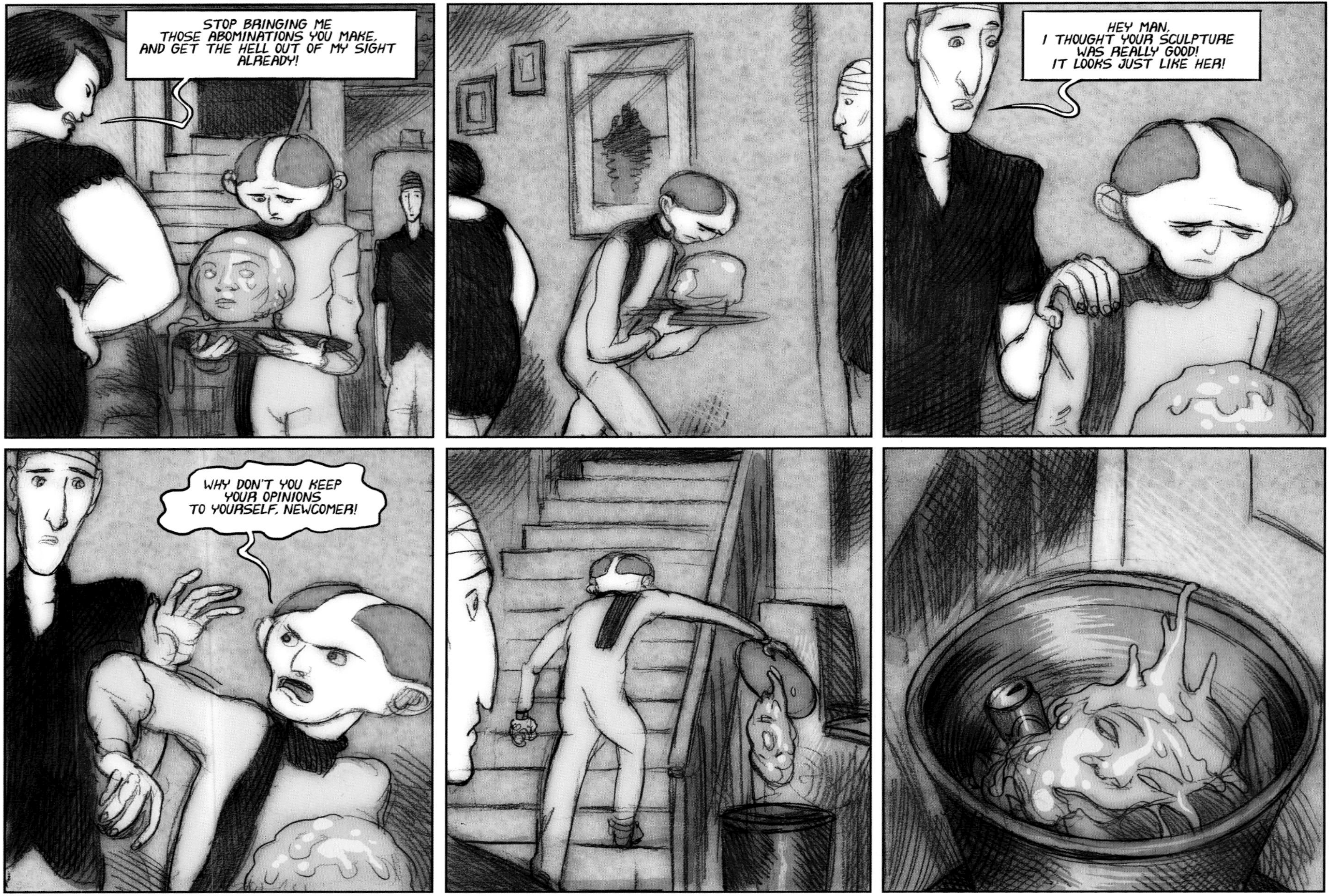
STOP BRINGING ME THOSE ABOMINATIONS YOU MAKE, AND GET THE HELL OUT OF MY SIGHT ALREADY!
HEY MAN, I THOUGHT YOUR SCULPTURE WAS REALLY GOOD! IT LOOKS JUST LIKE HER!
WHY DON'T YOU KEEP YOUR OPINIONS TO YOURSELF, NEWCOMER!

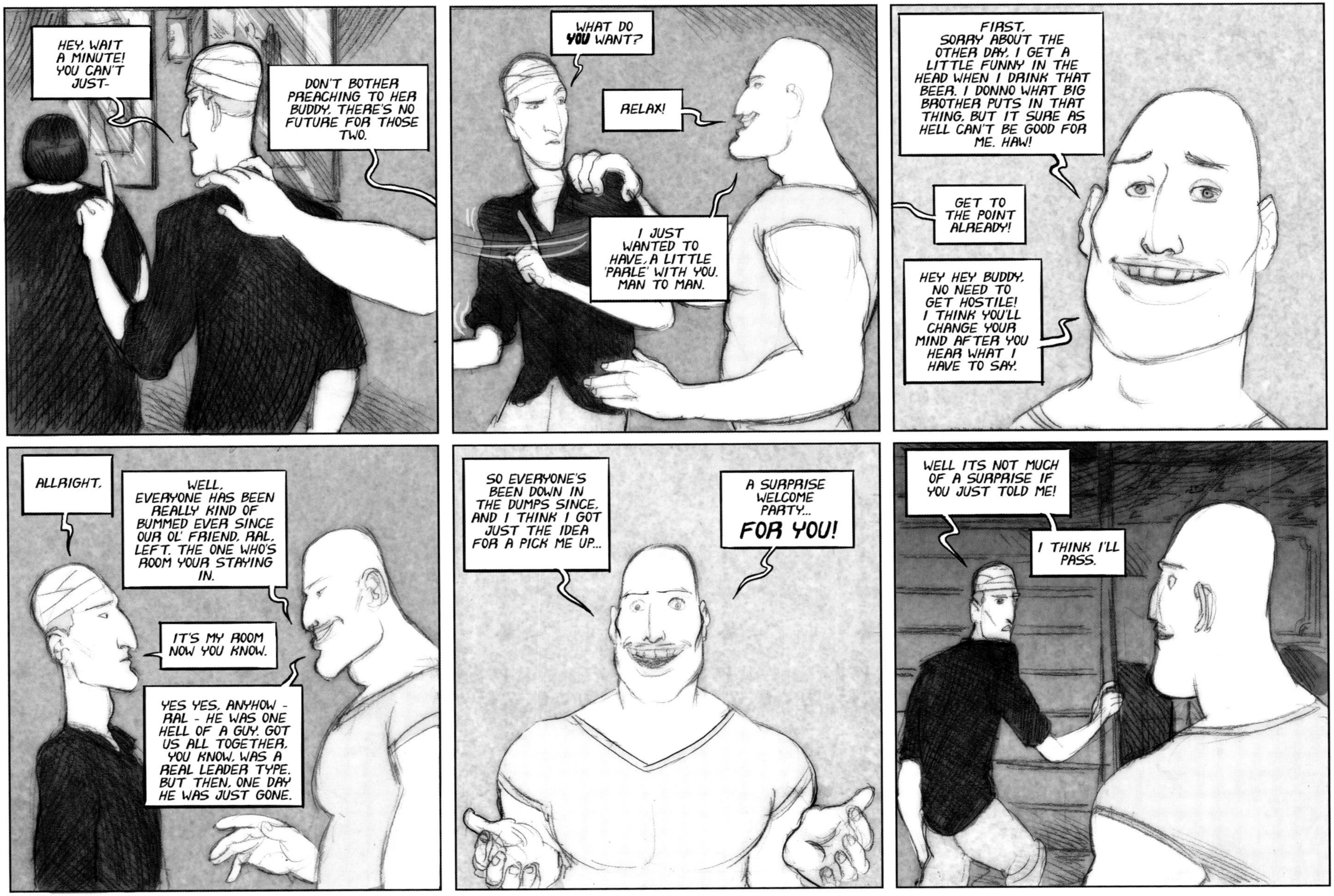
HEY, WAIT A MINUTE! YOU CAN'T JUST-
DON'T BOTHER PREACHING TO HER BUDDY, THERE'S NO FUTURE FOR THOSE TWO.
WHAT DO YOU WANT?
RELAX!
I JUST WANTED TO HAVE, A LITTLE 'PARLE' WITH YOU. MAN TO MAN.
FIRST, SORRY ABOUT THE OTHER DAY, I GET A LITTLE FUNNY IN THE HEAD WHEN I DRINK THAT BEER. I DONNO WHAT BIG BROTHER PUTS IN THAT THING, BUT IT SURE AS HELL CAN'T BE GOOD FOR ME. HAW!
GET TO THE POINT ALREADY!
HEY HEY BUDDY, NO NEED TO GET HOSTILE! I THINK YOU'LL CHANGE YOUR MIND AFTER YOU HEAR WHAT I HAVE TO SAY.
ALLRIGHT,
WELL, EVERYONE HAS BEEN REALLY KIND OF BUMMED EVER SINCE OUR OL' FRIEND, RAL, LEFT. THE ONE WHO'S ROOM YOUR STAYING IN.
IT'S MY ROOM NOW YOU KNOW.
YES YES, ANYHOW - RAL - HE WAS ONE HELL OF A GUY. GOT US ALL TOGETHER, YOU KNOW, WAS A REAL LEADER TYPE. BUT THEN, ONE DAY HE WAS JUST GONE.
SO EVERYONE'S BEEN DOWN IN THE DUMPS SINCE, AND I THINK I GOT JUST THE IDEA FOR A PICK ME UP...
A SURPRISE WELCOME PARTY... FOR YOU!
WELL ITS NOT MUCH OF A SURPRISE IF YOU JUST TOLD ME!
I THINK I'LL PASS.

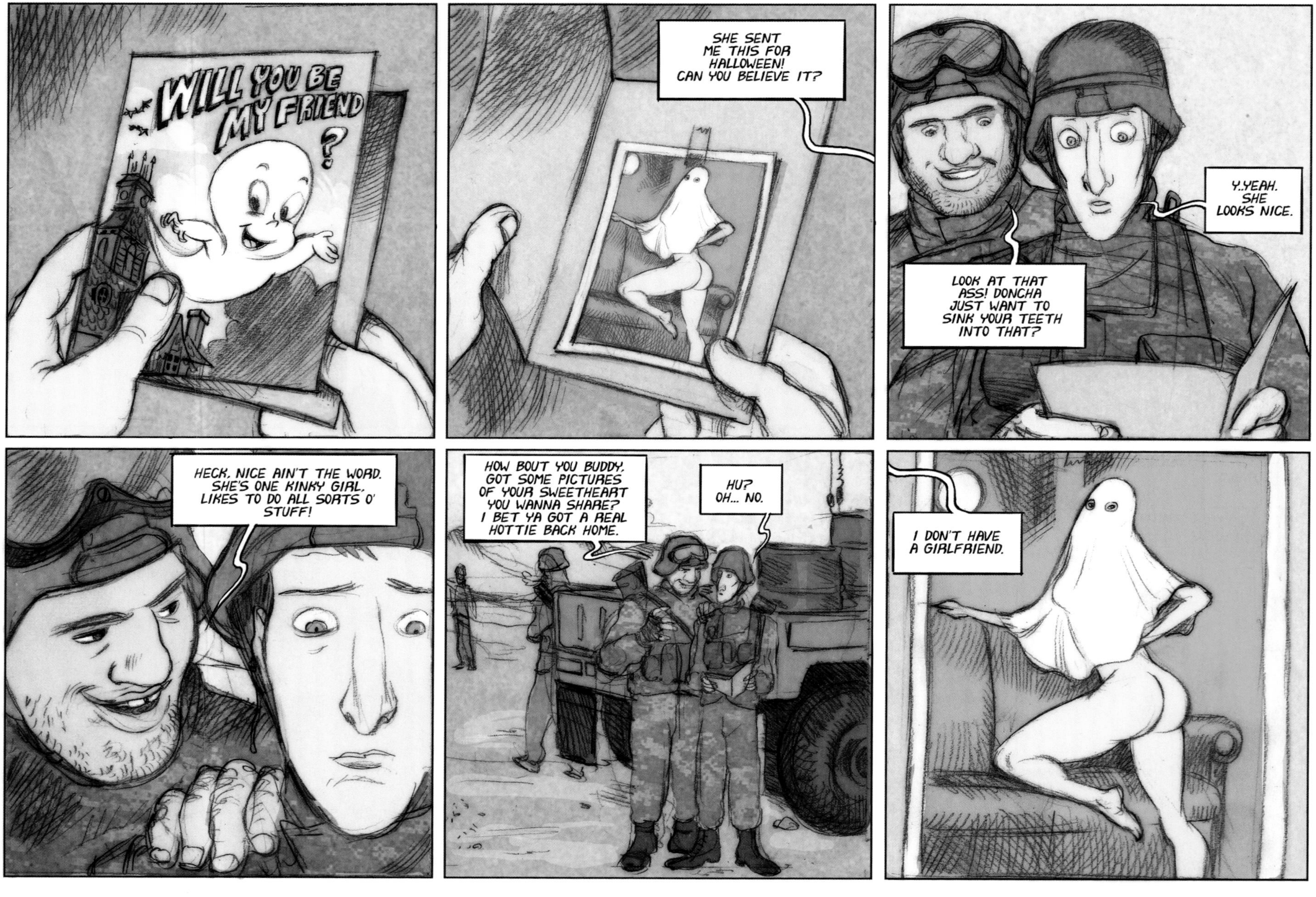
WILL YOU BE MY FRIEND ?
SHE SENT ME THIS FOR HALLOWEEN! CAN YOU BELIEVE IT?
LOOK AT THAT ASS! DONCHA JUST WANT TO SINK YOUR TEETH INTO THAT?
Y..YEAH. SHE LOOKS NICE.
HECK, NICE AIN'T THE WORD. SHE'S ONE KINKY GIRL, LIKES TO DO ALL SORTS O' STUFF!
HOW BOUT YOU BUDDY, GOT SOME PICTURES OF YOUR SWEETHEART YOU WANNA SHARE? I BET YA GOT A REAL HOTTIE BACK HOME.
HU? OH... NO.
I DON'T HAVE A GIRLFRIEND.

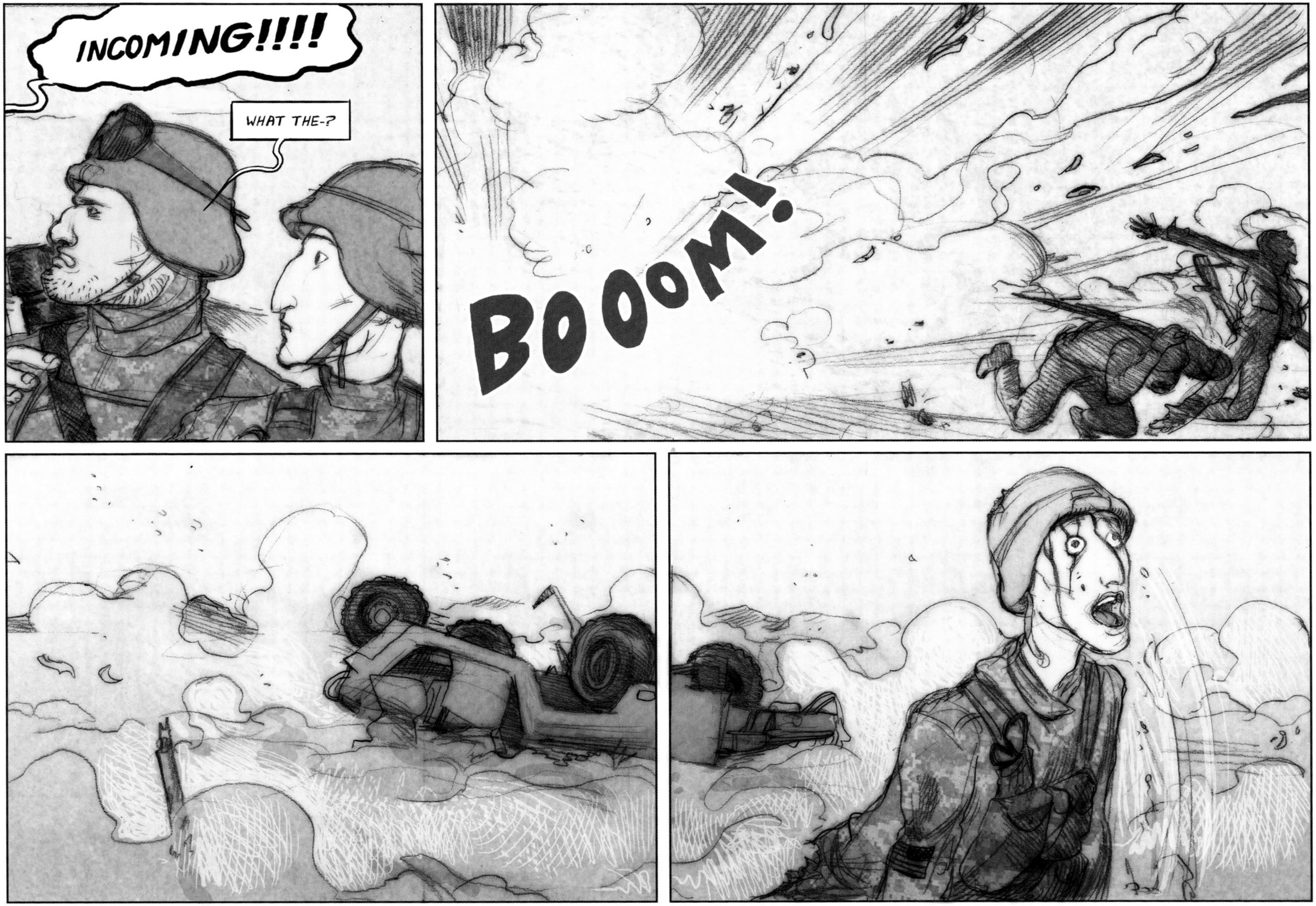
INCOMING!!!!
WHAT THE-?
BOOOM!

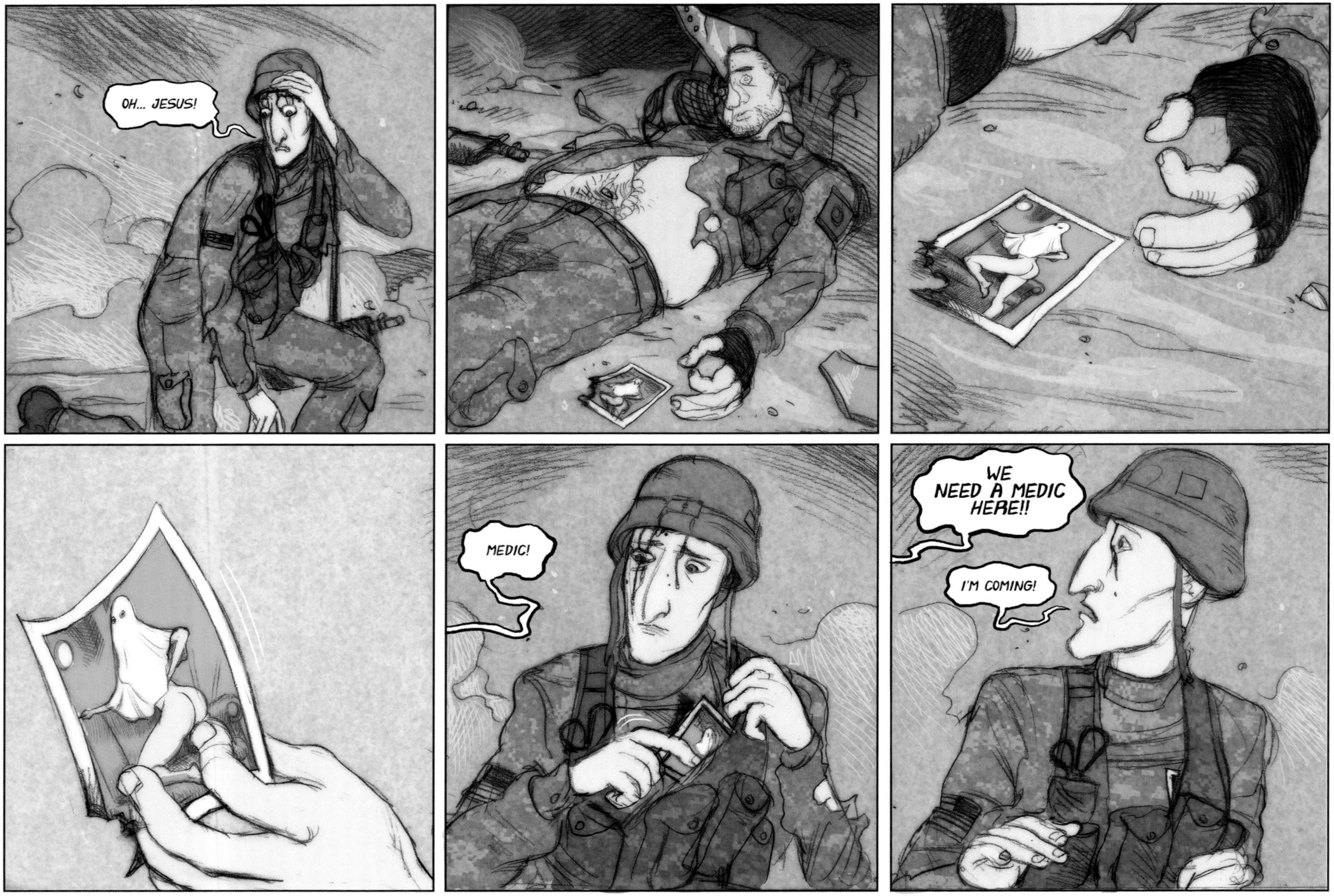
OH... JESUS!
MEDIC!
WE NEED A MEDIC HERE!!
I'M COMING!

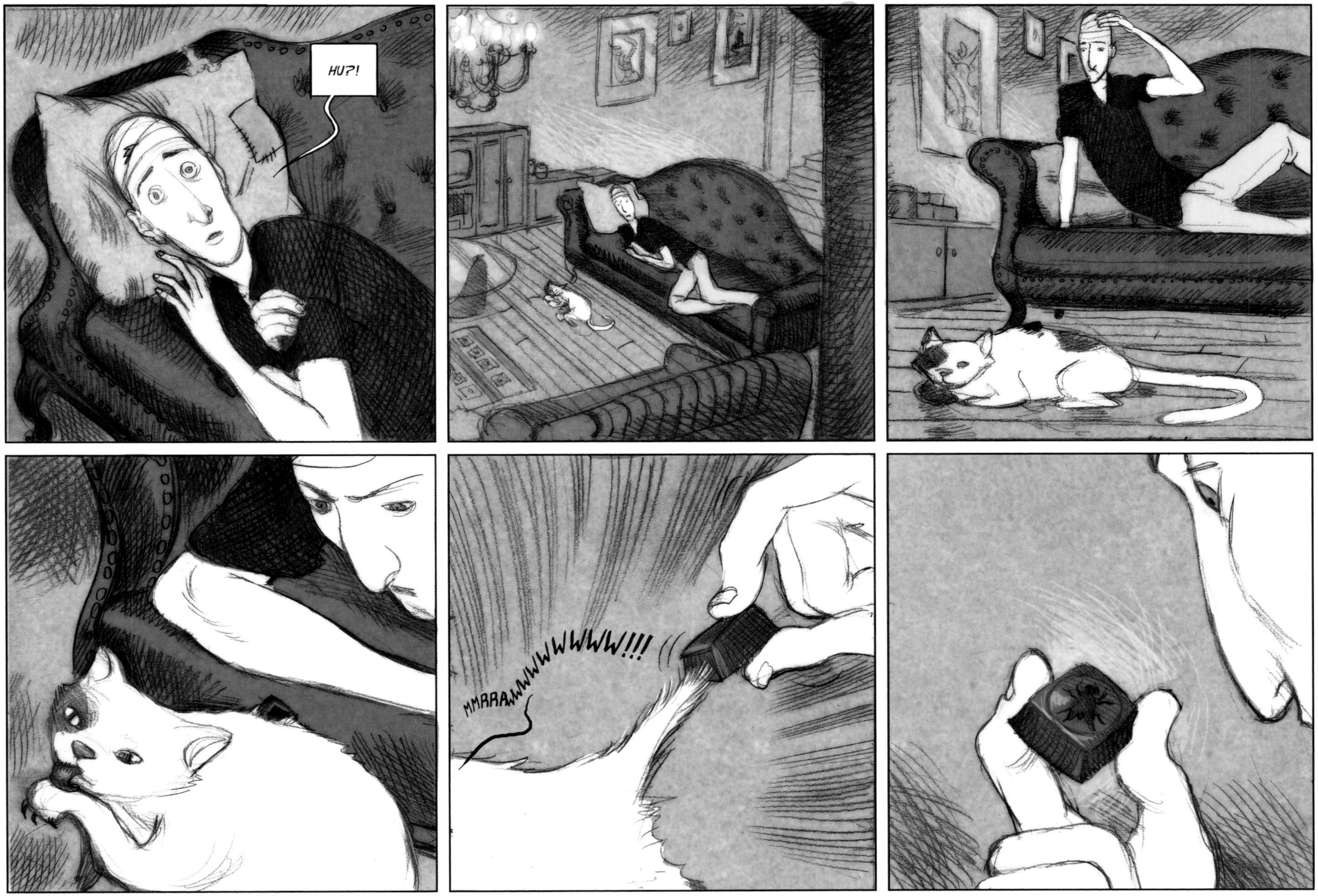
HU?!
MMRRAWWWWWWWWWW!!!

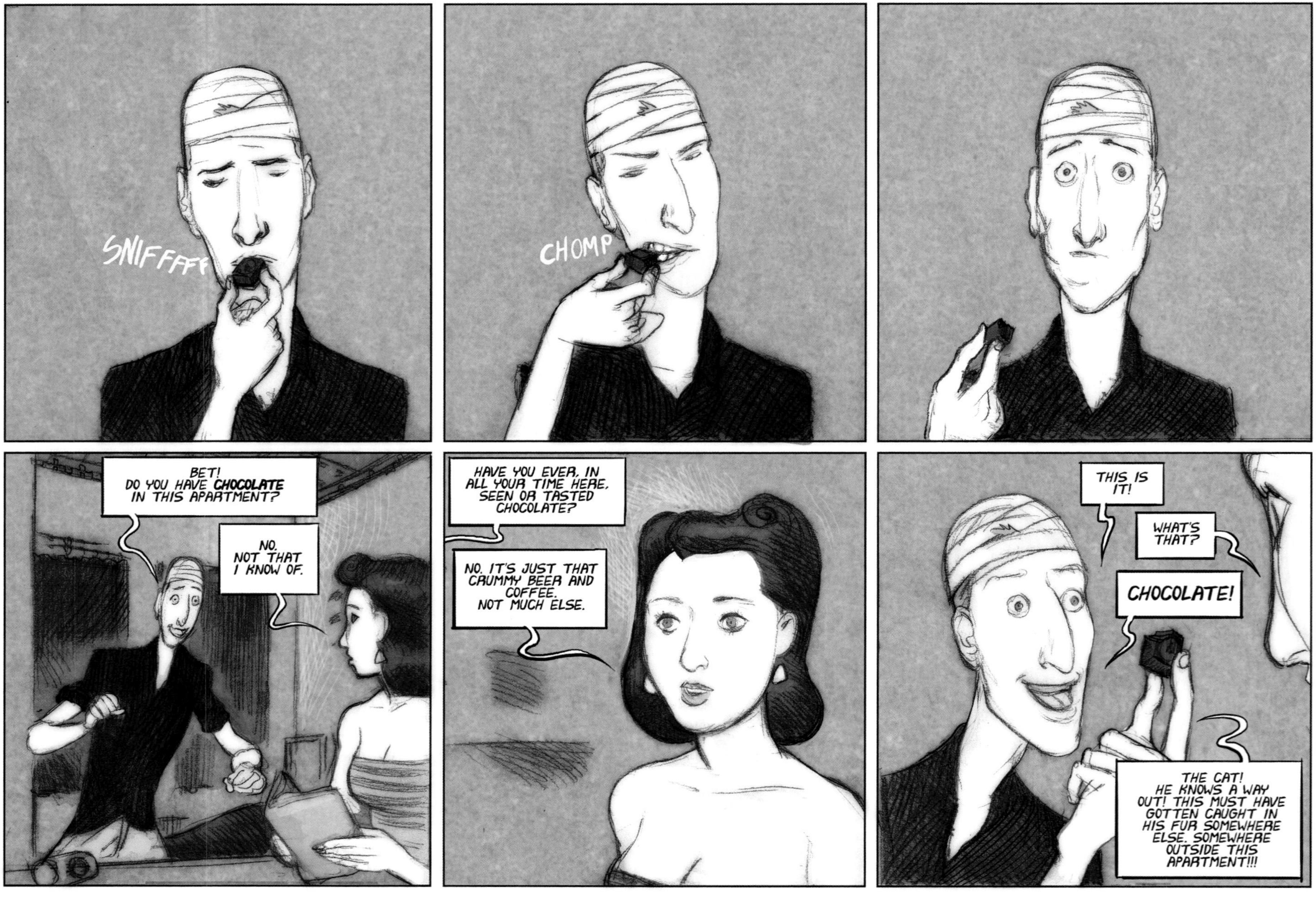
SNIFFFFF
CHOMP
BET! DO YOU HAVE CHOCOLATE IN THIS APARTMENT?
NO. NOT THAT I KNOW OF.
HAVE YOU EVER, IN ALL YOUR TIME HERE, SEEN OR TASTED CHOCOLATE?
NO. IT'S JUST THAT CRUMMY BEER AND COFFEE. NOT MUCH ELSE.
THIS IS IT!
WHAT'S THAT?
CHOCOLATE!
THE CAT! HE KNOWS A WAY OUT! THIS MUST HAVE GOTTEN CAUGHT IN HIS FUR SOMEWHERE ELSE. SOMEWHERE OUTSIDE THIS APARTMENT!!!

LATER...

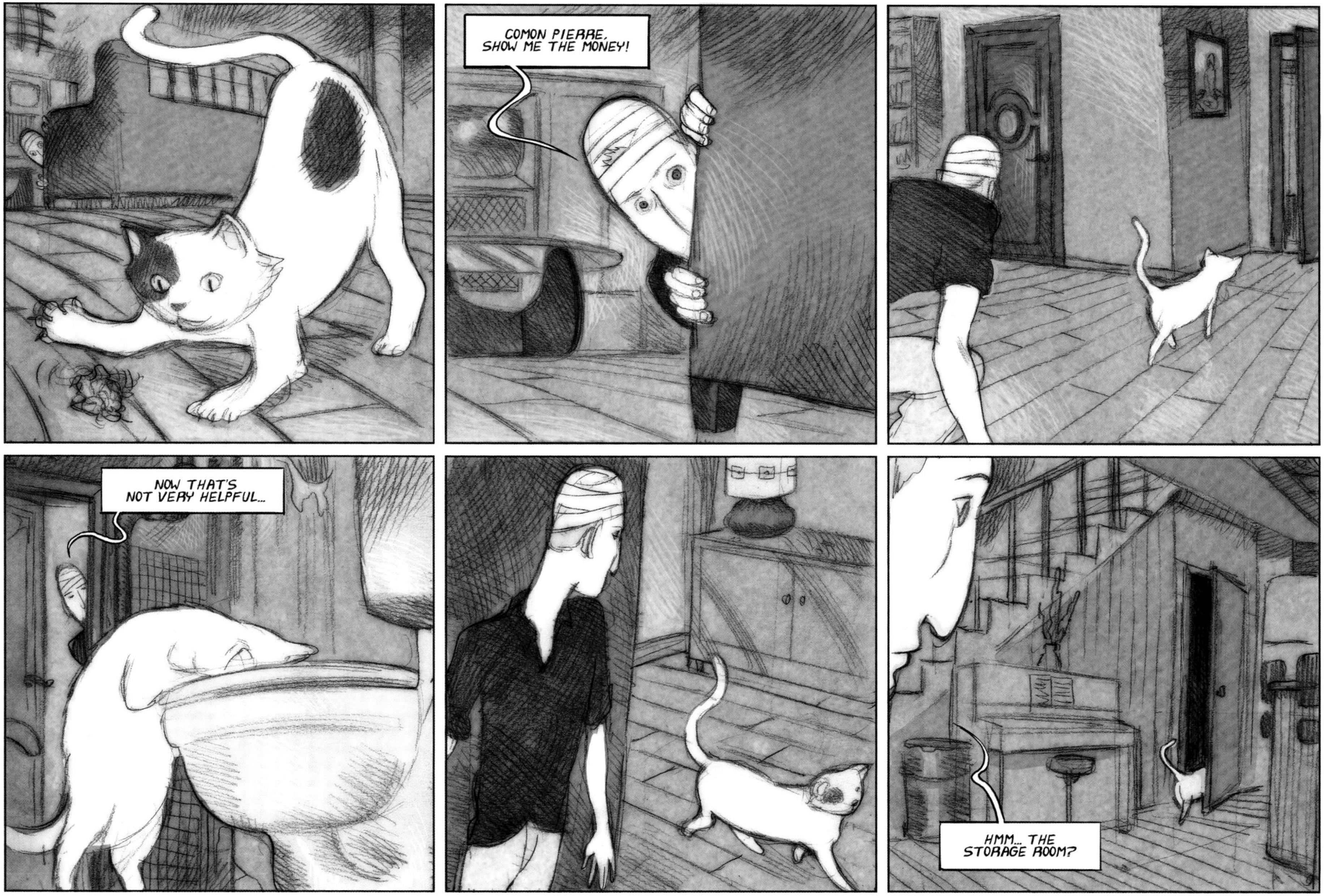
COMON PIERRE, SHOW ME THE MONEY!
NOW THAT'S NOT VERY HELPFUL...
HMM... THE STORAGE ROOM?

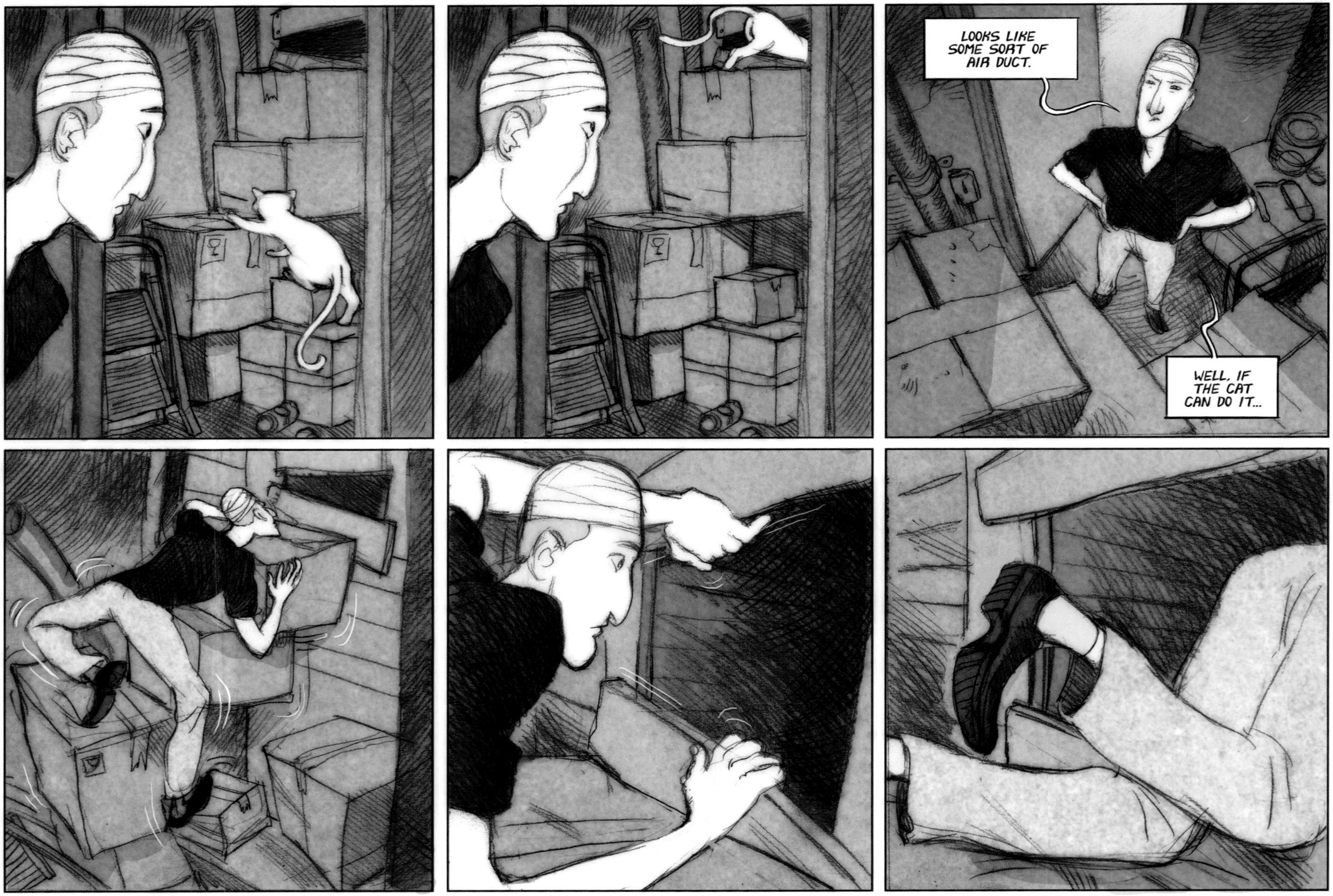
LOOKS LIKE SOME SORT OF AIR DUCT.
WELL, IF THE CAT CAN DO IT...

INCREDIBLE...

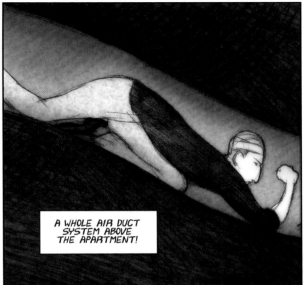

A WHOLE AIR DUCT SYSTEM ABOVE THE APARTMENT!

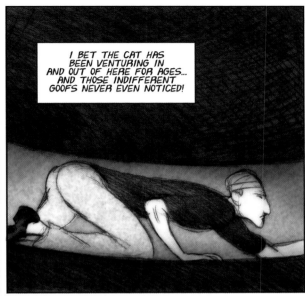

I BET THE CAT HAS BEEN VENTURING IN AND OUT OF HERE FOR AGES... AND THOSE INDIFFERENT GOOFS NEVER EVEN NOTICED!

IT MUST EXTEND QUITE FAR, PROBABLY INTO ANOTHER APARTMENT! OR MAYBE EVEN...

?!

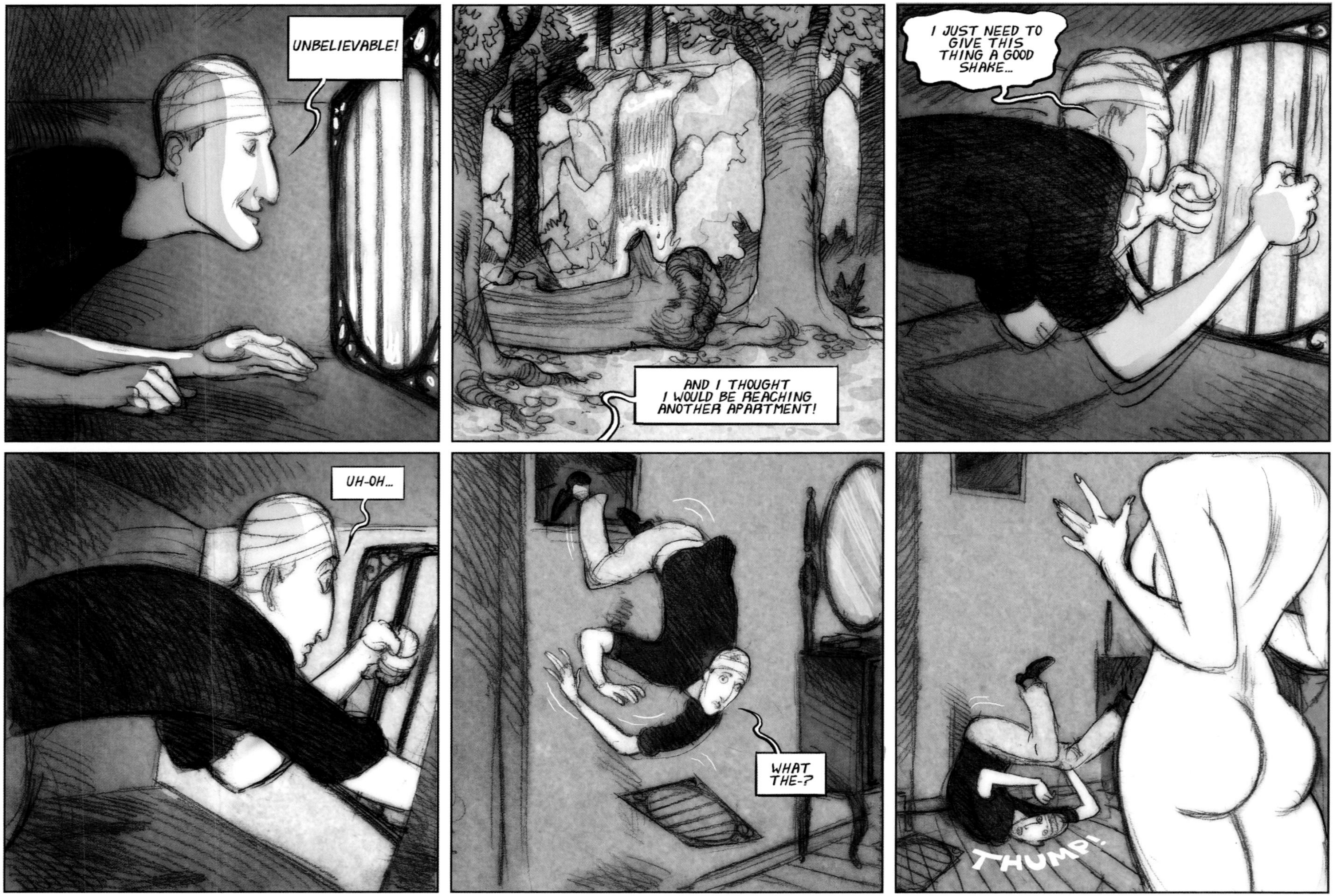
UNBELIEVABLE!
AND I THOUGHT I WOULD BE REACHING ANOTHER APARTMENT!
I JUST NEED TO GIVE THIS THING A GOOD SHAKE...
UH-OH...
WHAT THE-?
THUMP!

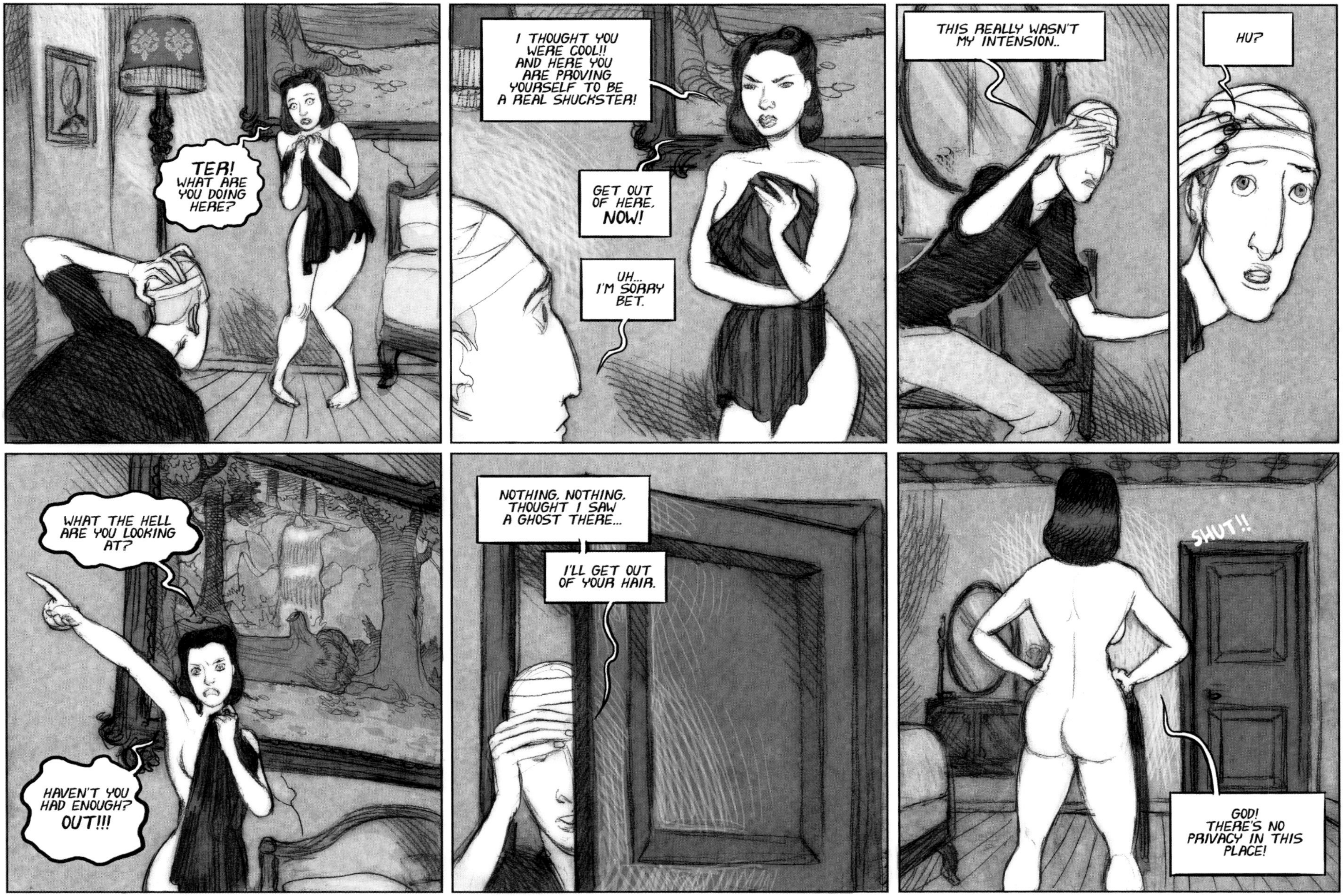
TER! WHAT ARE YOU DOING HERE?
I THOUGHT YOU WERE COOL!! AND HERE YOU ARE PROVING YOURSELF TO BE A REAL SHUCKSTER!
GET OUT OF HERE, NOW!
UH... I'M SORRY BET.
THIS REALLY WASN'T MY INTENSION..
HU?
WHAT THE HELL ARE YOU LOOKING AT?
HAVEN'T YOU HAD ENOUGH? OUT!!!
NOTHING, NOTHING, THOUGHT I SAW A GHOST THERE...
I'LL GET OUT OF YOUR HAIR.
SHUT!!
GOD! THERE'S NO PRIVACY IN THIS PLACE!

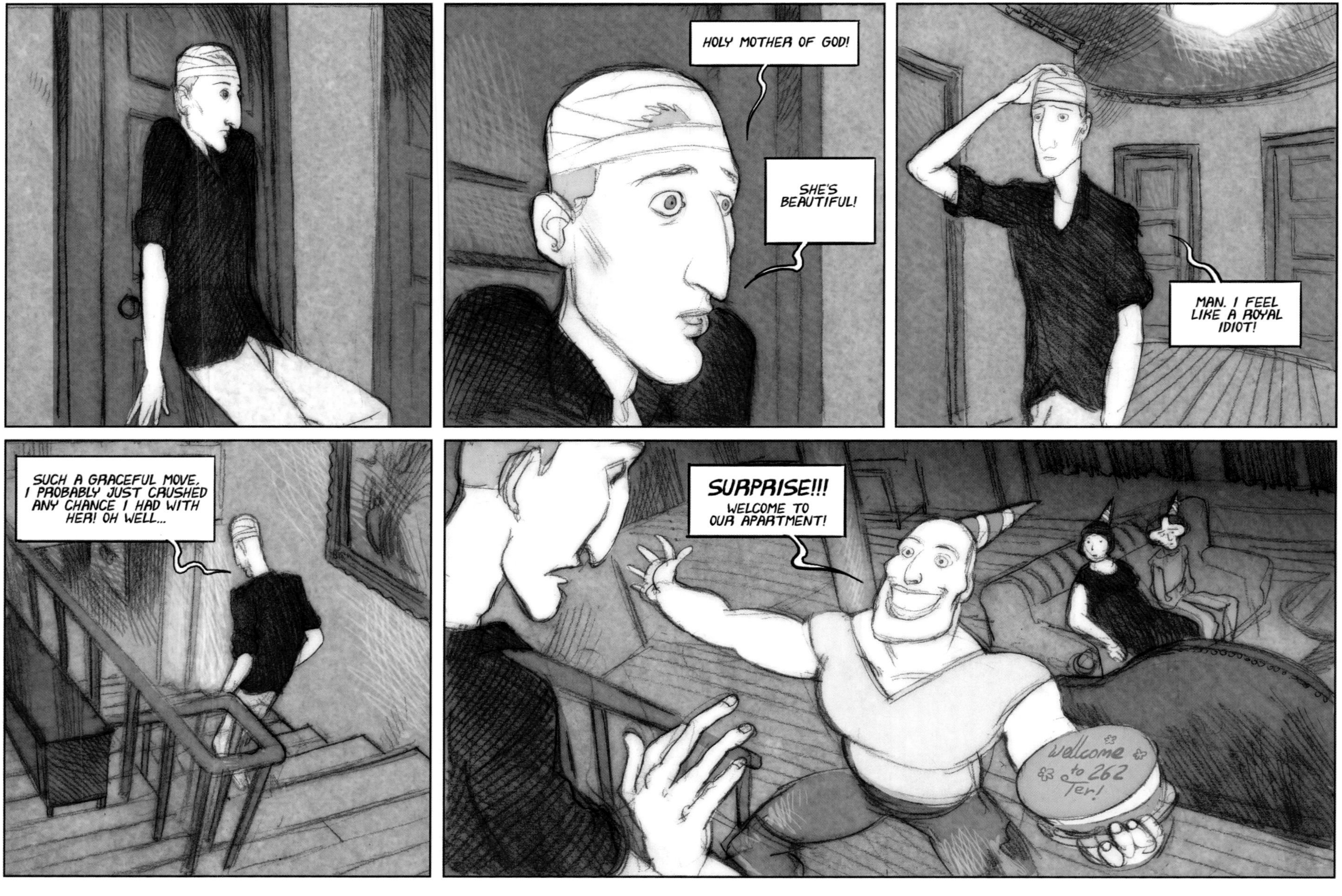
HOLY MOTHER OF GOD!
SHE'S BEAUTIFUL!
MAN. I FEEL LIKE A ROYAL IDIOT!
SUCH A GRACEFUL MOVE, I PROBABLY JUST CRUSHED ANY CHANCE I HAD WITH HER! OH WELL...
SURPRISE!!! WELCOME TO OUR APARTMENT!
Wellcome to 262 Ter!

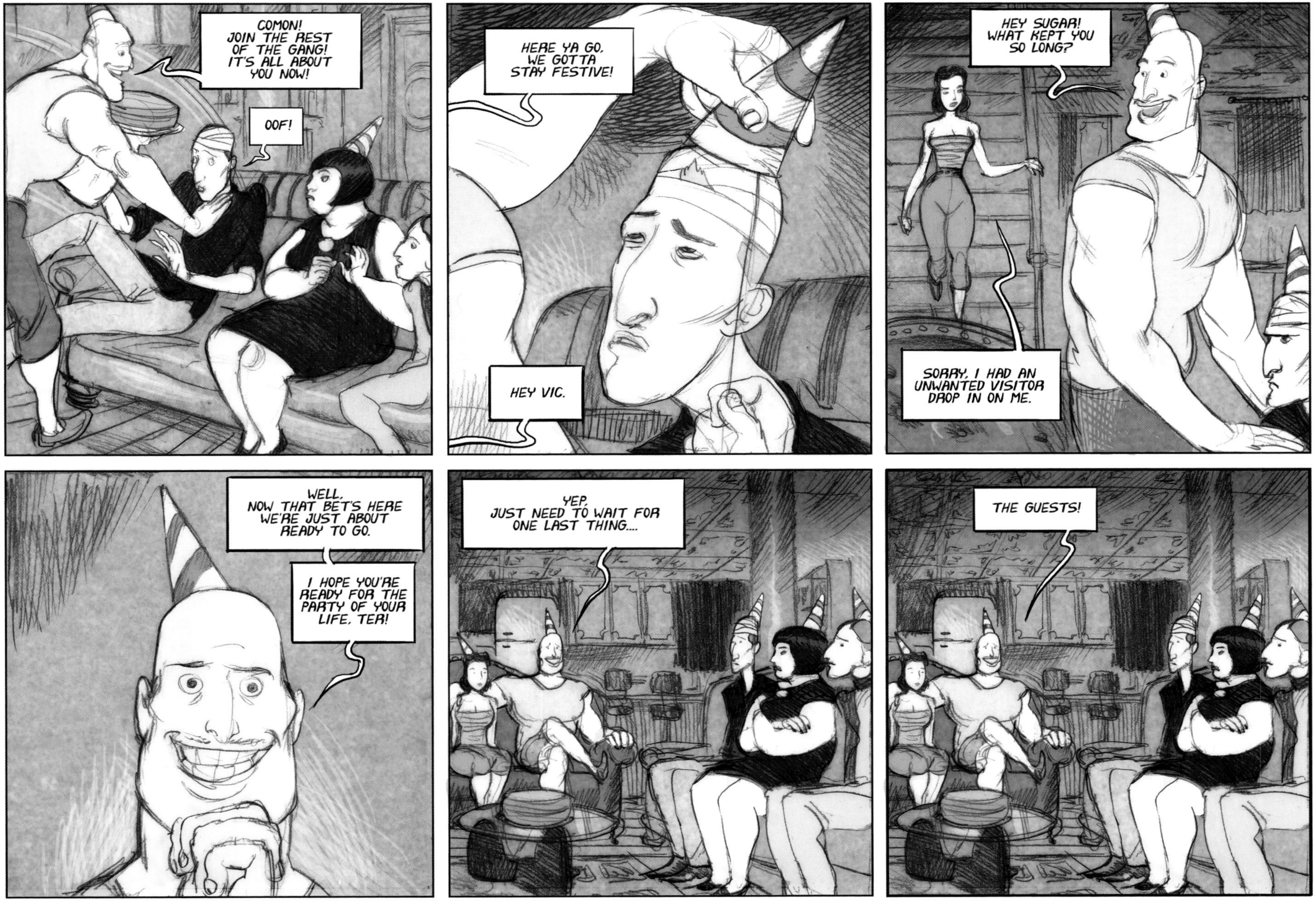
COMON! JOIN THE REST OF THE GANG! IT'S ALL ABOUT YOU NOW!
OOF!
HERE YA GO, WE GOTTA STAY FESTIVE!
HEY VIC.
HEY SUGAR! WHAT KEPT YOU SO LONG?
SORRY, I HAD AN UNWANTED VISITOR DROP IN ON ME.
WELL, NOW THAT BET'S HERE WE'RE JUST ABOUT READY TO GO.
I HOPE YOU'RE READY FOR THE PARTY OF YOUR LIFE, TER!
YEP, JUST NEED TO WAIT FOR ONE LAST THING....
THE GUESTS!

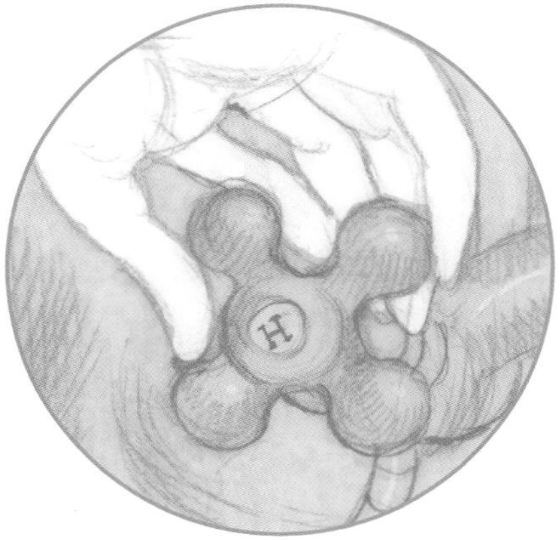
H

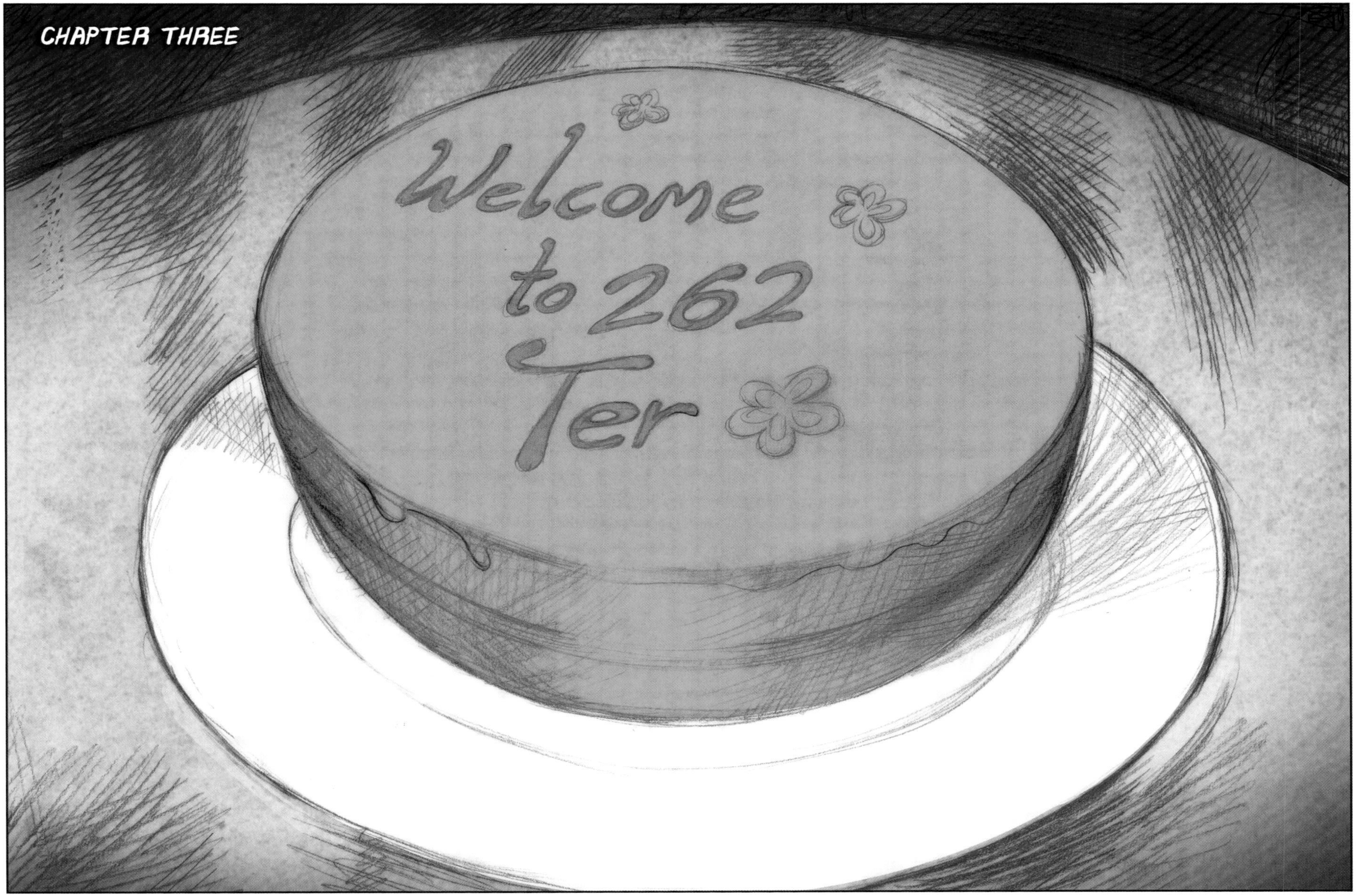
CHAPTER THREE
Welcome to 262 Ter

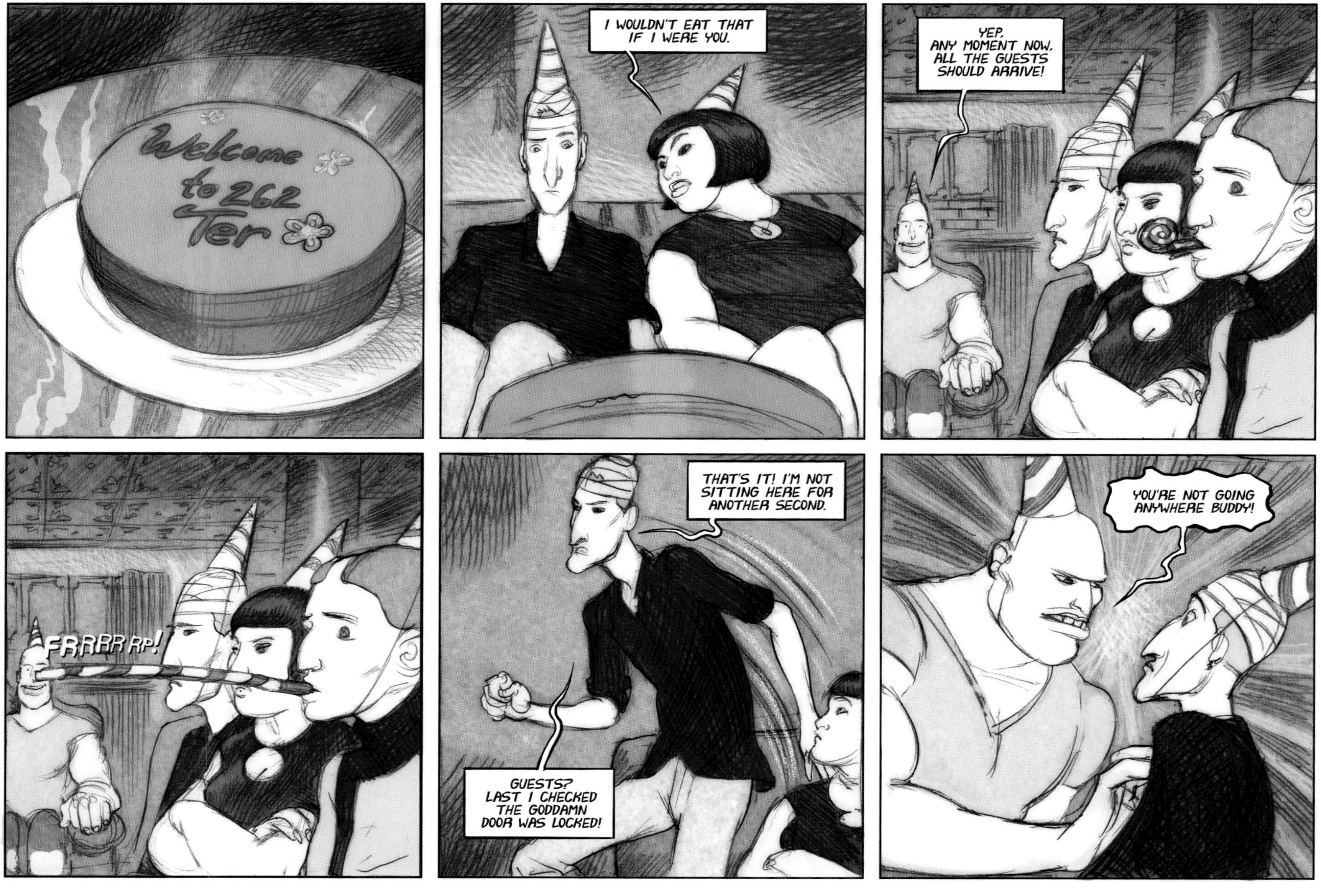
Welcome to 262 Ter
I WOULDN'T EAT THAT IF I WERE YOU.
YEP, ANY MOMENT NOW, ALL THE GUESTS SHOULD ARRIVE!
FRRRRR RP!
THAT'S IT! I'M NOT SITTING HERE FOR ANOTHER SECOND.
GUESTS? LAST I CHECKED THE GODDAMN DOOR WAS LOCKED!
YOU'RE NOT GOING ANYWHERE BUDDY!

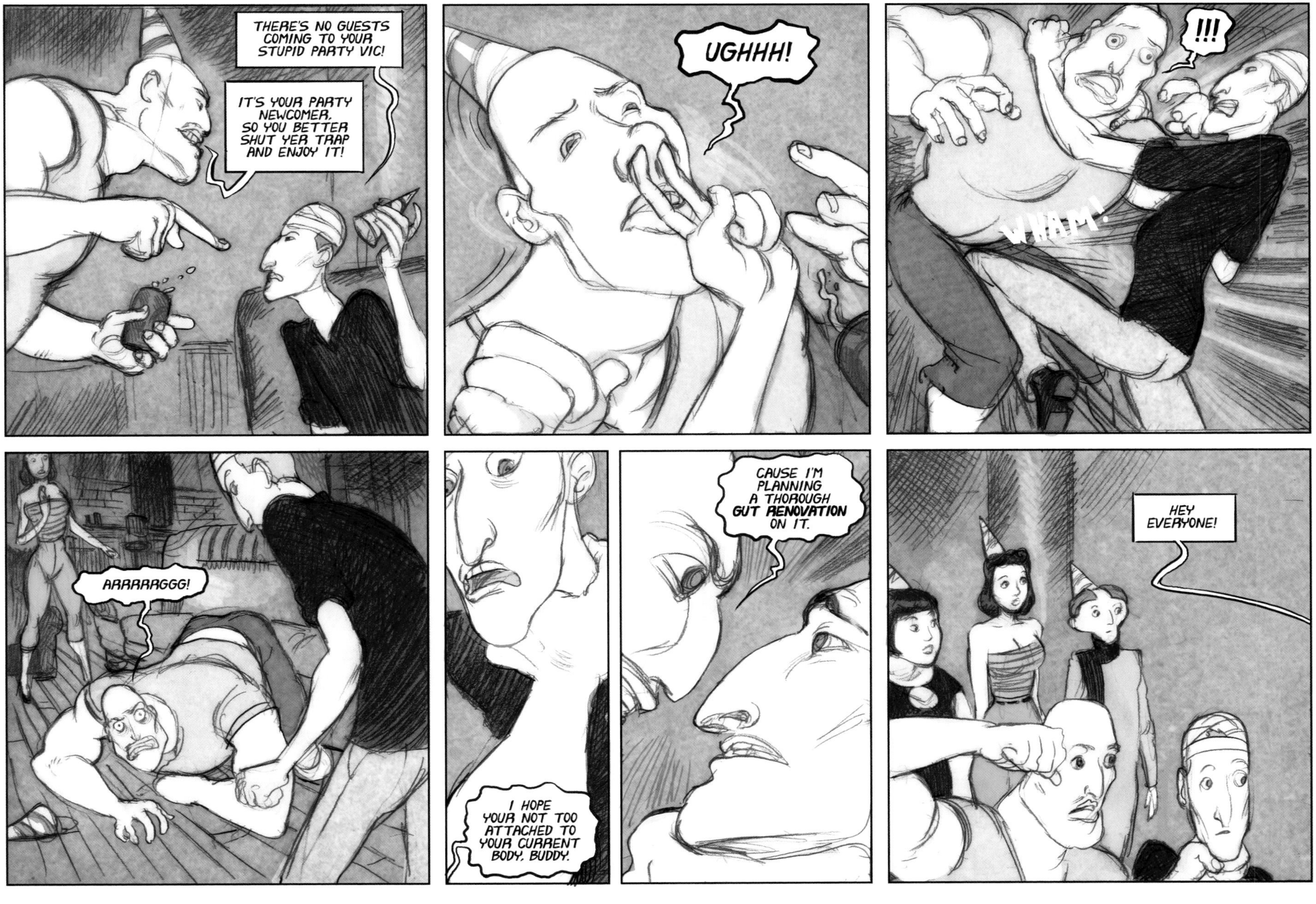
THERE'S NO GUESTS COMING TO YOUR STUPID PARTY VIC!
IT'S YOUR PARTY NEWCOMER, SO YOU BETTER SHUT YER TRAP AND ENJOY IT!
UGHHH!
!!!
WHAM!
ARRRRRRGGG!
I HOPE YOUR NOT TOO ATTACHED TO YOUR CURRENT BODY, BUDDY.
CAUSE I'M PLANNING A THOROUGH **GUT RENOVATION** ON IT.
HEY EVERYONE!

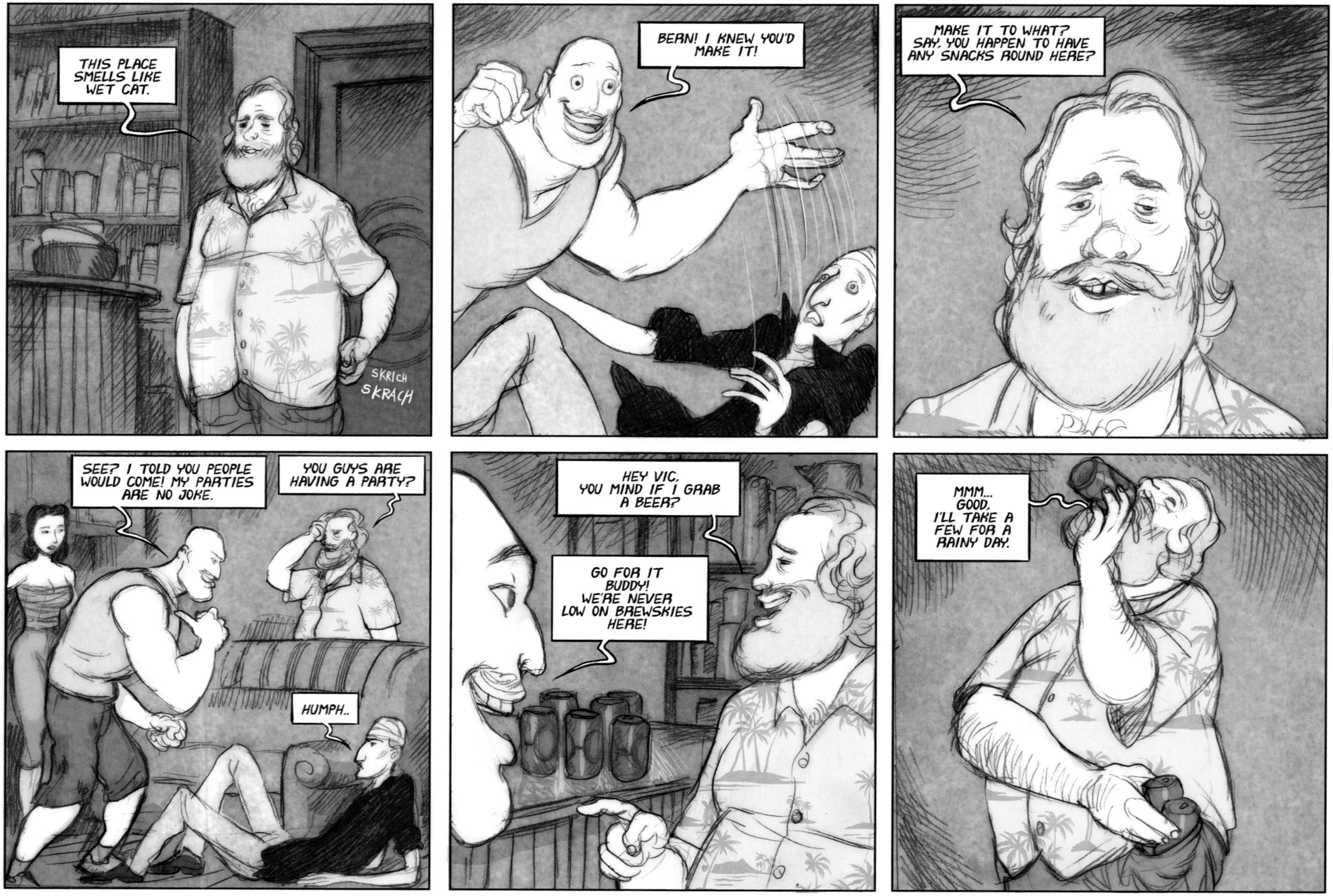
THIS PLACE SMELLS LIKE WET CAT.
SKRICH SKRACH
BERN! I KNEW YOU'D MAKE IT!
MAKE IT TO WHAT? SAY, YOU HAPPEN TO HAVE ANY SNACKS ROUND HERE?
SEE? I TOLD YOU PEOPLE WOULD COME! MY PARTIES ARE NO JOKE.
YOU GUYS ARE HAVING A PARTY?
HUMPH..
HEY VIC, YOU MIND IF I GRAB A BEER?
GO FOR IT BUDDY! WE'RE NEVER LOW ON BREWSKIES HERE!
MMM... GOOD. I'LL TAKE A FEW FOR A RAINY DAY.

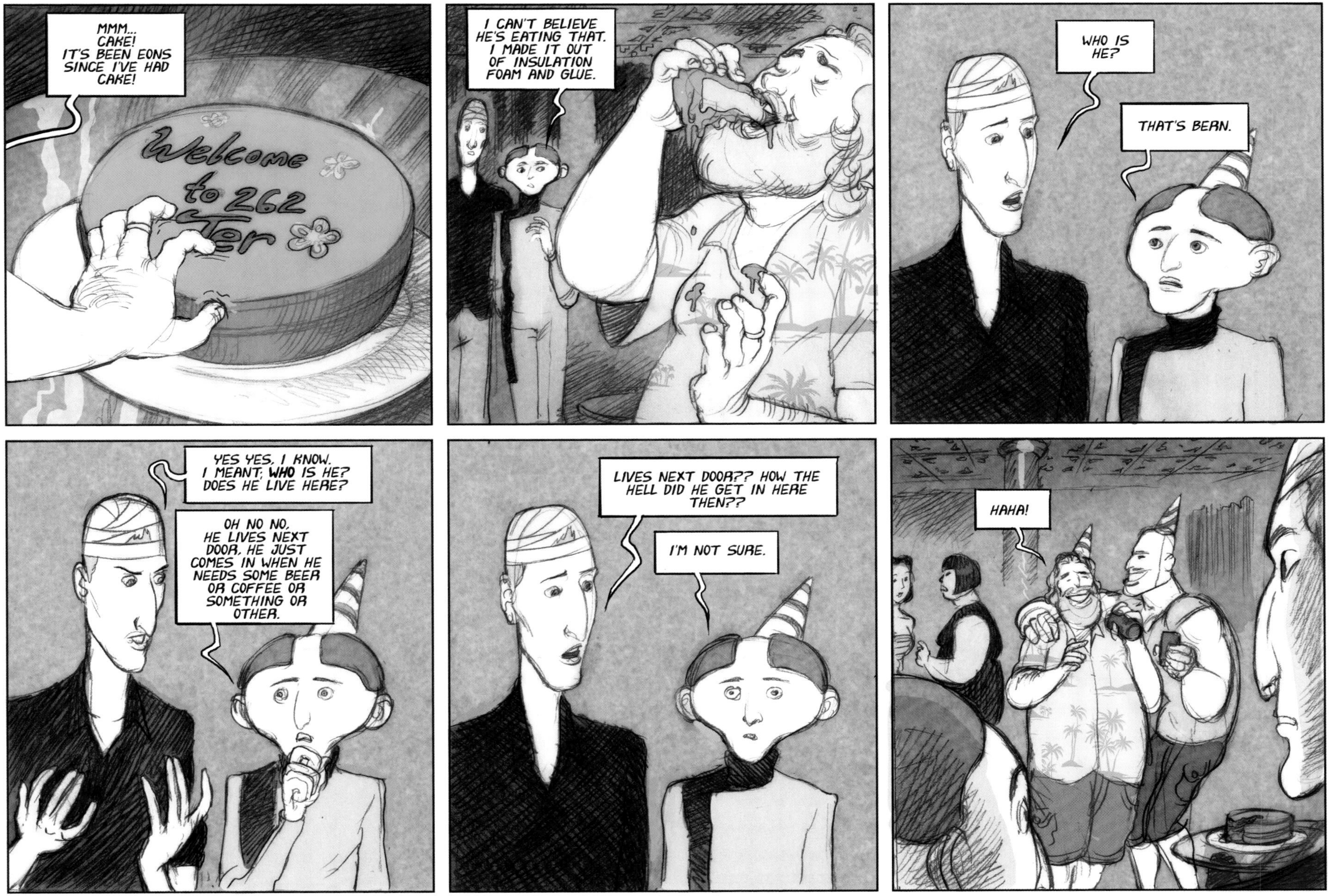
MMM... CAKE! IT'S BEEN EONS SINCE I'VE HAD CAKE!
Welcome to 262 Ter
I CAN'T BELIEVE HE'S EATING THAT. I MADE IT OUT OF INSULATION FOAM AND GLUE.
WHO IS HE?
THAT'S BERN.
YES YES, I KNOW. I MEANT; WHO IS HE? DOES HE LIVE HERE?
OH NO NO, HE LIVES NEXT DOOR, HE JUST COMES IN WHEN HE NEEDS SOME BEER OR COFFEE OR SOMETHING OR OTHER.
LIVES NEXT DOOR?? HOW THE HELL DID HE GET IN HERE THEN??
I'M NOT SURE.
HAHA!

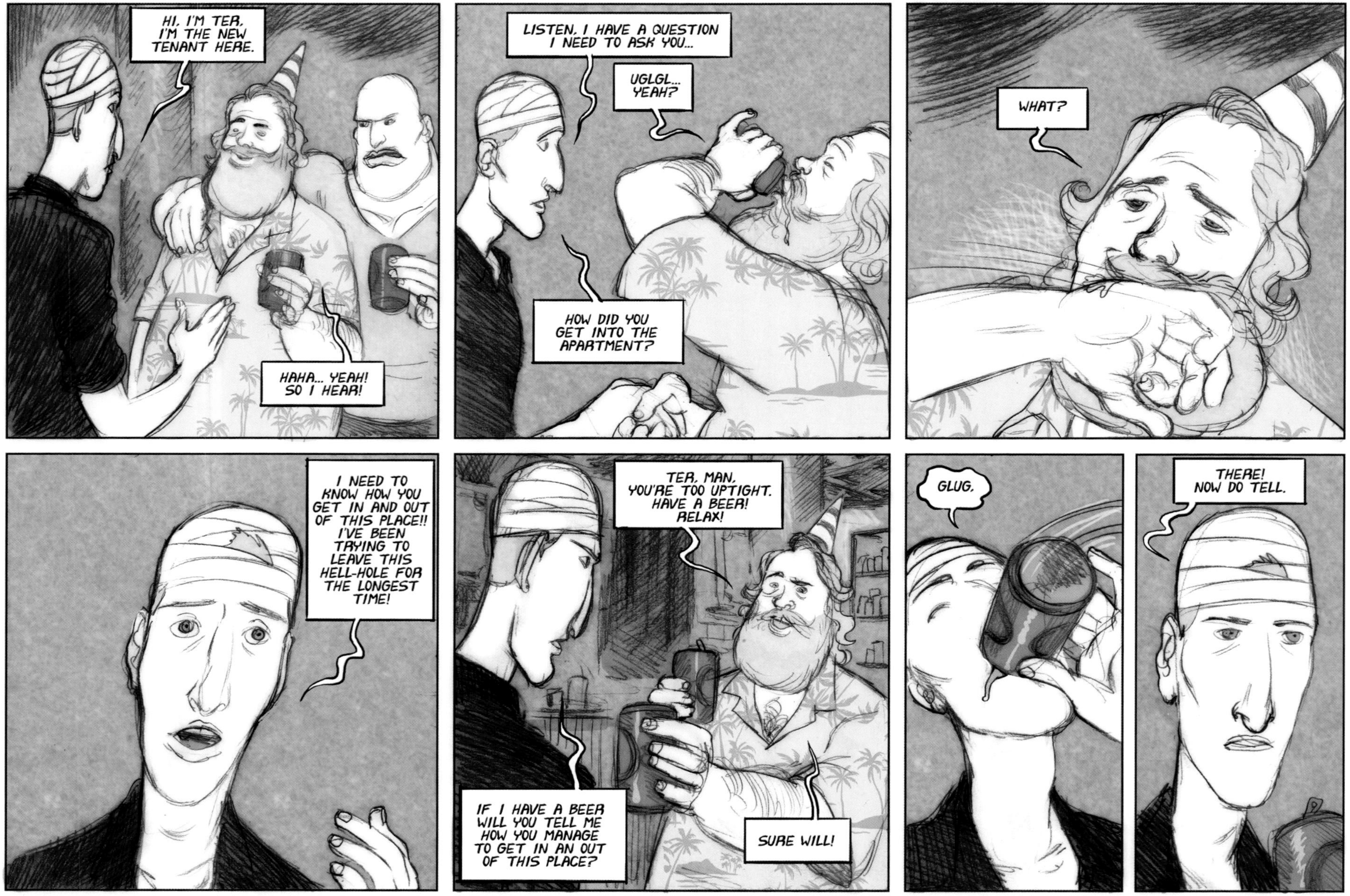

HI, I'M TER, I'M THE NEW TENANT HERE.
HAHA... YEAH! SO I HEAR!
LISTEN, I HAVE A QUESTION I NEED TO ASK YOU...
UGLGL... YEAH?
HOW DID YOU GET INTO THE APARTMENT?
WHAT?
I NEED TO KNOW HOW YOU GET IN AND OUT OF THIS PLACE!! I'VE BEEN TRYING TO LEAVE THIS HELL-HOLE FOR THE LONGEST TIME!
TER, MAN, YOU'RE TOO UPTIGHT. HAVE A BEER! RELAX!
IF I HAVE A BEER WILL YOU TELL ME HOW YOU MANAGE TO GET IN AN OUT OF THIS PLACE?
SURE WILL!
GLUG.
THERE! NOW DO TELL.

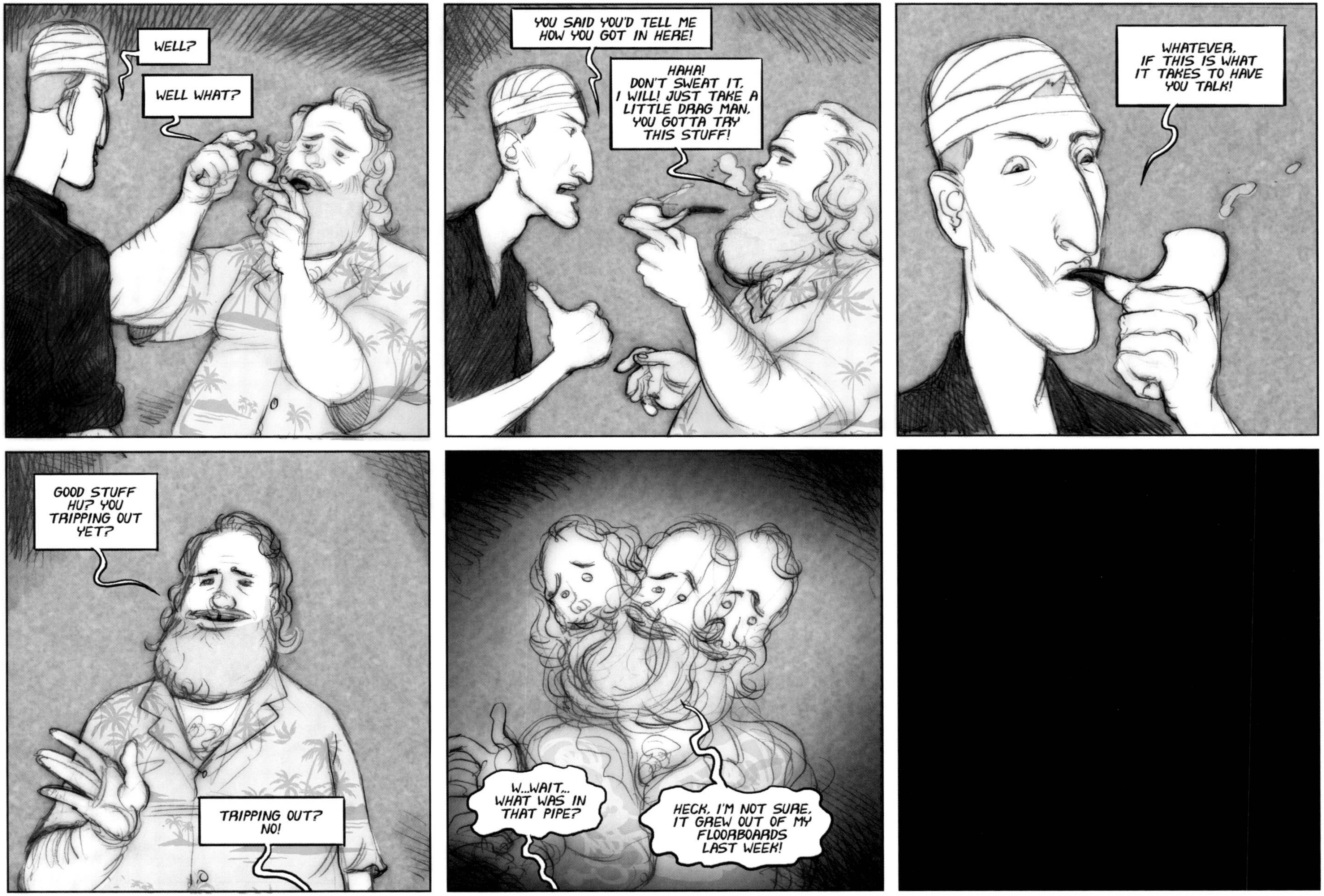
WELL?
WELL WHAT?
YOU SAID YOU'D TELL ME HOW YOU GOT IN HERE!
HAHA! DON'T SWEAT IT, I WILL! JUST TAKE A LITTLE DRAG MAN, YOU GOTTA TRY THIS STUFF!
WHATEVER, IF THIS IS WHAT IT TAKES TO HAVE YOU TALK!
GOOD STUFF HU? YOU TRIPPING OUT YET?
TRIPPING OUT? NO!
W...WAIT... WHAT WAS IN THAT PIPE?
HECK, I'M NOT SURE, IT GREW OUT OF MY FLOORBOARDS LAST WEEK!

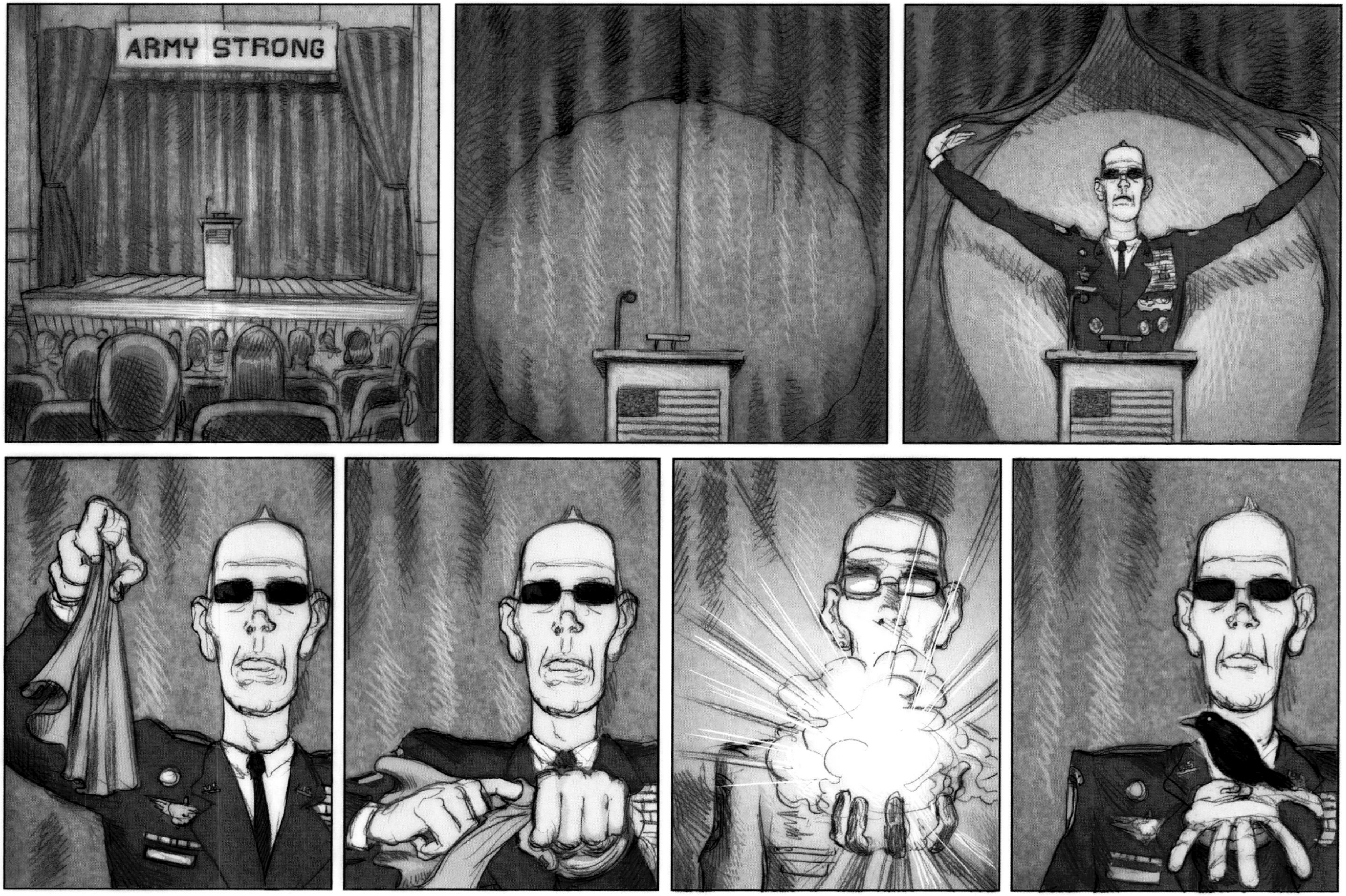
ARMY STRONG

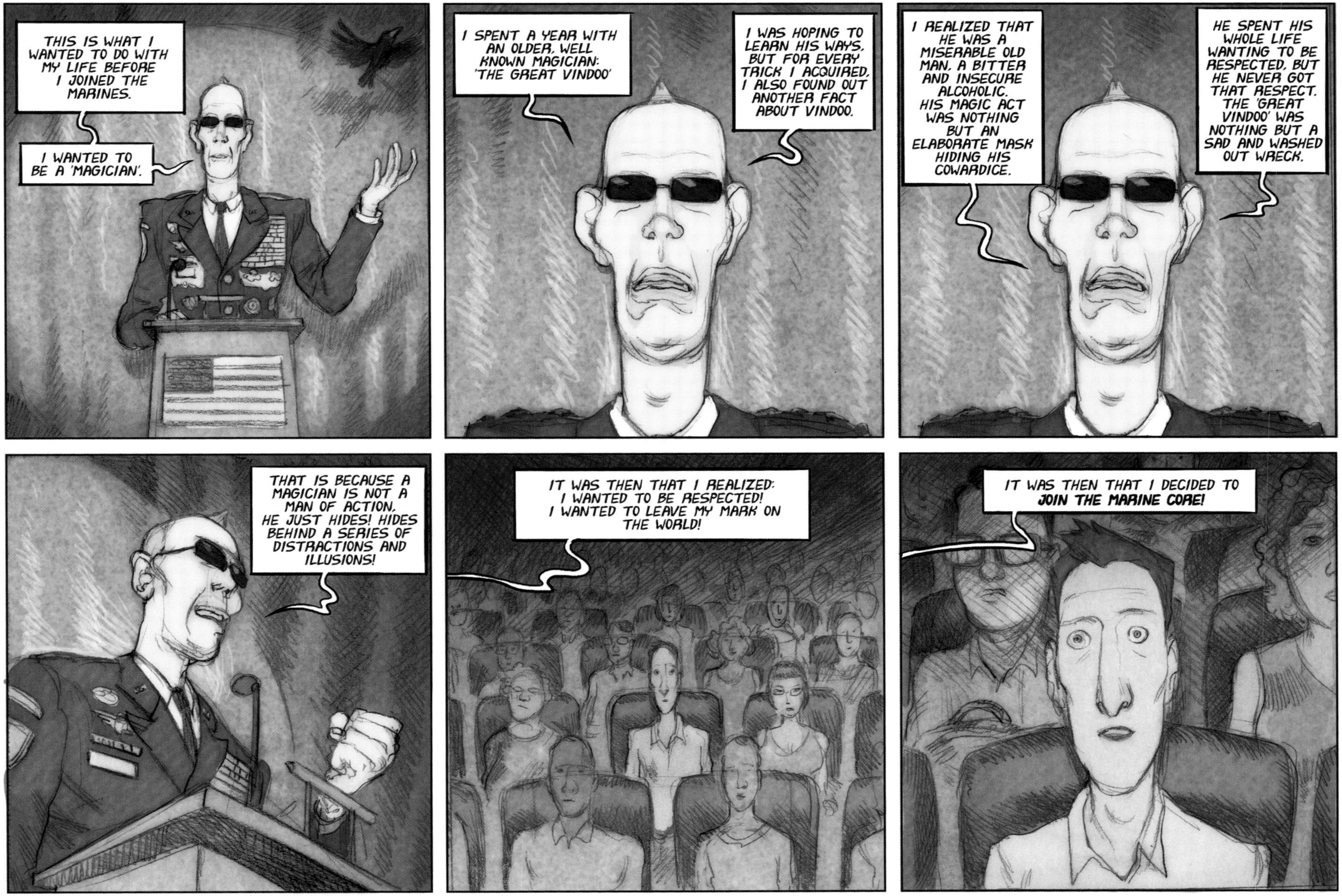
THIS IS WHAT I WANTED TO DO WITH MY LIFE BEFORE I JOINED THE MARINES.
I WANTED TO BE A 'MAGICIAN'.
I SPENT A YEAR WITH AN OLDER, WELL KNOWN MAGICIAN: 'THE GREAT VINDOO'
I WAS HOPING TO LEARN HIS WAYS, BUT FOR EVERY TRICK I ACQUIRED, I ALSO FOUND OUT ANOTHER FACT ABOUT VINDOO.
I REALIZED THAT HE WAS A MISERABLE OLD MAN, A BITTER AND INSECURE ALCOHOLIC. HIS MAGIC ACT WAS NOTHING BUT AN ELABORATE MASK HIDING HIS COWARDICE.
HE SPENT HIS WHOLE LIFE WANTING TO BE RESPECTED, BUT HE NEVER GOT THAT RESPECT. THE 'GREAT VINDOO' WAS NOTHING BUT A SAD AND WASHED OUT WRECK.
THAT IS BECAUSE A MAGICIAN IS NOT A MAN OF ACTION, HE JUST HIDES! HIDES BEHIND A SERIES OF DISTRACTIONS AND ILLUSIONS!
IT WAS THEN THAT I REALIZED: I WANTED TO BE RESPECTED! I WANTED TO LEAVE MY MARK ON THE WORLD!
IT WAS THEN THAT I DECIDED TO **JOIN THE MARINE CORE!**

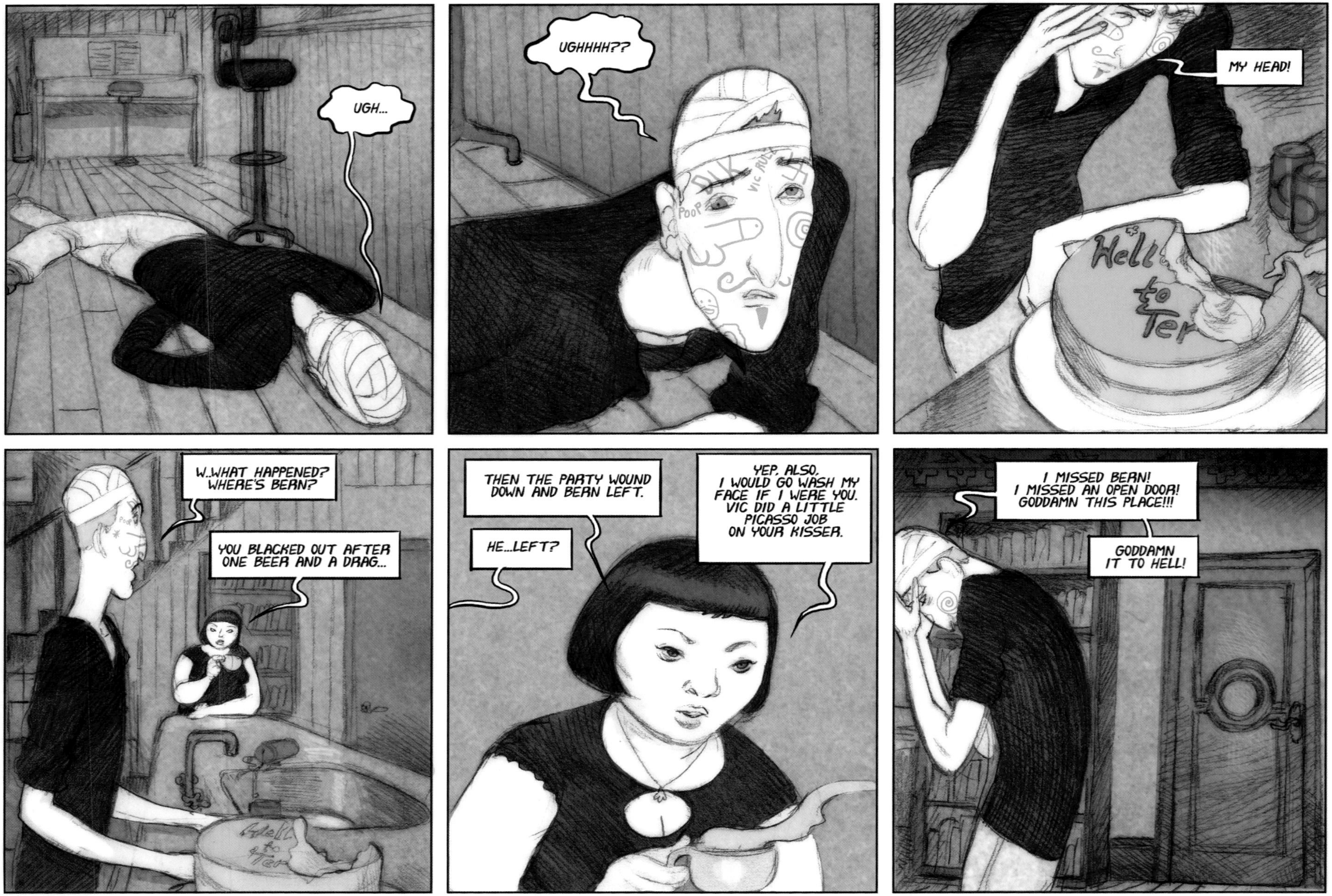
UGH...
UGHHHH??
MY HEAD!
Hell to Ter
W..WHAT HAPPENED? WHERE'S BERN?
YOU BLACKED OUT AFTER ONE BEER AND A DRAG...
THEN THE PARTY WOUND DOWN AND BERN LEFT.
HE...LEFT?
YEP, ALSO, I WOULD GO WASH MY FACE IF I WERE YOU. VIC DID A LITTLE PICASSO JOB ON YOUR KISSER.
I MISSED BERN! I MISSED AN OPEN DOOR! GODDAMN THIS PLACE!!!
GODDAMN IT TO HELL!

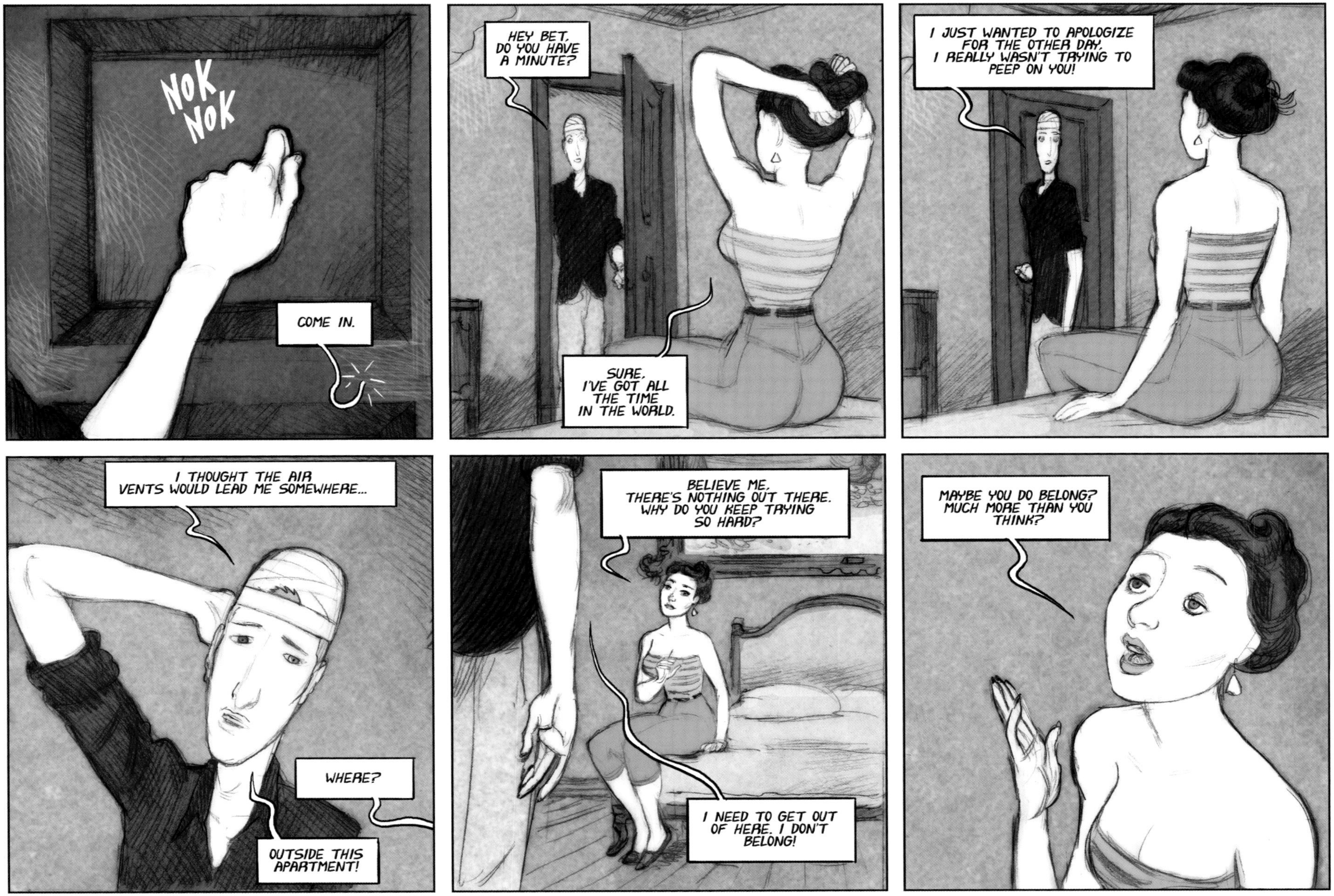
NOK NOK
COME IN.
HEY BET, DO YOU HAVE A MINUTE?
SURE, I'VE GOT ALL THE TIME IN THE WORLD.
I JUST WANTED TO APOLOGIZE FOR THE OTHER DAY, I REALLY WASN'T TRYING TO PEEP ON YOU!
I THOUGHT THE AIR VENTS WOULD LEAD ME SOMEWHERE...
WHERE?
OUTSIDE THIS APARTMENT!
BELIEVE ME, THERE'S NOTHING OUT THERE. WHY DO YOU KEEP TRYING SO HARD?
I NEED TO GET OUT OF HERE. I DON'T BELONG!
MAYBE YOU DO BELONG? MUCH MORE THAN YOU THINK?

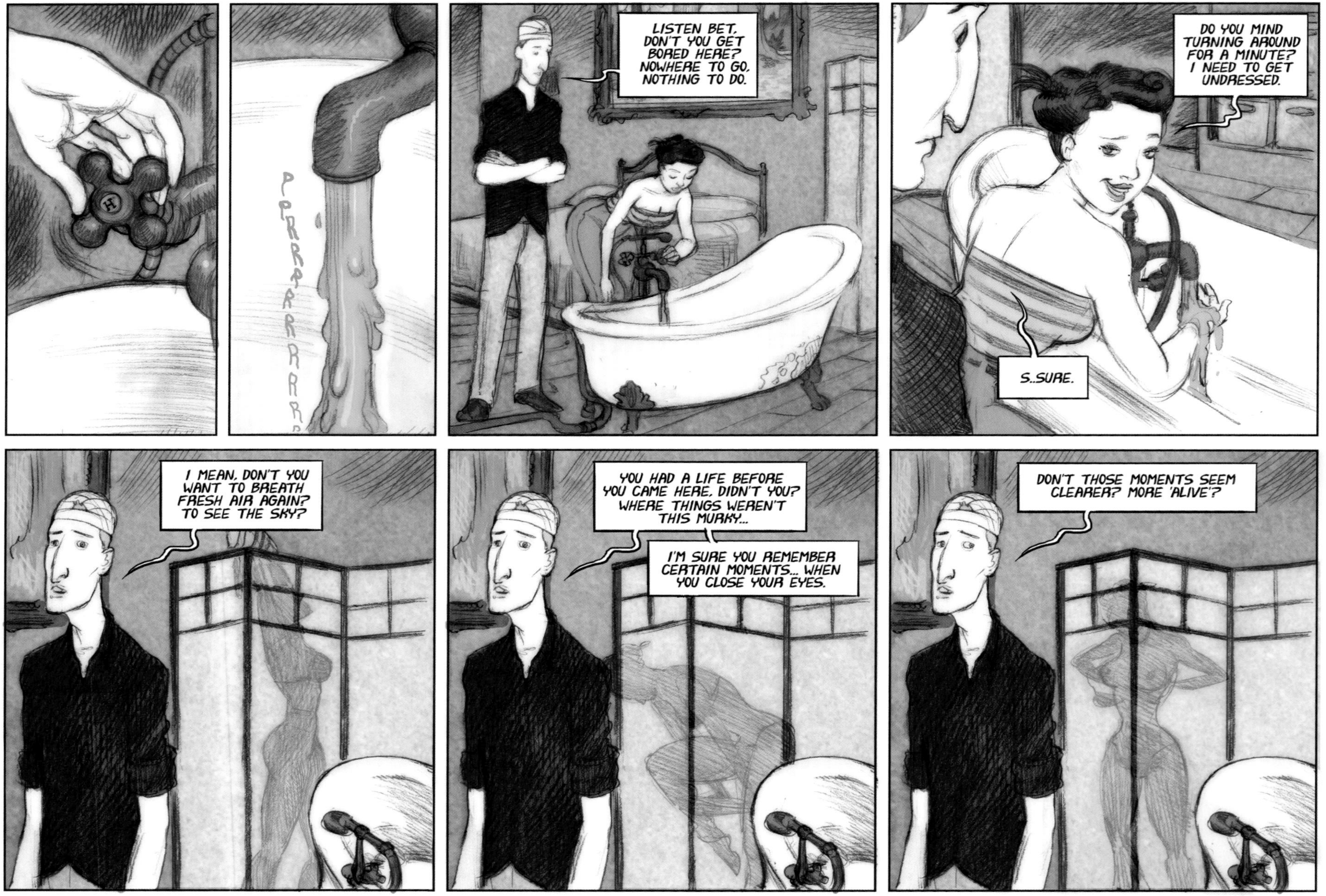
PPRRRRRRRR
LISTEN BET, DON'T YOU GET BORED HERE? NOWHERE TO GO, NOTHING TO DO.
DO YOU MIND TURNING AROUND FOR A MINUTE? I NEED TO GET UNDRESSED.
S..SURE.
I MEAN, DON'T YOU WANT TO BREATH FRESH AIR AGAIN? TO SEE THE SKY?
YOU HAD A LIFE BEFORE YOU CAME HERE, DIDN'T YOU? WHERE THINGS WEREN'T THIS MURKY...
I'M SURE YOU REMEMBER CERTAIN MOMENTS... WHEN YOU CLOSE YOUR EYES.
DON'T THOSE MOMENTS SEEM CLEARER? MORE 'ALIVE'?

YOU CAN TURN AROUND NOW. KEEP GOING...

OH, WELL I WAS SAYING - MEMORIES, DON'T THEY HAUNT YOU HERE? DON'T THEY MAKE YOU MISS IT ALL?

MY MEMORIES?

IT'S MOSTLY HAZE. I DO REMEMBER BEING A LITTLE GIRL, SMALLER THEN EVERYONE. BEING TEASED AND LAUGHED AT.

THEN GROWING UP ALL OF A SUDDEN, FILLING OUT. NONE OF MY CLOTHES FITTING.

UHE...UHE...UHE

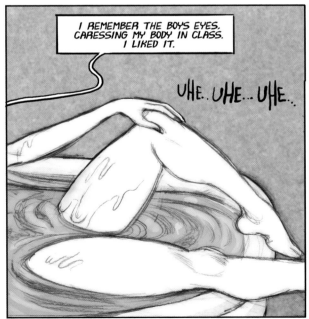

I REMEMBER THE BOYS EYES, CARESSING MY BODY IN CLASS. I LIKED IT.

UHE..UHE...UHE..

I USED TO PULL MY SKIRT UP, HIGHER AND HIGHER... WATCH THEIR EYES GET WIDER.

UHE...UHE...UHE...UHE...UHE...UH

WHAT THE HELL IS THAT NOISE?

..UHE...UHE...UHE...UHE...

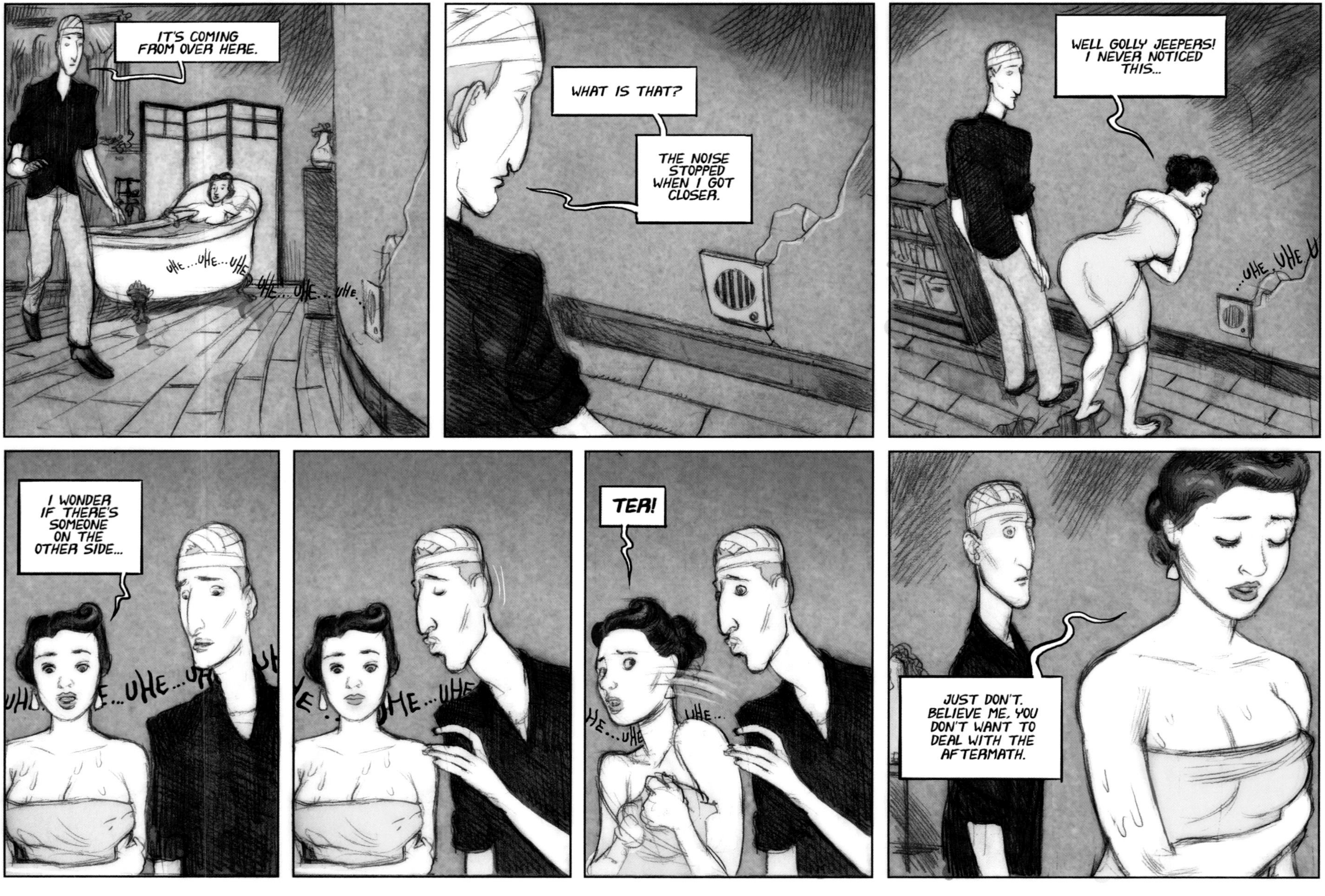
IT'S COMING FROM OVER HERE.
UHE...UHE...UHE...UHE...UHE...UHE...
WHAT IS THAT?
THE NOISE STOPPED WHEN I GOT CLOSER.
WELL GOLLY JEEPERS! I NEVER NOTICED THIS...
...UHE, UHE
I WONDER IF THERE'S SOMEONE ON THE OTHER SIDE...
UHE...UHE...
TER!
JUST DON'T. BELIEVE ME, YOU DON'T WANT TO DEAL WITH THE AFTERMATH.

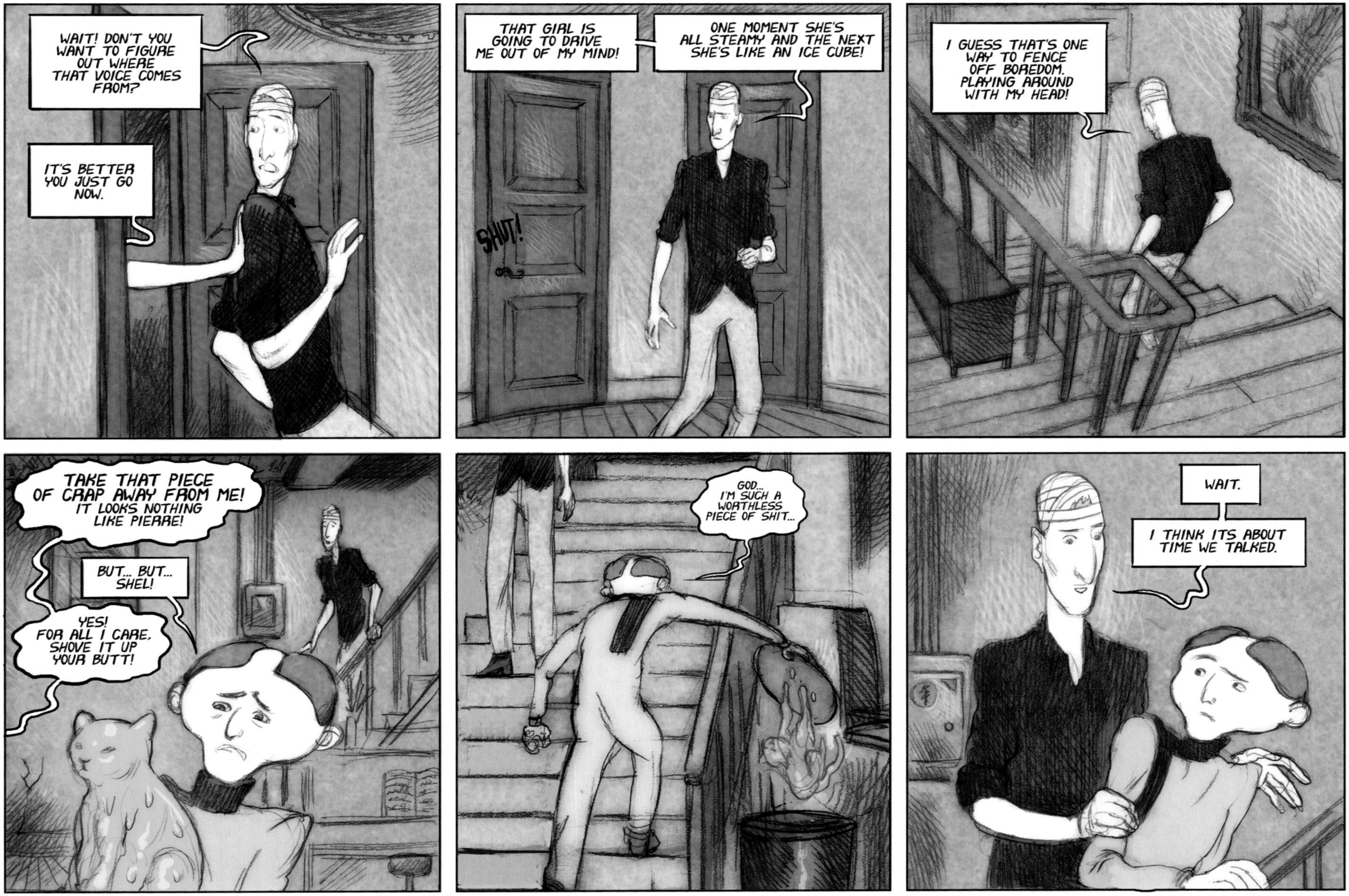
WAIT! DON'T YOU WANT TO FIGURE OUT WHERE THAT VOICE COMES FROM?
IT'S BETTER YOU JUST GO NOW.
THAT GIRL IS GOING TO DRIVE ME OUT OF MY MIND!
ONE MOMENT SHE'S ALL STEAMY AND THE NEXT SHE'S LIKE AN ICE CUBE!
SHUT!
I GUESS THAT'S ONE WAY TO FENCE OFF BOREDOM. PLAYING AROUND WITH MY HEAD!
TAKE THAT PIECE OF CRAP AWAY FROM ME! IT LOOKS NOTHING LIKE PIERRE!
BUT... BUT... SHEL!
YES! FOR ALL I CARE, SHOVE IT UP YOUR BUTT!
GOD... I'M SUCH A WORTHLESS PIECE OF SHIT...
WAIT.
I THINK ITS ABOUT TIME WE TALKED.

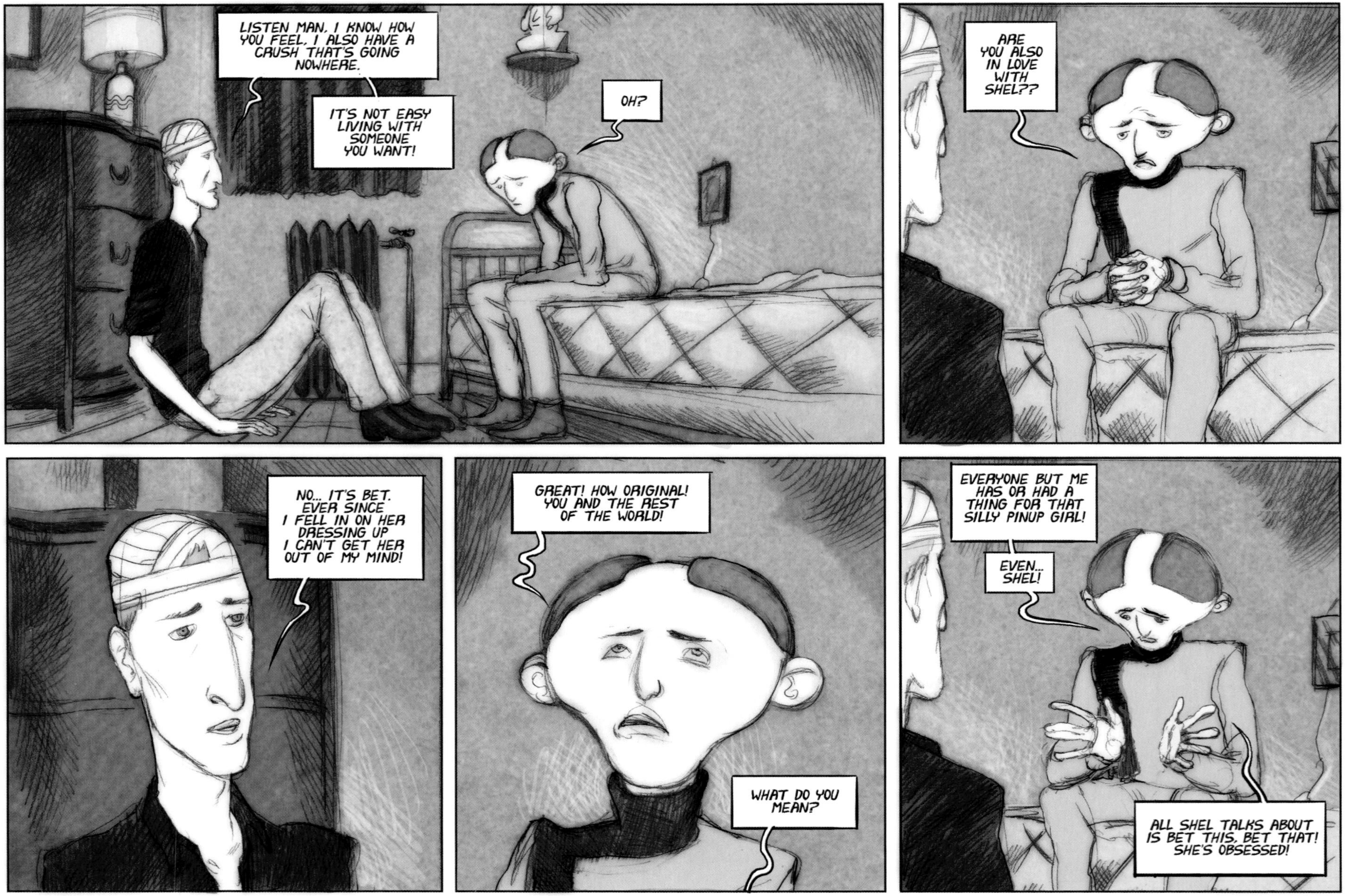
LISTEN MAN, I KNOW HOW YOU FEEL, I ALSO HAVE A CRUSH THAT'S GOING NOWHERE.
IT'S NOT EASY LIVING WITH SOMEONE YOU WANT!
OH?
ARE YOU ALSO IN LOVE WITH SHEL??
NO... IT'S BET. EVER SINCE I FELL IN ON HER DRESSING UP I CAN'T GET HER OUT OF MY MIND!
GREAT! HOW ORIGINAL! YOU AND THE REST OF THE WORLD!
WHAT DO YOU MEAN?
EVERYONE BUT ME HAS OR HAD A THING FOR THAT SILLY PINUP GIRL!
EVEN... SHEL!
ALL SHEL TALKS ABOUT IS BET THIS, BET THAT! SHE'S OBSESSED!

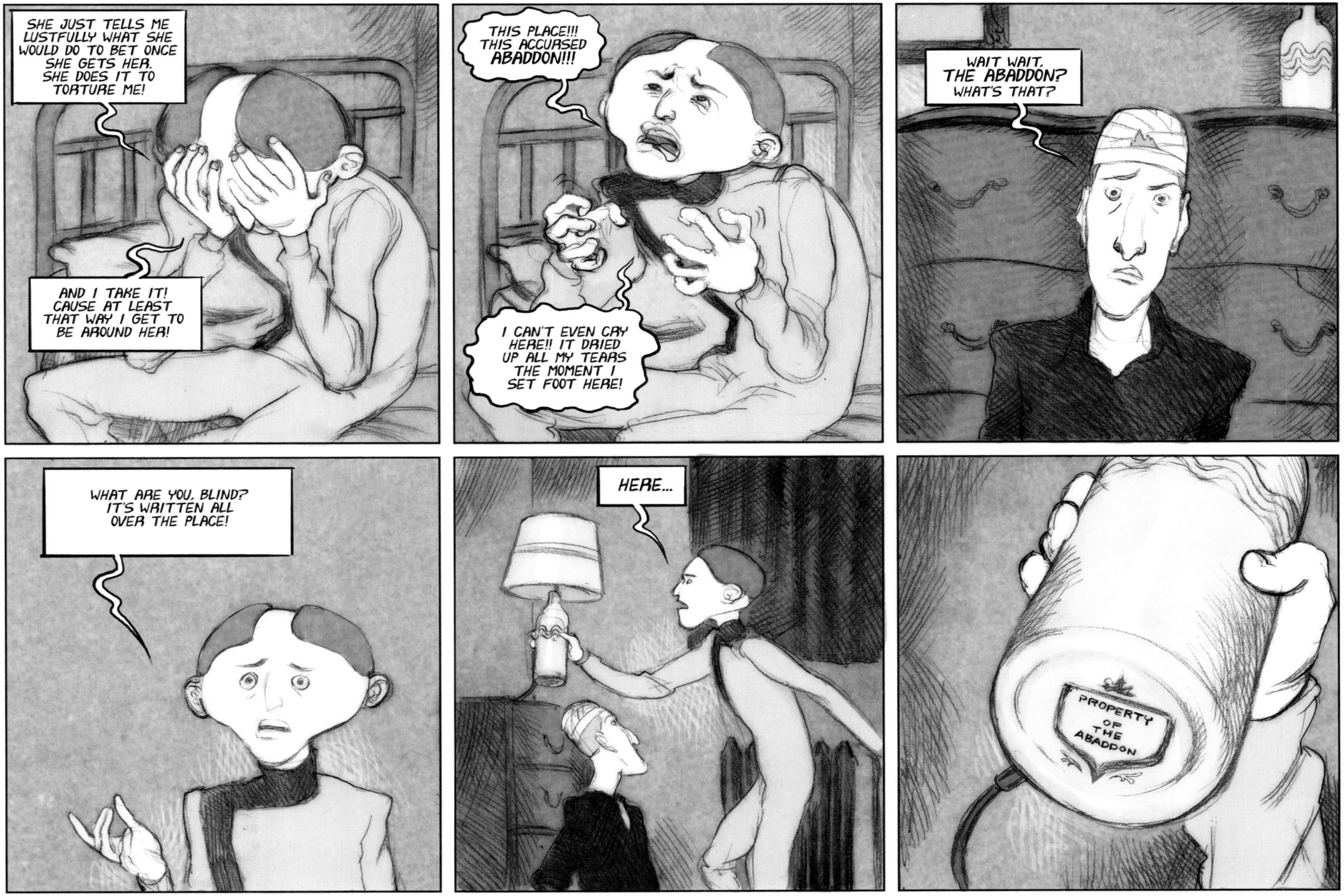
SHE JUST TELLS ME LUSTFULLY WHAT SHE WOULD DO TO BET ONCE SHE GETS HER. SHE DOES IT TO TORTURE ME!
AND I TAKE IT! CAUSE AT LEAST THAT WAY I GET TO BE AROUND HER!
THIS PLACE!!! THIS ACCURSED ABADDON!!!
I CAN'T EVEN CRY HERE!! IT DRIED UP ALL MY TEARS THE MOMENT I SET FOOT HERE!
WAIT WAIT. THE ABADDON? WHAT'S THAT?
WHAT ARE YOU, BLIND? IT'S WRITTEN ALL OVER THE PLACE!
HERE...
PROPERTY OF THE ABADDON

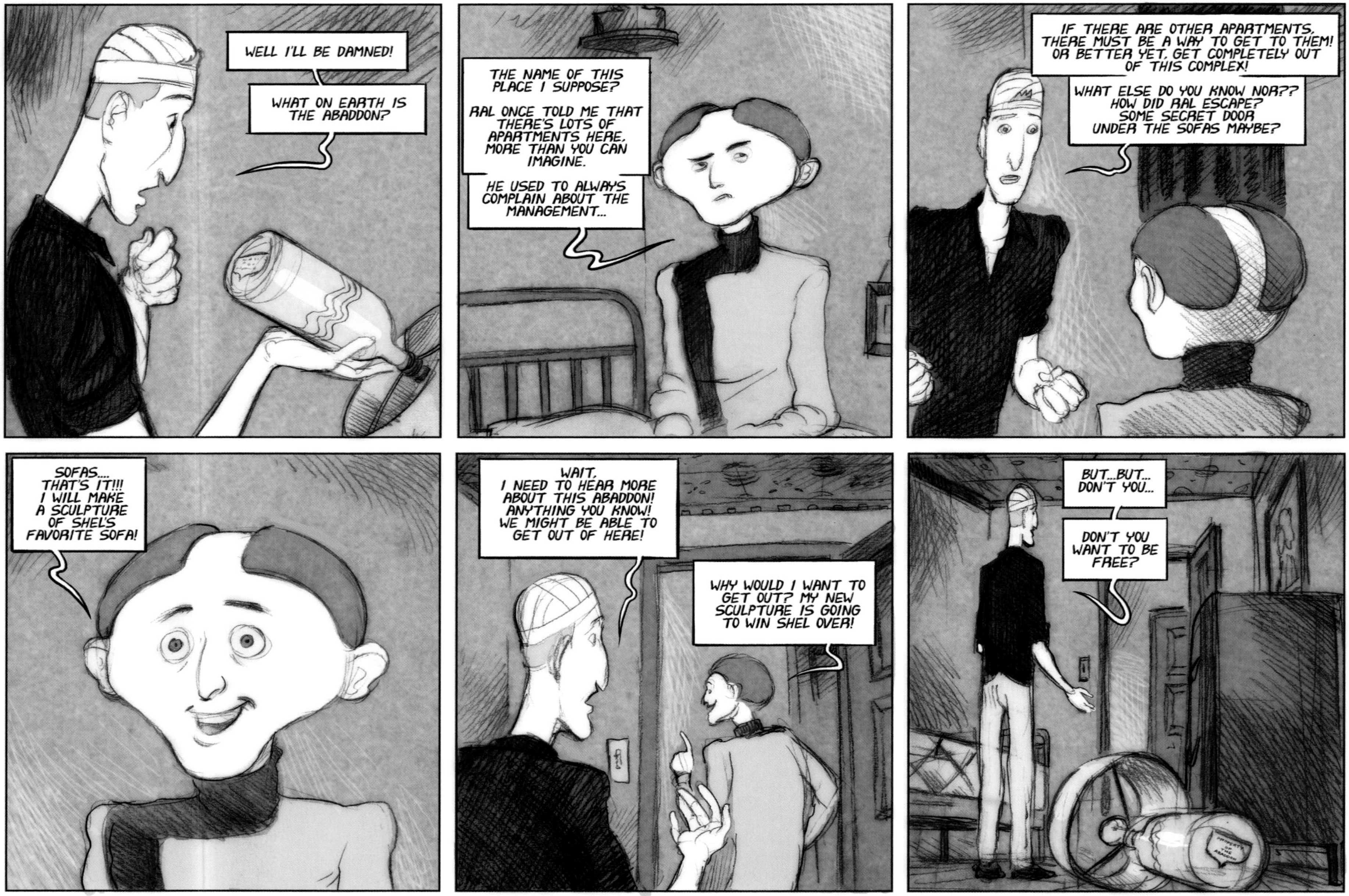
WELL I'LL BE DAMNED!
WHAT ON EARTH IS THE ABADDON?
THE NAME OF THIS PLACE I SUPPOSE?
RAL ONCE TOLD ME THAT THERE'S LOTS OF APARTMENTS HERE. MORE THAN YOU CAN IMAGINE.
HE USED TO ALWAYS COMPLAIN ABOUT THE MANAGEMENT...
IF THERE ARE OTHER APARTMENTS, THERE MUST BE A WAY TO GET TO THEM! OR BETTER YET, GET COMPLETELY OUT OF THIS COMPLEX!
WHAT ELSE DO YOU KNOW NOR?? HOW DID RAL ESCAPE? SOME SECRET DOOR UNDER THE SOFAS MAYBE?
SOFAS.... THAT'S IT!!! I WILL MAKE A SCULPTURE OF SHEL'S FAVORITE SOFA!
WAIT, I NEED TO HEAR MORE ABOUT THIS ABADDON! ANYTHING YOU KNOW! WE MIGHT BE ABLE TO GET OUT OF HERE!
WHY WOULD I WANT TO GET OUT? MY NEW SCULPTURE IS GOING TO WIN SHEL OVER!
BUT...BUT... DON'T YOU...
DON'T YOU WANT TO BE FREE?

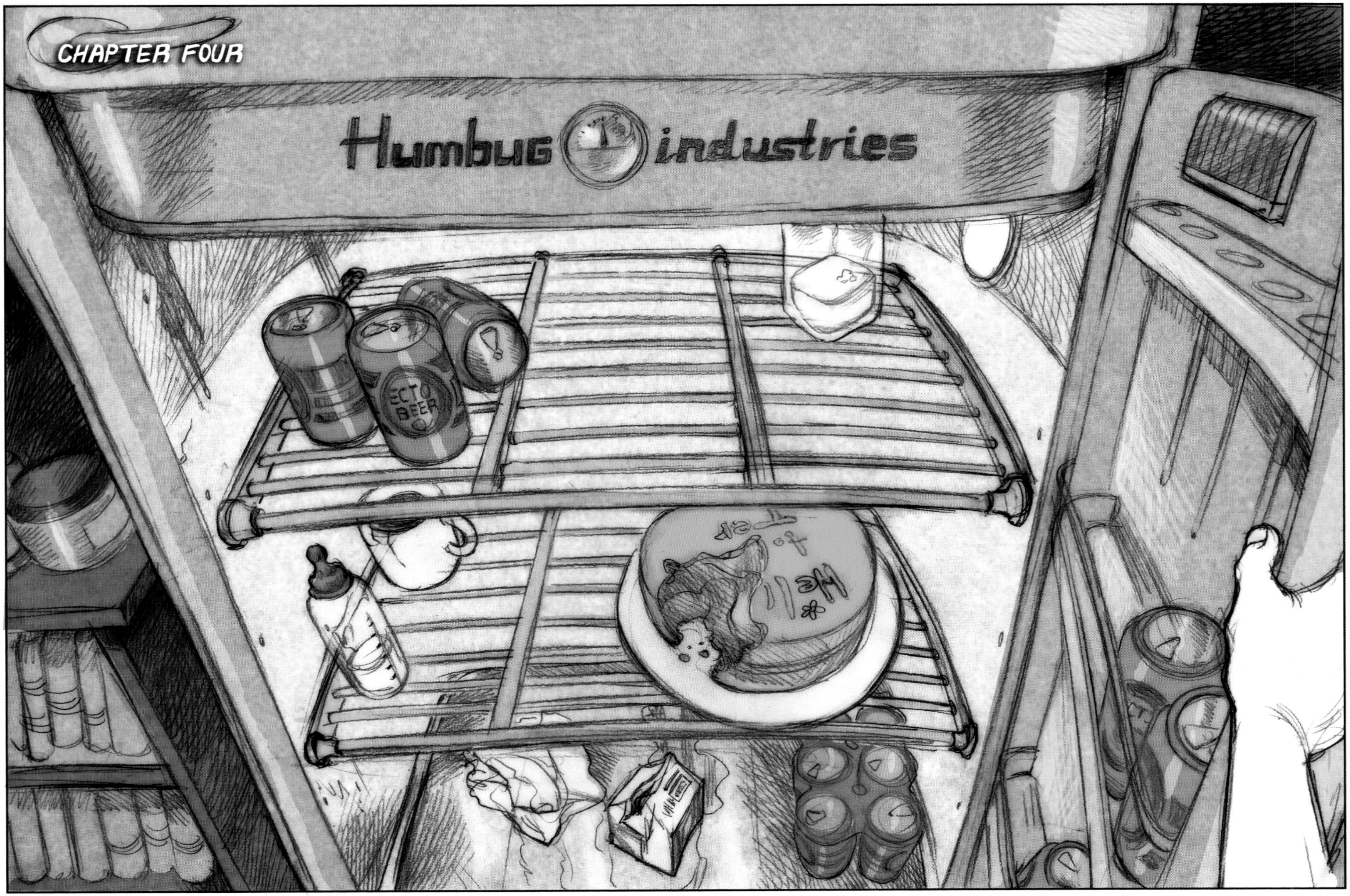
CHAPTER FOUR
Humbug industries
ECTO BEER

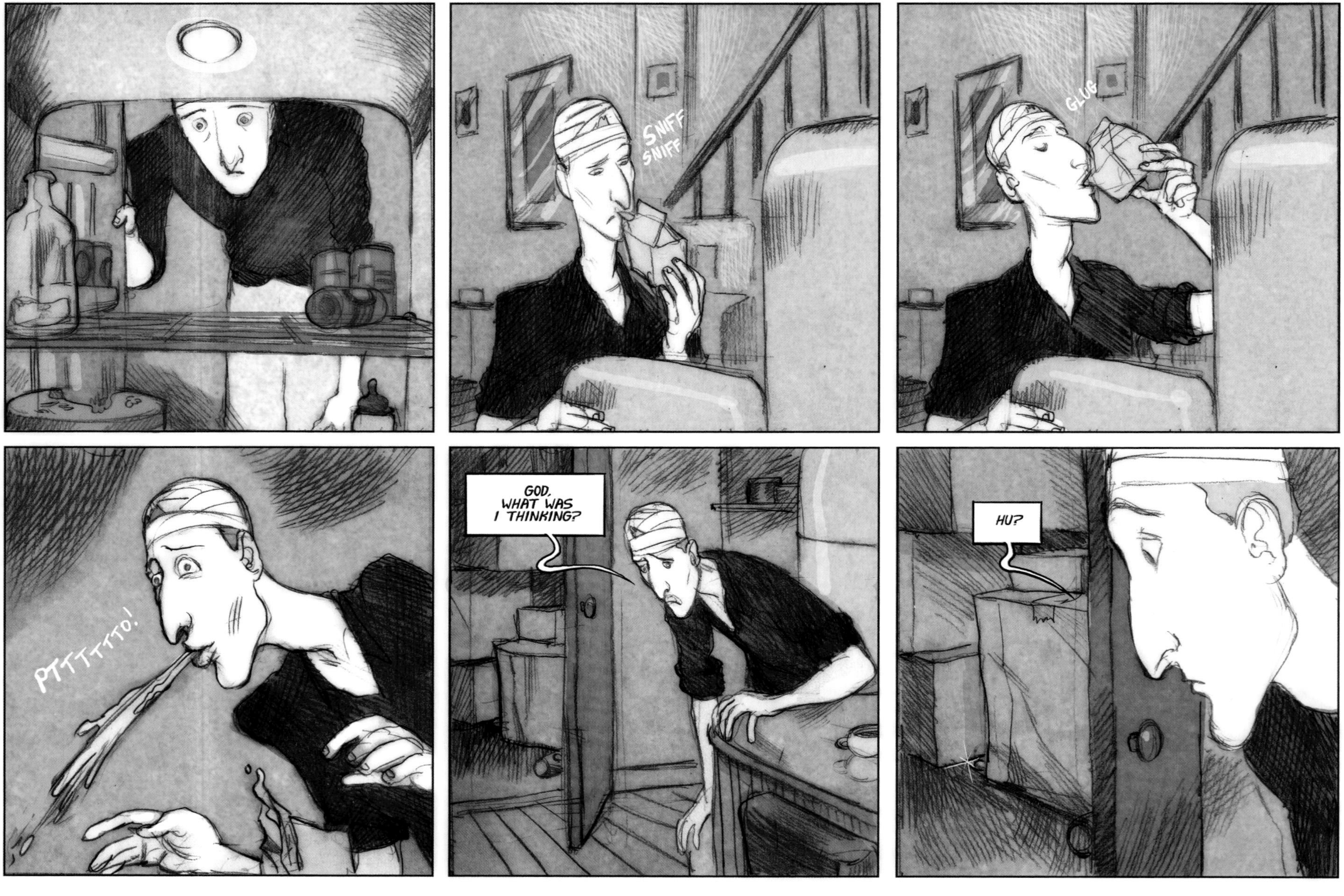
SNIFF
SNIFF
GLUG
PTTTTTTO!
GOD, WHAT WAS I THINKING?
HU?

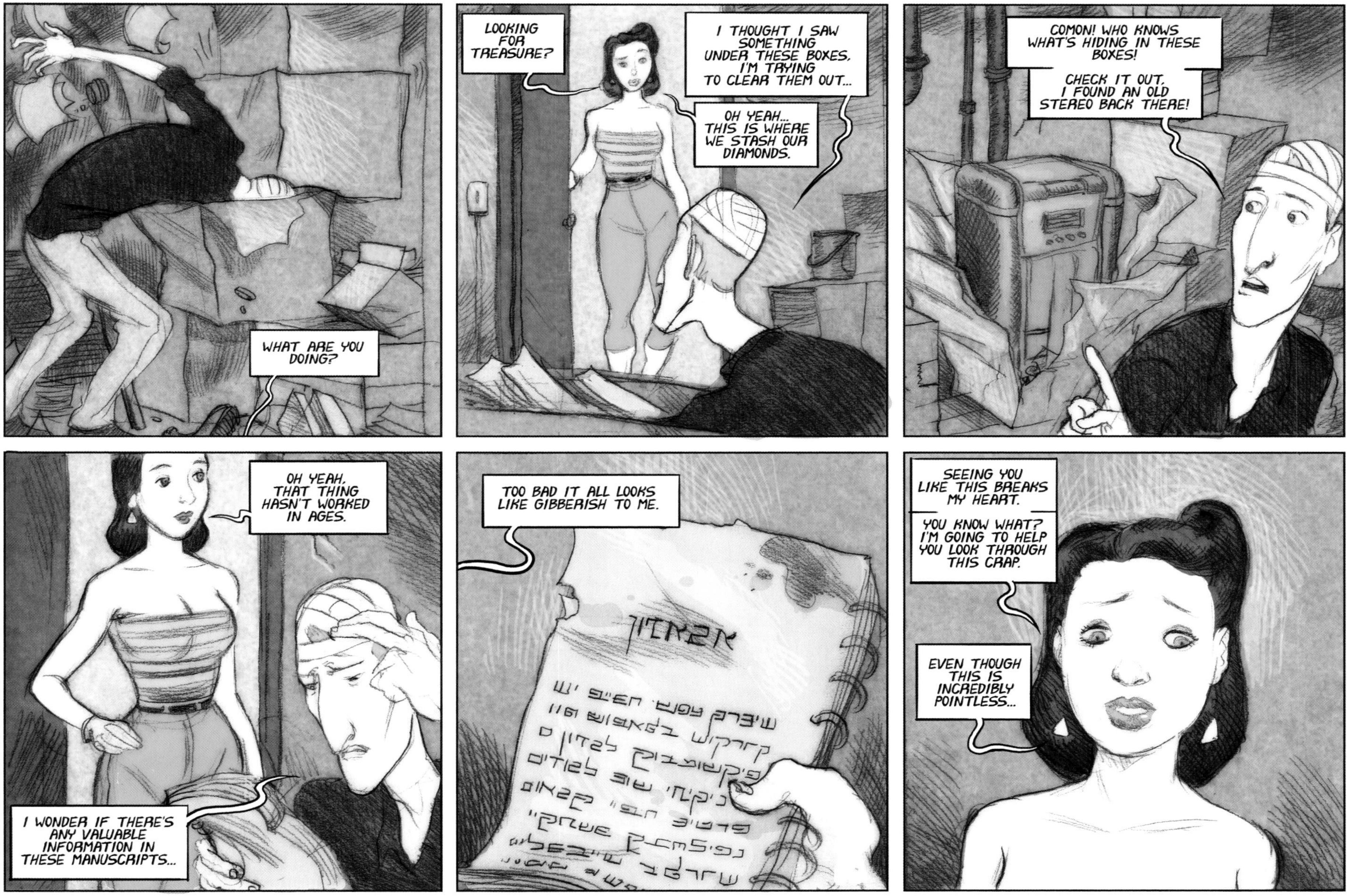
WHAT ARE YOU DOING?
LOOKING FOR TREASURE?
I THOUGHT I SAW SOMETHING UNDER THESE BOXES, I'M TRYING TO CLEAR THEM OUT...
OH YEAH... THIS IS WHERE WE STASH OUR DIAMONDS.
COMON! WHO KNOWS WHAT'S HIDING IN THESE BOXES!
CHECK IT OUT, I FOUND AN OLD STEREO BACK THERE!
OH YEAH, THAT THING HASN'T WORKED IN AGES.
I WONDER IF THERE'S ANY VALUABLE INFORMATION IN THESE MANUSCRIPTS...
TOO BAD IT ALL LOOKS LIKE GIBBERISH TO ME.
SEEING YOU LIKE THIS BREAKS MY HEART.
YOU KNOW WHAT? I'M GOING TO HELP YOU LOOK THROUGH THIS CRAP.
EVEN THOUGH THIS IS INCREDIBLY POINTLESS...

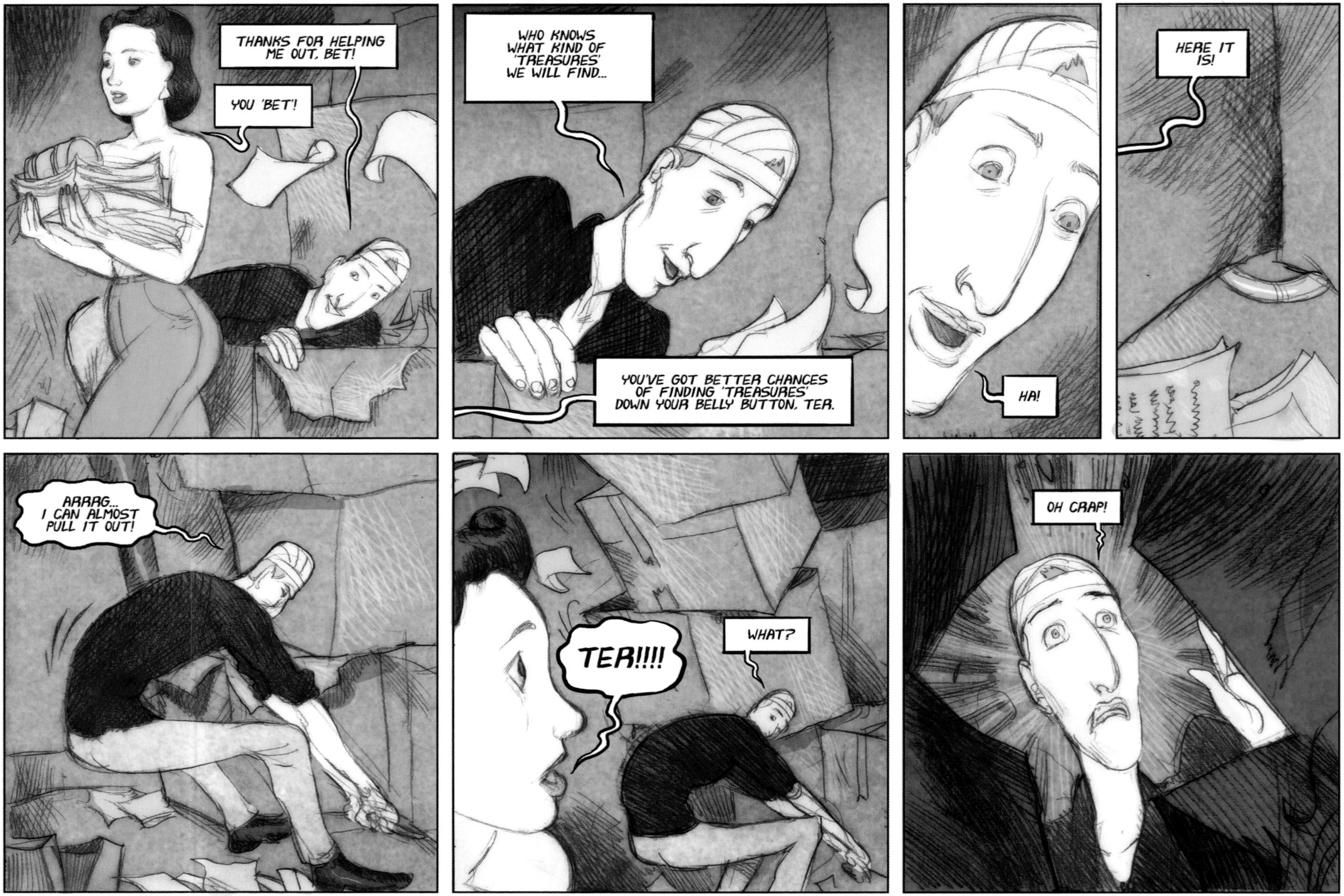
THANKS FOR HELPING ME OUT, BET!
YOU 'BET'!
WHO KNOWS WHAT KIND OF 'TREASURES' WE WILL FIND...
YOU'VE GOT BETTER CHANCES OF FINDING 'TREASURES' DOWN YOUR BELLY BUTTON, TER.
HA!
HERE IT IS!
ARRRG... I CAN ALMOST PULL IT OUT!
TER!!!!
WHAT?
OH CRAP!

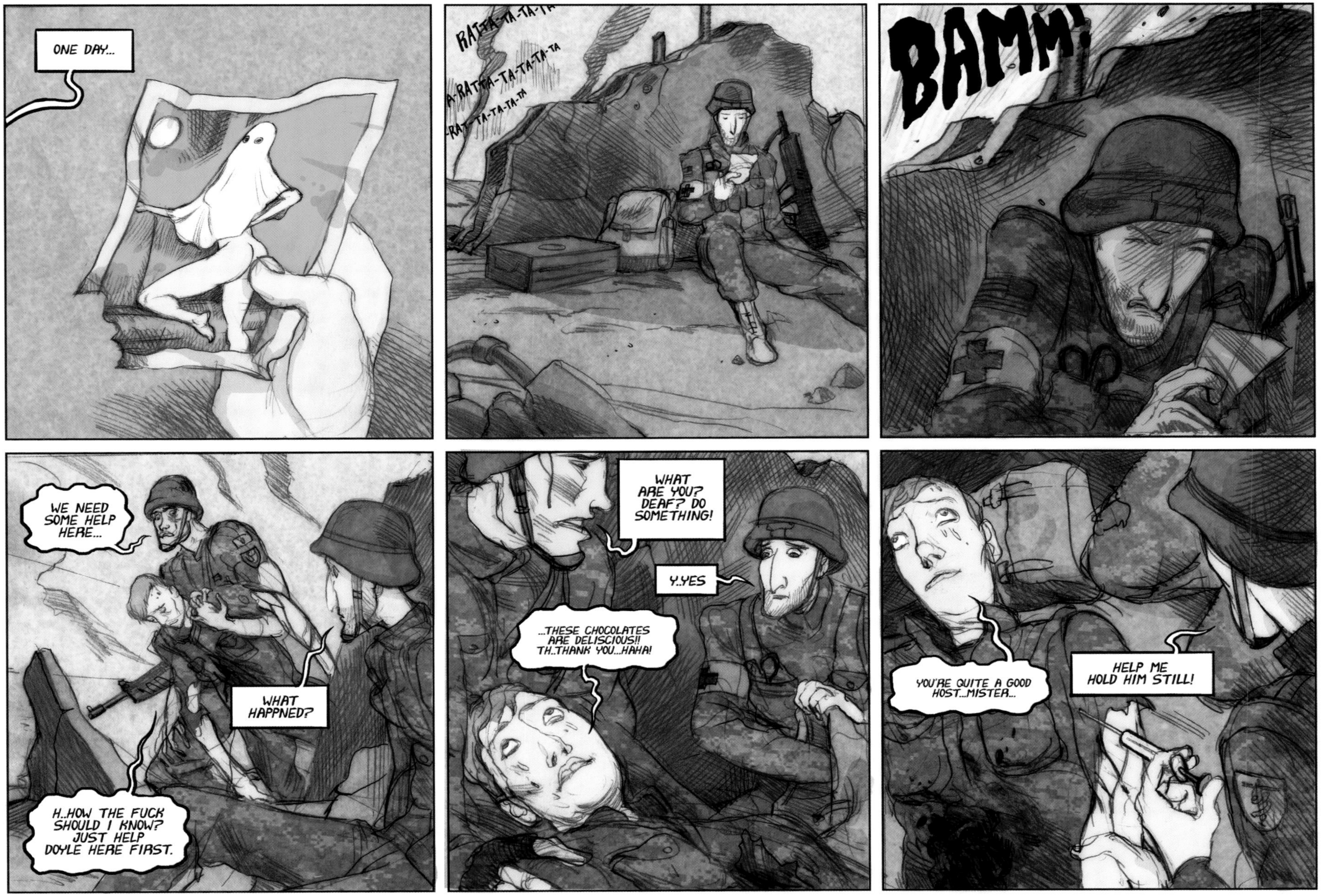
ONE DAY...
RAT-TA-TA-TA
A-RAT-TA-TA-TA-TA-TA
-RAT-TA-TA-TA-TA
BAMM!
WE NEED SOME HELP HERE...
WHAT HAPPNED?
H..HOW THE FUCK SHOULD I KNOW? JUST HELP DOYLE HERE FIRST.
WHAT ARE YOU? DEAF? DO SOMETHING!
Y..YES
...THESE CHOCOLATES ARE DELISCIOUS!! TH..THANK YOU...HAHA!
YOU'RE QUITE A GOOD HOST...MISTER...
HELP ME HOLD HIM STILL!

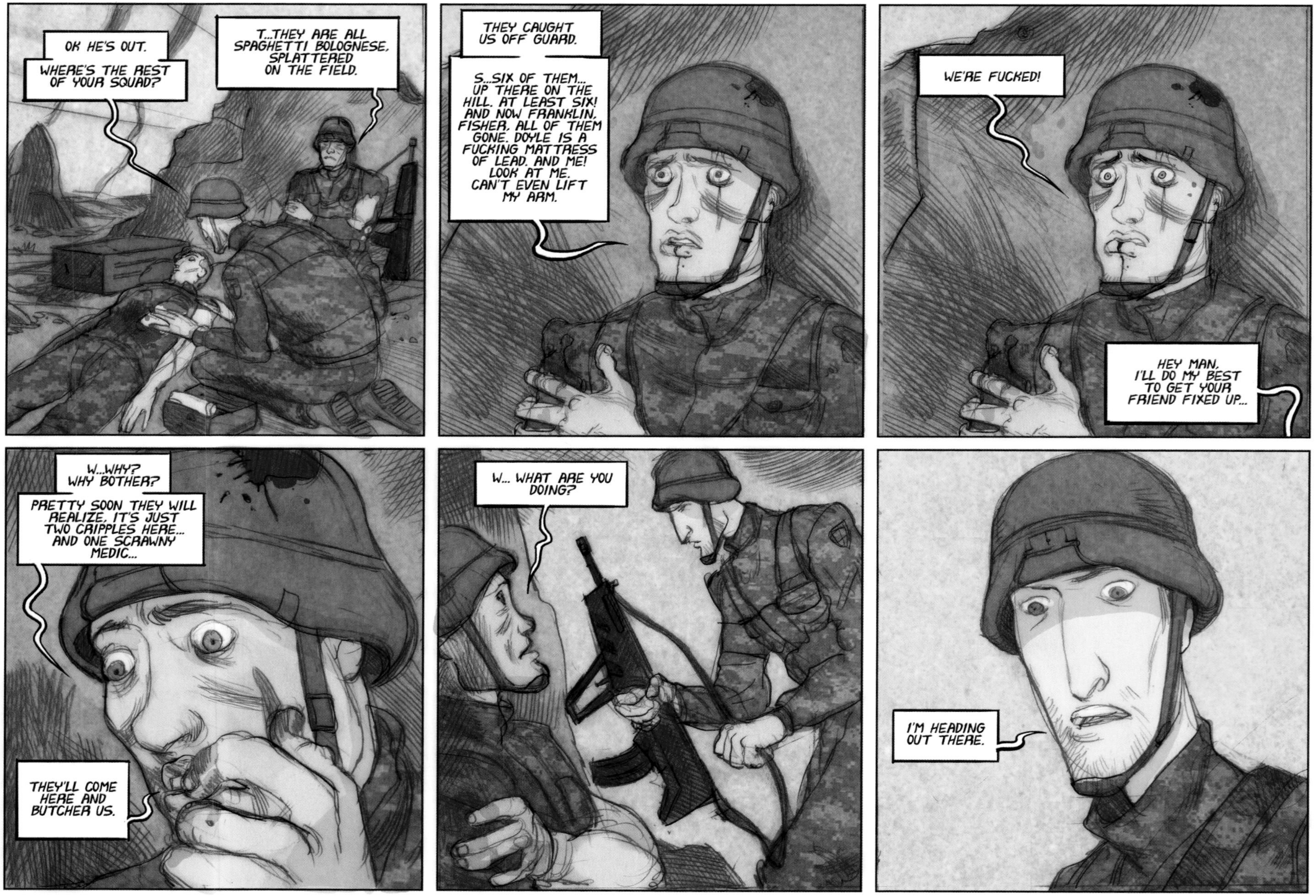
OK HE'S OUT.
WHERE'S THE REST OF YOUR SQUAD?
T...THEY ARE ALL SPAGHETTI BOLOGNESE, SPLATTERED ON THE FIELD.
THEY CAUGHT US OFF GUARD.
S...SIX OF THEM... UP THERE ON THE HILL. AT LEAST SIX! AND NOW FRANKLIN, FISHER, ALL OF THEM GONE. DOYLE IS A FUCKING MATTRESS OF LEAD. AND ME! LOOK AT ME. CAN'T EVEN LIFT MY ARM.
WE'RE FUCKED!
HEY MAN, I'LL DO MY BEST TO GET YOUR FRIEND FIXED UP...
W...WHY? WHY BOTHER?
PRETTY SOON THEY WILL REALIZE. IT'S JUST TWO CRIPPLES HERE... AND ONE SCRAWNY MEDIC...
THEY'LL COME HERE AND BUTCHER US.
W... WHAT ARE YOU DOING?
I'M HEADING OUT THERE.

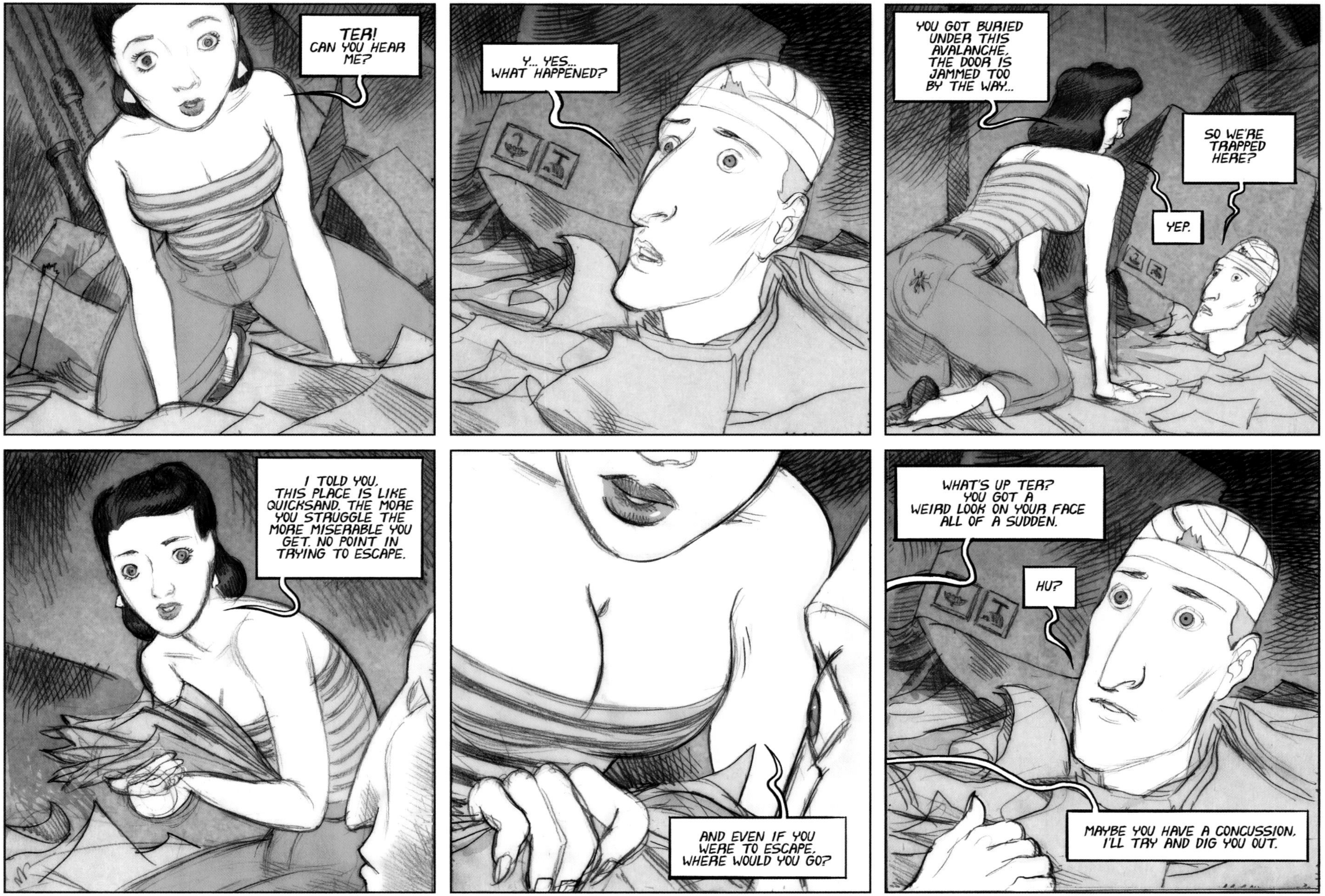
TER! CAN YOU HEAR ME?
Y... YES... WHAT HAPPENED?
YOU GOT BURIED UNDER THIS AVALANCHE, THE DOOR IS JAMMED TOO BY THE WAY...
SO WE'RE TRAPPED HERE?
YEP.
I TOLD YOU, THIS PLACE IS LIKE QUICKSAND. THE MORE YOU STRUGGLE THE MORE MISERABLE YOU GET. NO POINT IN TRYING TO ESCAPE.
AND EVEN IF YOU WERE TO ESCAPE, WHERE WOULD YOU GO?
WHAT'S UP TER? YOU GOT A WEIRD LOOK ON YOUR FACE ALL OF A SUDDEN.
HU?
MAYBE YOU HAVE A CONCUSSION, I'LL TRY AND DIG YOU OUT.

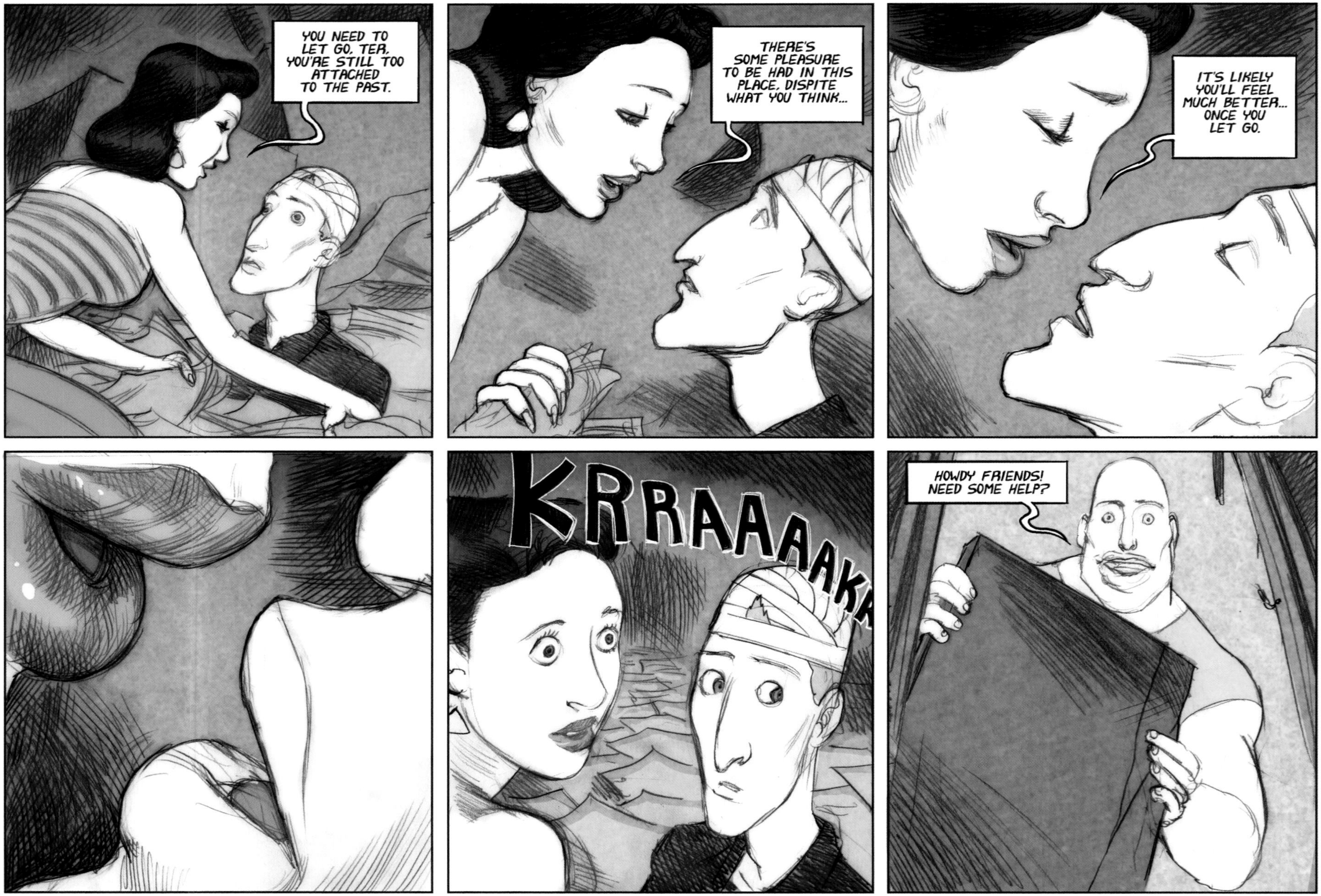
YOU NEED TO LET GO, TER. YOU'RE STILL TOO ATTACHED TO THE PAST.
THERE'S SOME PLEASURE TO BE HAD IN THIS PLACE, DISPITE WHAT YOU THINK...
IT'S LIKELY YOU'LL FEEL MUCH BETTER... ONCE YOU LET GO.
KRRAAAAK
HOWDY FRIENDS! NEED SOME HELP?

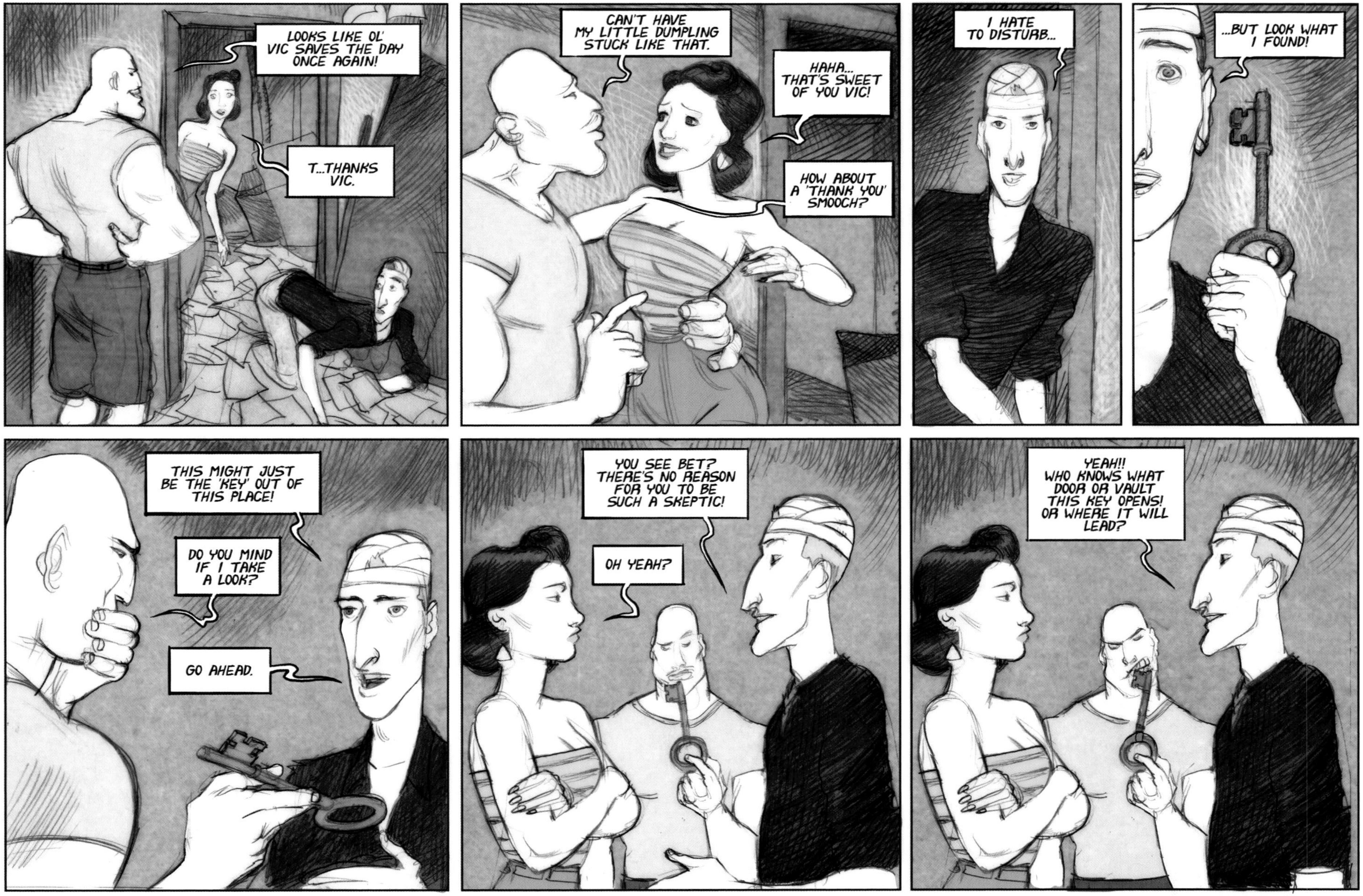
LOOKS LIKE OL' VIC SAVES THE DAY ONCE AGAIN!
T...THANKS VIC.
CAN'T HAVE MY LITTLE DUMPLING STUCK LIKE THAT.
HAHA... THAT'S SWEET OF YOU VIC!
HOW ABOUT A 'THANK YOU' SMOOCH?
I HATE TO DISTURB...
...BUT LOOK WHAT I FOUND!
THIS MIGHT JUST BE THE 'KEY' OUT OF THIS PLACE!
DO YOU MIND IF I TAKE A LOOK?
GO AHEAD.
YOU SEE BET? THERE'S NO REASON FOR YOU TO BE SUCH A SKEPTIC!
OH YEAH?
YEAH!! WHO KNOWS WHAT DOOR OR VAULT THIS KEY OPENS! OR WHERE IT WILL LEAD?

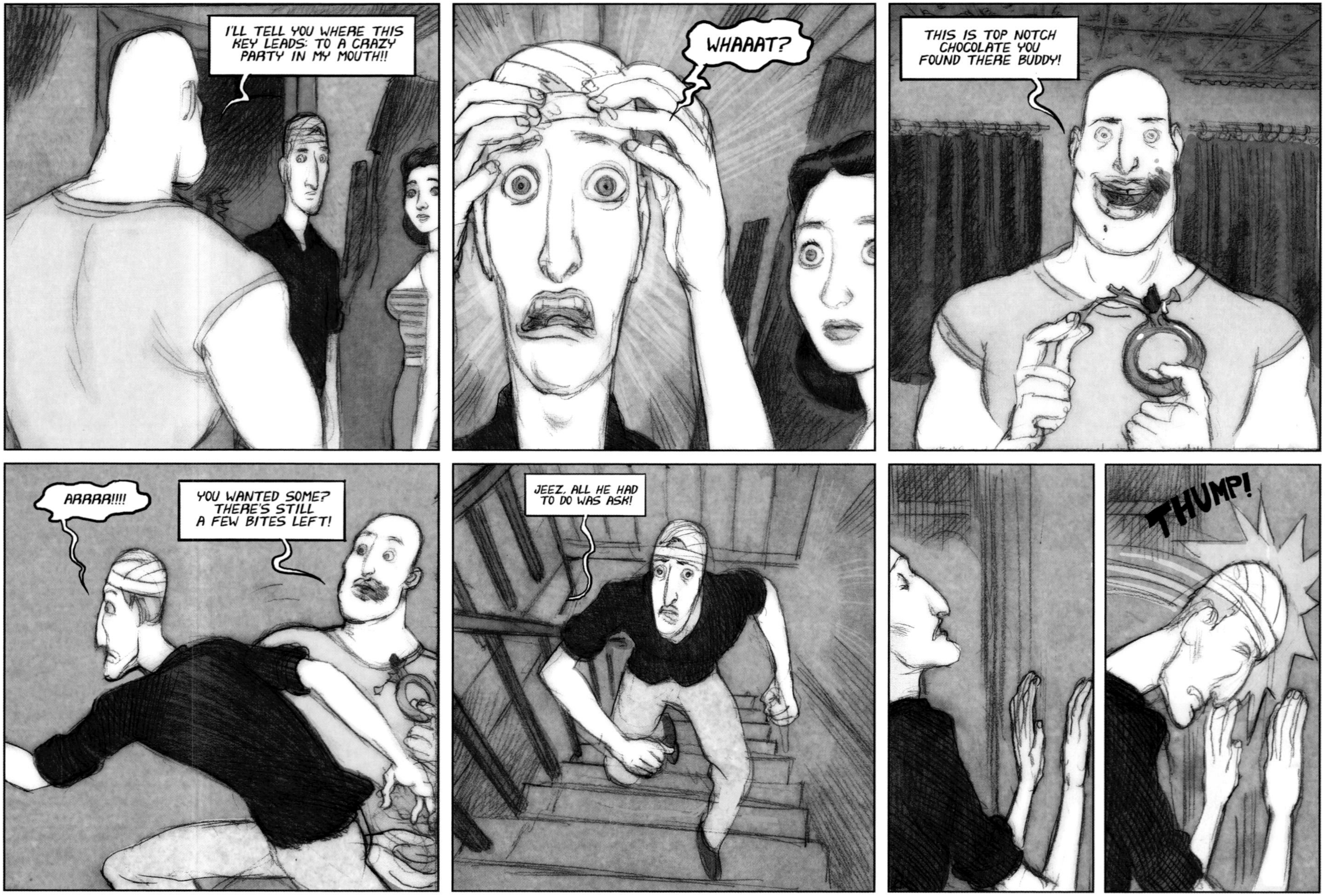
I'LL TELL YOU WHERE THIS KEY LEADS: TO A CRAZY PARTY IN MY MOUTH!!
WHAAAT?
THIS IS TOP NOTCH CHOCOLATE YOU FOUND THERE BUDDY!
ARRRR!!!!
YOU WANTED SOME? THERE'S STILL A FEW BITES LEFT!
JEEZ. ALL HE HAD TO DO WAS ASK!
THUMP!

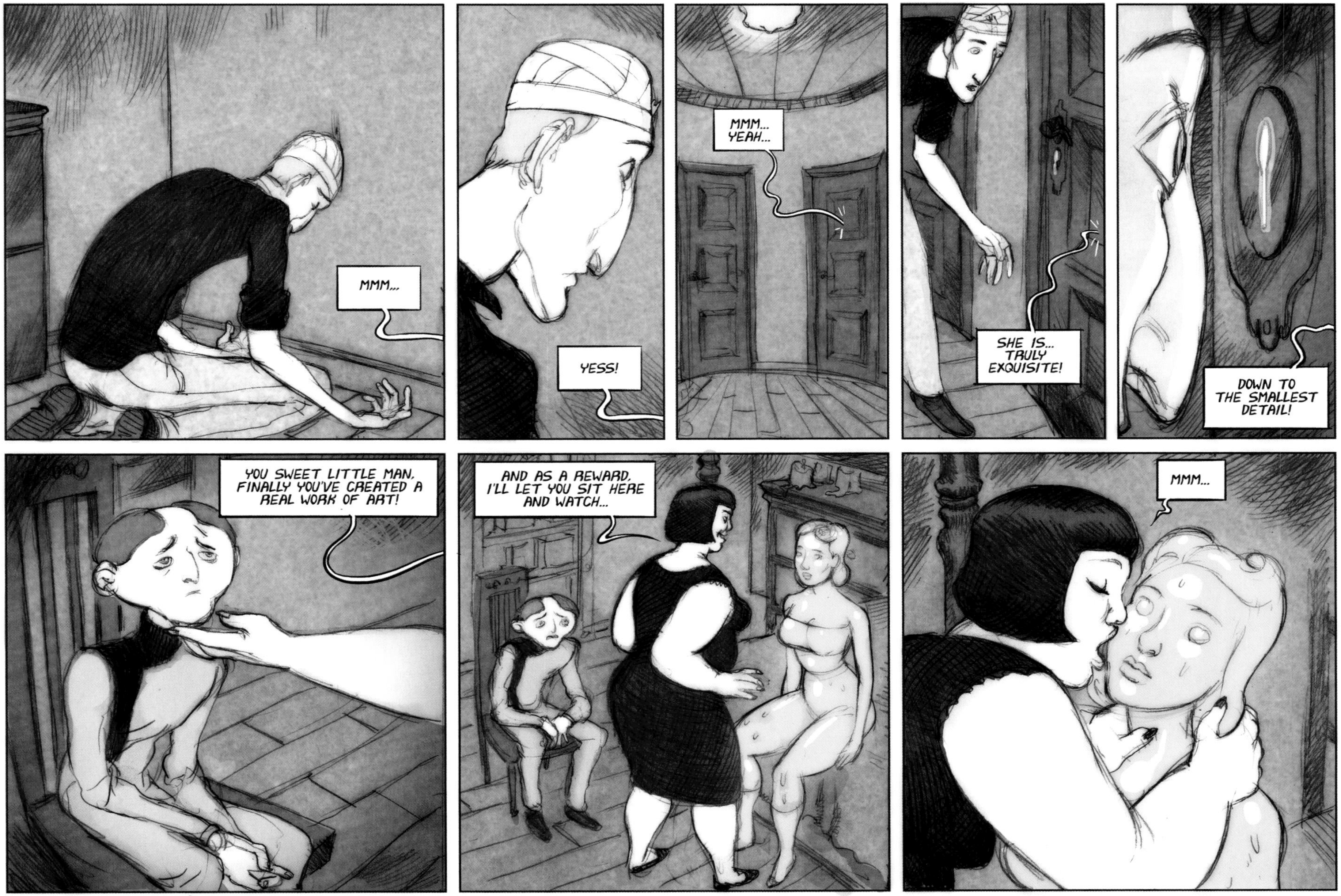
MMM...
YESS!
MMM... YEAH...
SHE IS... TRULY EXQUISITE!
DOWN TO THE SMALLEST DETAIL!
YOU SWEET LITTLE MAN, FINALLY YOU'VE CREATED A REAL WORK OF ART!
AND AS A REWARD, I'LL LET YOU SIT HERE AND WATCH...
MMM...

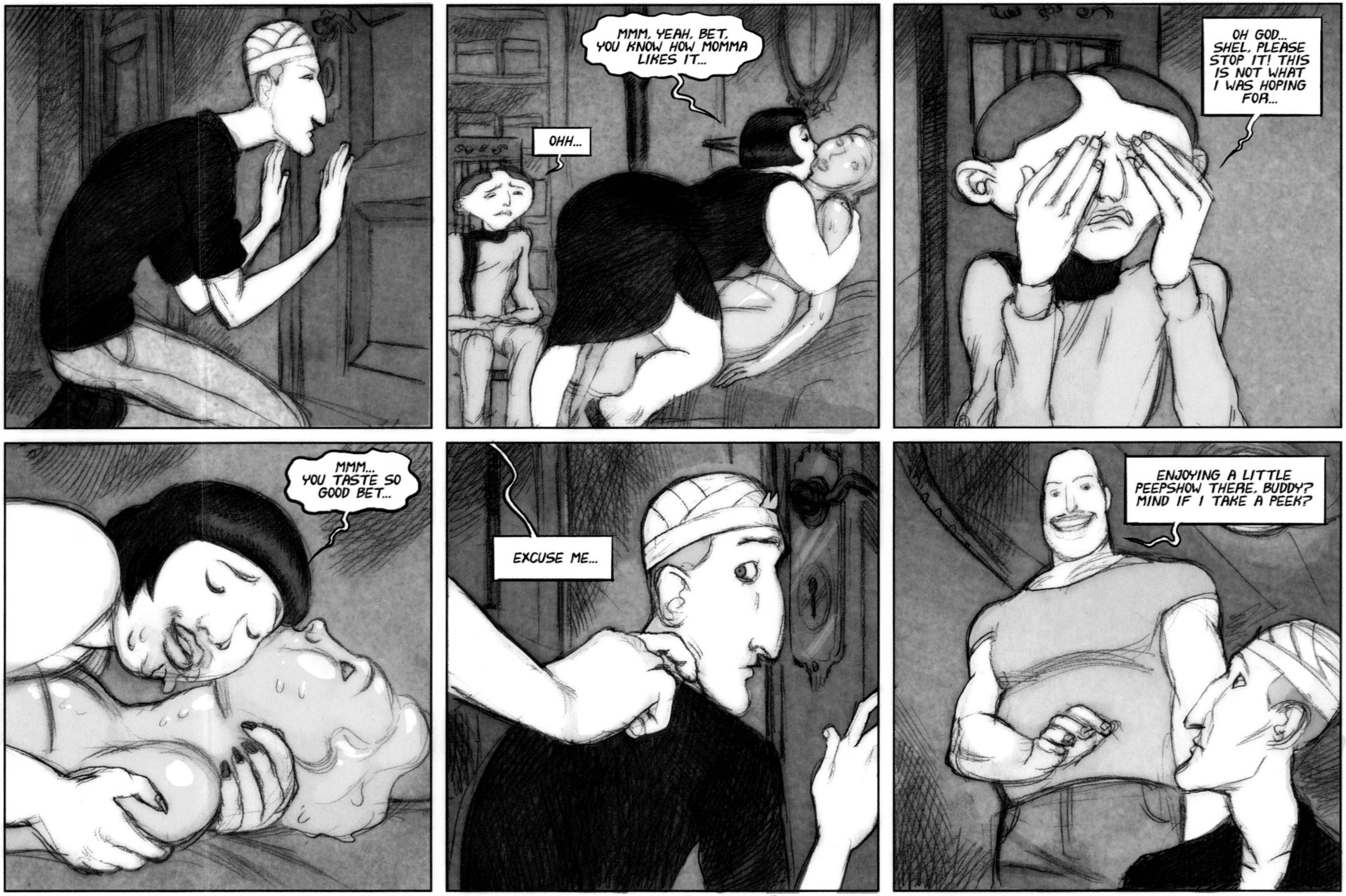
MMM, YEAH, BET, YOU KNOW HOW MOMMA LIKES IT...
OHH...
OH GOD... SHEL, PLEASE STOP IT! THIS IS NOT WHAT I WAS HOPING FOR...
MMM... YOU TASTE SO GOOD BET...
EXCUSE ME...
ENJOYING A LITTLE PEEPSHOW THERE, BUDDY? MIND IF I TAKE A PEEK?

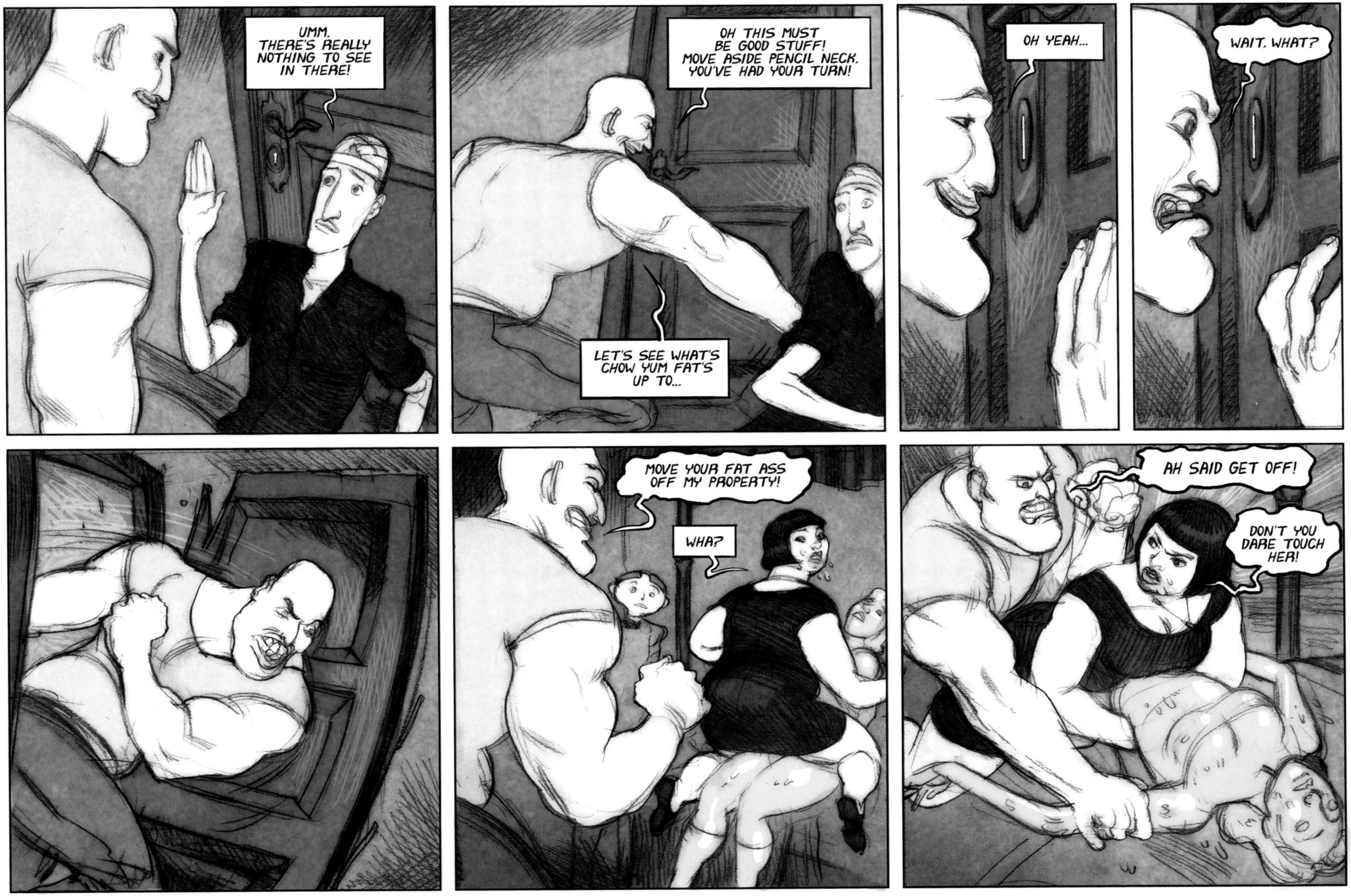
UMM. THERE'S REALLY NOTHING TO SEE IN THERE!
OH THIS MUST BE GOOD STUFF! MOVE ASIDE PENCIL NECK. YOU'VE HAD YOUR TURN!
LET'S SEE WHAT'S CHOW YUM FAT'S UP TO...
OH YEAH...
WAIT, WHAT?
MOVE YOUR FAT ASS OFF MY PROPERTY!
WHA?
AH SAID GET OFF!
DON'T YOU DARE TOUCH HER!

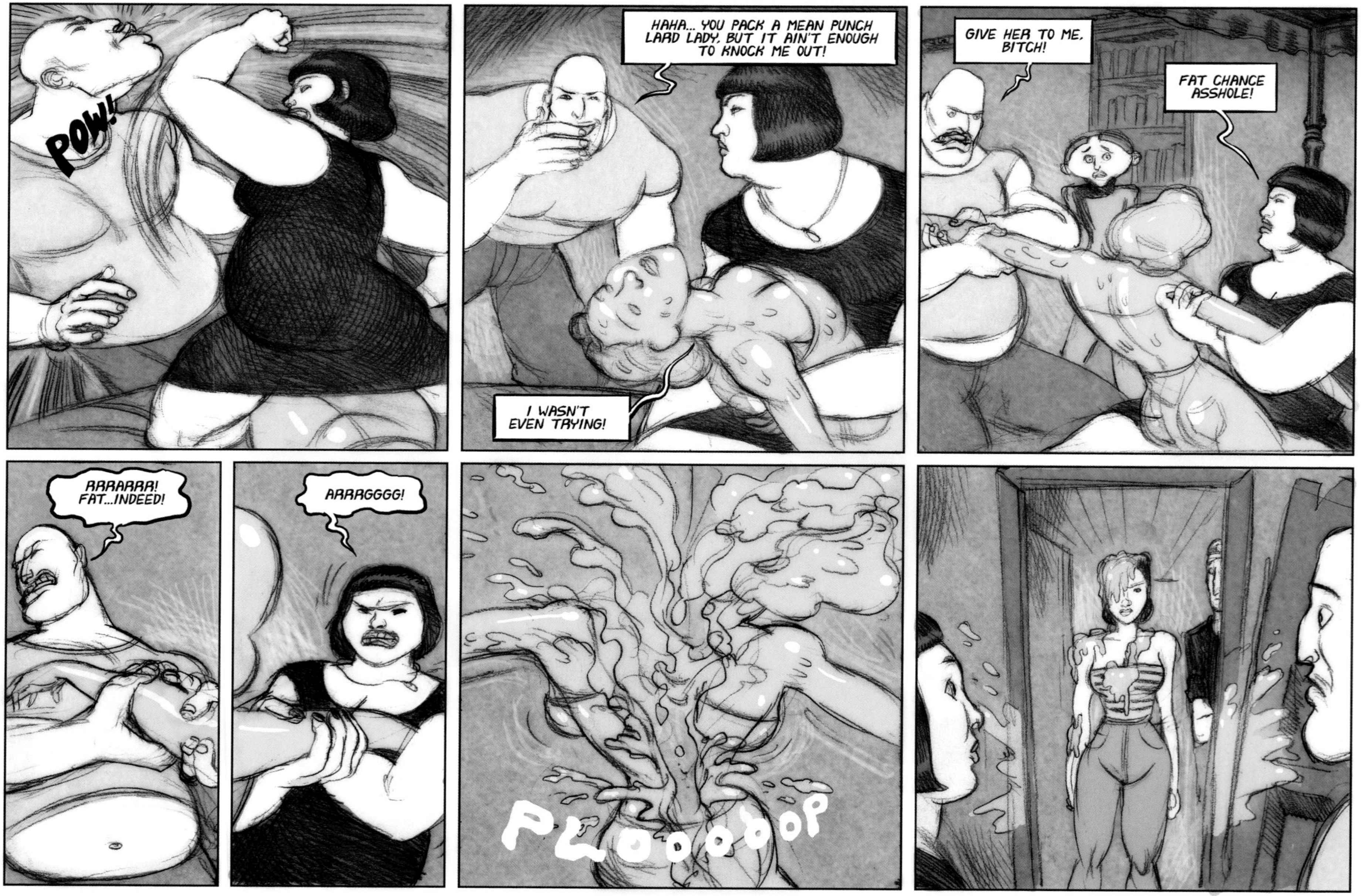
POW!
HAHA... YOU PACK A MEAN PUNCH LARD LADY, BUT IT AIN'T ENOUGH TO KNOCK ME OUT!
I WASN'T EVEN TRYING!
GIVE HER TO ME, BITCH!
FAT CHANCE ASSHOLE!
RRRARRR! FAT...INDEED!
ARRRGGGG!
PLOOOOOP

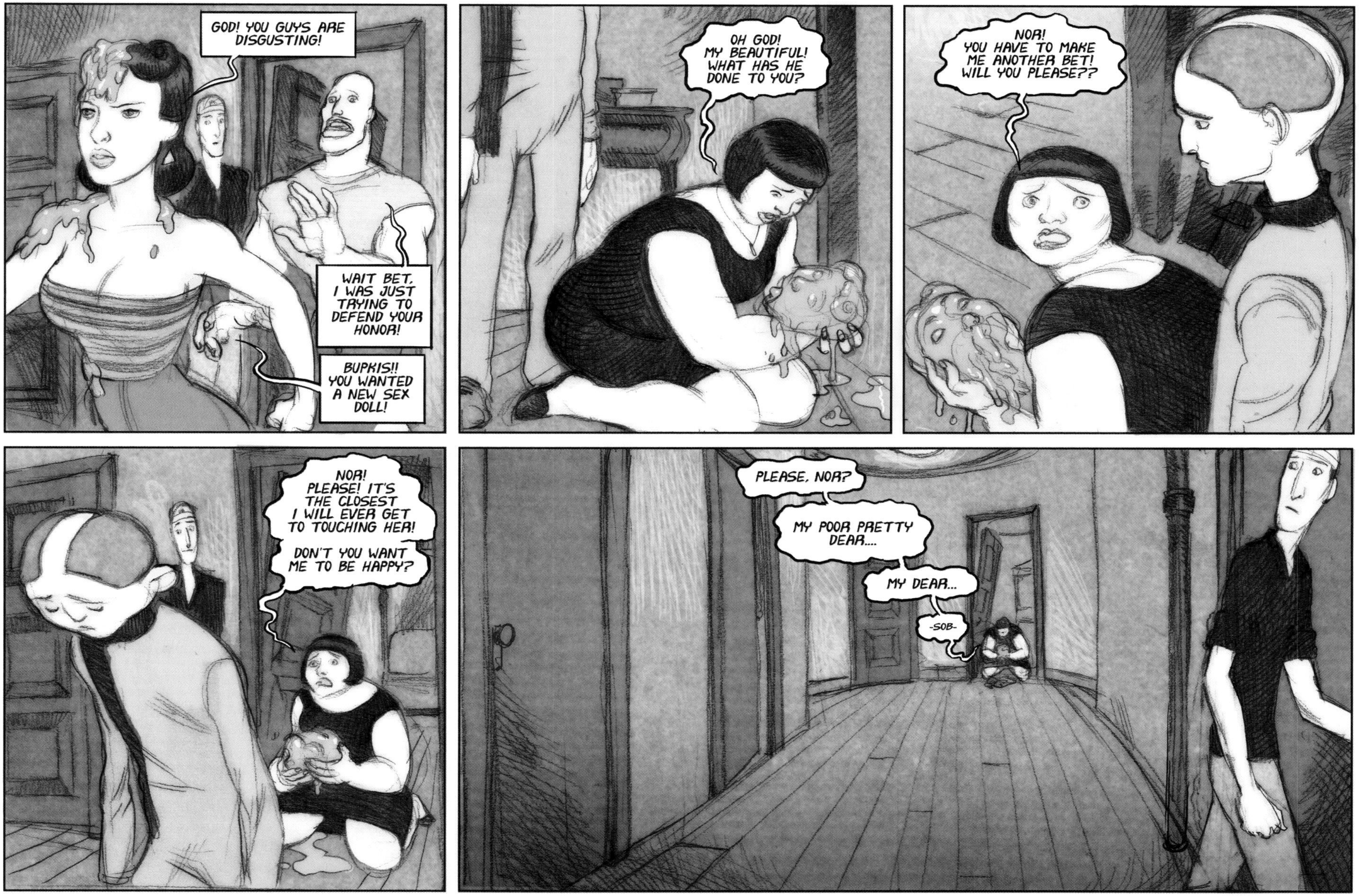
GOD! YOU GUYS ARE DISGUSTING!
WAIT BET, I WAS JUST TRYING TO DEFEND YOUR HONOR!
BUPKIS!! YOU WANTED A NEW SEX DOLL!
OH GOD! MY BEAUTIFUL! WHAT HAS HE DONE TO YOU?
NOR! YOU HAVE TO MAKE ME ANOTHER BET! WILL YOU PLEASE??
NOR! PLEASE! IT'S THE CLOSEST I WILL EVER GET TO TOUCHING HER!
DON'T YOU WANT ME TO BE HAPPY?
PLEASE, NOR?
MY POOR PRETTY DEAR....
MY DEAR...
-SOB-

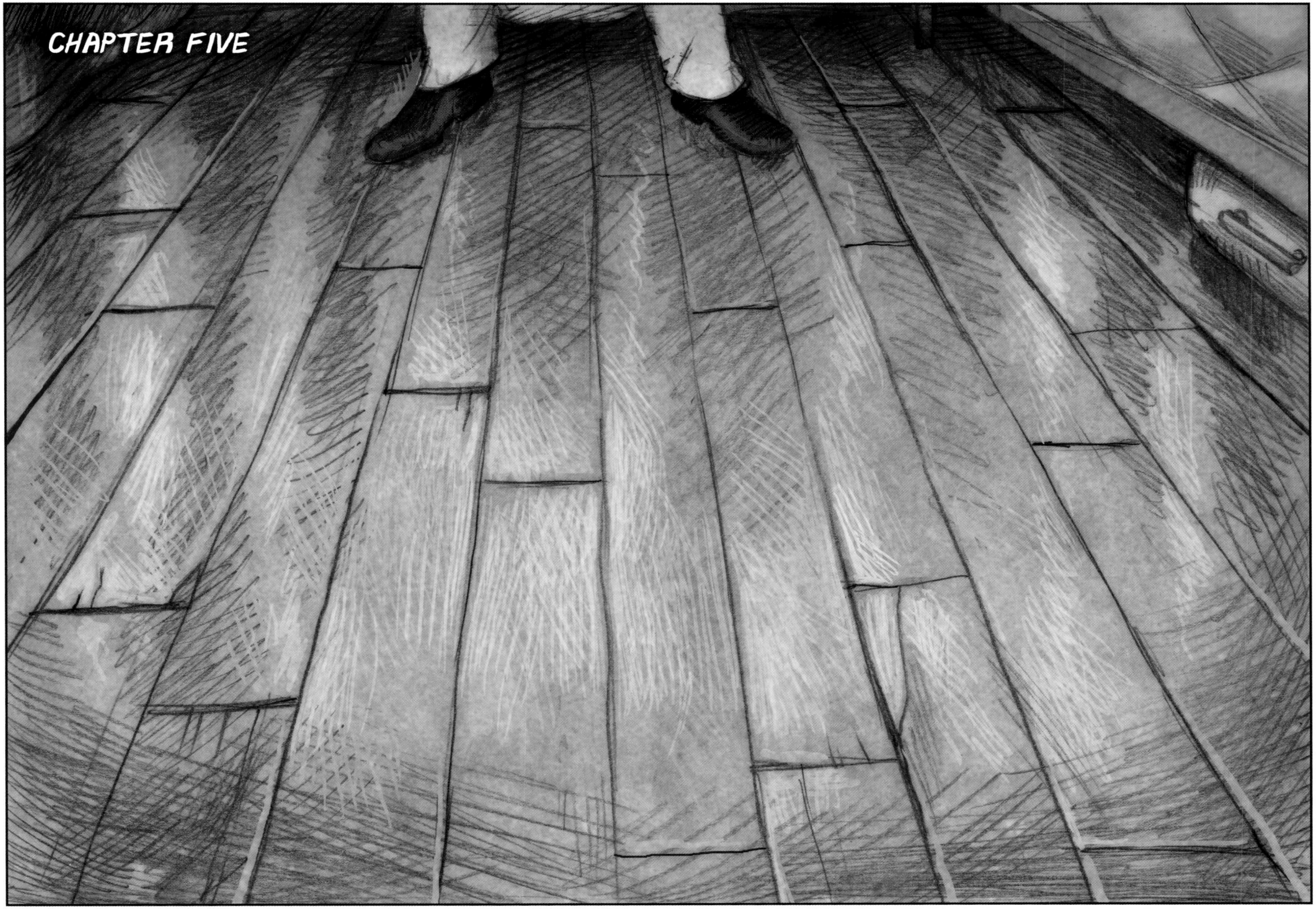
CHAPTER FIVE

I'VE GIVEN UP.

I SIMPLY CAN'T GET OUT.
BET SAID THIS PLACE IS LIKE A PIT
OF QUICKSAND, AND IT'S TRUE: THE MORE
I STRUGGLE THE LESS I MOVE.

BUT MAYBE THERE'S STILL SOMETHING I CAN DO.
SOMETHING TO MAKE THIS PLACE MORE TOLERABLE.

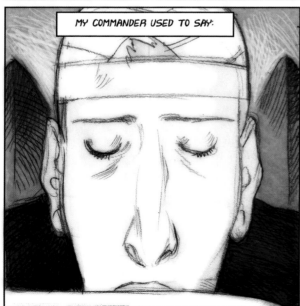

MY COMMANDER USED TO SAY:

IN ORDER TO HAVE YOUR MEN FIGHT
THE ENEMY, THEY MUST FIRST
CEASE TO FIGHT EACH OTHER.

I NEED TO FIND SOMETHING TO GET THEM OUT OF
THEIR MISERY. EVEN FOR JUST A LITTLE WHILE...

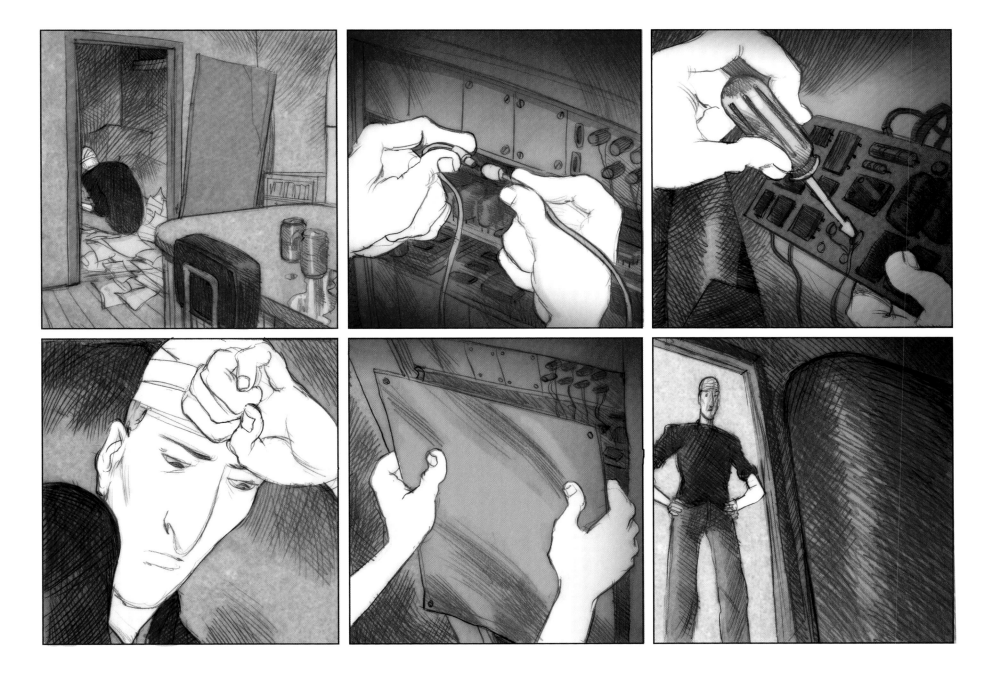

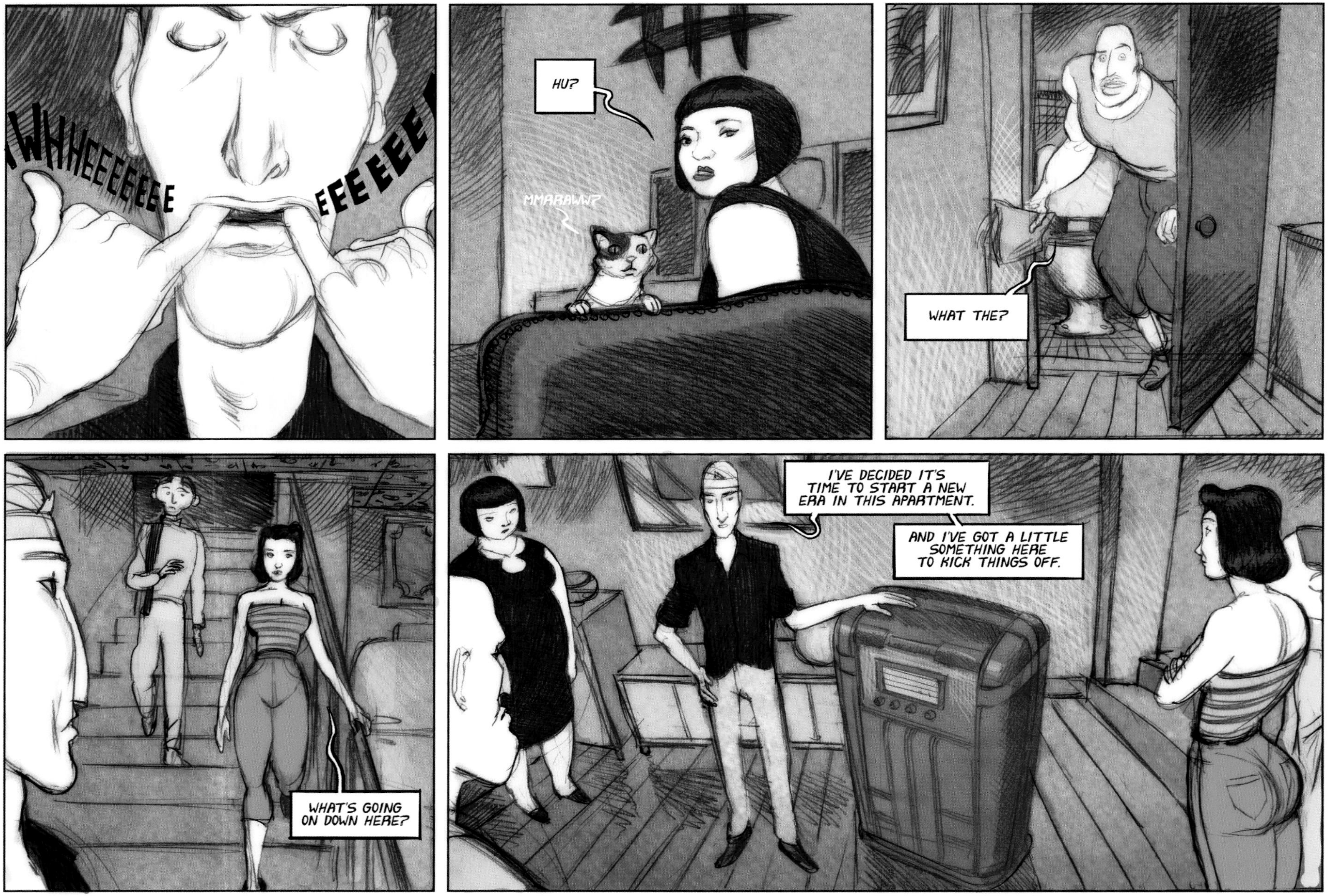
WHHEEEEEEE
EEEEEEE
HU?
MMARAWW?
WHAT THE?
WHAT'S GOING ON DOWN HERE?
I'VE DECIDED IT'S TIME TO START A NEW ERA IN THIS APARTMENT.
AND I'VE GOT A LITTLE SOMETHING HERE TO KICK THINGS OFF.

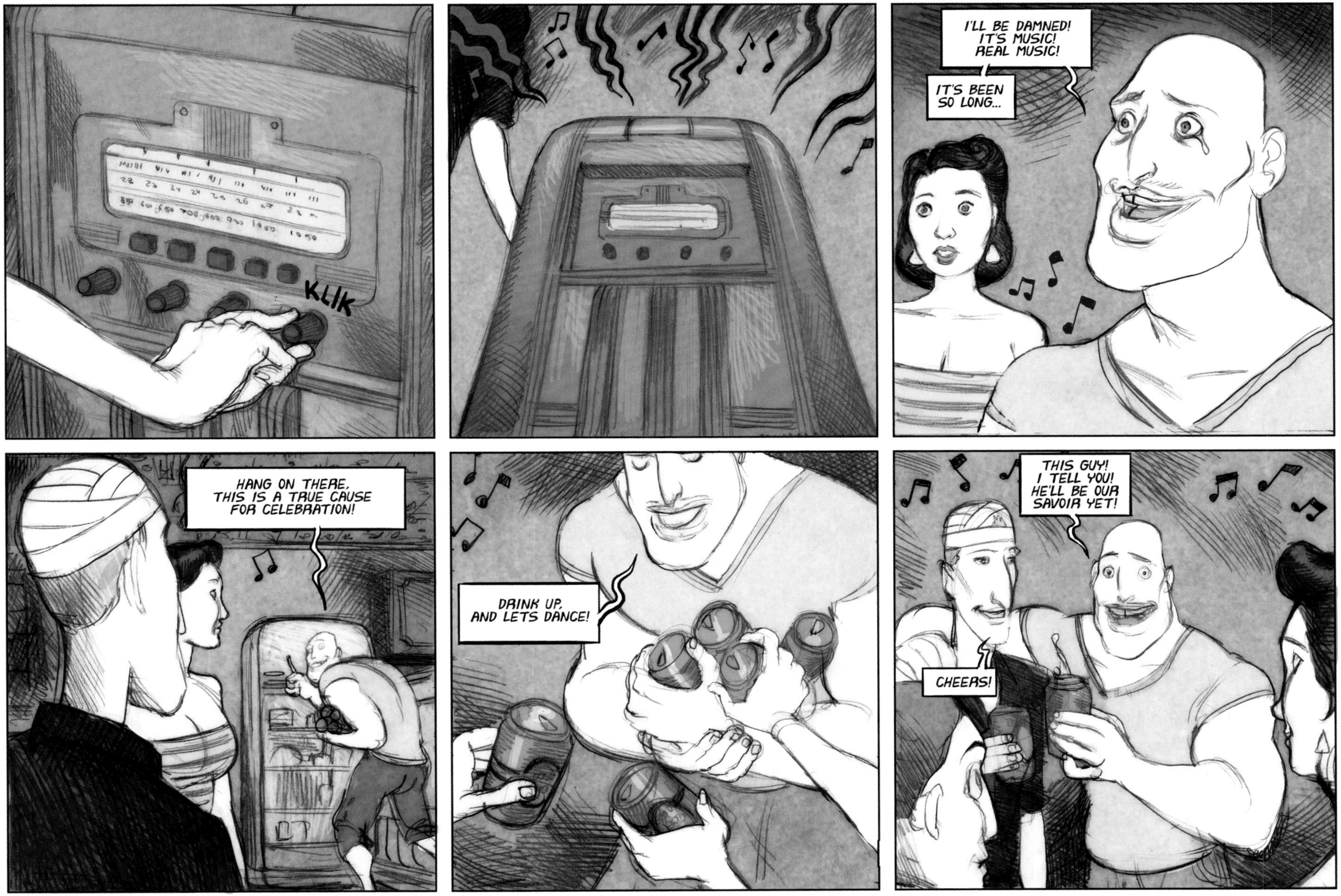
KLIK
I'LL BE DAMNED! IT'S MUSIC! REAL MUSIC!
IT'S BEEN SO LONG...
HANG ON THERE, THIS IS A TRUE CAUSE FOR CELEBRATION!
DRINK UP, AND LETS DANCE!
THIS GUY! I TELL YOU! HE'LL BE OUR SAVOIR YET!
CHEERS!

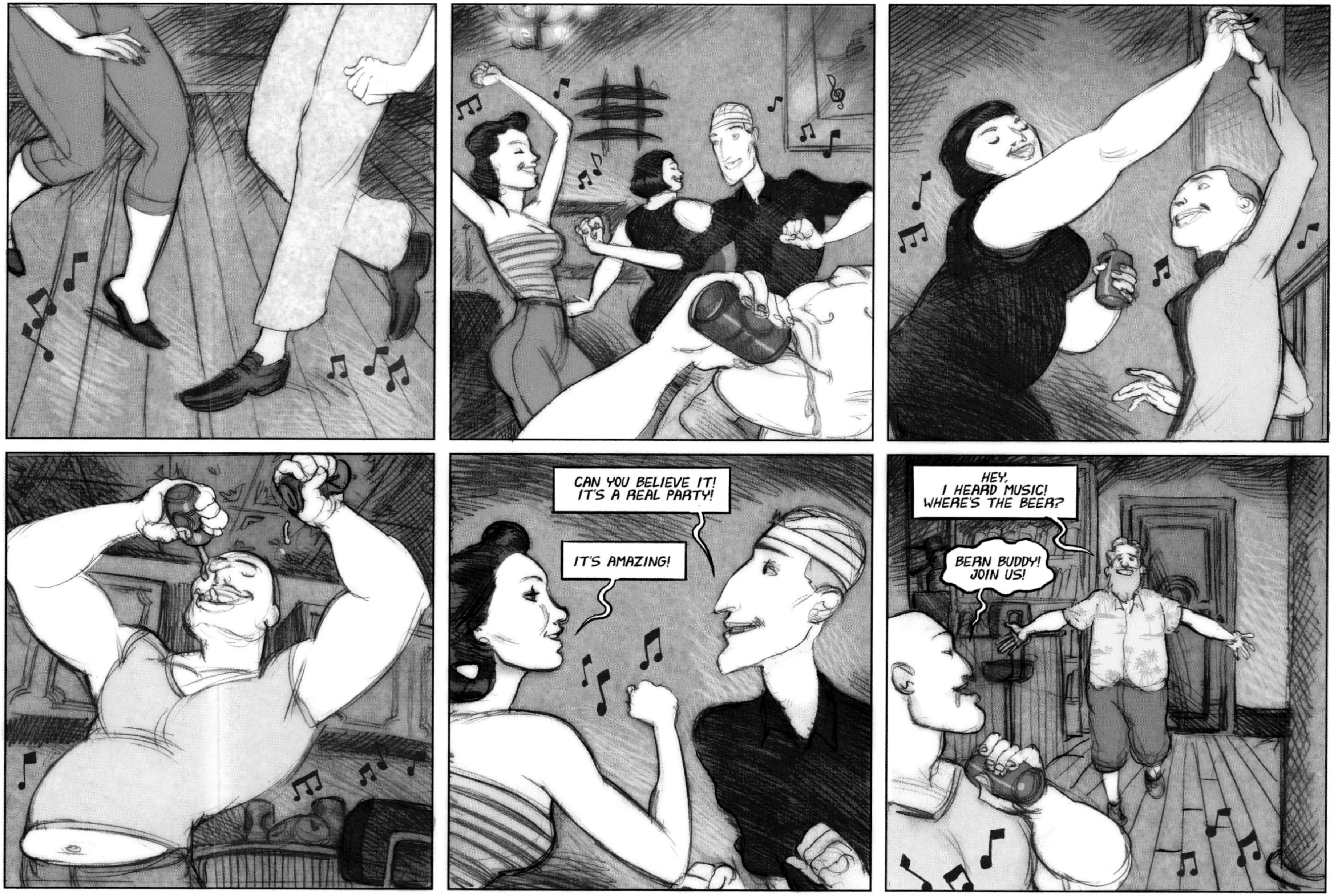
CAN YOU BELIEVE IT! IT'S A REAL PARTY!
IT'S AMAZING!
HEY, I HEARD MUSIC! WHERE'S THE BEER?
BERN BUDDY! JOIN US!

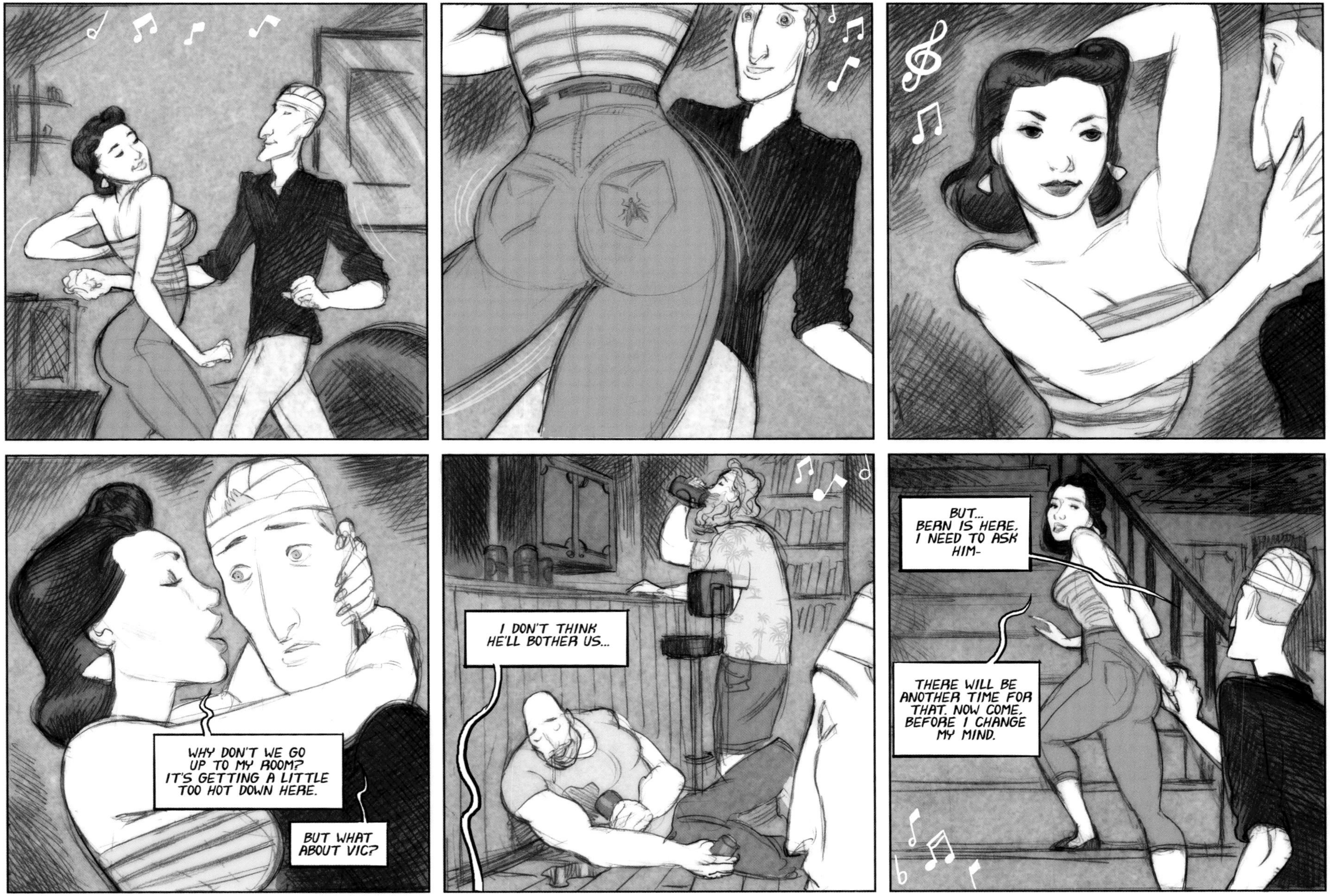
WHY DON'T WE GO UP TO MY ROOM? IT'S GETTING A LITTLE TOO HOT DOWN HERE.
BUT WHAT ABOUT VIC?
I DON'T THINK HE'LL BOTHER US...
BUT... BERN IS HERE. I NEED TO ASK HIM-
THERE WILL BE ANOTHER TIME FOR THAT. NOW COME, BEFORE I CHANGE MY MIND.

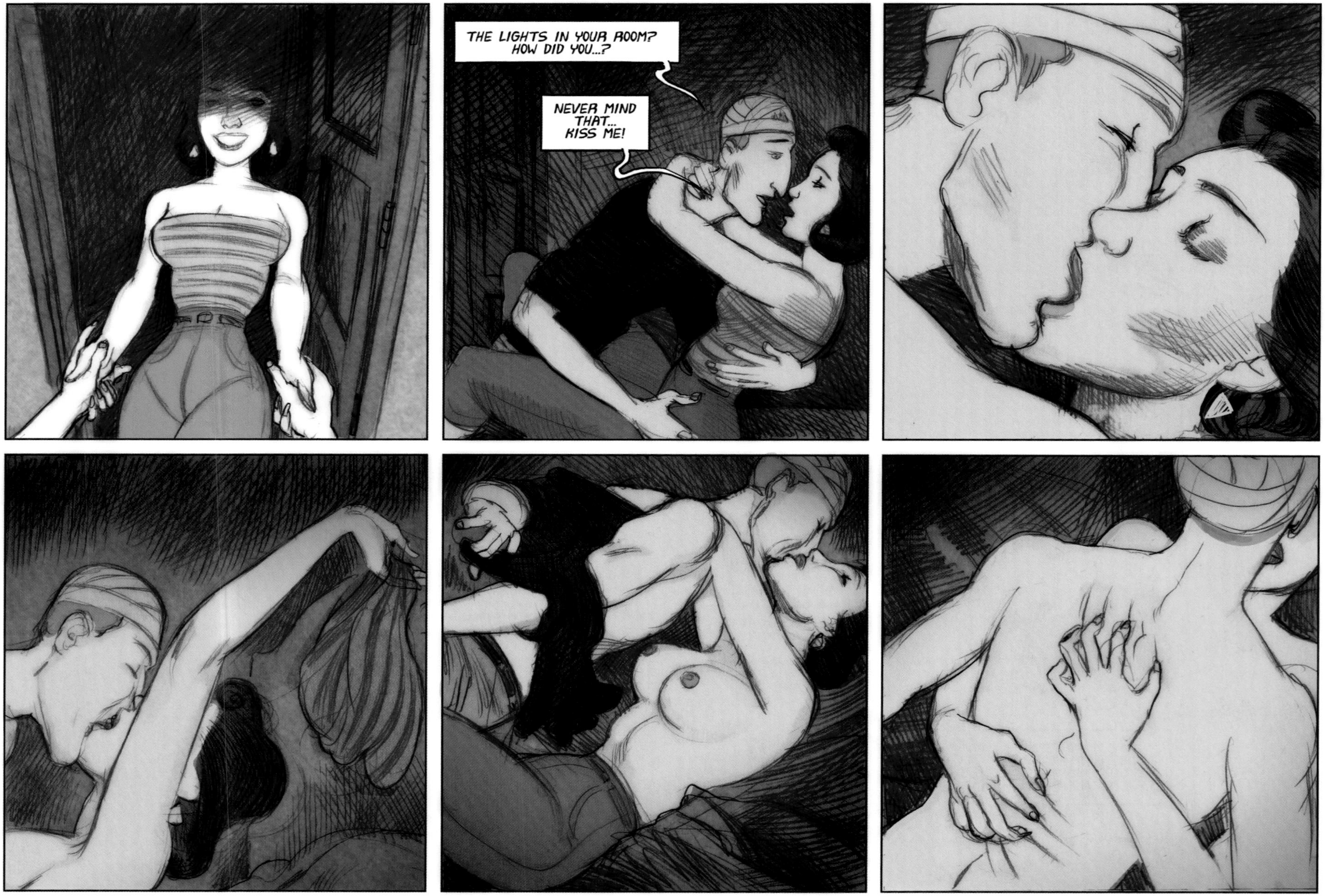
THE LIGHTS IN YOUR ROOM? HOW DID YOU...?
NEVER MIND THAT... KISS ME!

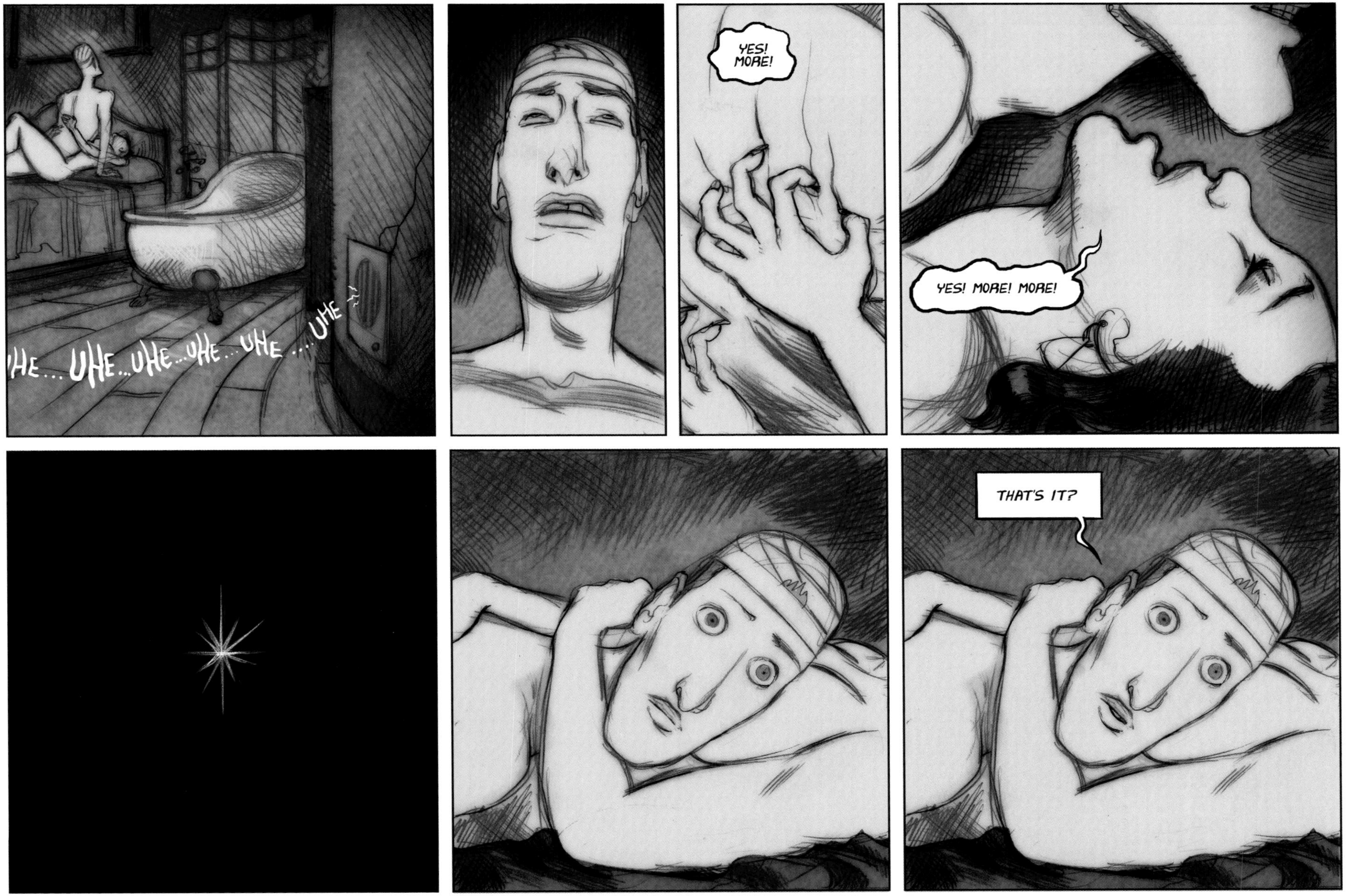
UHE... UHE... UHE... UHE... UHE ... UHE
YES! MORE!
YES! MORE! MORE!
THAT'S IT?

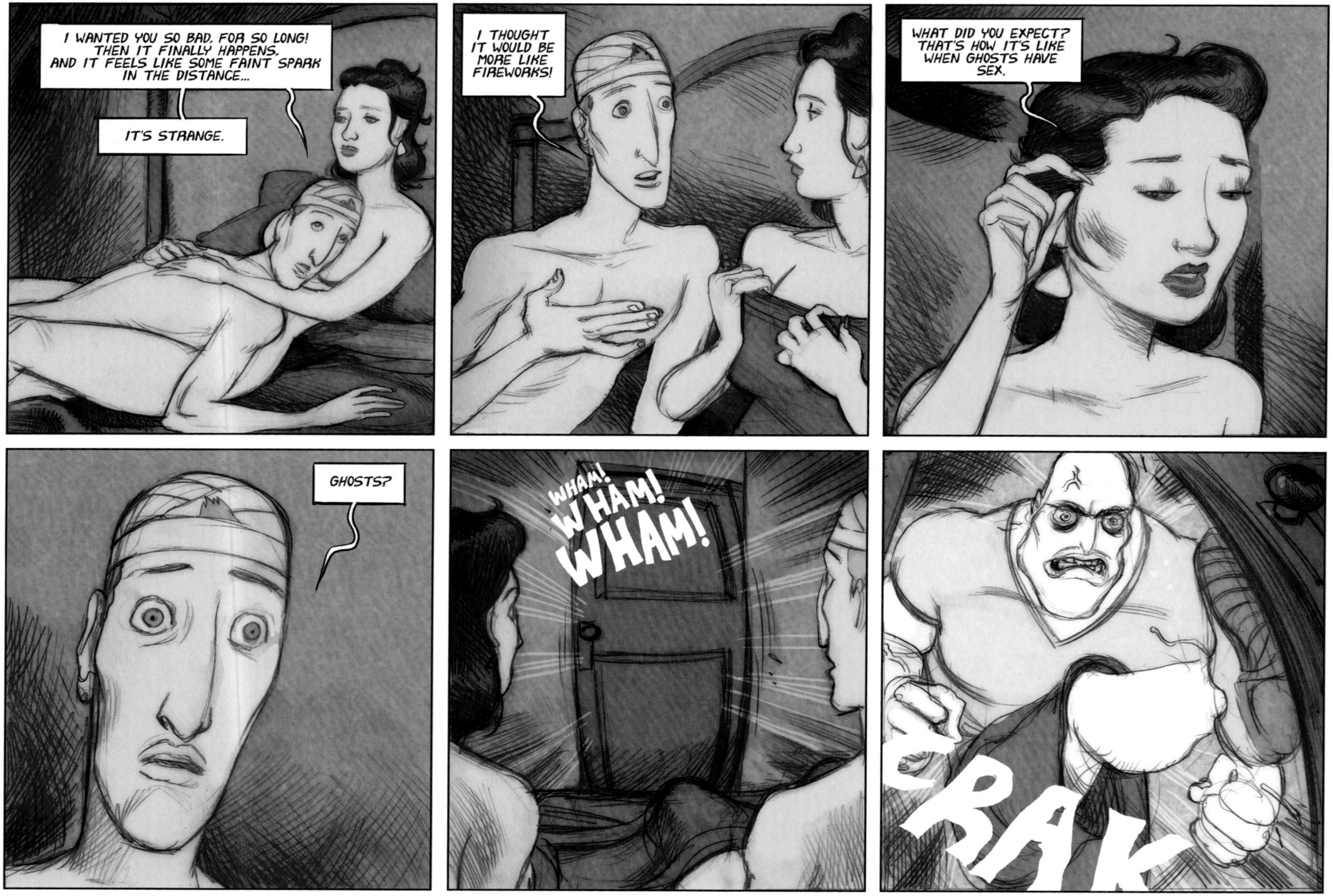

I WANTED YOU SO BAD, FOR SO LONG! THEN IT FINALLY HAPPENS, AND IT FEELS LIKE SOME FAINT SPARK IN THE DISTANCE...
IT'S STRANGE.
I THOUGHT IT WOULD BE MORE LIKE FIREWORKS!
WHAT DID YOU EXPECT? THAT'S HOW IT'S LIKE WHEN GHOSTS HAVE SEX.
GHOSTS?
WHAM! WHAM! WHAM!
RAK

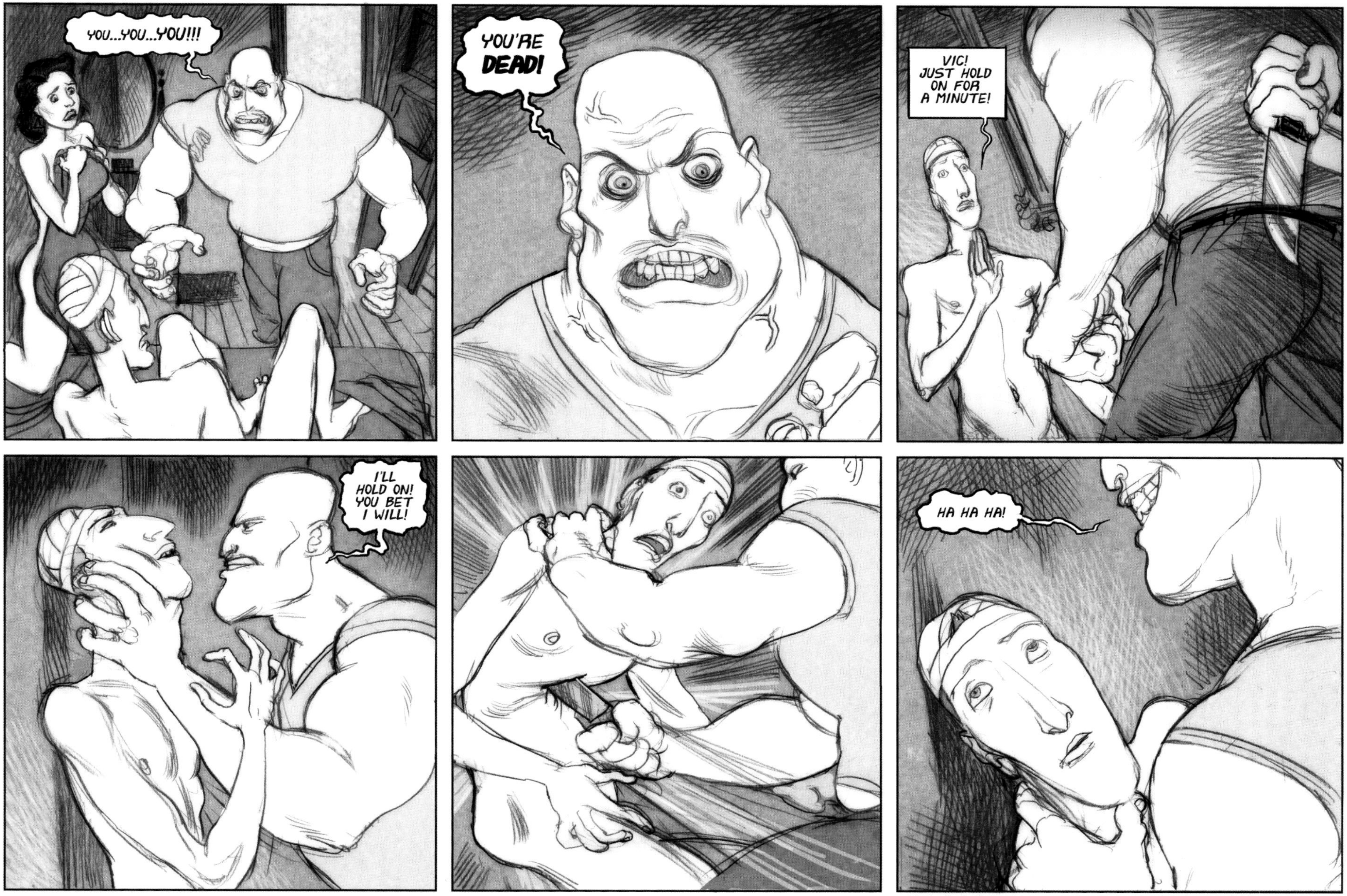
YOU...YOU...YOU!!!
YOU'RE DEAD!
VIC! JUST HOLD ON FOR A MINUTE!
I'LL HOLD ON! YOU BET I WILL!
HA HA HA!

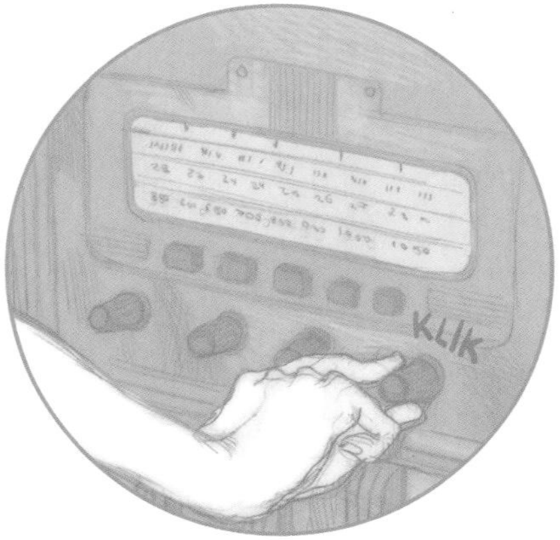
KLIK

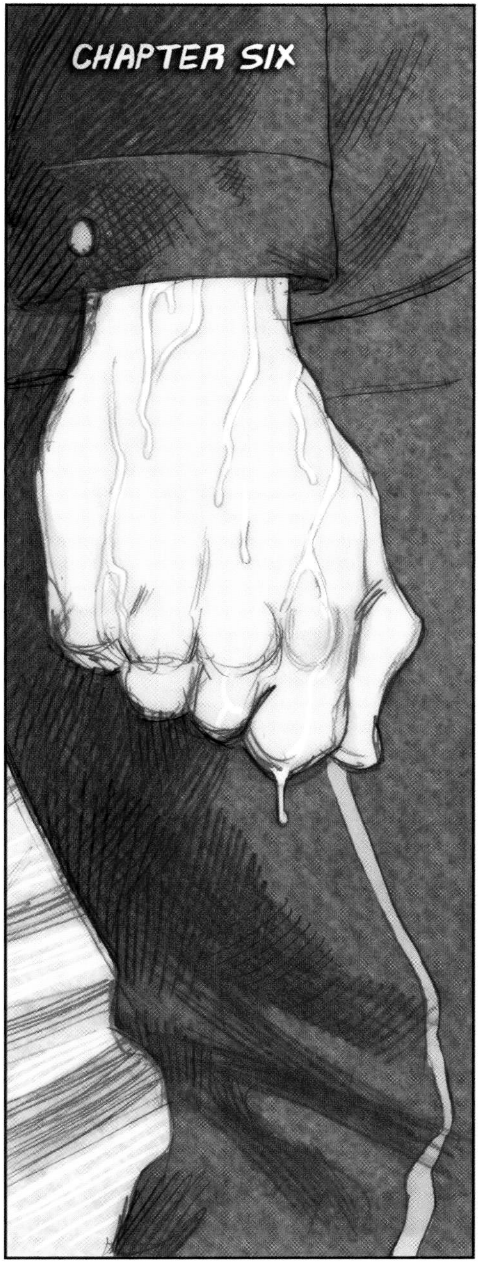
CHAPTER SIX
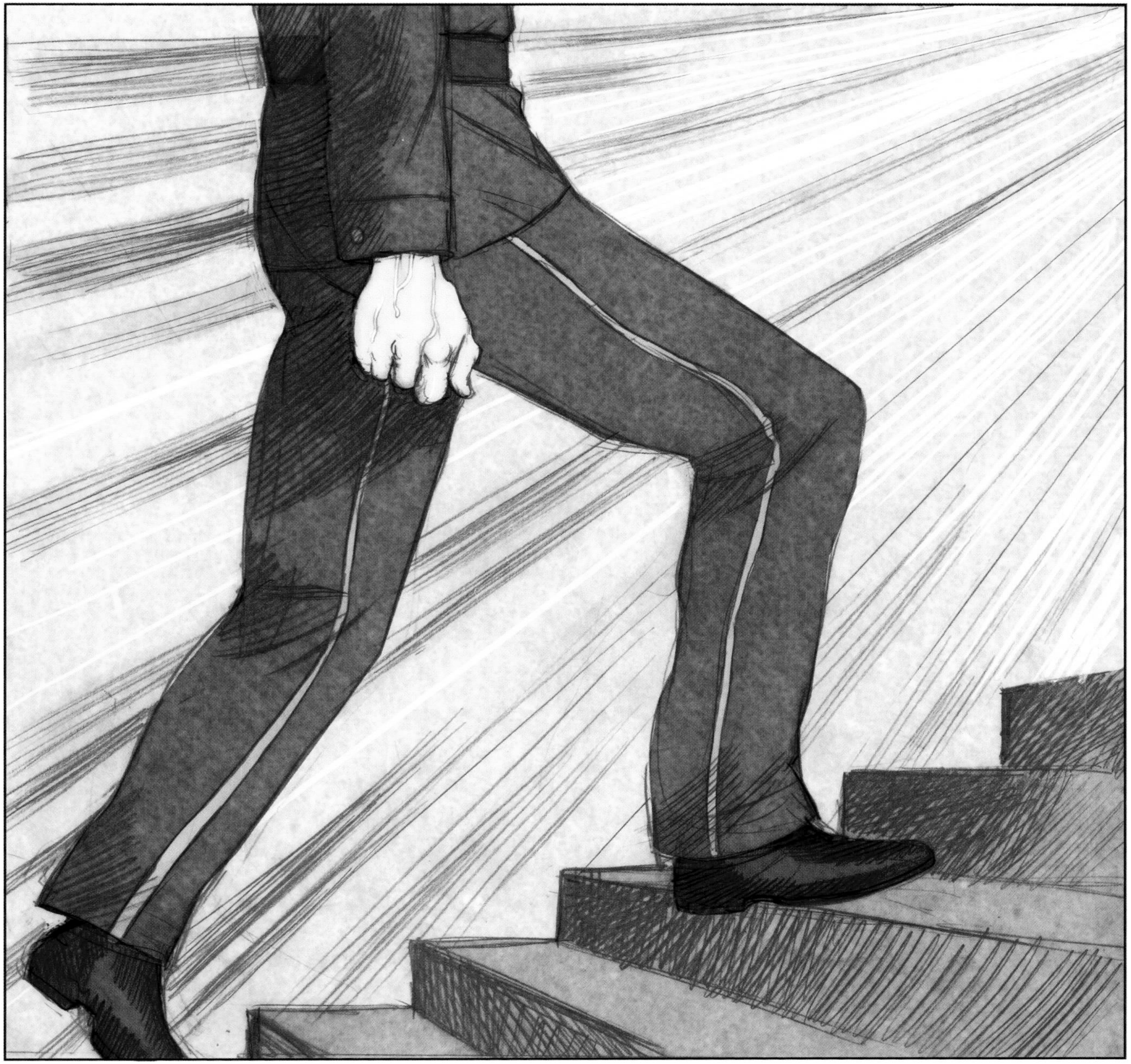

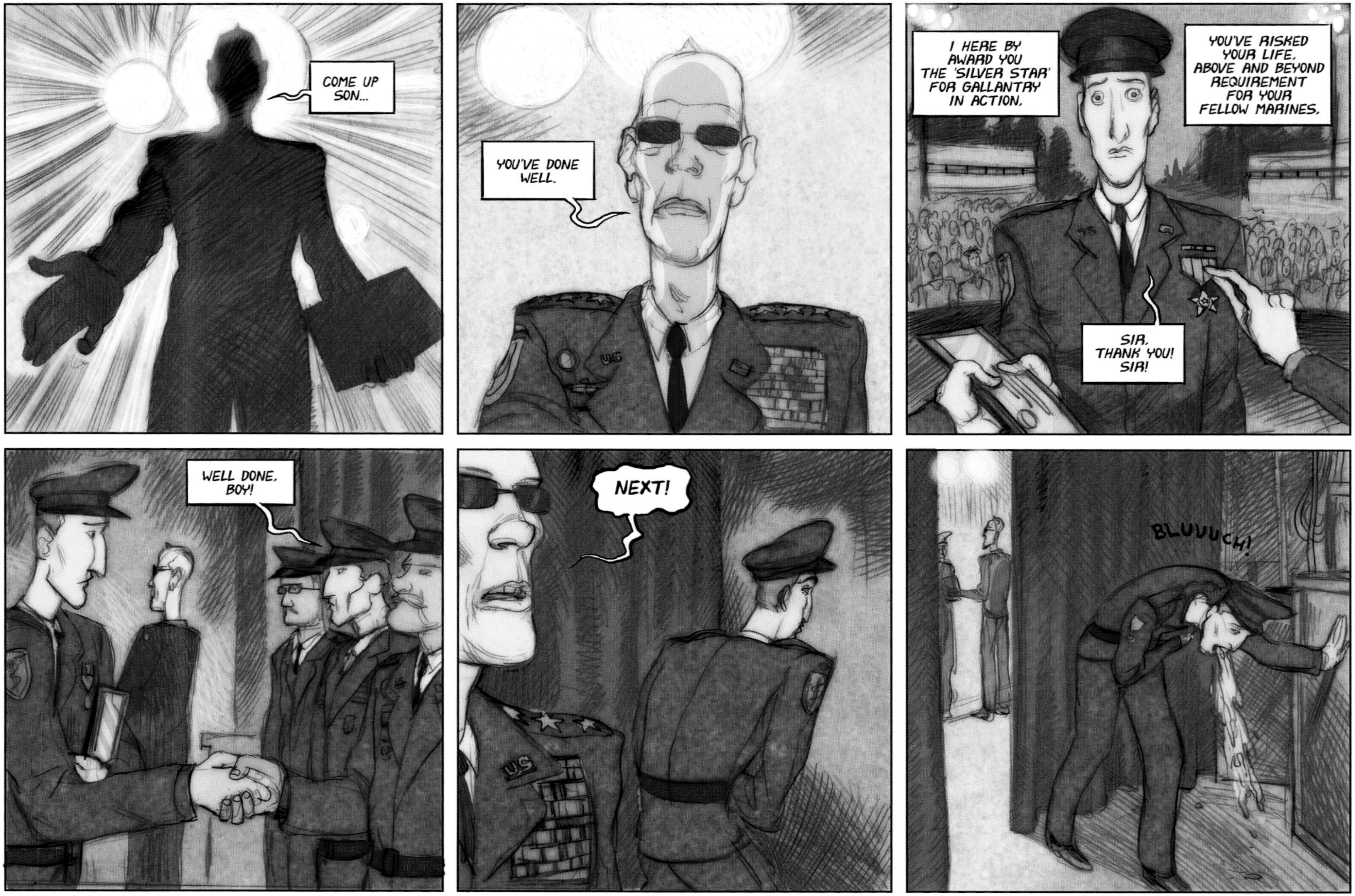
COME UP SON...
YOU'VE DONE WELL.
I HERE BY AWARD YOU THE 'SILVER STAR' FOR GALLANTRY IN ACTION.
YOU'VE RISKED YOUR LIFE, ABOVE AND BEYOND REQUIREMENT FOR YOUR FELLOW MARINES.
SIR, THANK YOU! SIR!
WELL DONE, BOY!
NEXT!
BLUUUCH!

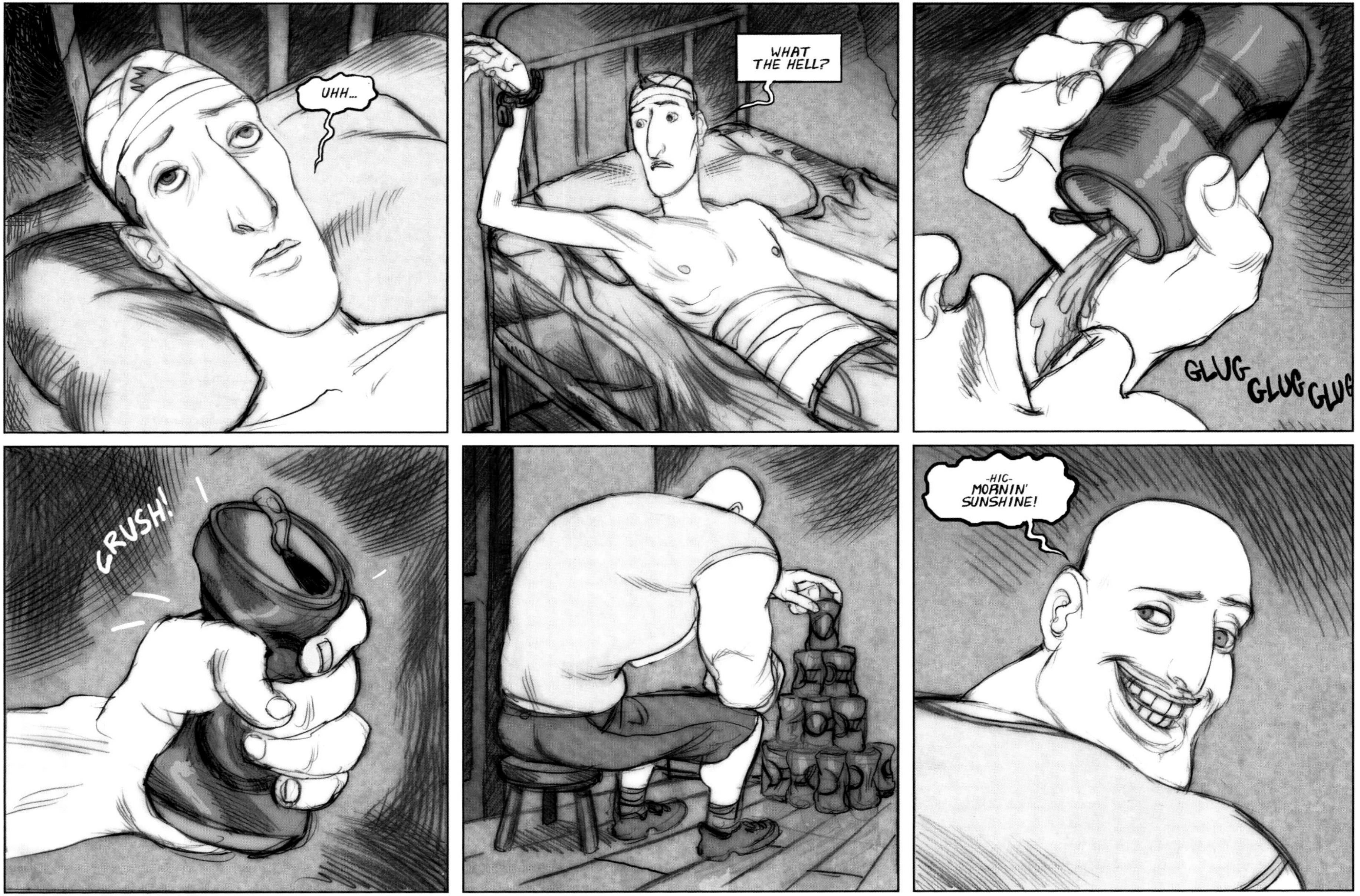
UHH...
WHAT THE HELL?
GLUG GLUG GLUG
CRUSH!
-HIC- MORNIN' SUNSHINE!

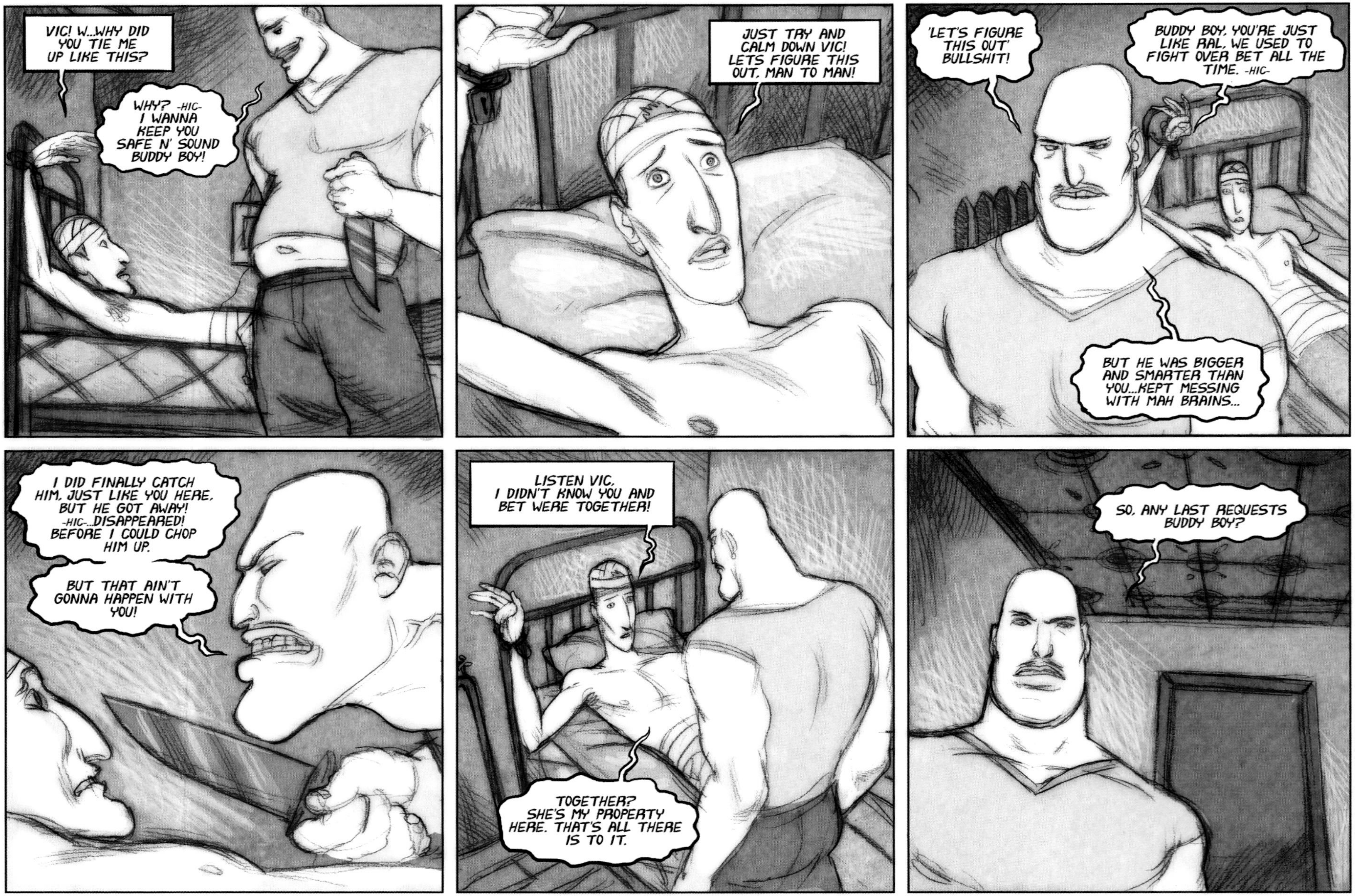
VIC! W...WHY DID YOU TIE ME UP LIKE THIS?
WHY? -HIC- I WANNA KEEP YOU SAFE N' SOUND BUDDY BOY!
JUST TRY AND CALM DOWN VIC! LETS FIGURE THIS OUT, MAN TO MAN!
'LET'S FIGURE THIS OUT' BULLSHIT!
BUDDY BOY, YOU'RE JUST LIKE RAL, WE USED TO FIGHT OVER BET ALL THE TIME. -HIC-
BUT HE WAS BIGGER AND SMARTER THAN YOU...KEPT MESSING WITH MAH BRAINS...
I DID FINALLY CATCH HIM, JUST LIKE YOU HERE, BUT HE GOT AWAY! -HIC-...DISAPPEARED! BEFORE I COULD CHOP HIM UP.
BUT THAT AIN'T GONNA HAPPEN WITH YOU!
LISTEN VIC, I DIDN'T KNOW YOU AND BET WERE TOGETHER!
TOGETHER? SHE'S MY PROPERTY HERE. THAT'S ALL THERE IS TO IT.
SO, ANY LAST REQUESTS BUDDY BOY?

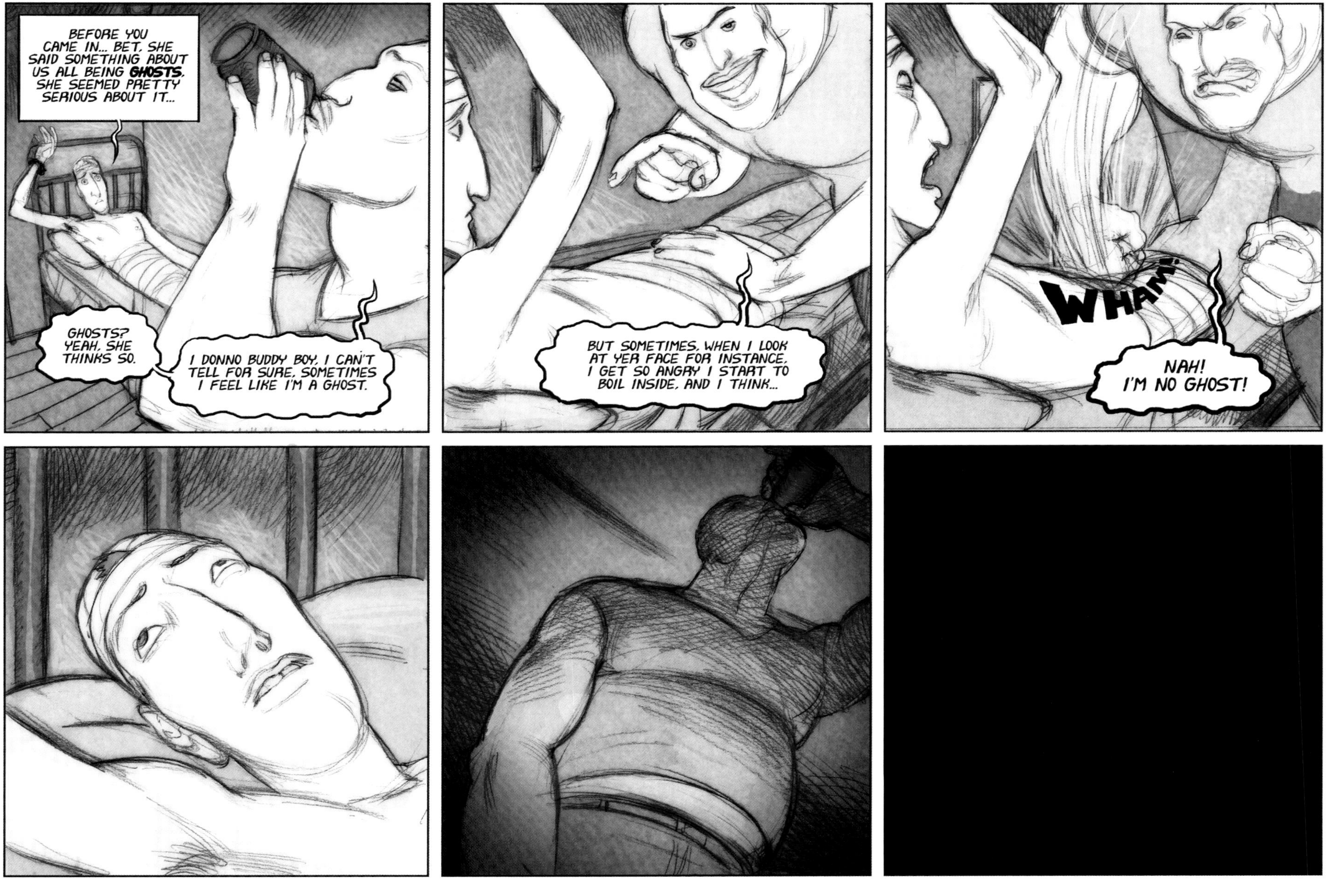
BEFORE YOU CAME IN... BET, SHE SAID SOMETHING ABOUT US ALL BEING **GHOSTS**, SHE SEEMED PRETTY SERIOUS ABOUT IT...
GHOSTS? YEAH, SHE THINKS SO.
I DONNO BUDDY BOY, I CAN'T TELL FOR SURE, SOMETIMES I FEEL LIKE I'M A GHOST.
BUT SOMETIMES, WHEN I LOOK AT YER FACE FOR INSTANCE, I GET SO ANGRY I START TO BOIL INSIDE, AND I THINK...
WHAM!
NAH! I'M NO GHOST!

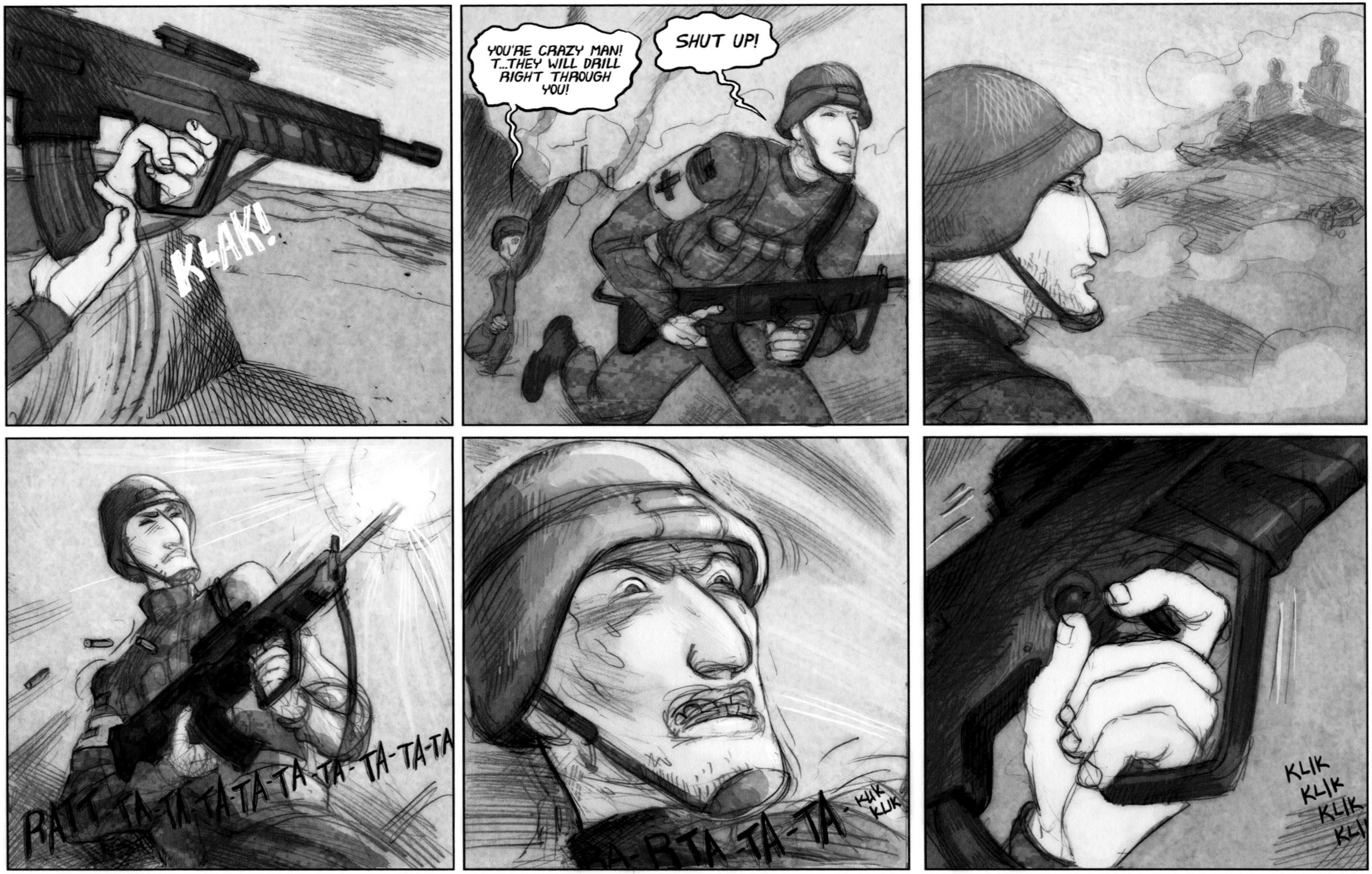
KLAK!
YOU'RE CRAZY MAN! T...THEY WILL DRILL RIGHT THROUGH YOU!
SHUT UP!
RATT-TA-TA-TA-TA-TA-TA-TA-TA-TA
A-RTA-TA-TA-
KLIK KLIK
KLIK
KLIK
KLIK
KLI

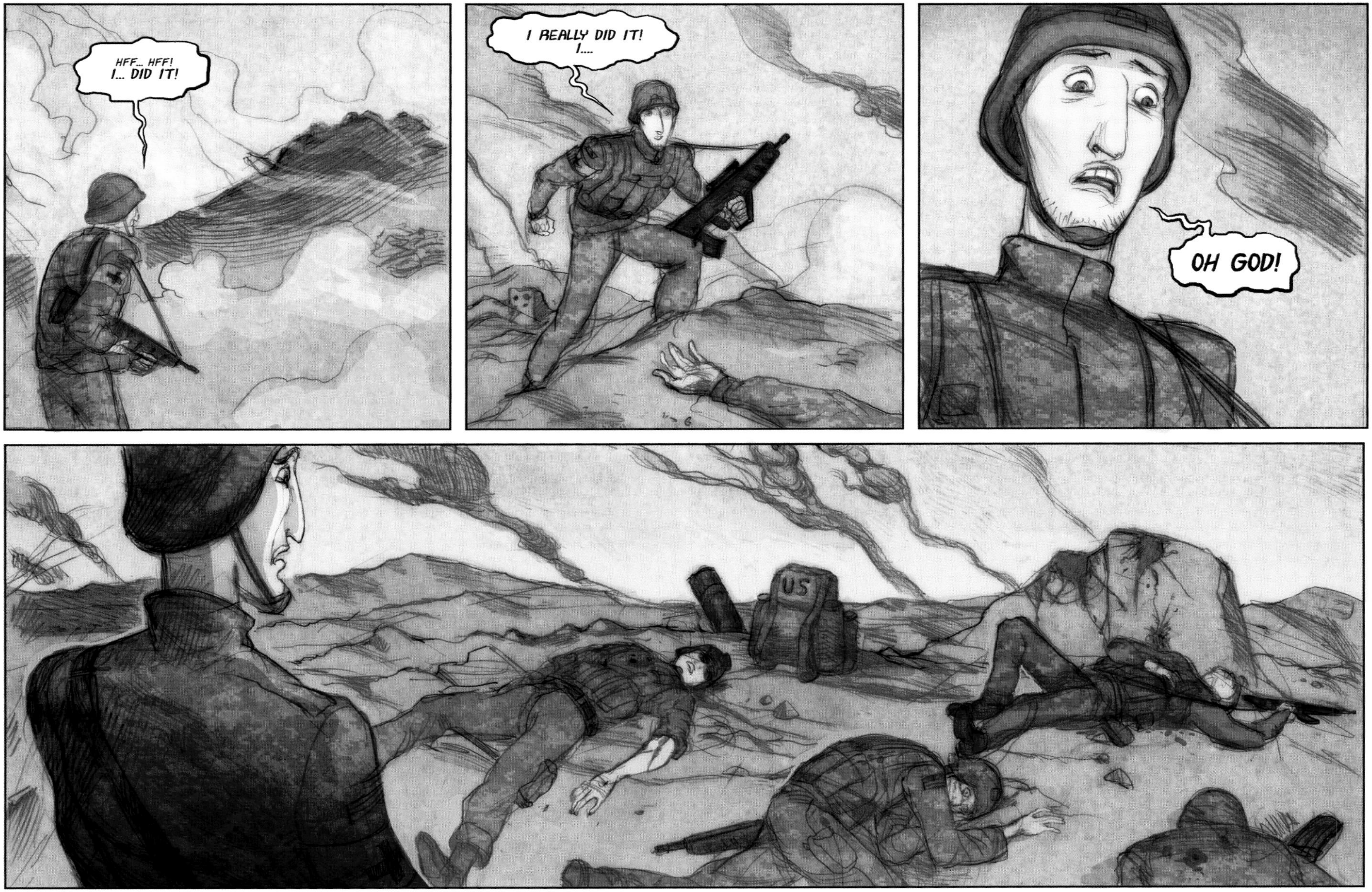
HFF... HFF!
I... DID IT!
I REALLY DID IT!
I....
OH GOD!

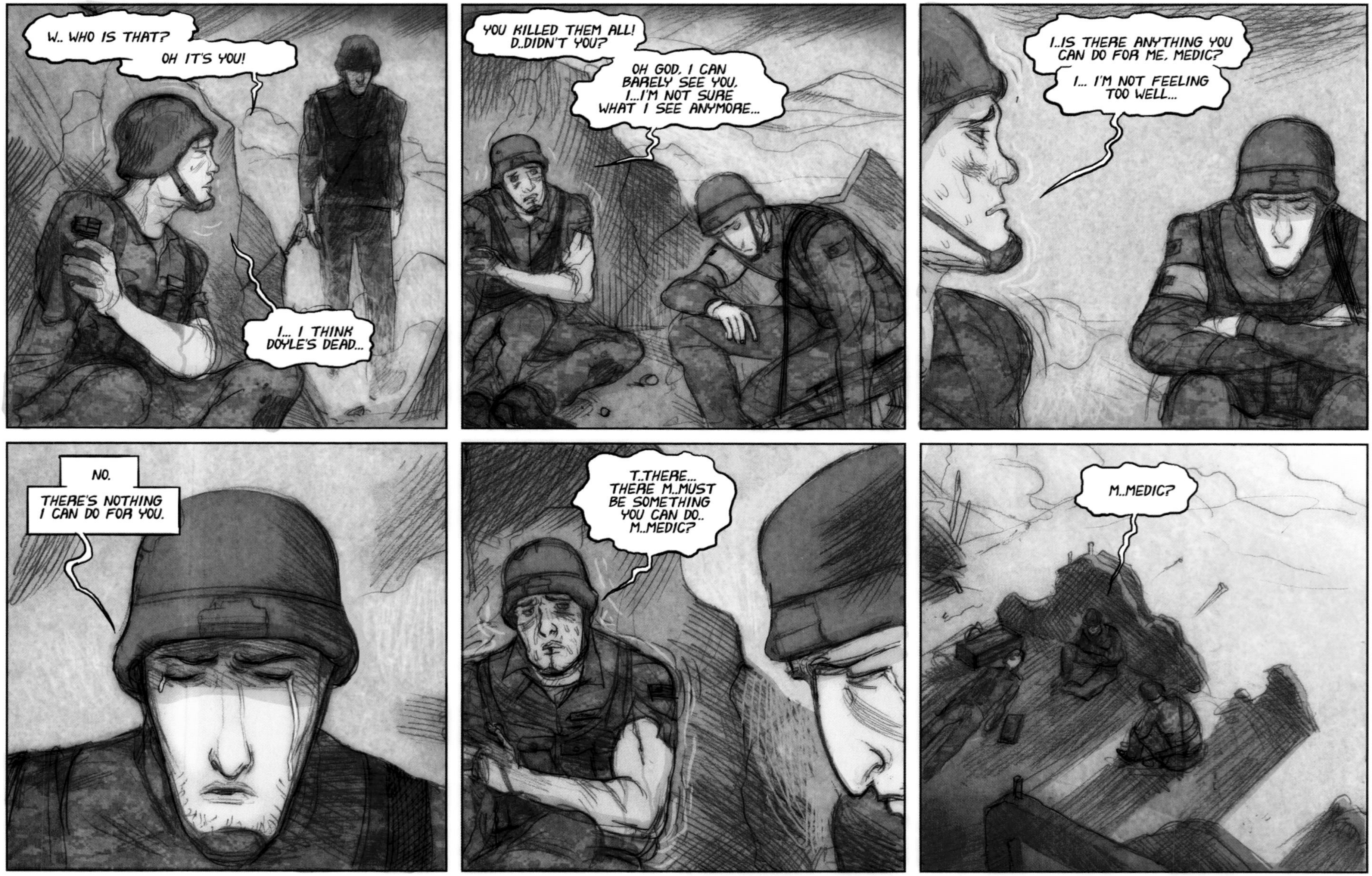
W.. WHO IS THAT?
OH IT'S YOU!
I... I THINK DOYLE'S DEAD...
YOU KILLED THEM ALL! D..DIDN'T YOU?
OH GOD, I CAN BARELY SEE YOU, I...I'M NOT SURE WHAT I SEE ANYMORE...
I..IS THERE ANYTHING YOU CAN DO FOR ME, MEDIC?
I... I'M NOT FEELING TOO WELL...
NO.
THERE'S NOTHING I CAN DO FOR YOU.
T..THERE... THERE M..MUST BE SOMETHING YOU CAN DO.. M..MEDIC?
M..MEDIC?

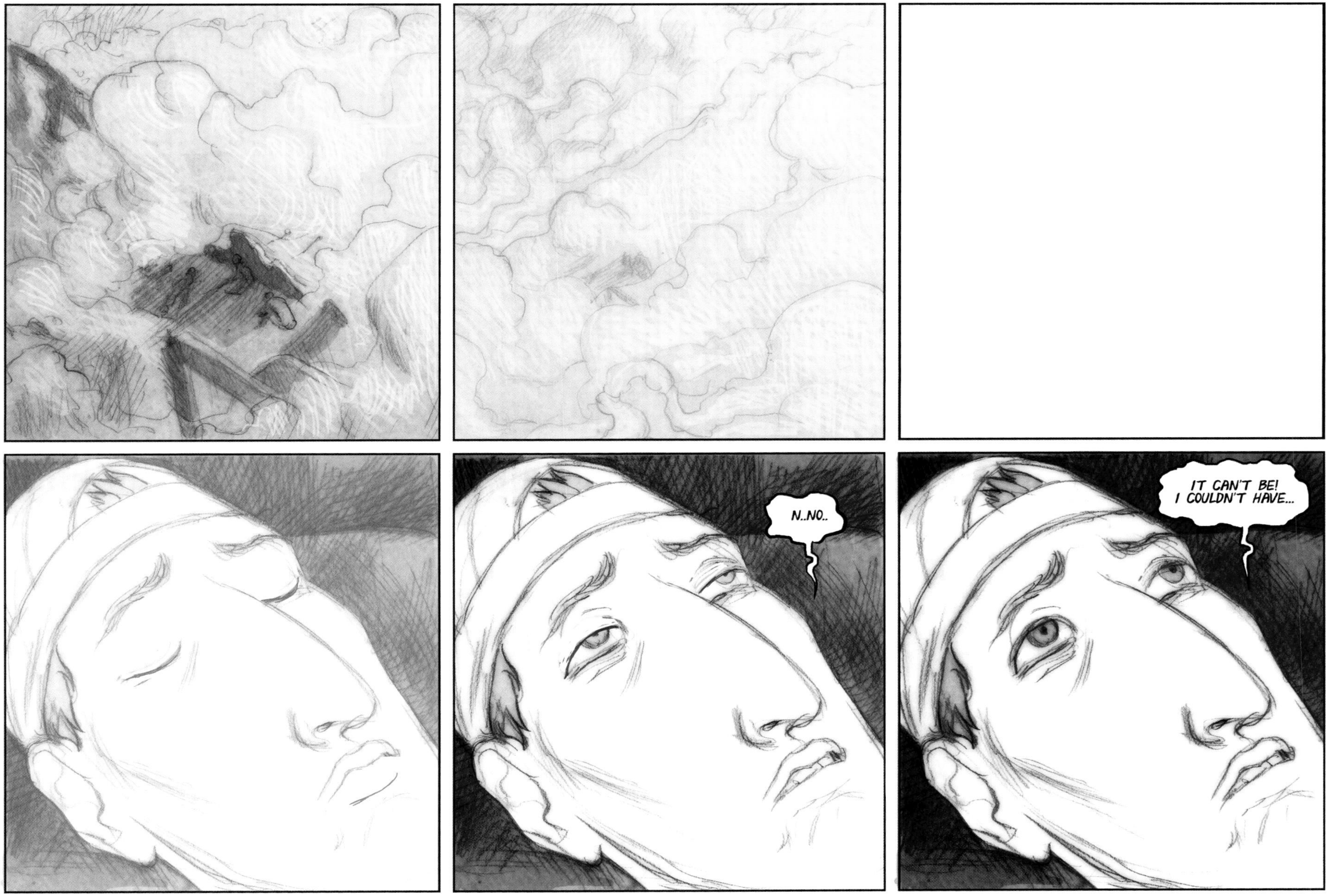
N..NO..
IT CAN'T BE!
I COULDN'T HAVE...

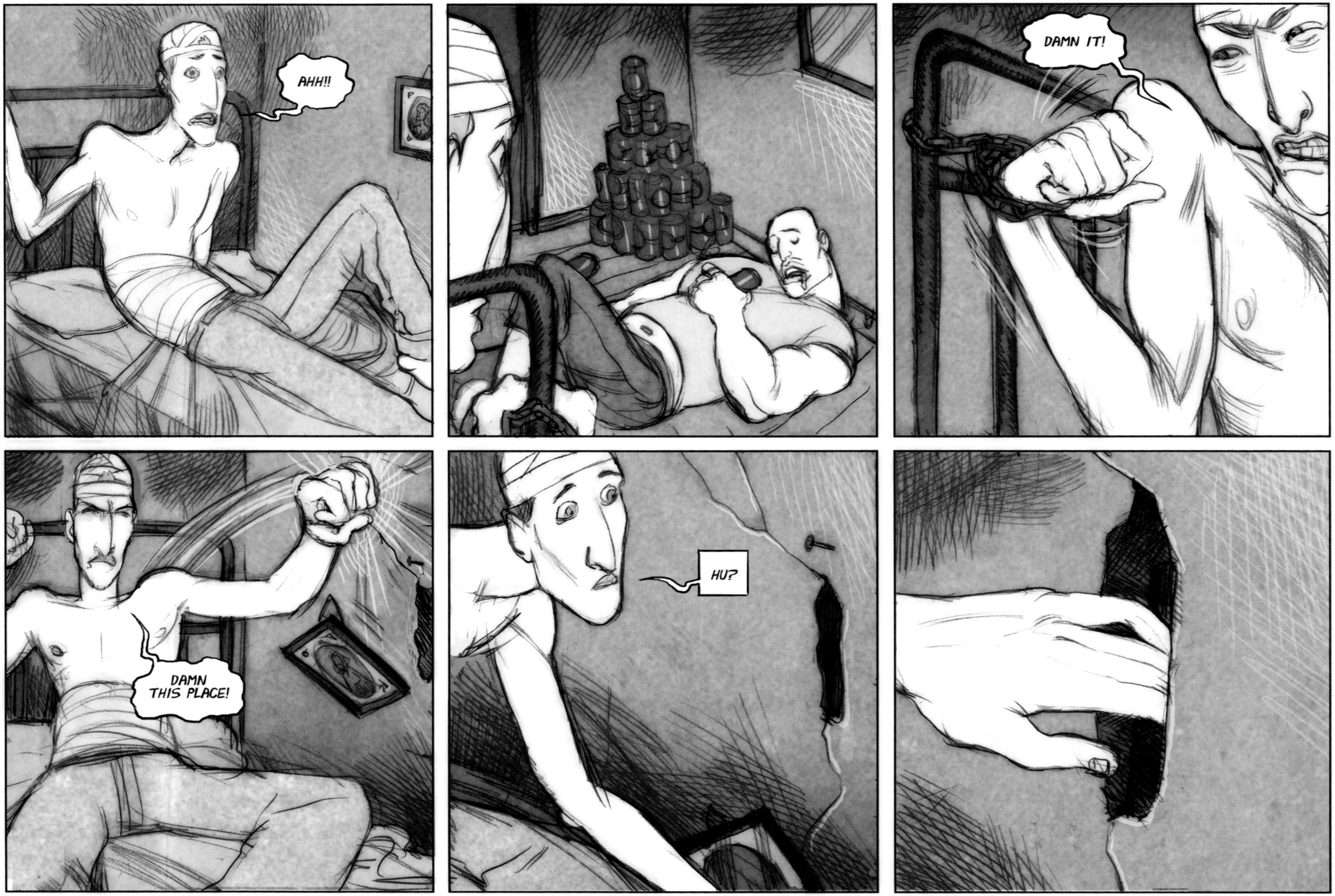
AHH!!
DAMN IT!
DAMN THIS PLACE!
HU?

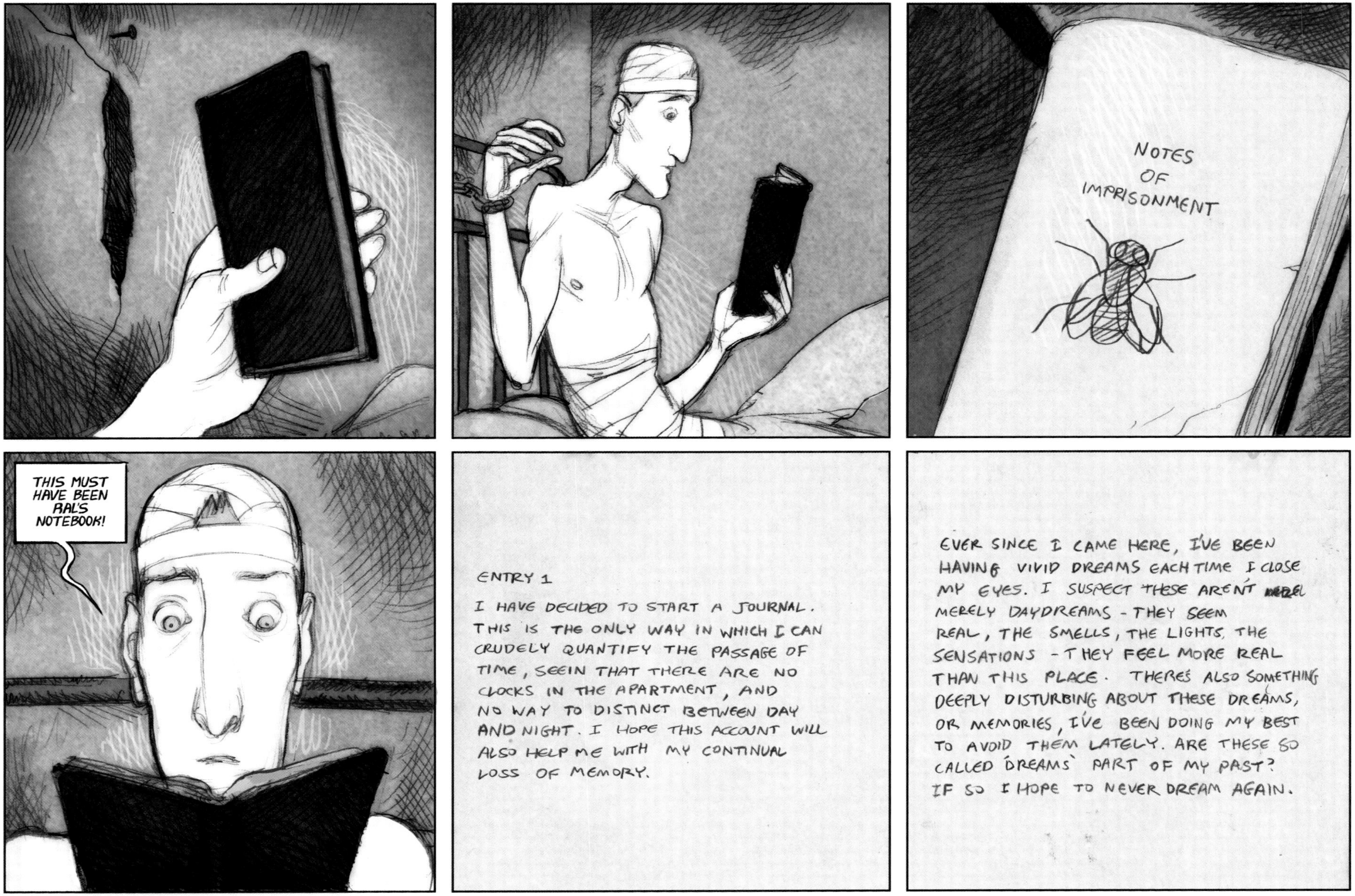
NOTES OF IMPRISONMENT
THIS MUST HAVE BEEN RAL'S NOTEBOOK!
ENTRY 1
I HAVE DECIDED TO START A JOURNAL. THIS IS THE ONLY WAY IN WHICH I CAN CRUDELY QUANTIFY THE PASSAGE OF TIME, SEEIN THAT THERE ARE NO CLOCKS IN THE APARTMENT, AND NO WAY TO DISTINCT BETWEEN DAY AND NIGHT. I HOPE THIS ACCOUNT WILL ALSO HELP ME WITH MY CONTINUAL LOSS OF MEMORY.
EVER SINCE I CAME HERE, I'VE BEEN HAVING VIVID DREAMS EACH TIME I CLOSE MY EYES. I SUSPECT THESE AREN'T MERELY DAYDREAMS - THEY SEEM REAL, THE SMELLS, THE LIGHTS, THE SENSATIONS - THEY FEEL MORE REAL THAN THIS PLACE. THERE'S ALSO SOMETHING DEEPLY DISTURBING ABOUT THESE DREAMS, OR MEMORIES, I'VE BEEN DOING MY BEST TO AVOID THEM LATELY. ARE THESE SO CALLED 'DREAMS' PART OF MY PAST? IF SO I HOPE TO NEVER DREAM AGAIN.

ENTRY 6

I'VE HAD A VISION OF MYSELF HITTING A WOMAN ~~PUNCHING~~ AND CHOKING HER. SHE WAS BEGGING ME FOR MERCY BUT I JUST HIT HER HARDER, FEELING FLUSHED WITH ANGER. WE WERE WEARING WHITE COATS, HER MOUTH WAS BLEEDING ALL OVER HER STARCHED, WHITE COLLAR. I WOKE UP SHAKING.

ENTRY 8

I HAVE FOUND OUT THAT THIS PLACE IS CALLED 'THE ABADDON', IT'S HARD TO SAY HOW OLD IT IS, BUT I ASSUME THAT IT MAY BE MORE THAN 200 YEARS OLD. MY 'ROOMMATES' ARE BEING LESS THAN COOPERATIVE IN HELPING ME FIND OUT MORE ABOUT THE HISTORY OF THE PLACE. THEY ALSO HAVE ABSOLUTELY NO DESIRE TO ESCAPE. THEY HAVE FULLY SURRENDERED THEMSELVS TO THE DECAYING SPIRIT OF THIS PLACE, THEY HAVE A VERY VAGUE IDEA OF HOW LONG THEY HAVE LIVED HERE OR THE DETAILS OF THEIR LIVES PRIOR TO COMING HERE.

THE MOST COOPERATIVE OF THE GROUP IS **BET**, WHICH I SUSPECT IS DEVELOPING AN INFATUATION WITH ME SHE'S INDISPUTABLY ATTRACTIVE, HOWEVER I SIMPLY CAN'T ALLOW MYSELF TO GET INVOLVED WITH HER WHILE I STILL REASERCH 'THE ABADDON'.

ENTRY 17

IT'S BEEN QUITE MISRABLE HERE LATELY. I'M LOCKED IN HERE WITH A GROUP OF DEMENTED LUNATICS. THERE IS NEVER ANY PEACE AND QUIET HERE - JUST A SERIES OF CONFRONTATIONS AND AWKWARD INTERACTIONS. IT IS AS IF SOMEONE HAS CAREFULLY PICKED THE MOST DYSFUNCTIONAL AND INCOMPATIBLE PEOPLE TO LIVE TOGETHER. THIS REMINDS ME OF A PLAY I READ ONCE... WHAT WAS IT CALLED? DAMN MY BLASTED MIND! IT'S GETTING FOGGIER BY THE DAY. REGARDLESS, THIS PATHETIC GROUP OF MORONS SEEM TO HAVE TAKEN A LIKING TO ME, THEY ARE SO THICK THEY CAN'T DETECT MY ABSOLUTE CONTEMPT TOWARDS THEM.

ENTRY 26

BET AND I HAVE BEEN SNEAKING INTO HER ROOM DURING VIC'S DRUNKEN BLACKOUTS BET LIKES IT WHEN I'M ROUGH WITH HER, TODAY I HIT HER REAL HARD ON THE MOUTH THEN SHOVED HER HEAD INTO THE WALL. STRANGELY ENOUGH, SHE DIDN'T BLEED. SHE WANTS TO ~~MAKE~~ HAVE SEX EACH TIME I ROUGH HER UP, BUT I FEEL NO DESIRE. I'M GETTING DISTRACTED LATELY, I NEED ~~CONCENTRATE~~ TO FOCUS ON MY ESCAPE.

ENTRY 66

PLEASE, KILL ME.
PLEASE, KILL ME.

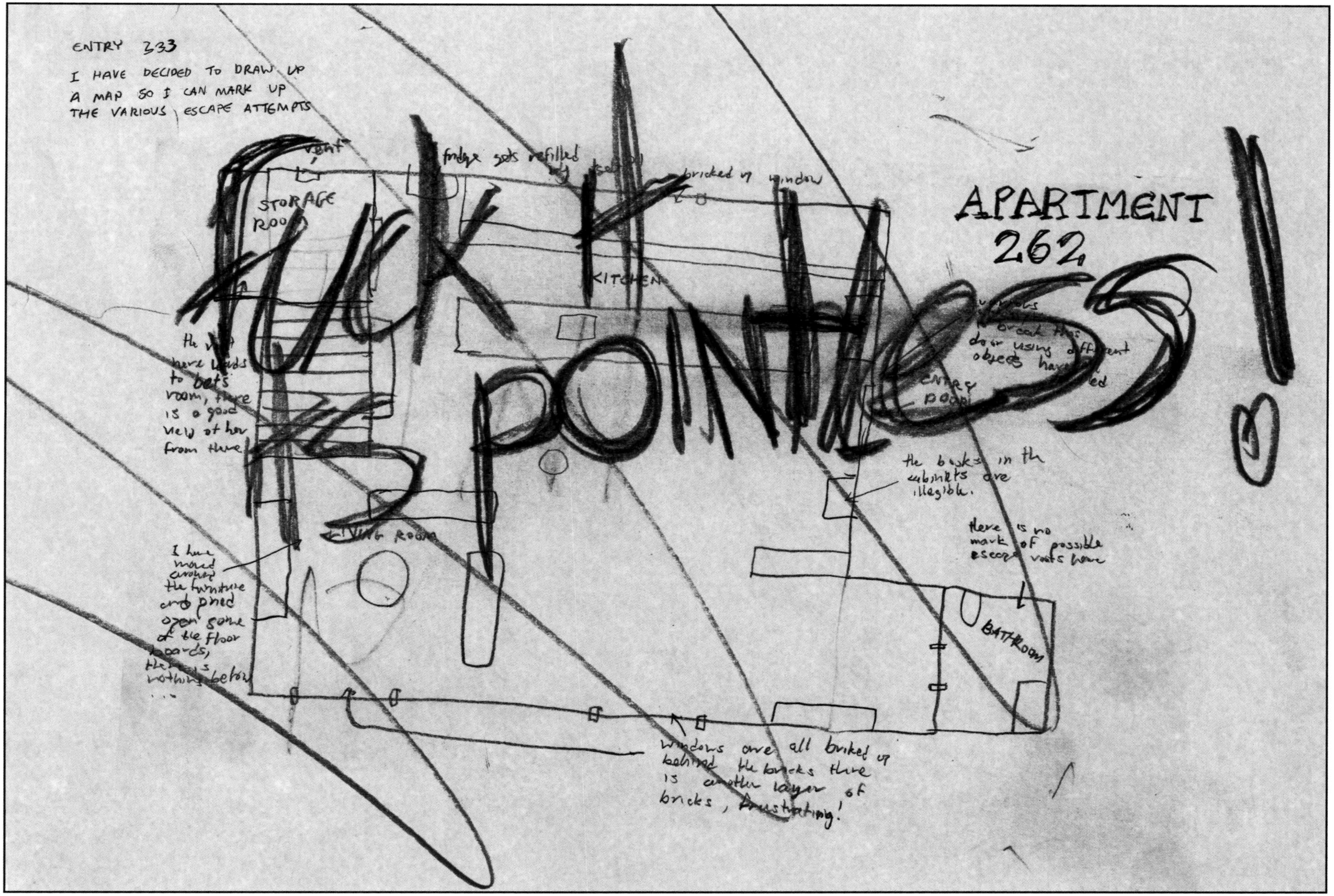
ENTRY 333
I HAVE DECIDED TO DRAW UP A MAP SO I CAN MARK UP THE VARIOUS ESCAPE ATTEMPTS
vent
bricked up window
STORAGE ROOM
KITCHEN
APARTMENT 262
FUCK
POINTLESS!
ENTRY ROOM
LIVING ROOM
BATHROOM
the books in the cabinets are illegible.
there is no mark of possible escape routs here
I have moved around the furniture and pried open some of the floor boards, there is nothing below . . .
windows are all bricked up behind the bricks there is another layer of bricks, frustrating!

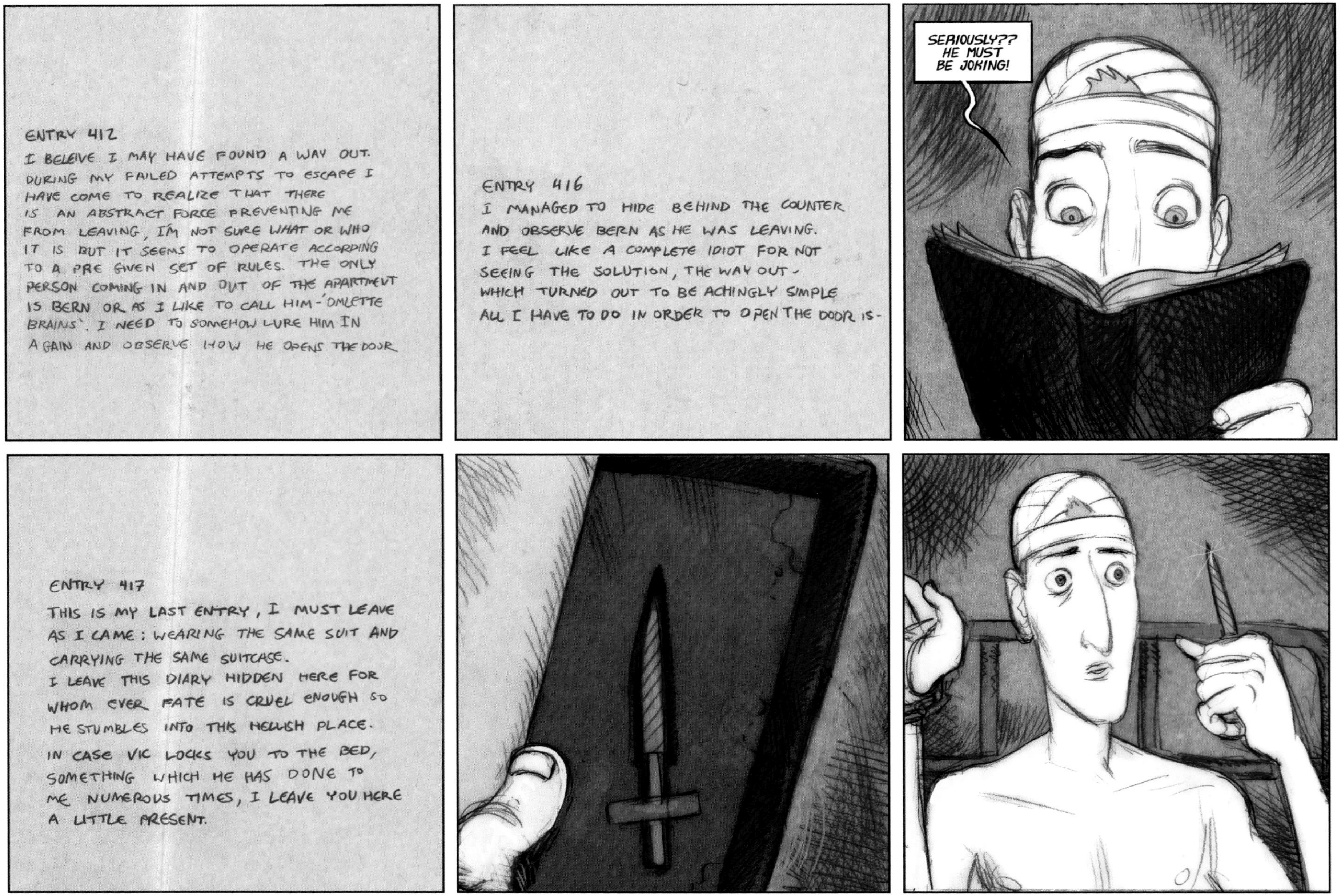
ENTRY 412
I BELEIVE I MAY HAVE FOUND A WAY OUT.
DURING MY FAILED ATTEMPTS TO ESCAPE I HAVE COME TO REALIZE THAT THERE IS AN ABSTRACT FORCE PREVENTING ME FROM LEAVING, I'M NOT SURE WHAT OR WHO IT IS BUT IT SEEMS TO OPERATE ACCORDING TO A PRE GIVEN SET OF RULES. THE ONLY PERSON COMING IN AND OUT OF THE APARTMENT IS BERN OR AS I LIKE TO CALL HIM-'OMLETTE BRAINS'. I NEED TO SOMEHOW LURE HIM IN AGAIN AND OBSERVE HOW HE OPENS THE DOOR
ENTRY 416
I MANAGED TO HIDE BEHIND THE COUNTER AND OBSERVE BERN AS HE WAS LEAVING.
I FEEL LIKE A COMPLETE IDIOT FOR NOT SEEING THE SOLUTION, THE WAY OUT - WHICH TURNED OUT TO BE ACHINGLY SIMPLE
ALL I HAVE TO DO IN ORDER TO OPEN THE DOOR IS-
SERIOUSLY?? HE MUST BE JOKING!
ENTRY 417
THIS IS MY LAST ENTRY, I MUST LEAVE AS I CAME: WEARING THE SAME SUIT AND CARRYING THE SAME SUITCASE.
I LEAVE THIS DIARY HIDDEN HERE FOR WHOM EVER FATE IS CRUEL ENOUGH SO HE STUMBLES INTO THIS HELLISH PLACE.
IN CASE VIC LOCKS YOU TO THE BED, SOMETHING WHICH HE HAS DONE TO ME NUMEROUS TIMES, I LEAVE YOU HERE A LITTLE PRESENT.

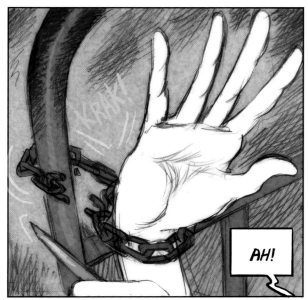

AH!

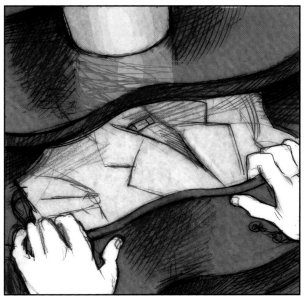

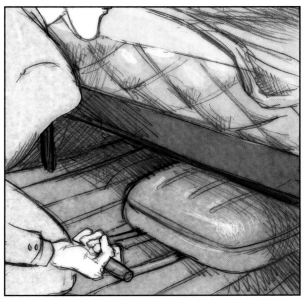

GOODBYE OL' VIC, GOODBYE AND GOOD RIDDANCE!

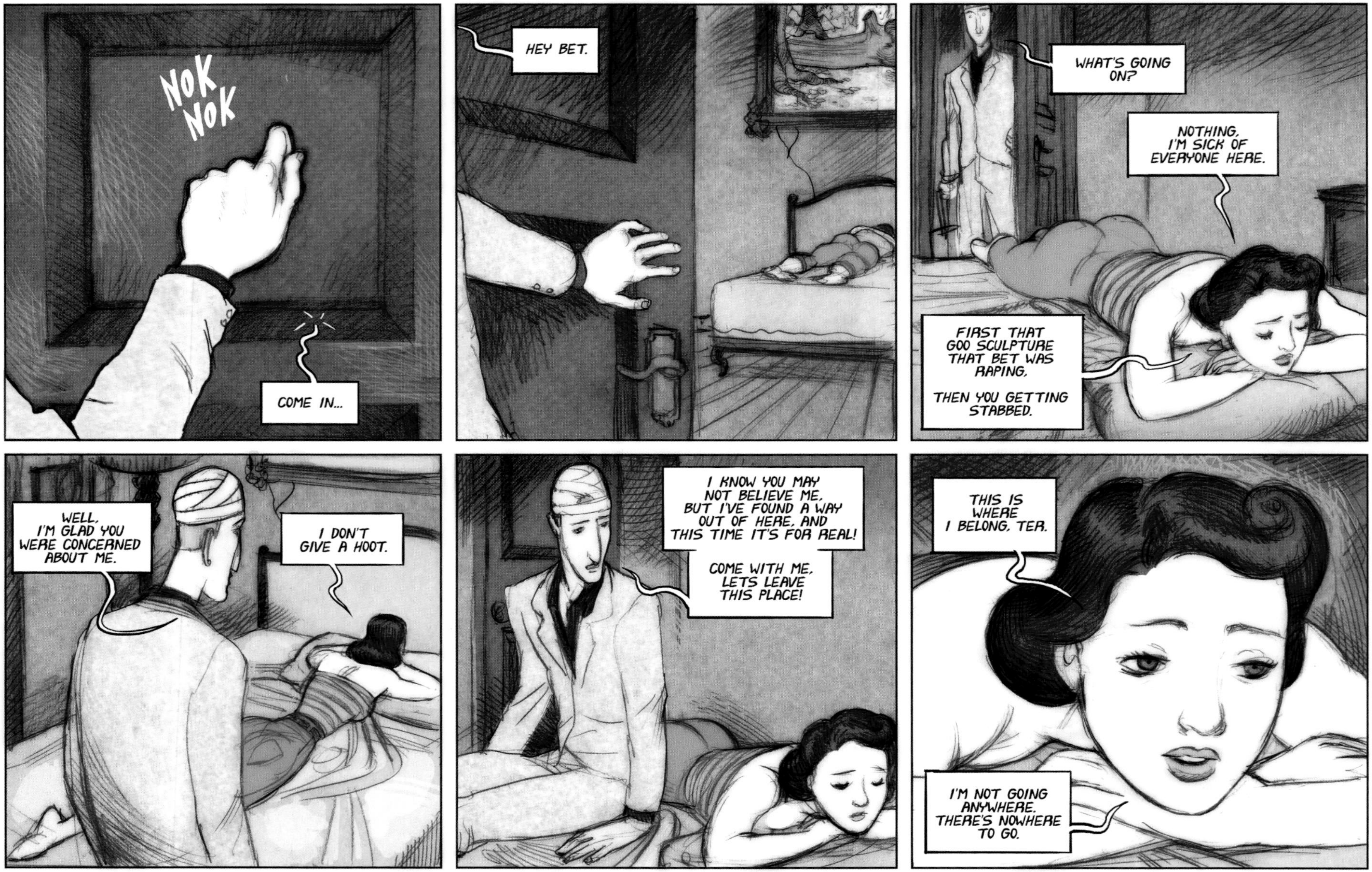
NOK NOK
COME IN...
HEY BET.
WHAT'S GOING ON?
NOTHING, I'M SICK OF EVERYONE HERE.
FIRST THAT GOO SCULPTURE THAT BET WAS RAPING,
THEN YOU GETTING STABBED.
WELL, I'M GLAD YOU WERE CONCERNED ABOUT ME.
I DON'T GIVE A HOOT.
I KNOW YOU MAY NOT BELIEVE ME, BUT I'VE FOUND A WAY OUT OF HERE, AND THIS TIME IT'S FOR REAL!
COME WITH ME, LETS LEAVE THIS PLACE!
THIS IS WHERE I BELONG, TER.
I'M NOT GOING ANYWHERE. THERE'S NOWHERE TO GO.

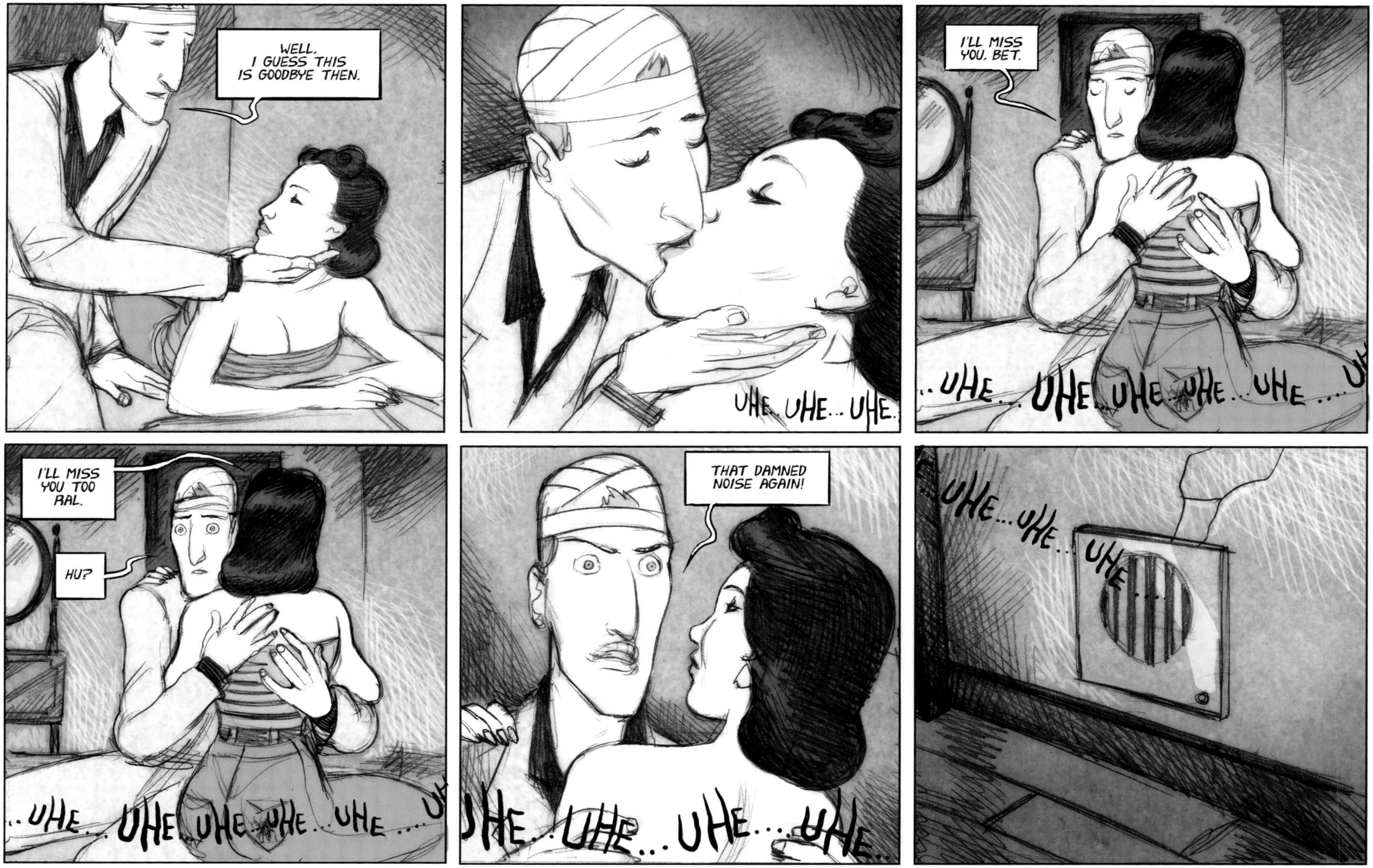
WELL, I GUESS THIS IS GOODBYE THEN.
UHE... UHE... UHE...
I'LL MISS YOU, BET.
...UHE... UHE... UHE... UHE... UHE... UH
I'LL MISS YOU TOO RAL.
HU?
...UHE... UHE... UHE... UHE... UHE... UH
UHE... UHE... UHE... UHE...
THAT DAMNED NOISE AGAIN!
UHE... UHE... UHE...

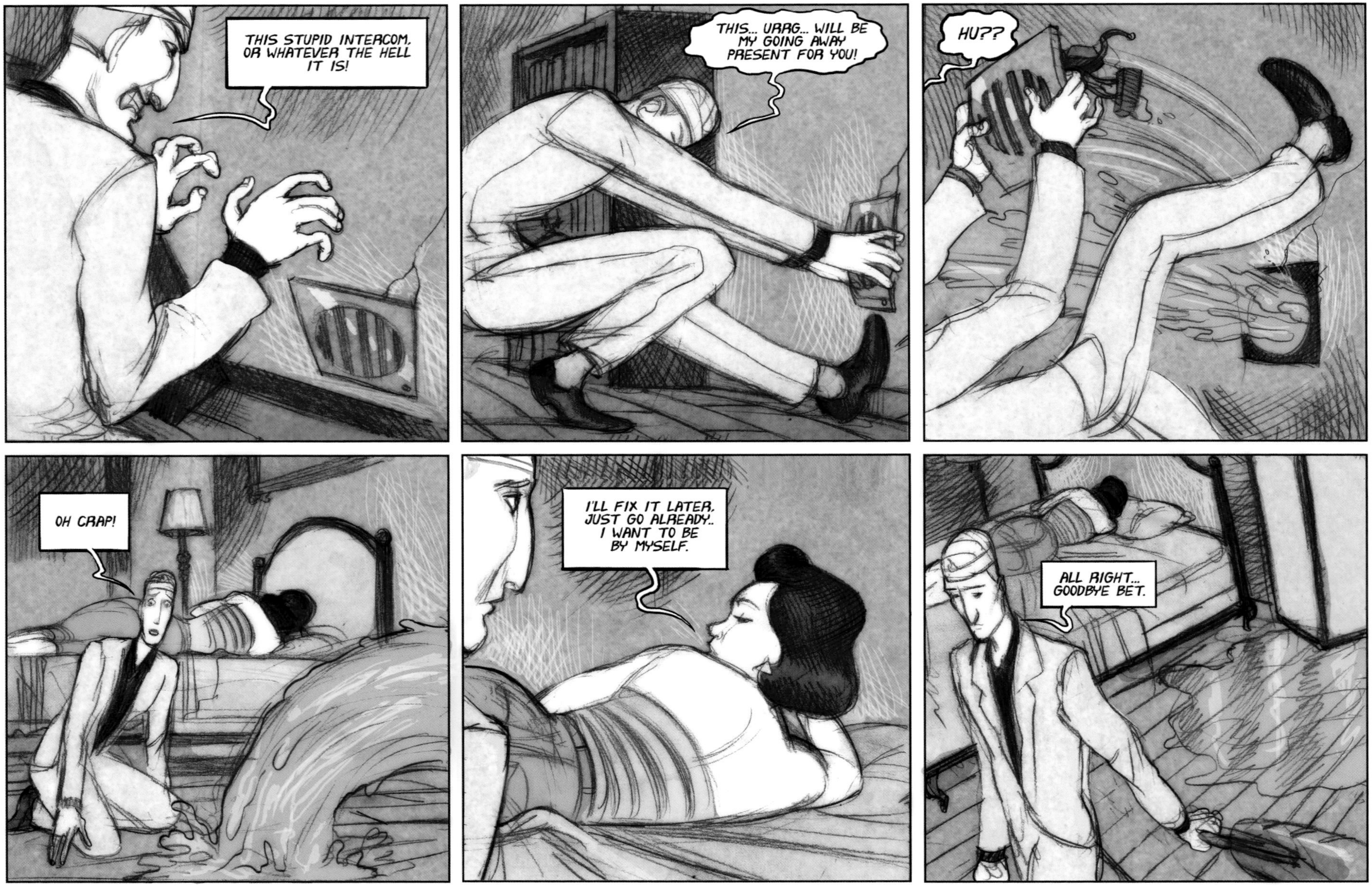
THIS STUPID INTERCOM, OR WHATEVER THE HELL IT IS!
THIS... URRG... WILL BE MY GOING AWAY PRESENT FOR YOU!
HU??
OH CRAP!
I'LL FIX IT LATER, JUST GO ALREADY.. I WANT TO BE BY MYSELF.
ALL RIGHT... GOODBYE BET.

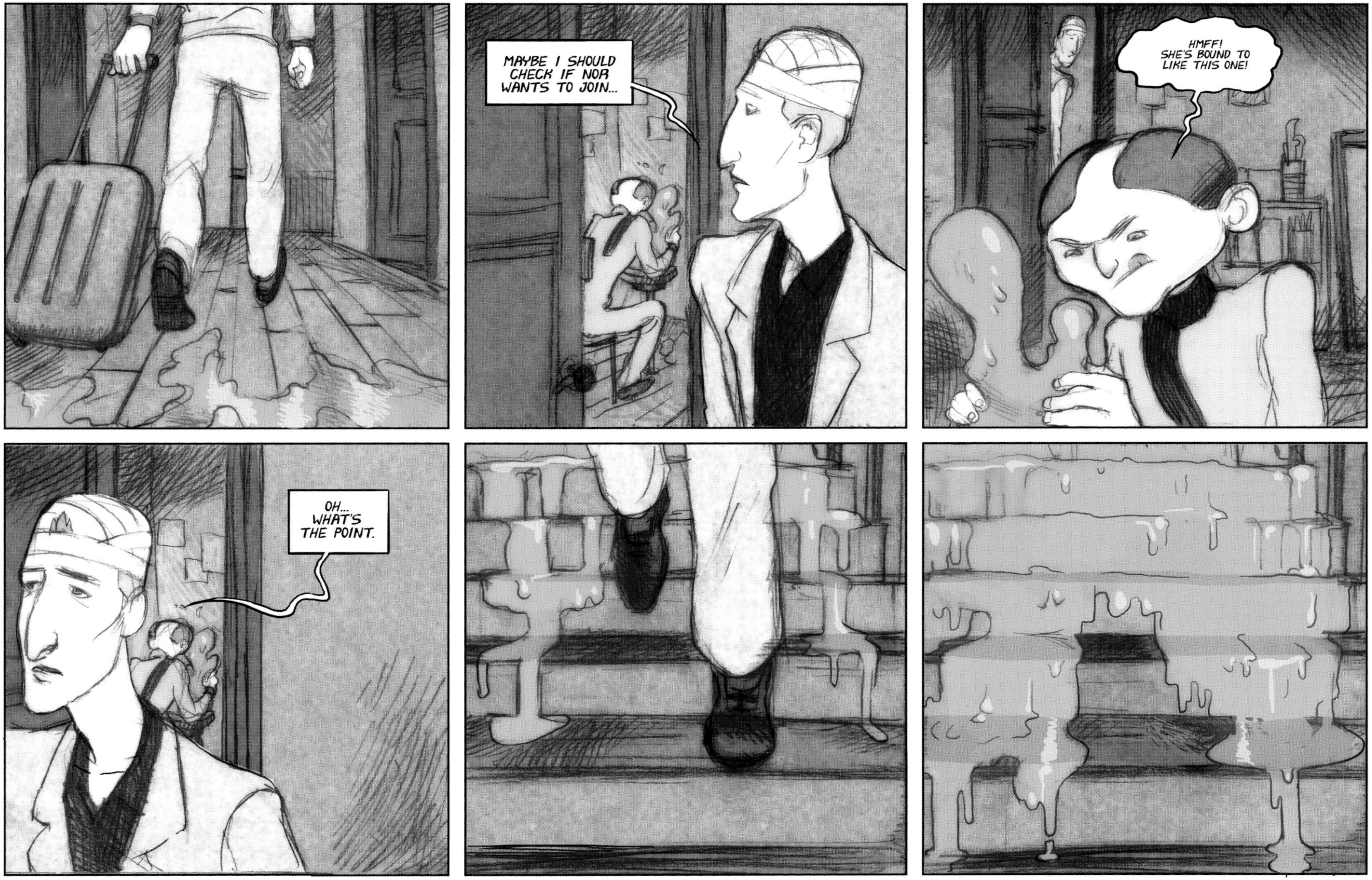
MAYBE I SHOULD CHECK IF NOR WANTS TO JOIN...
HMFF! SHE'S BOUND TO LIKE THIS ONE!
OH... WHAT'S THE POINT.

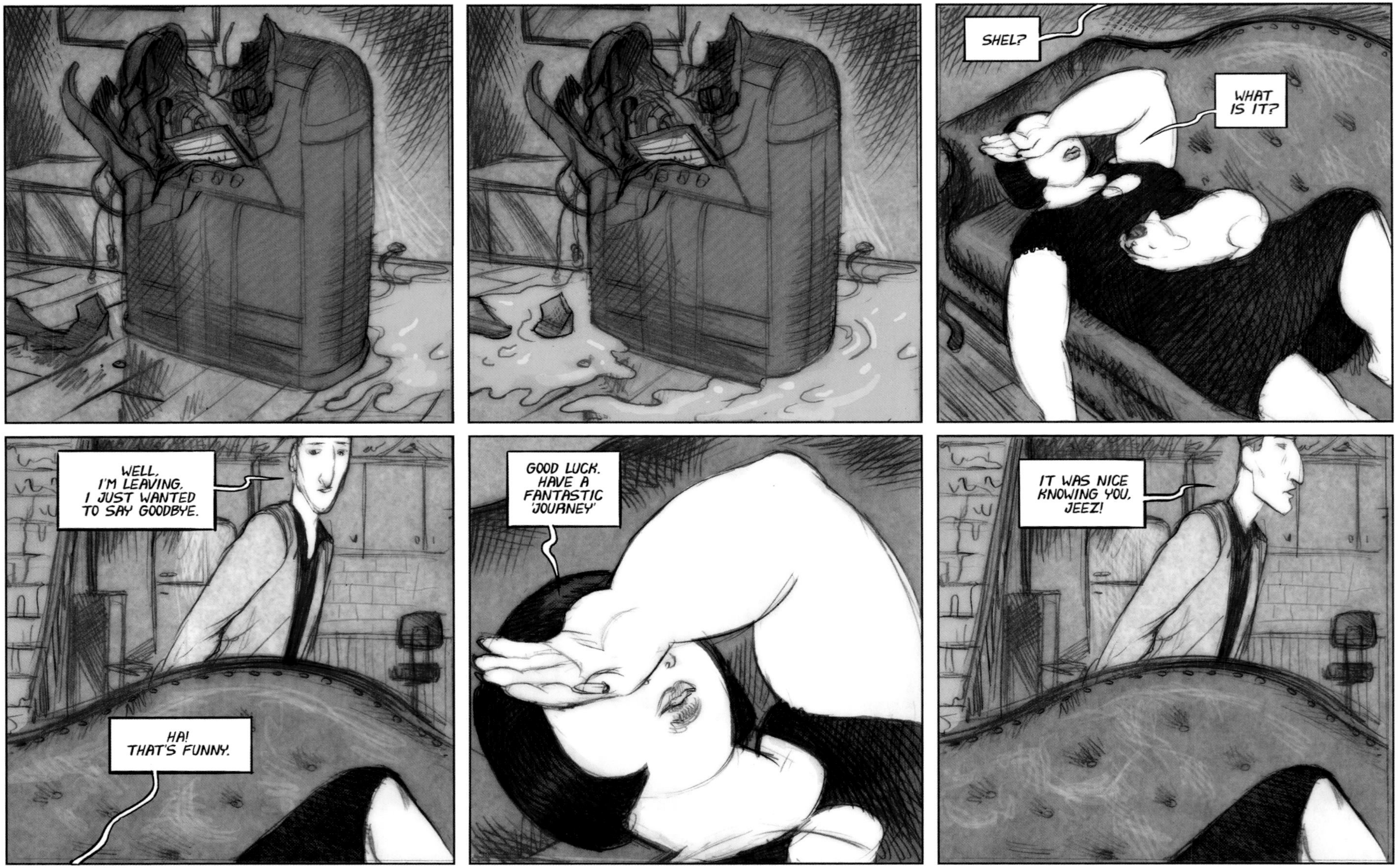
SHEL?
WHAT IS IT?
WELL, I'M LEAVING. I JUST WANTED TO SAY GOODBYE.
HA! THAT'S FUNNY.
GOOD LUCK. HAVE A FANTASTIC 'JOURNEY'
IT WAS NICE KNOWING YOU, JEEZ!

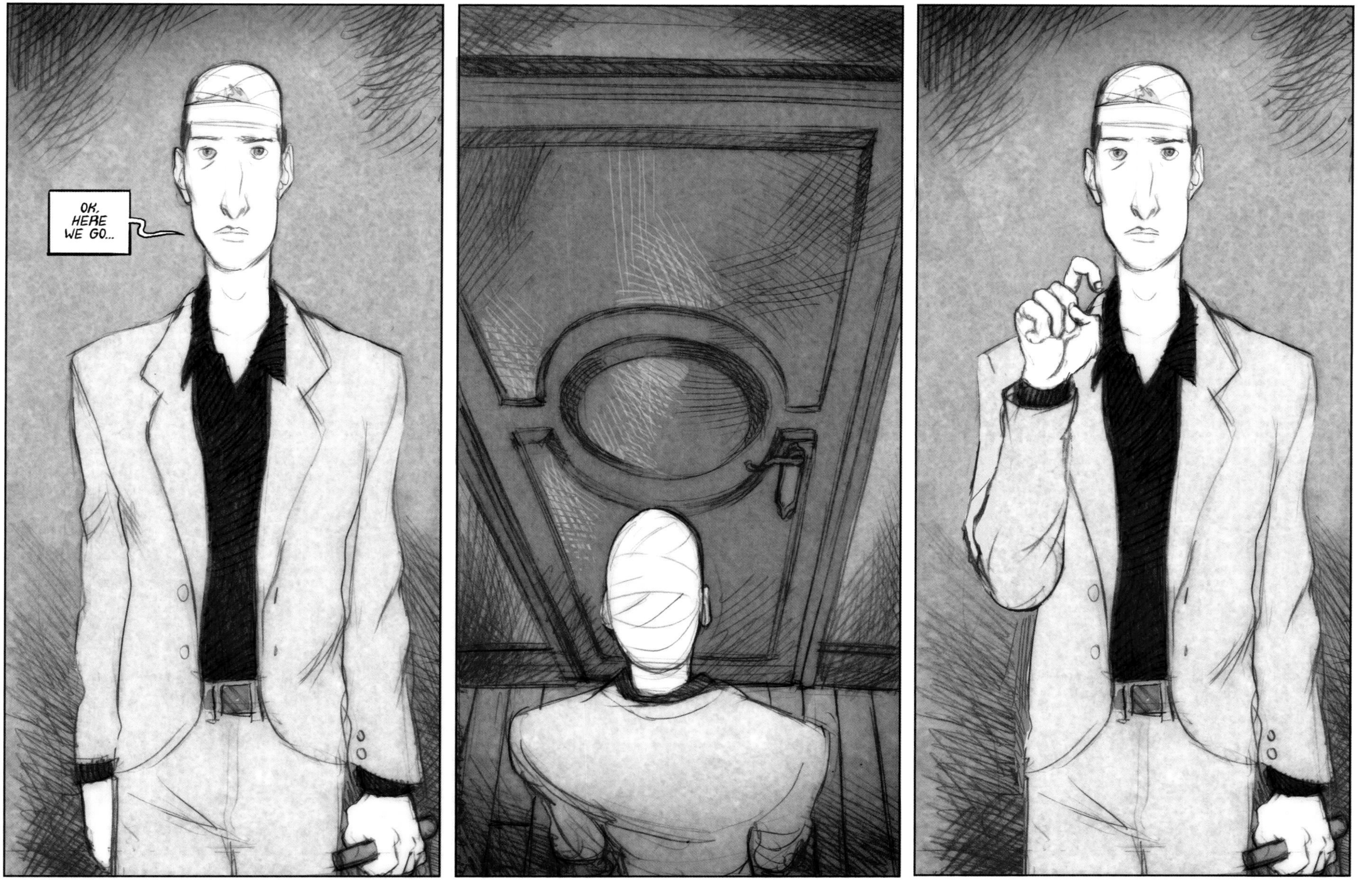
OK, HERE WE GO...

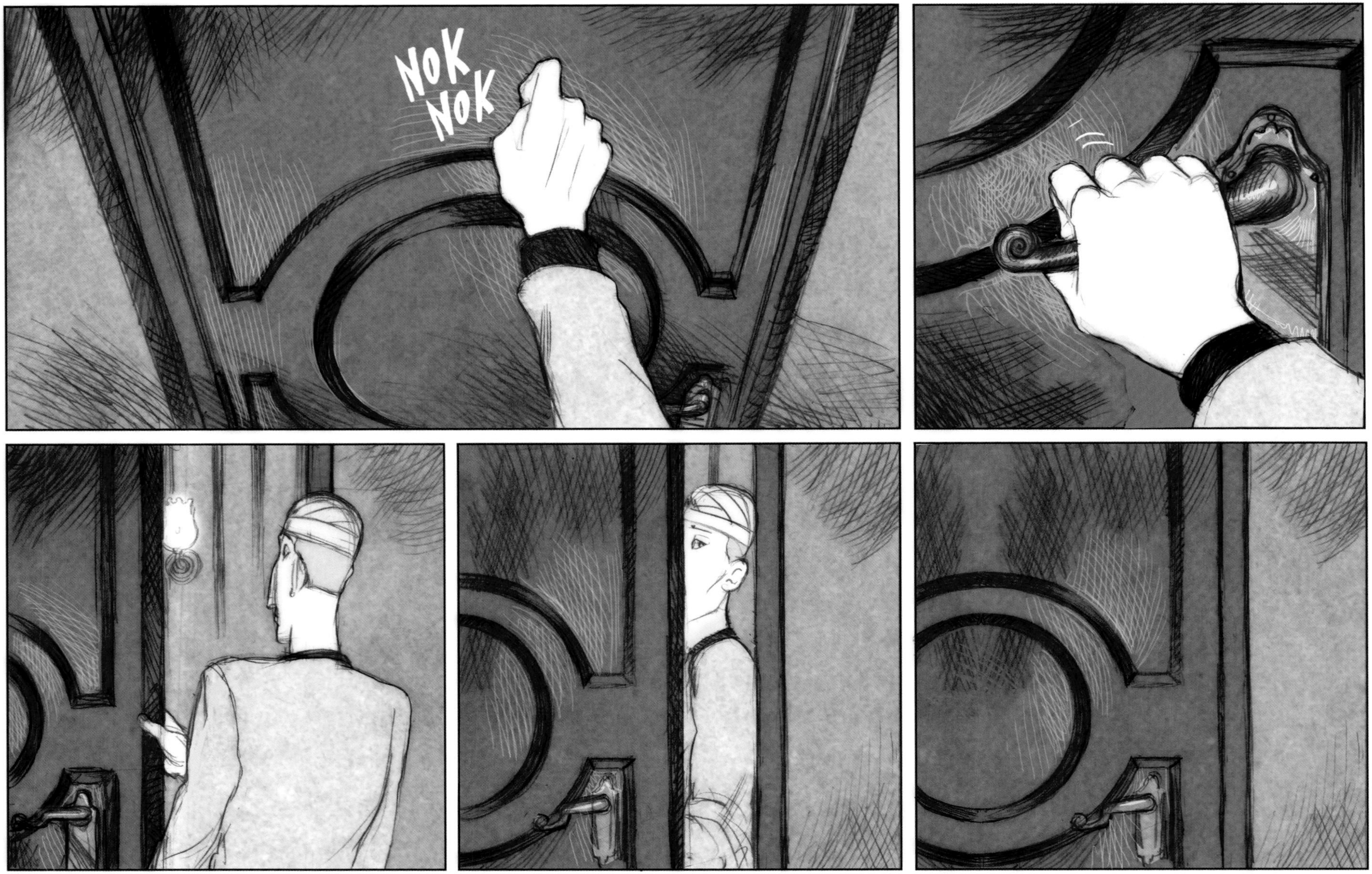
NOK NOK

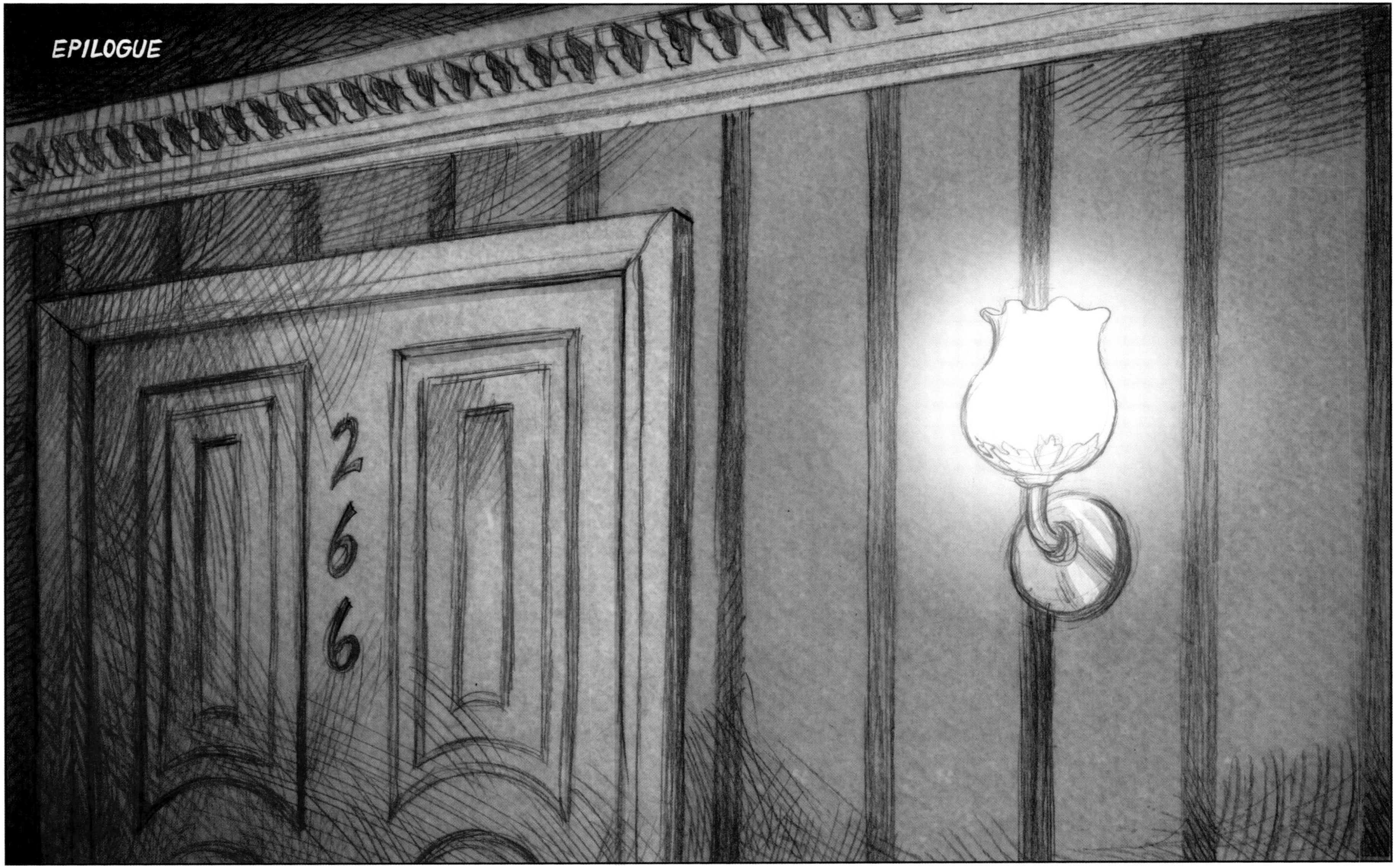
EPILOGUE
266

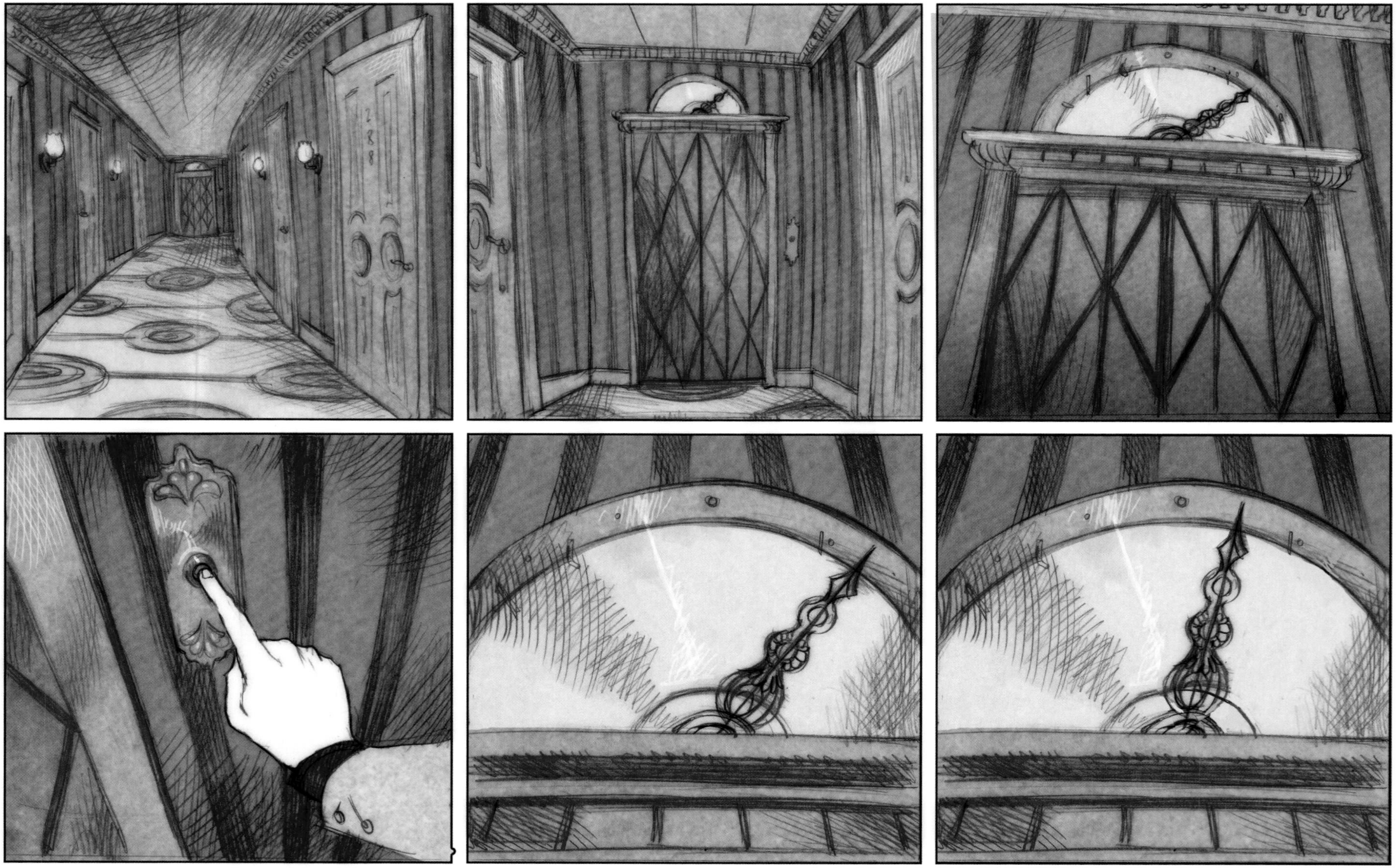

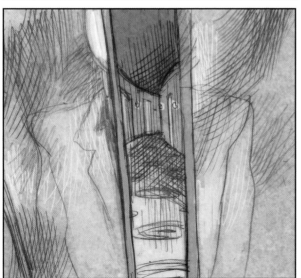

SIR,
YOU DROPPED
SOMETHING
ON THE GROUND.

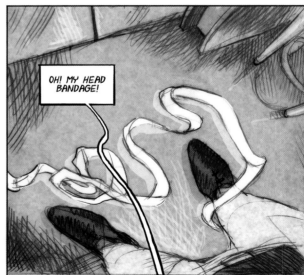

OH! MY HEAD
BANDAGE!

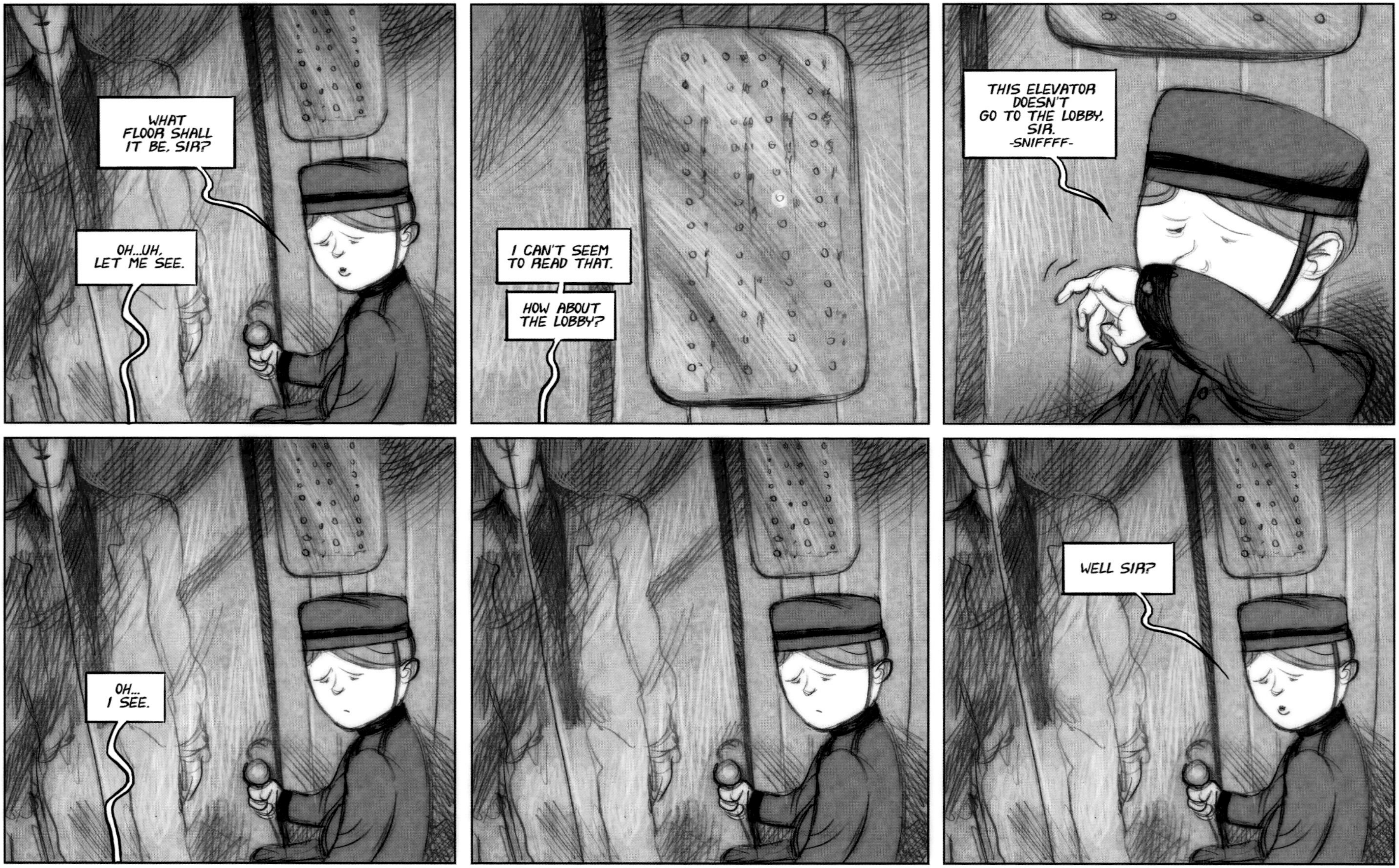
WHAT FLOOR SHALL IT BE, SIR?
OH...UH, LET ME SEE.
I CAN'T SEEM TO READ THAT.
HOW ABOUT THE LOBBY?
THIS ELEVATOR DOESN'T GO TO THE LOBBY, SIR. -SNIFFFF-
OH... I SEE.
WELL SIR?

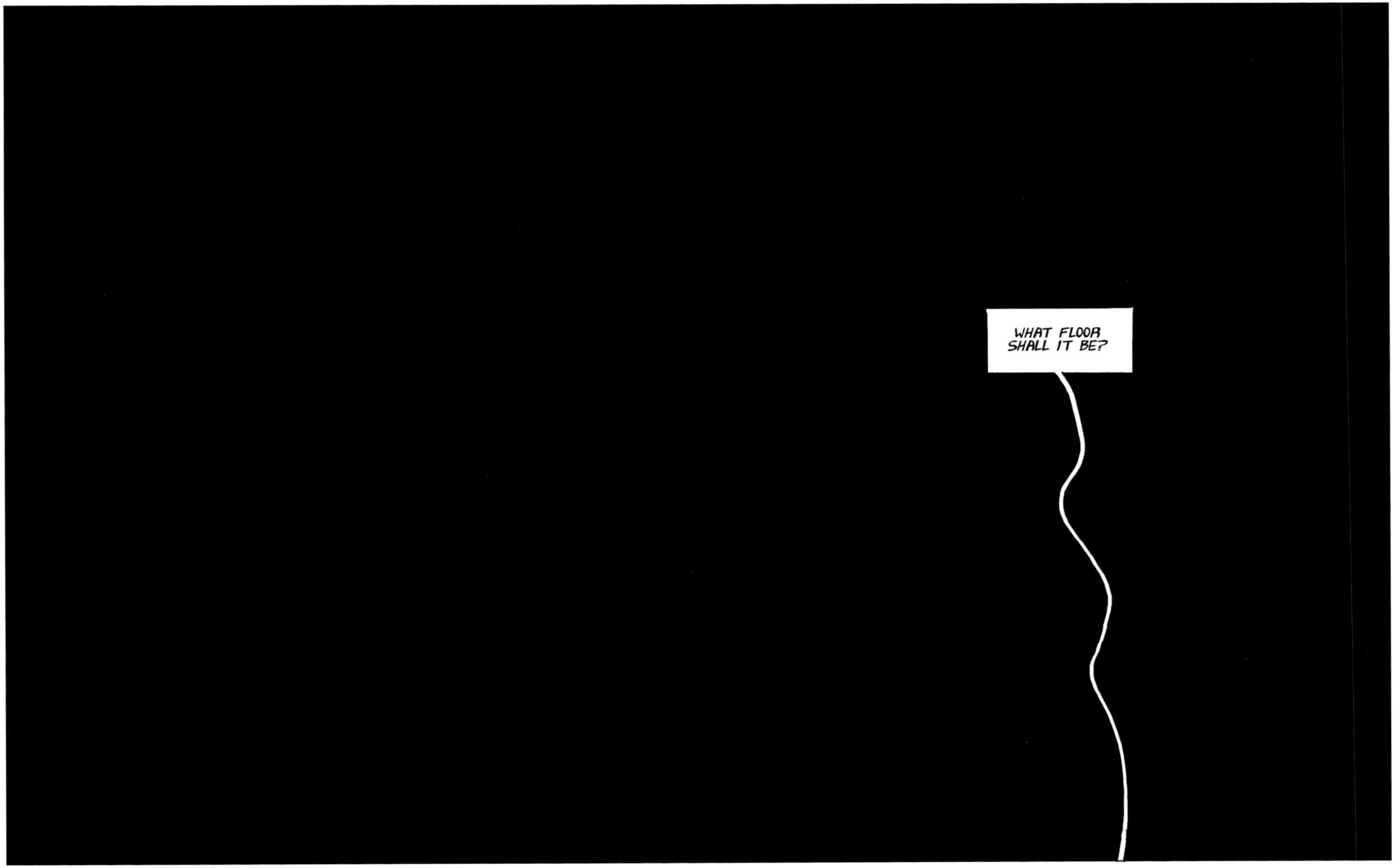
WHAT FLOOR SHALL IT BE?

PART TWO

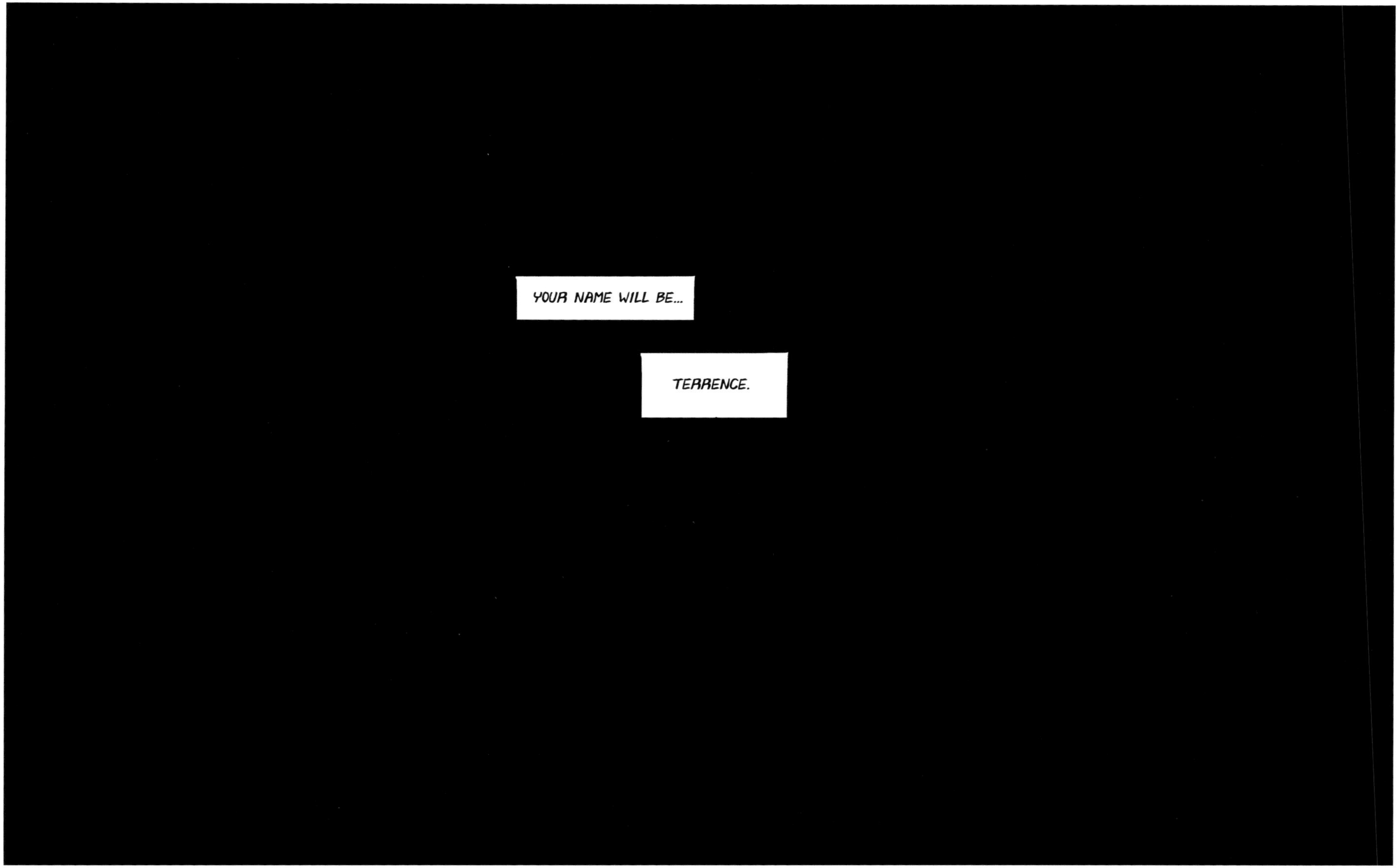
YOUR NAME WILL BE...
TERRENCE.

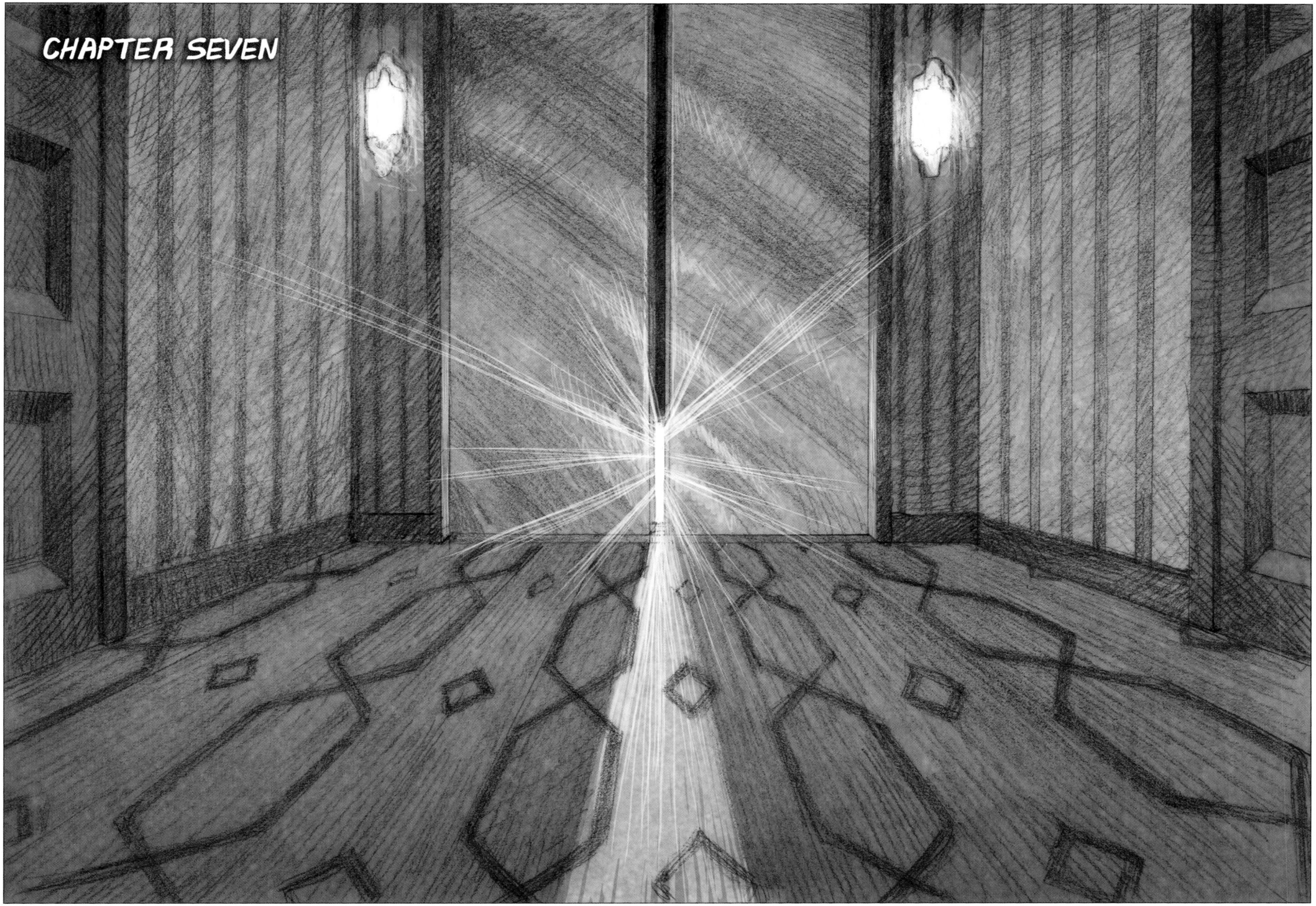
CHAPTER SEVEN

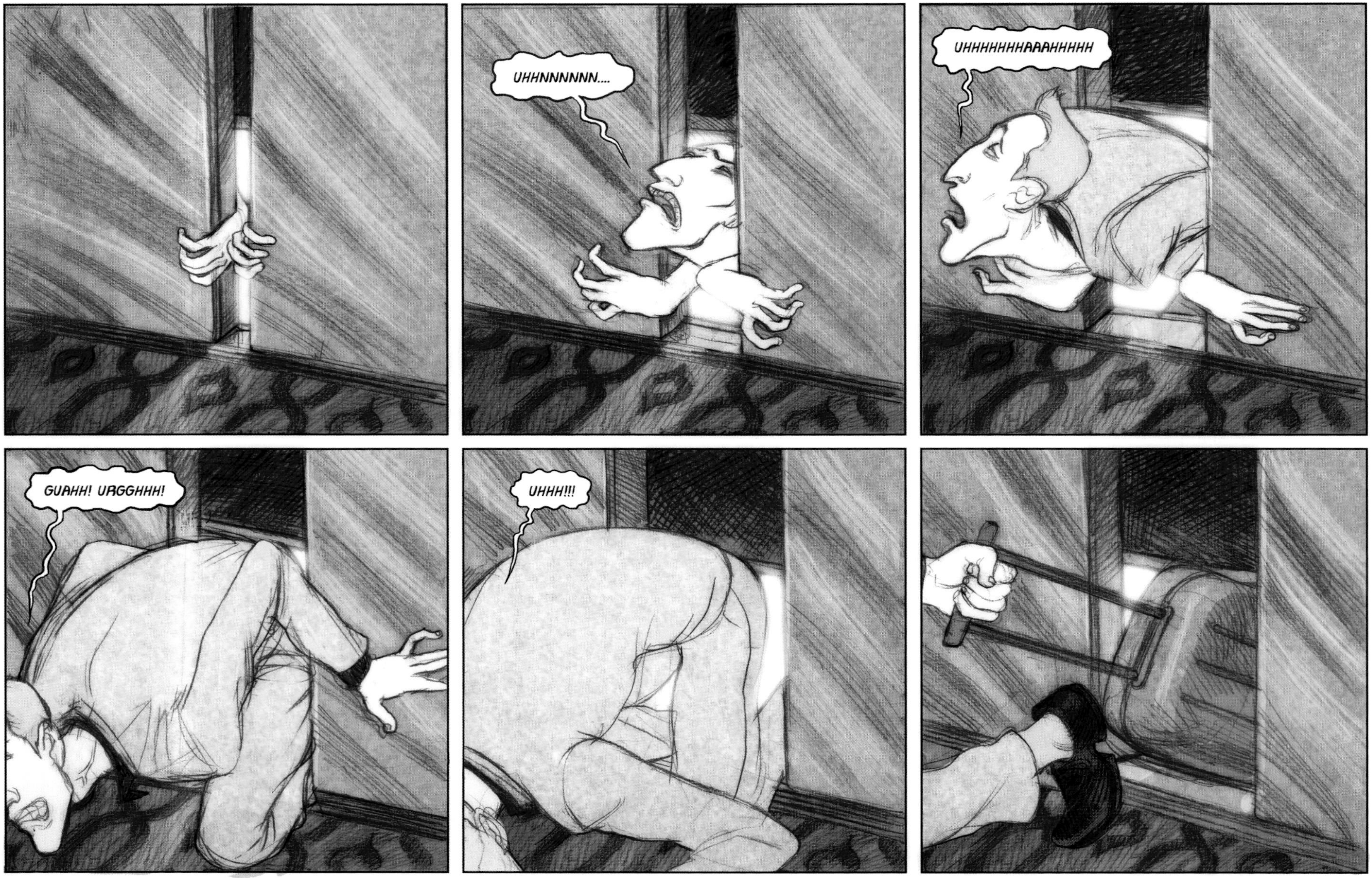
UHHNNNNNN....
UHHHHHHHAAAHHHHH
GUAHH! URGGHHH!
UHHH!!!

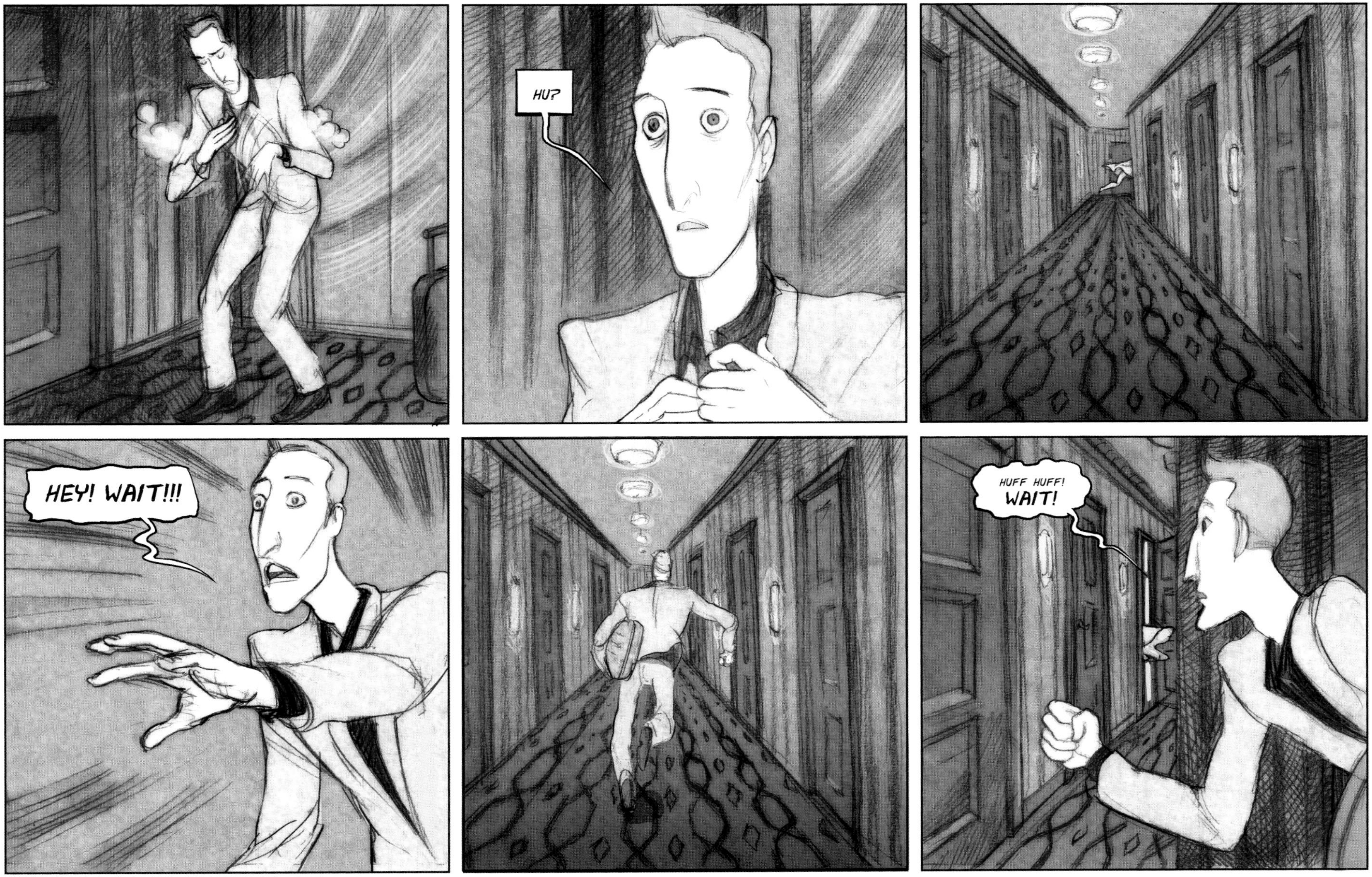
HU?
HEY! WAIT!!!
HUFF HUFF!
WAIT!

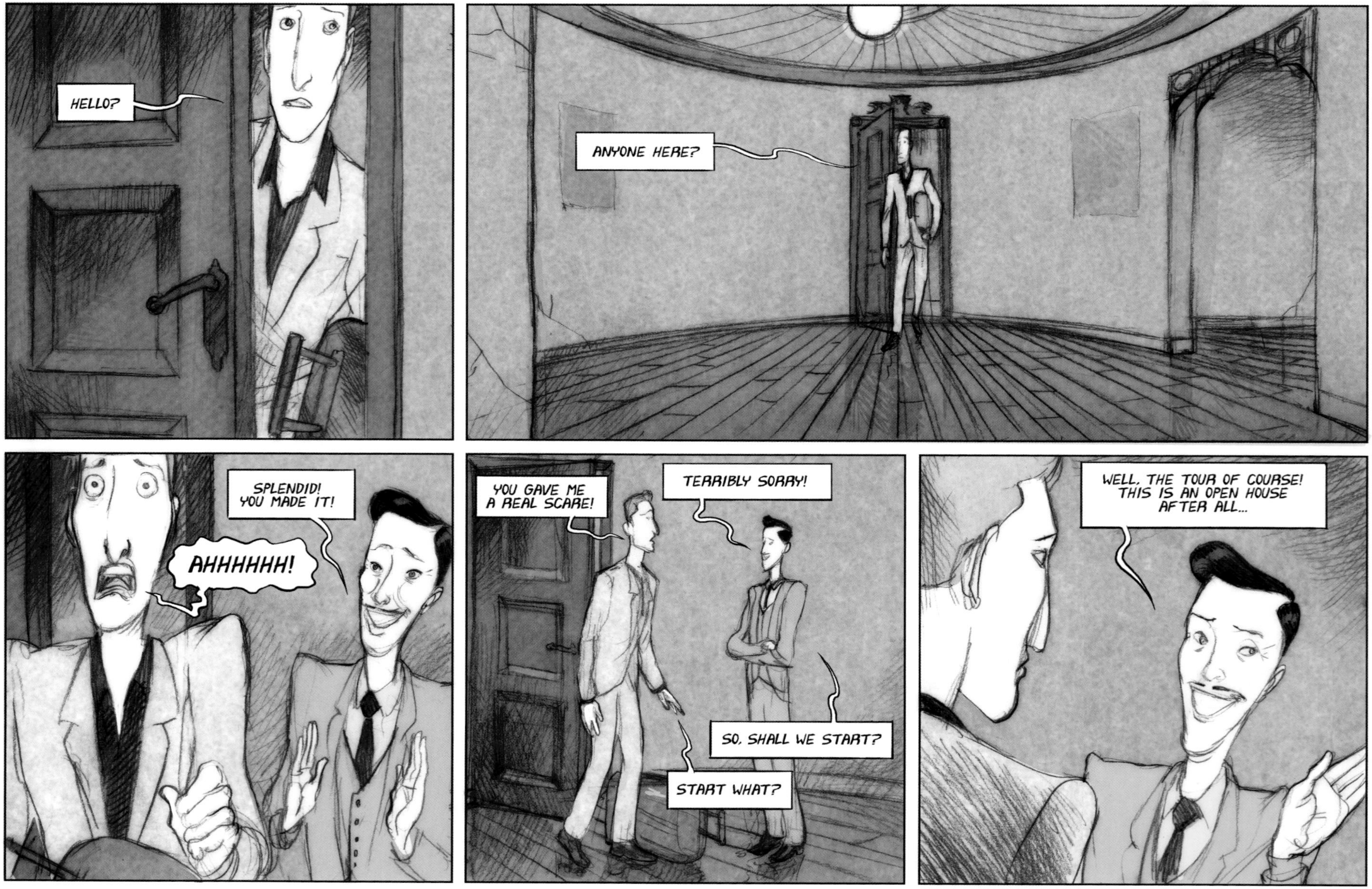
HELLO?
ANYONE HERE?
SPLENDID! YOU MADE IT!
AHHHHHH!
YOU GAVE ME A REAL SCARE!
TERRIBLY SORRY!
SO, SHALL WE START?
START WHAT?
WELL, THE TOUR OF COURSE! THIS IS AN OPEN HOUSE AFTER ALL...

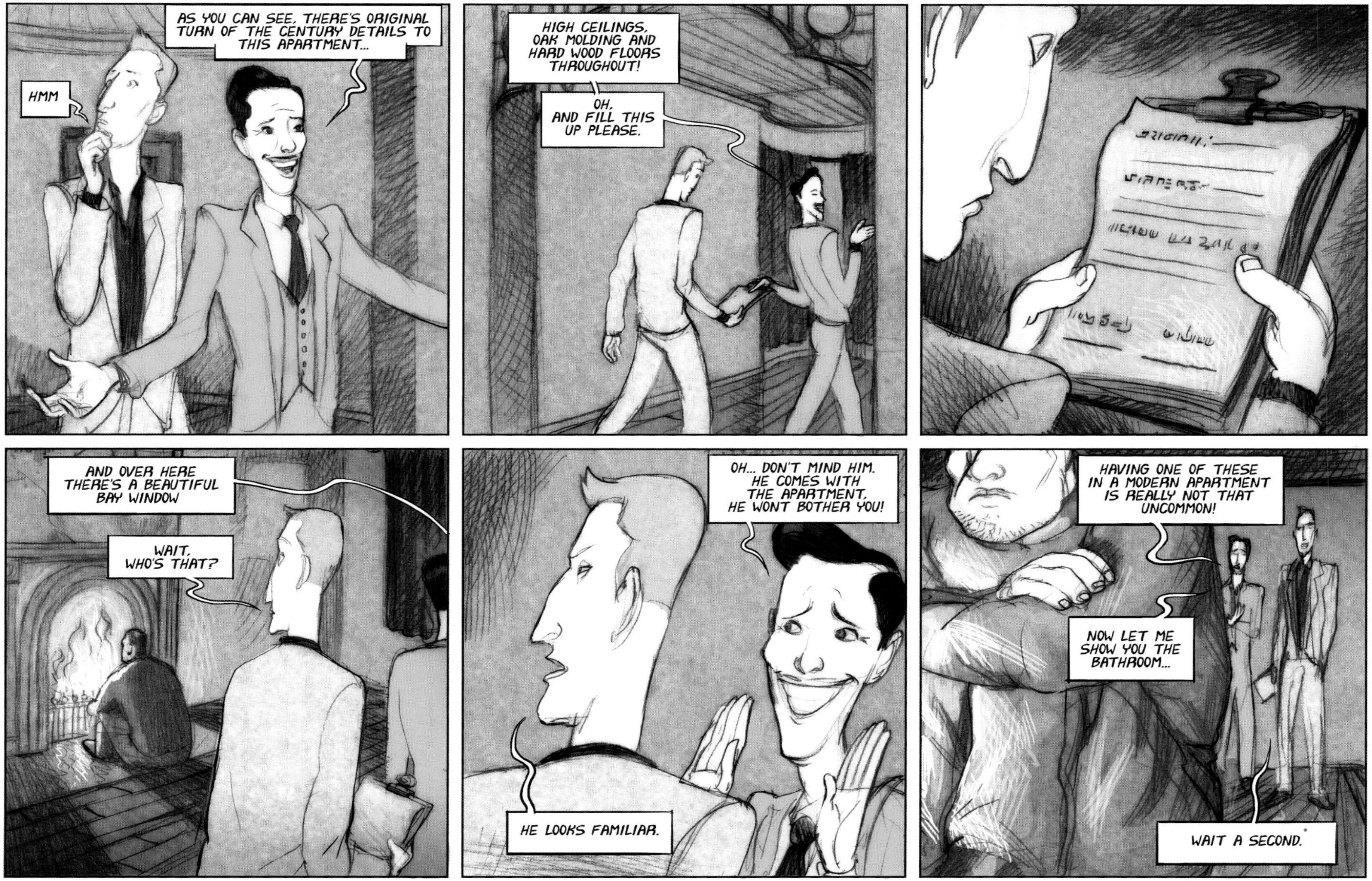

AS YOU CAN SEE, THERE'S ORIGINAL TURN OF THE CENTURY DETAILS TO THIS APARTMENT...
HMM
HIGH CEILINGS, OAK MOLDING AND HARD WOOD FLOORS THROUGHOUT!
OH, AND FILL THIS UP PLEASE.
AND OVER HERE THERE'S A BEAUTIFUL BAY WINDOW
WAIT, WHO'S THAT?
OH... DON'T MIND HIM. HE COMES WITH THE APARTMENT. HE WONT BOTHER YOU!
HE LOOKS FAMILIAR.
HAVING ONE OF THESE IN A MODERN APARTMENT IS REALLY NOT THAT UNCOMMON!
NOW LET ME SHOW YOU THE BATHROOM...
WAIT A SECOND.

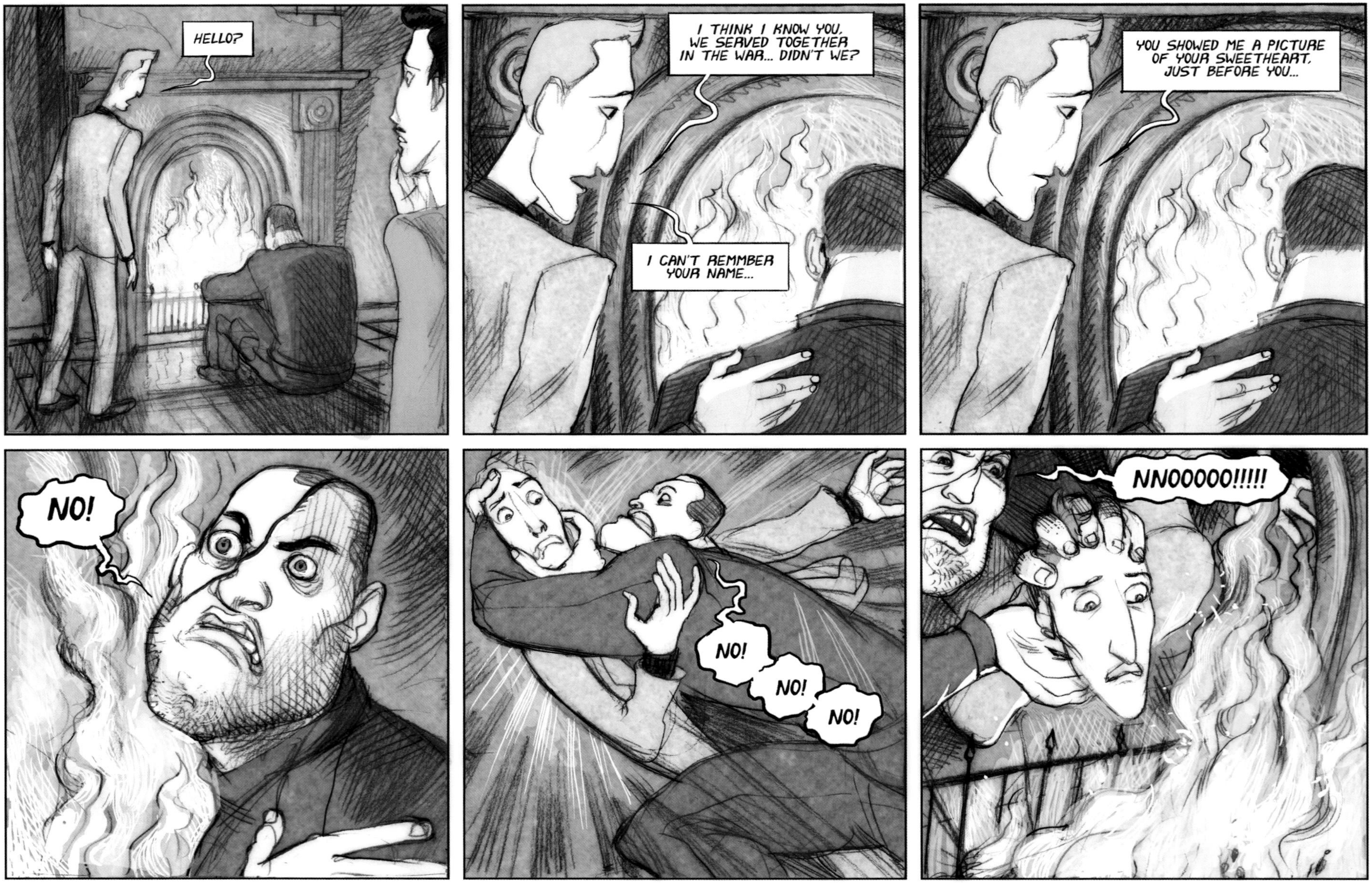
HELLO?
I THINK I KNOW YOU, WE SERVED TOGETHER IN THE WAR... DIDN'T WE?
I CAN'T REMMBER YOUR NAME...
YOU SHOWED ME A PICTURE OF YOUR SWEETHEART, JUST BEFORE YOU...
NO!
NO!
NO!
NO!
NNOOOOO!!!!!

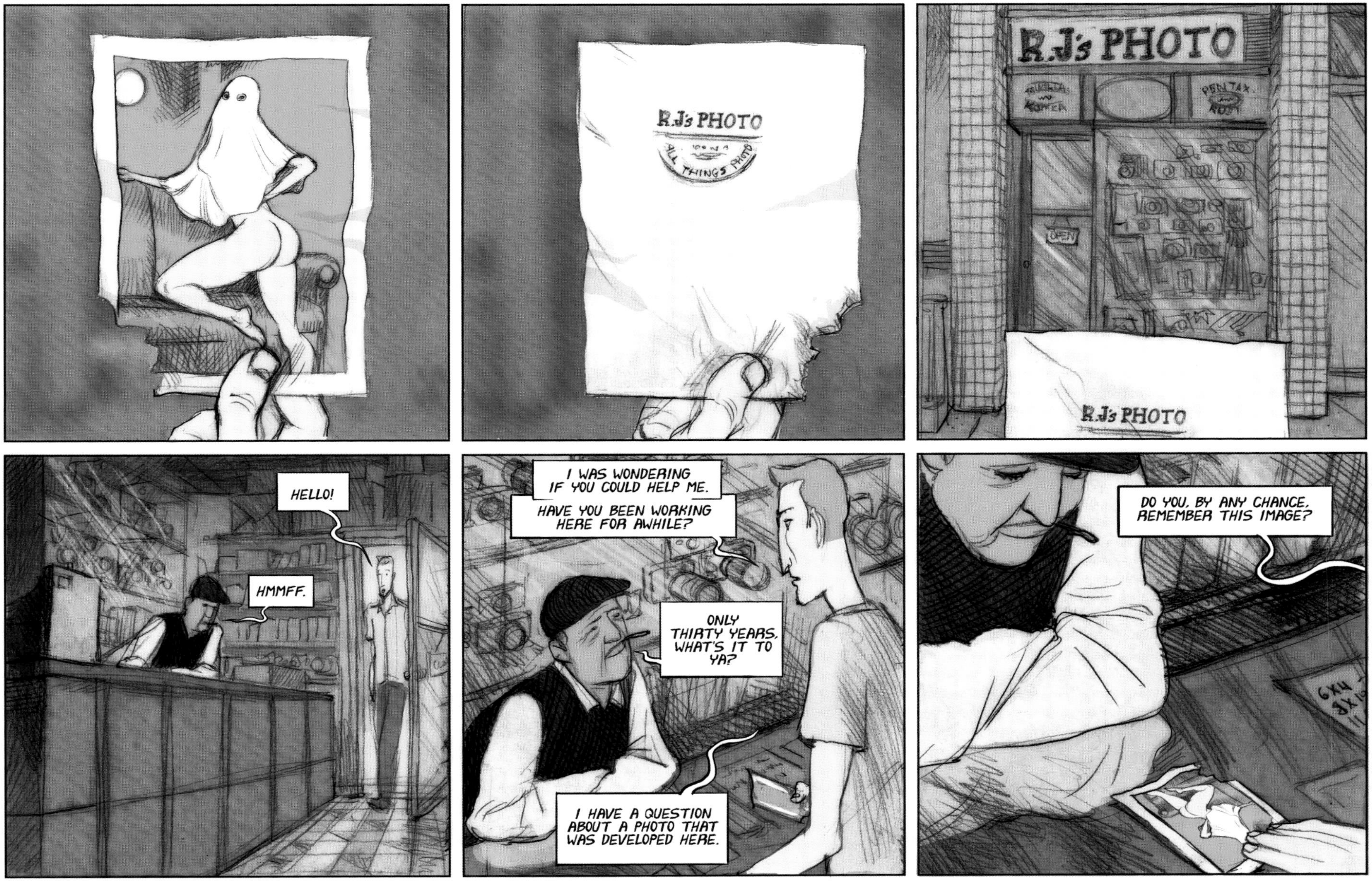

R.J's PHOTO
R.J's PHOTO
R.J's PHOTO
HELLO!
HMMFF.
I WAS WONDERING IF YOU COULD HELP ME.
HAVE YOU BEEN WORKING HERE FOR AWHILE?
ONLY THIRTY YEARS, WHAT'S IT TO YA?
I HAVE A QUESTION ABOUT A PHOTO THAT WAS DEVELOPED HERE.
DO YOU, BY ANY CHANCE, REMEMBER THIS IMAGE?

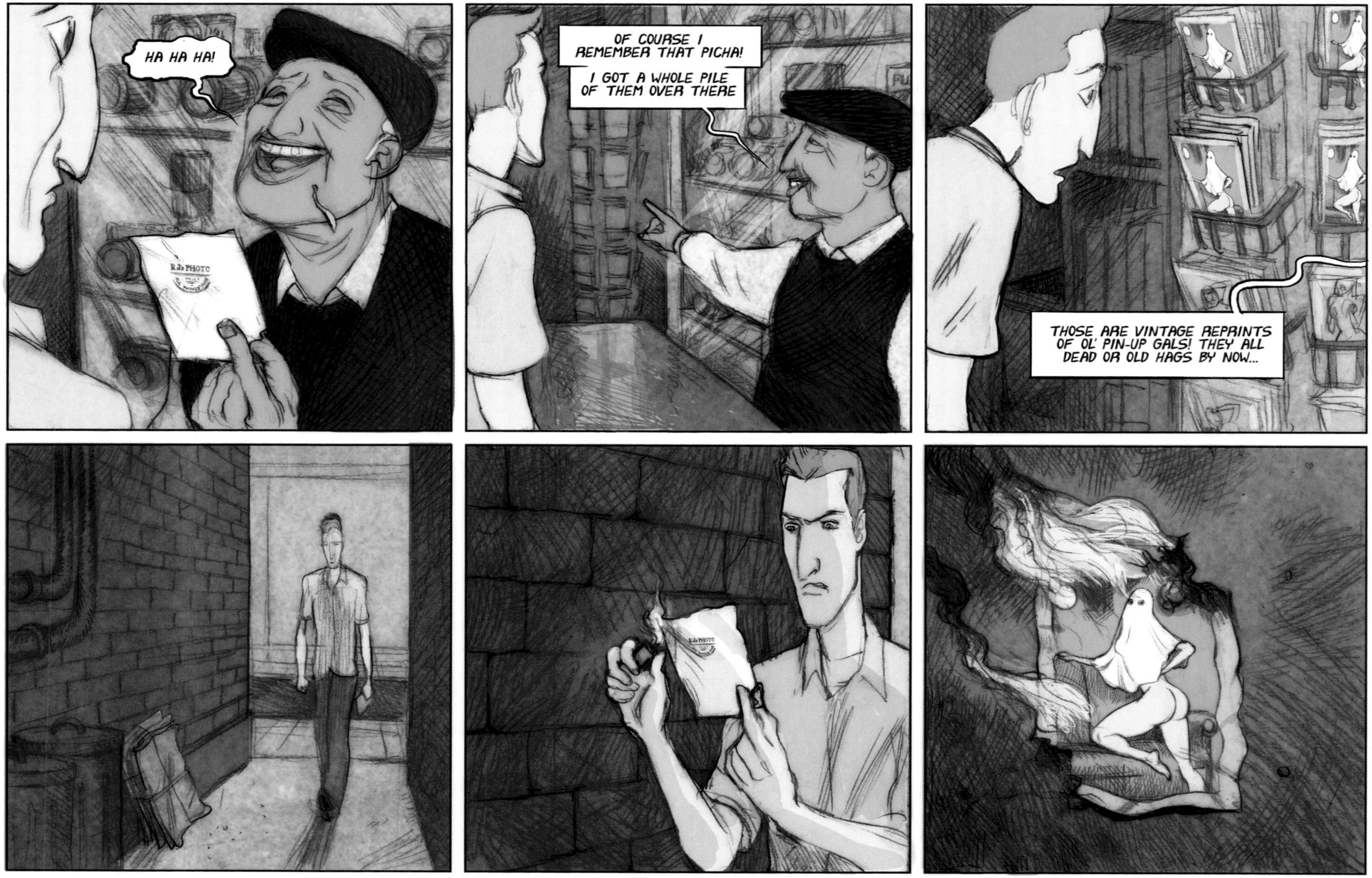
HA HA HA!
R.J.'s PHOTO
OF COURSE I REMEMBER THAT PICHA!
I GOT A WHOLE PILE OF THEM OVER THERE
THOSE ARE VINTAGE REPRINTS OF OL' PIN-UP GALS! THEY ALL DEAD OR OLD HAGS BY NOW...

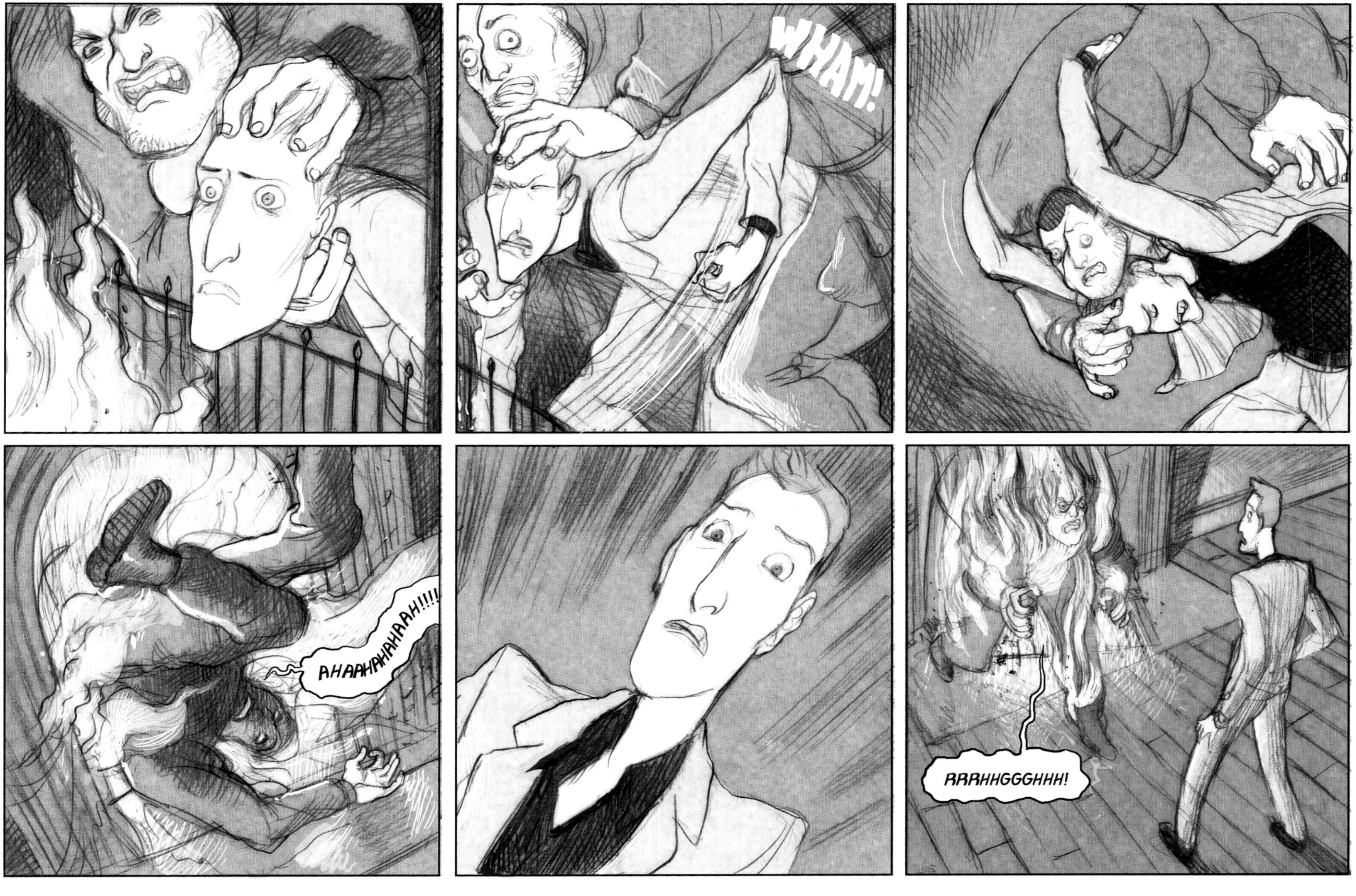
WHAM!
AHAAHAHAHAAH!!!!
RRRHHGGGHHH!

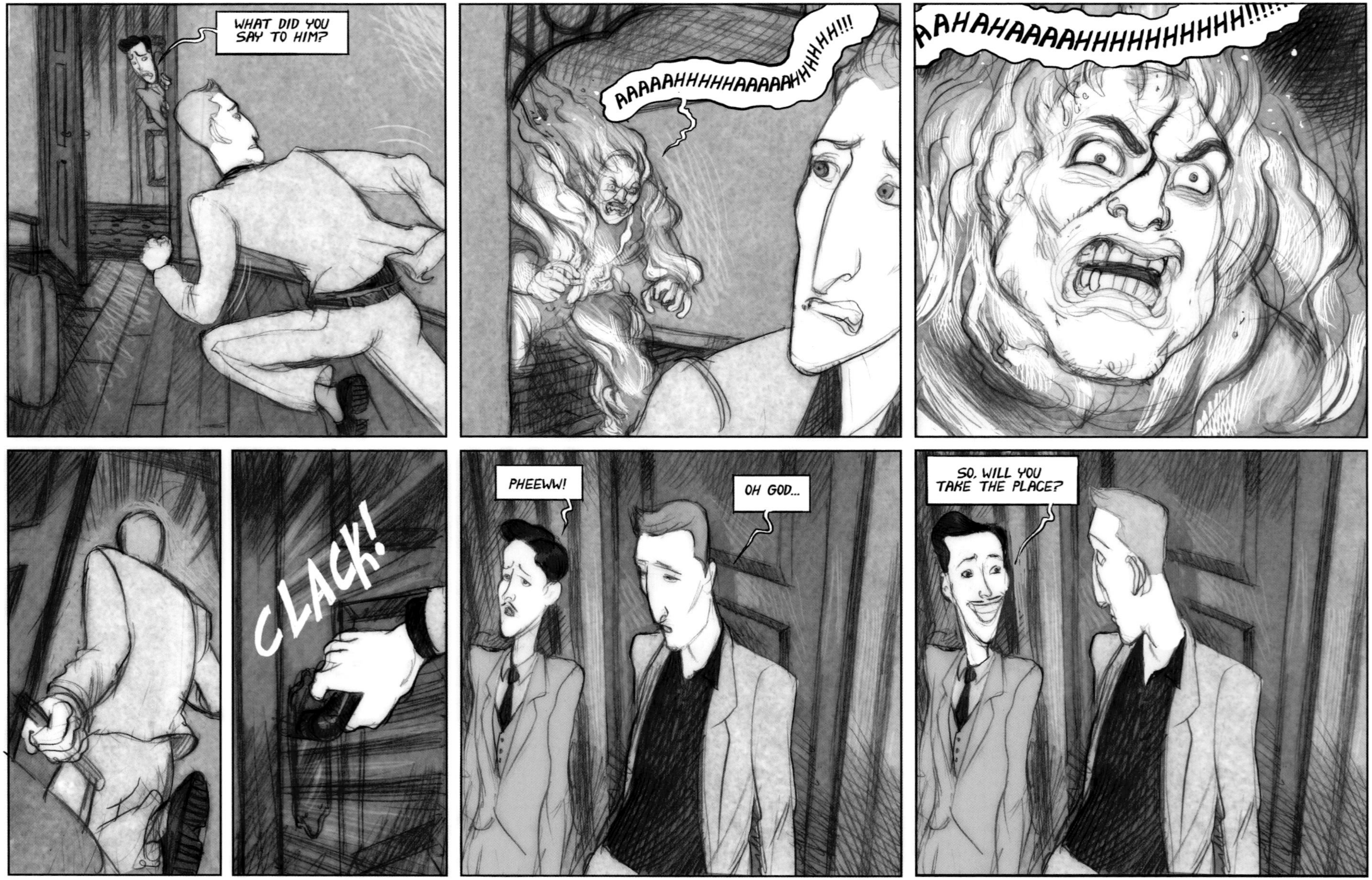
WHAT DID YOU SAY TO HIM?
AAAAAHHHHHAAAAAAHHHHH!!!
AAHAHAAAAAHHHHHHHHHH!!!!!
CLACK!
PHEEWW!
OH GOD...
SO, WILL YOU TAKE THE PLACE?

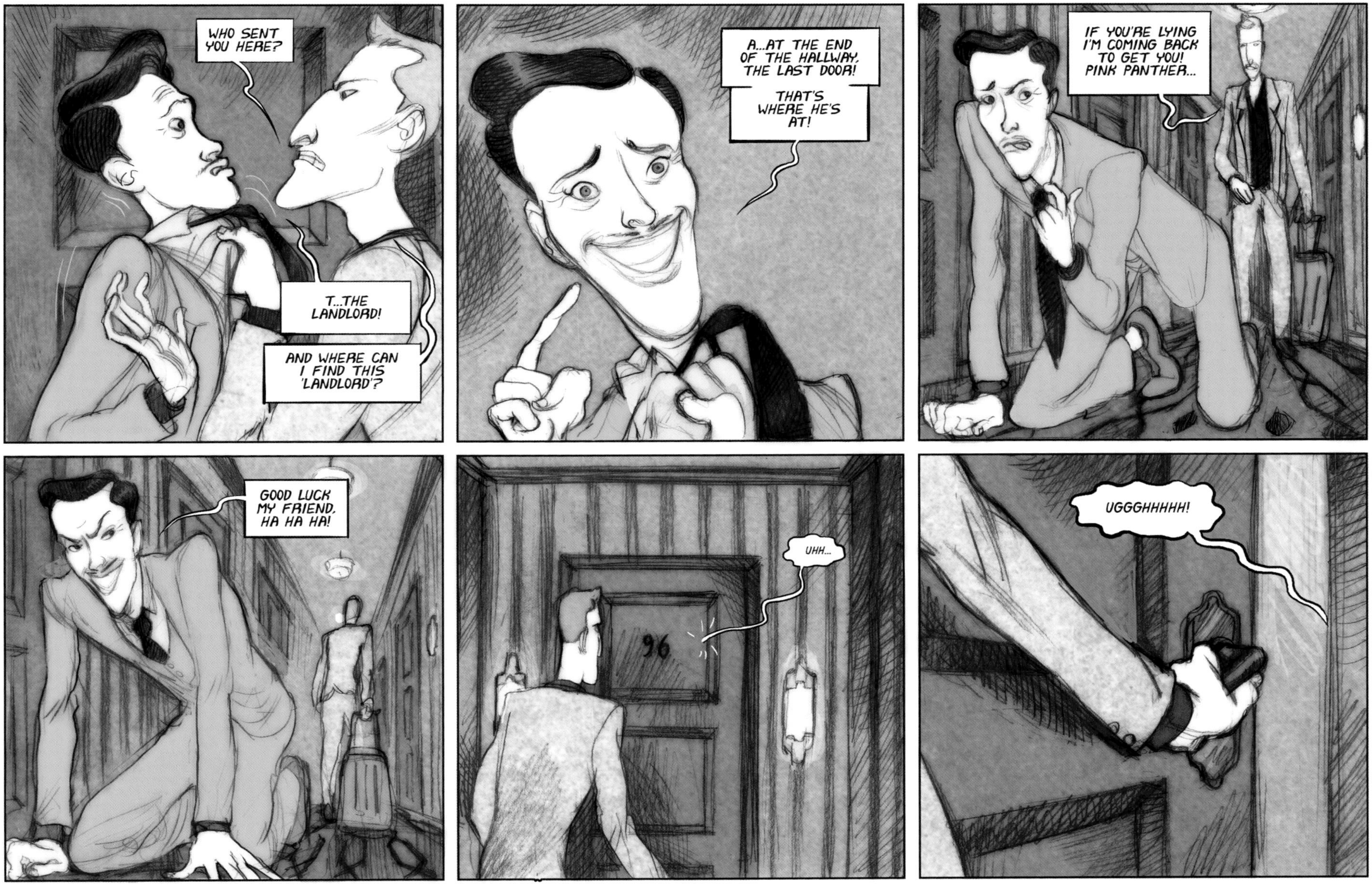
WHO SENT YOU HERE?
T...THE LANDLORD!
AND WHERE CAN I FIND THIS 'LANDLORD'?
A...AT THE END OF THE HALLWAY, THE LAST DOOR!
THAT'S WHERE HE'S AT!
IF YOU'RE LYING I'M COMING BACK TO GET YOU! PINK PANTHER...
GOOD LUCK MY FRIEND. HA HA HA!
UHH...
96
UGGGHHHHH!

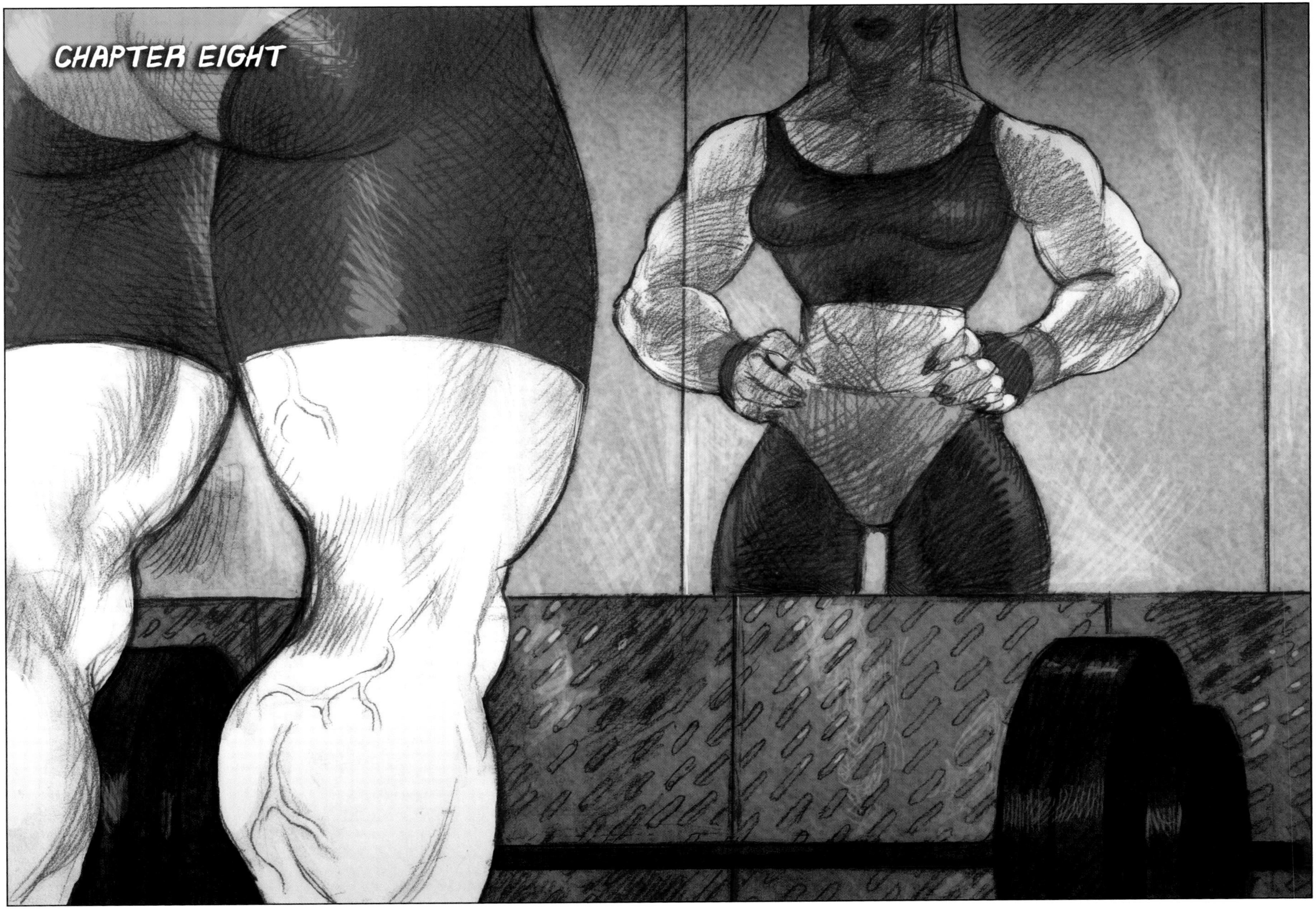
CHAPTER EIGHT

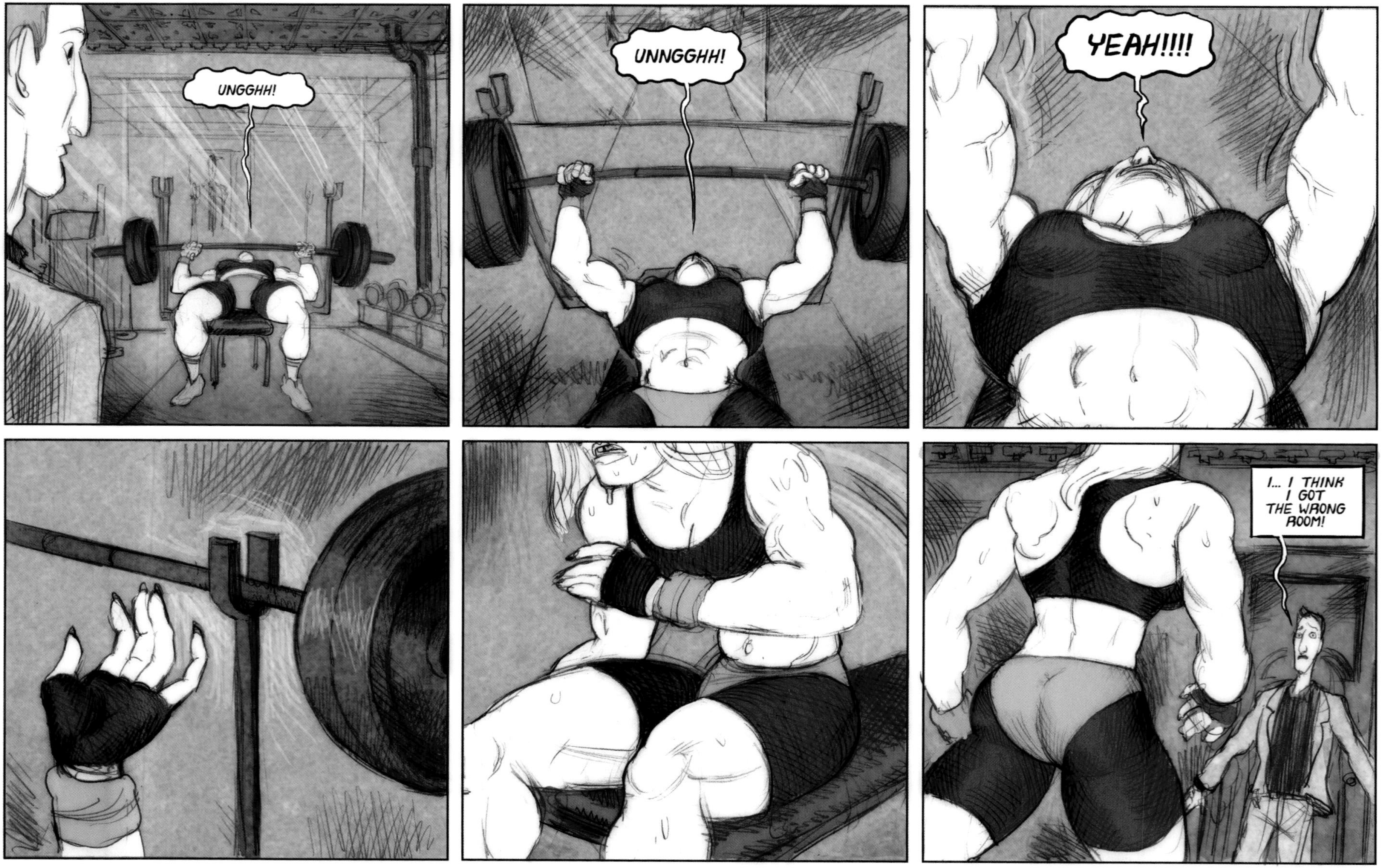
UNGGHH!
UNNGGHH!
YEAH!!!!
I... I THINK I GOT THE WRONG ROOM!

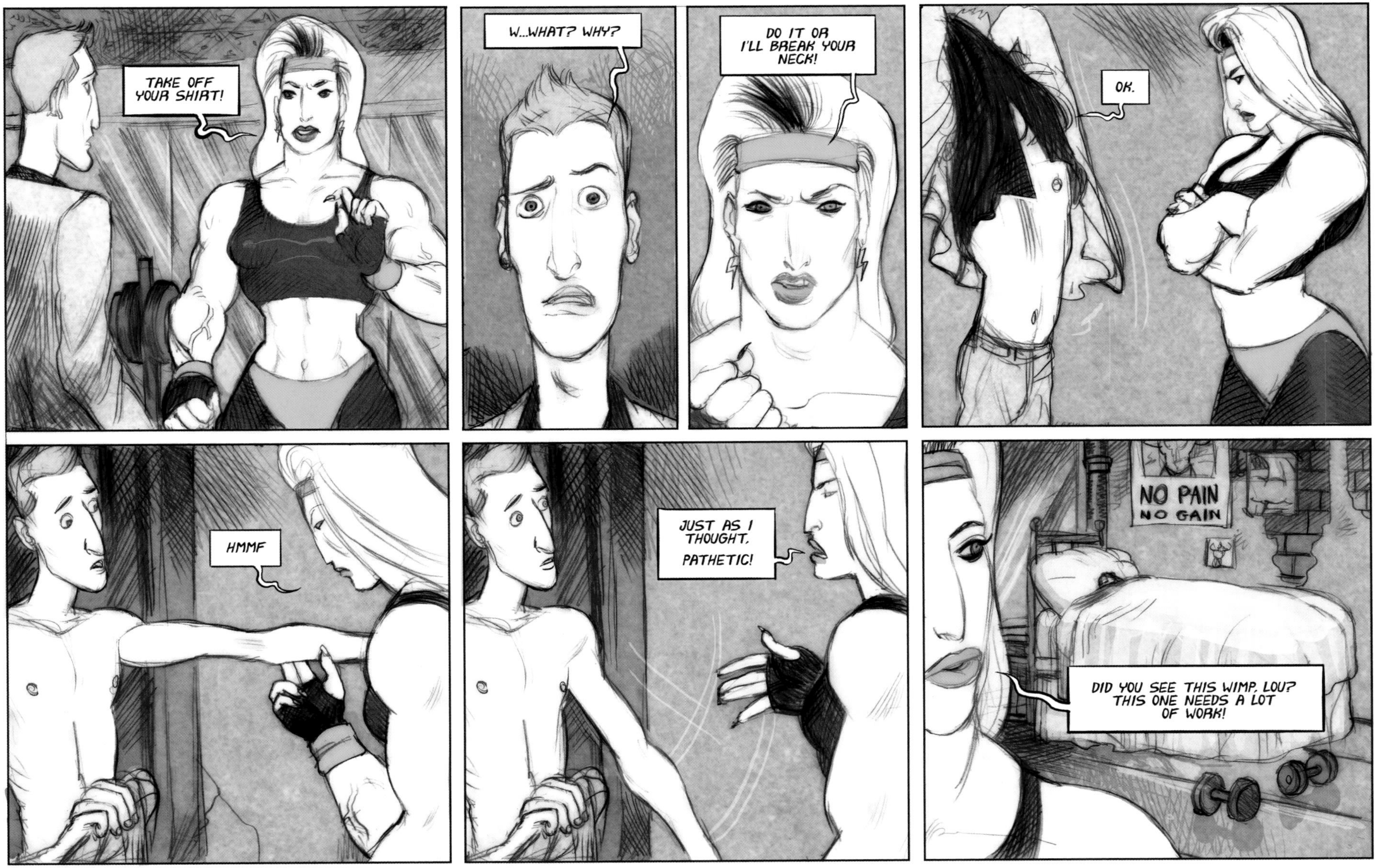
TAKE OFF YOUR SHIRT!
W...WHAT? WHY?
DO IT OR I'LL BREAK YOUR NECK!
OK.
HMMF
JUST AS I THOUGHT, PATHETIC!
NO PAIN NO GAIN
DID YOU SEE THIS WIMP, LOU? THIS ONE NEEDS A LOT OF WORK!

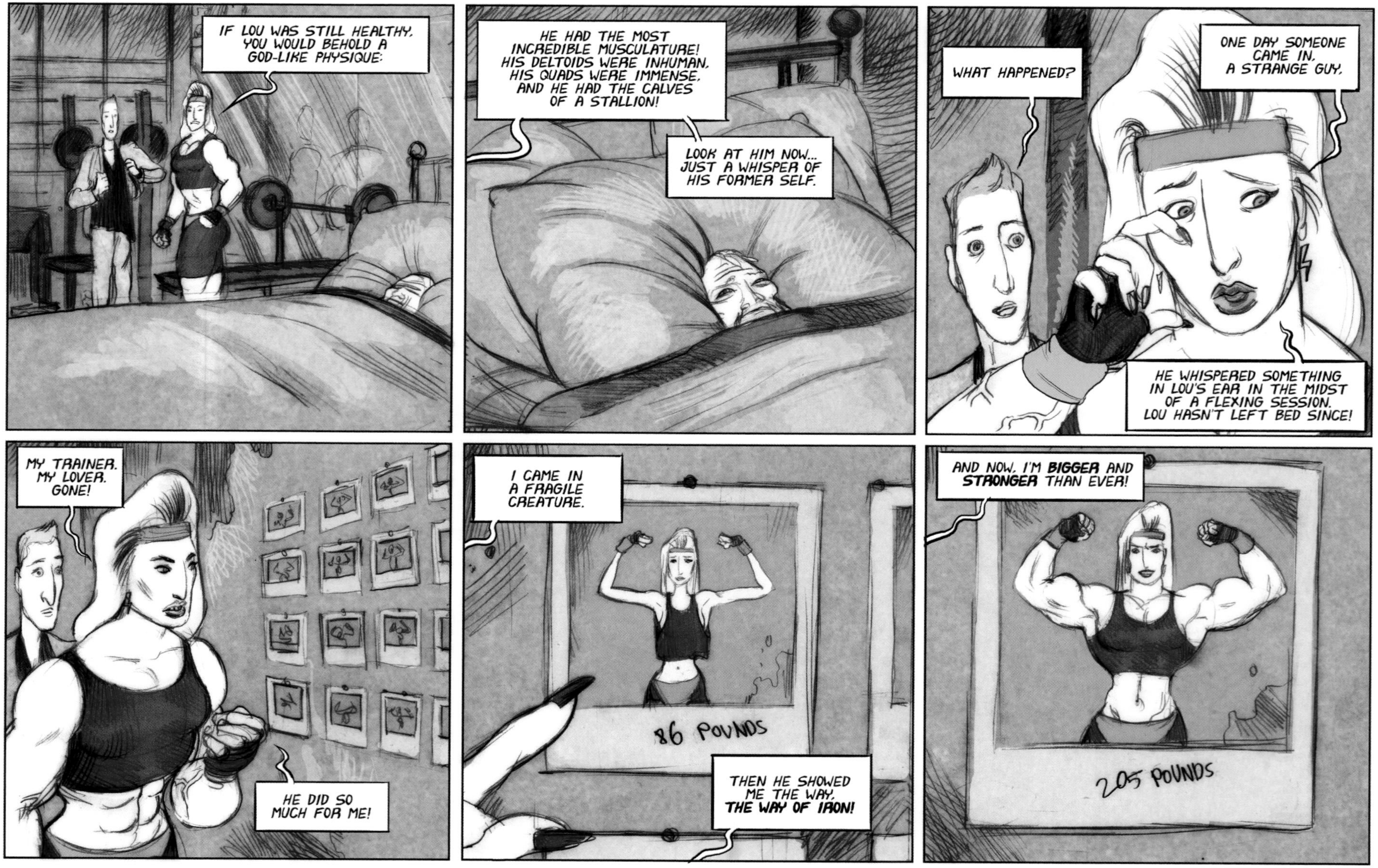
IF LOU WAS STILL HEALTHY, YOU WOULD BEHOLD A GOD-LIKE PHYSIQUE:
HE HAD THE MOST INCREDIBLE MUSCULATURE! HIS DELTOIDS WERE INHUMAN, HIS QUADS WERE IMMENSE, AND HE HAD THE CALVES OF A STALLION!
LOOK AT HIM NOW... JUST A WHISPER OF HIS FORMER SELF.
WHAT HAPPENED?
ONE DAY SOMEONE CAME IN, A STRANGE GUY,
HE WHISPERED SOMETHING IN LOU'S EAR IN THE MIDST OF A FLEXING SESSION. LOU HASN'T LEFT BED SINCE!
MY TRAINER. MY LOVER. GONE!
HE DID SO MUCH FOR ME!
I CAME IN A FRAGILE CREATURE.
86 POUNDS
THEN HE SHOWED ME THE WAY, THE WAY OF IRON!
AND NOW, I'M BIGGER AND STRONGER THAN EVER!
205 POUNDS

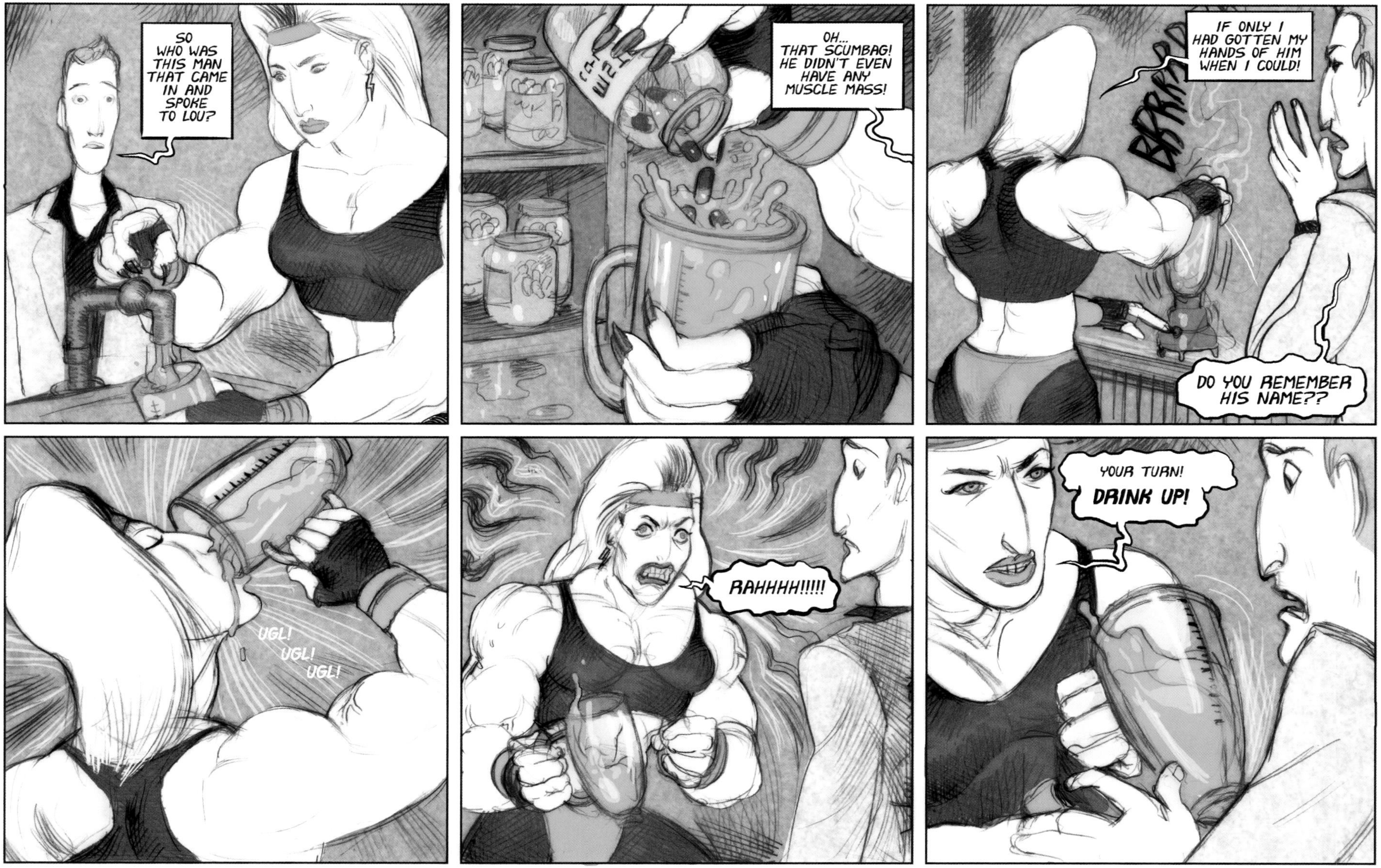
SO WHO WAS THIS MAN THAT CAME IN AND SPOKE TO LOU?
OH... THAT SCÜMBAG! HE DIDN'T EVEN HAVE ANY MUSCLE MASS!
IF ONLY I HAD GOTTEN MY HANDS OF HIM WHEN I COULD!
DO YOU REMEMBER HIS NAME??
UGL! UGL! UGL!
RAHHHH!!!!!
YOUR TURN!
DRINK UP!

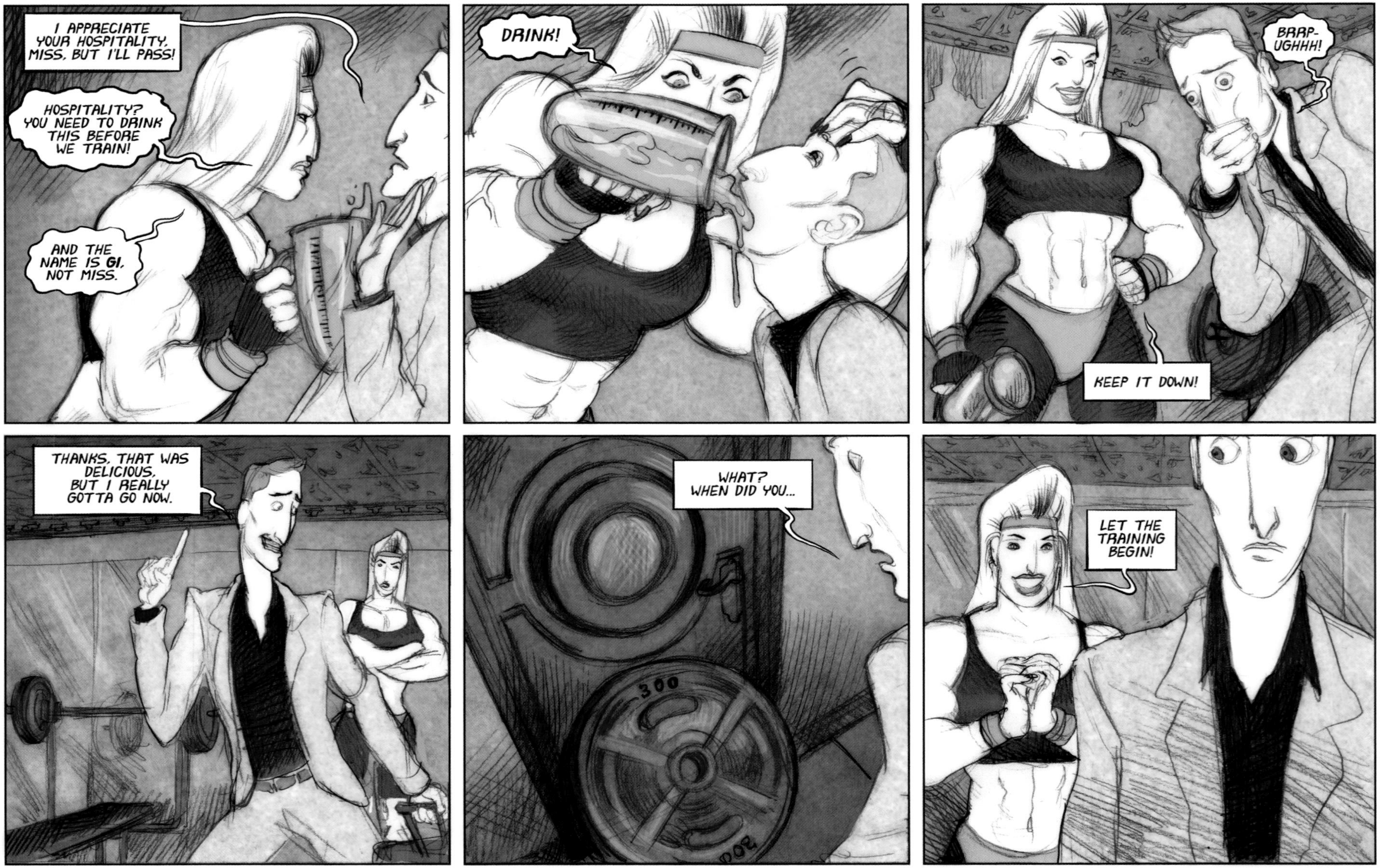
I APPRECIATE YOUR HOSPITALITY, MISS, BUT I'LL PASS!
HOSPITALITY? YOU NEED TO DRINK THIS BEFORE WE TRAIN!
AND THE NAME IS **GI**, NOT MISS.
DRINK!
BRRP-UGHHH!
KEEP IT DOWN!
THANKS, THAT WAS DELICIOUS, BUT I REALLY GOTTA GO NOW.
WHAT? WHEN DID YOU...
300
LET THE TRAINING BEGIN!

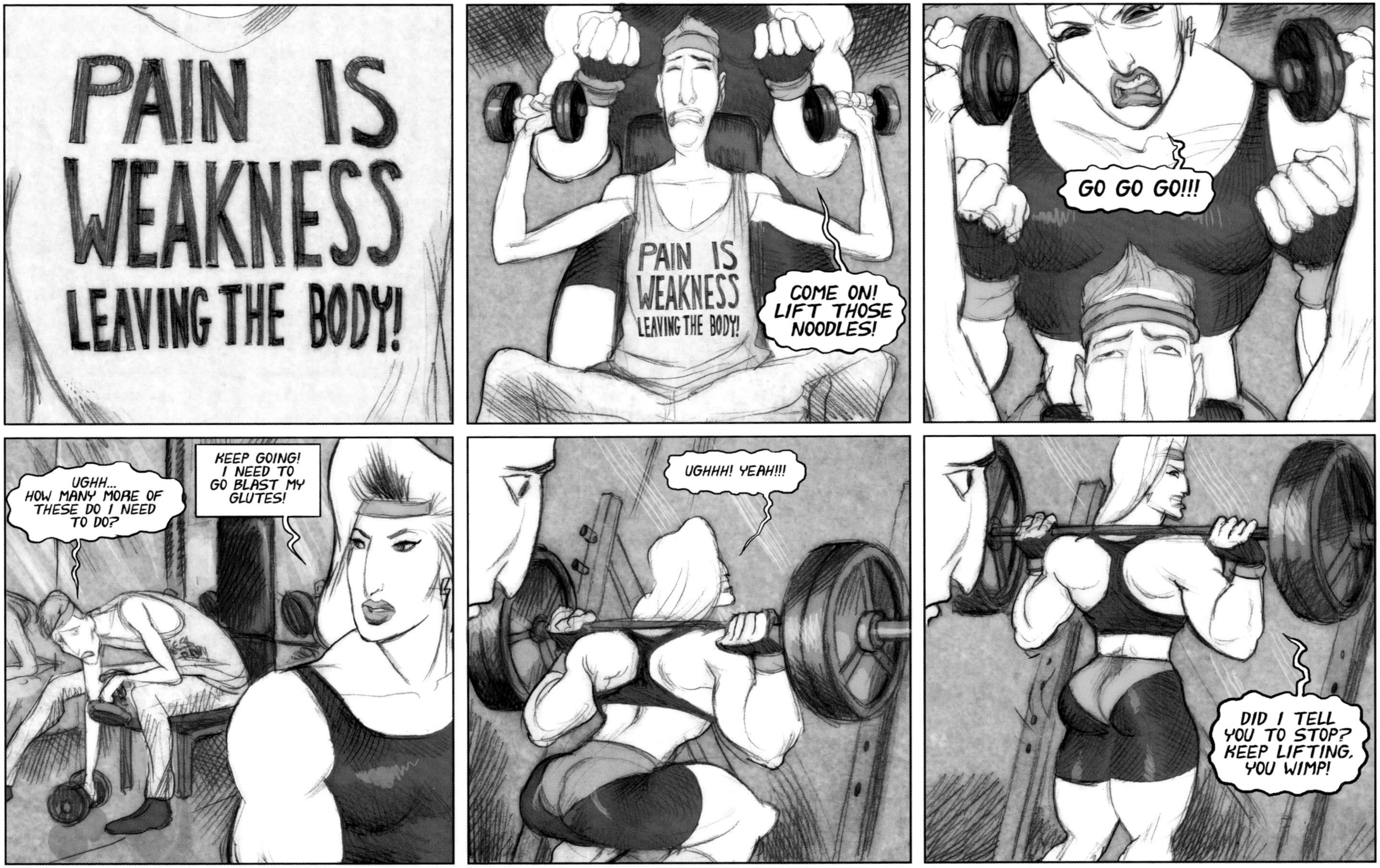
PAIN IS WEAKNESS LEAVING THE BODY!
PAIN IS WEAKNESS LEAVING THE BODY!
COME ON! LIFT THOSE NOODLES!
GO GO GO!!!
UGHH... HOW MANY MORE OF THESE DO I NEED TO DO?
KEEP GOING! I NEED TO GO BLAST MY GLUTES!
UGHHH! YEAH!!!
DID I TELL YOU TO STOP? KEEP LIFTING, YOU WIMP!

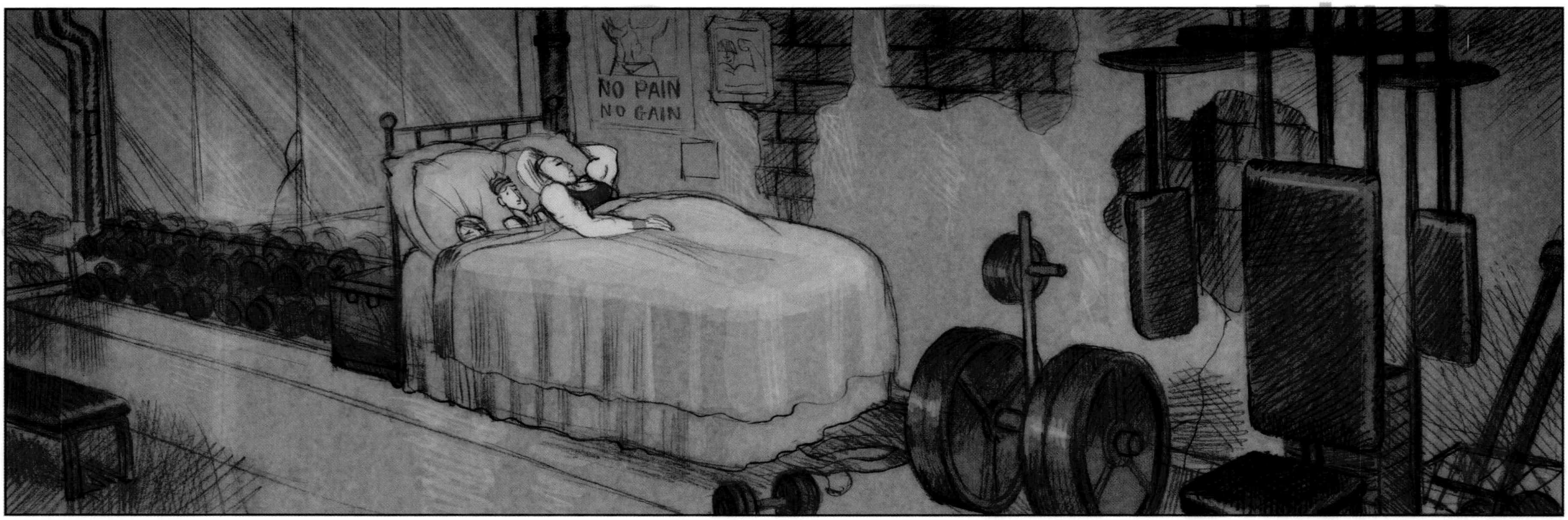
NO PAIN
NO GAIN

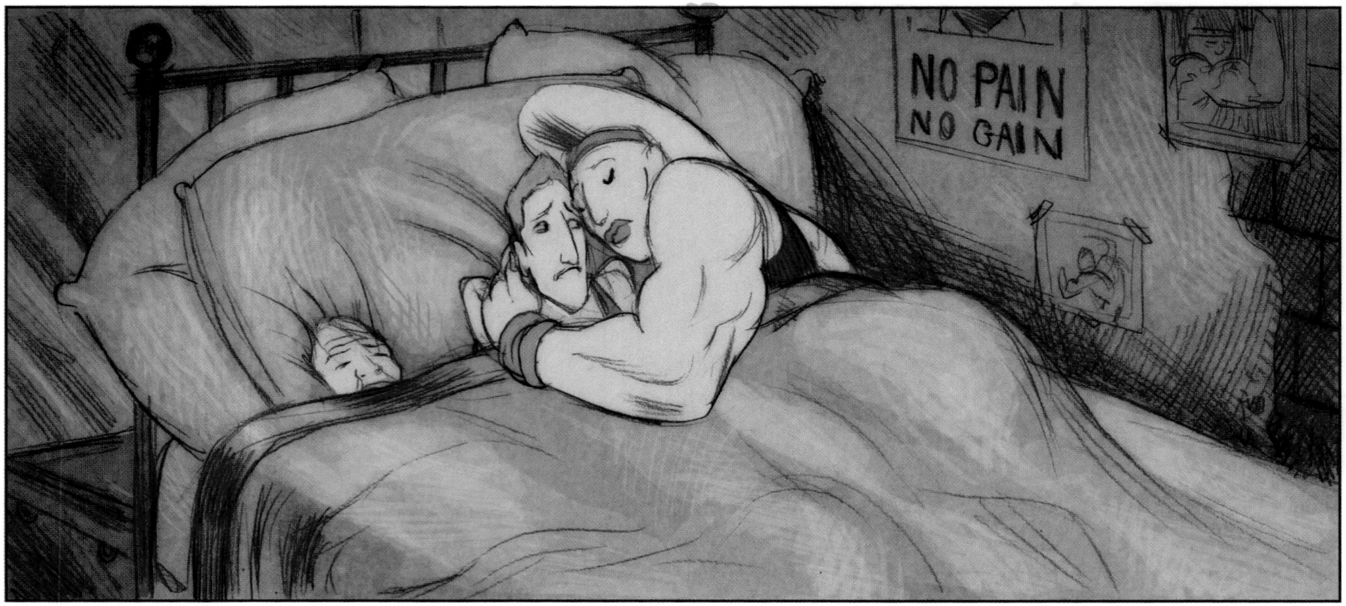
NO PAIN
NO GAIN

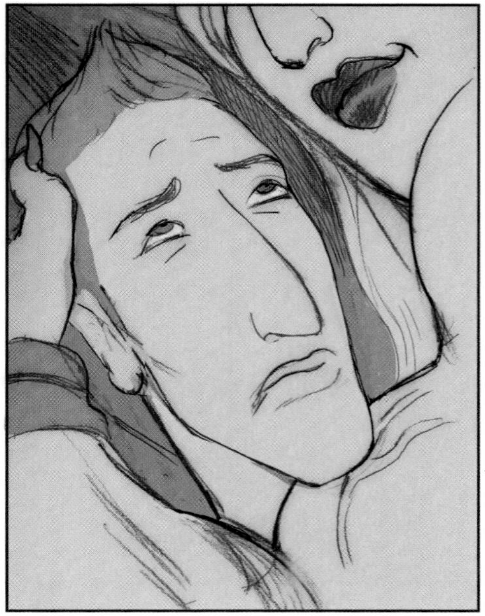

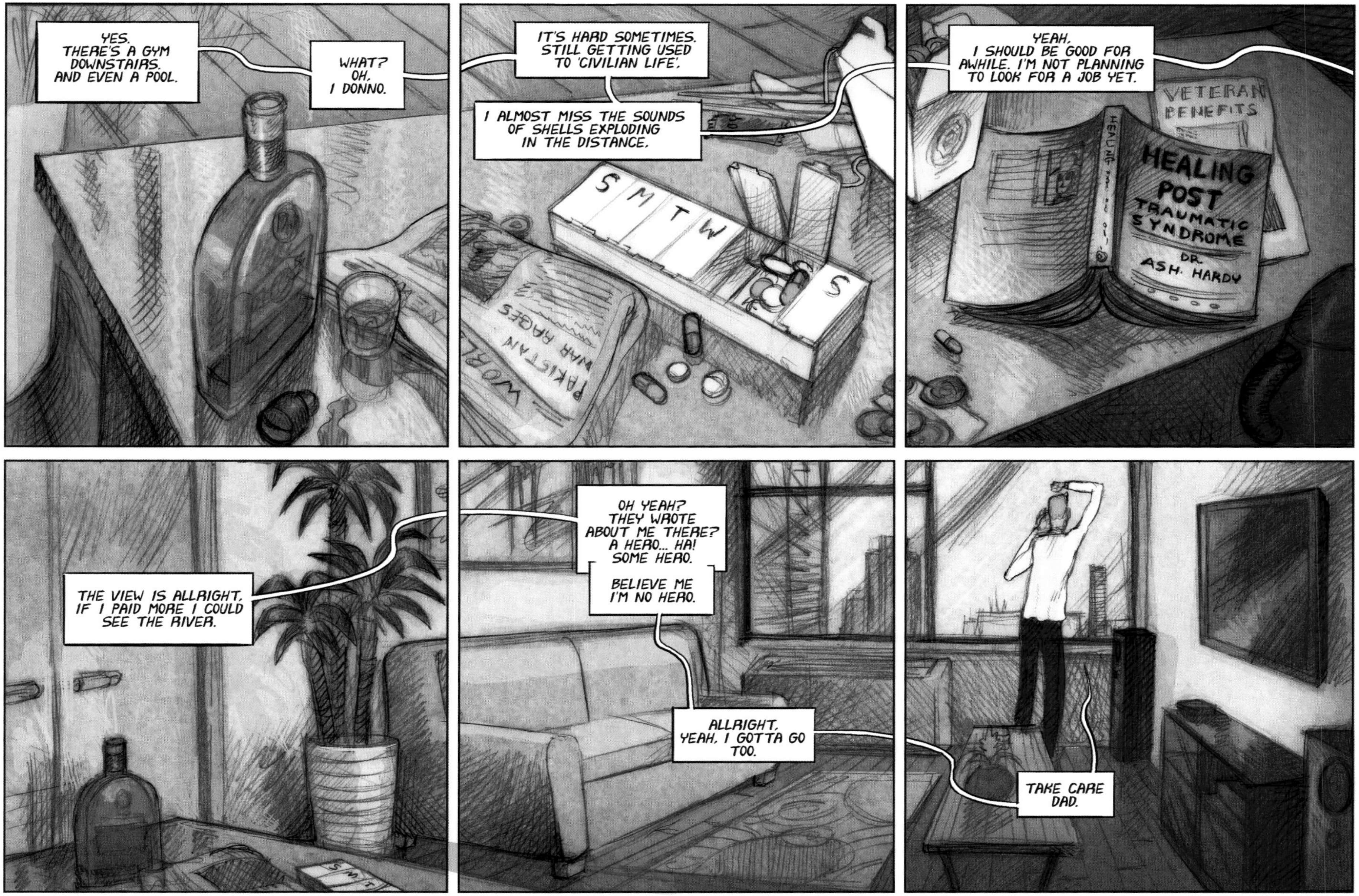
YES. THERE'S A GYM DOWNSTAIRS. AND EVEN A POOL.
WHAT? OH, I DONNO.
IT'S HARD SOMETIMES. STILL GETTING USED TO 'CIVILIAN LIFE'.
I ALMOST MISS THE SOUNDS OF SHELLS EXPLODING IN THE DISTANCE.
S M T W S
PAKISTAN WAR RAGES
YEAH, I SHOULD BE GOOD FOR AWHILE. I'M NOT PLANNING TO LOOK FOR A JOB YET.
VETERAN BENEFITS
HEALING POST TRAUMATIC SYNDROME
DR. ASH. HARDY
THE VIEW IS ALLRIGHT. IF I PAID MORE I COULD SEE THE RIVER.
OH YEAH? THEY WROTE ABOUT ME THERE? A HERO... HA! SOME HERO.
BELIEVE ME I'M NO HERO.
ALLRIGHT. YEAH, I GOTTA GO TOO.
TAKE CARE DAD.

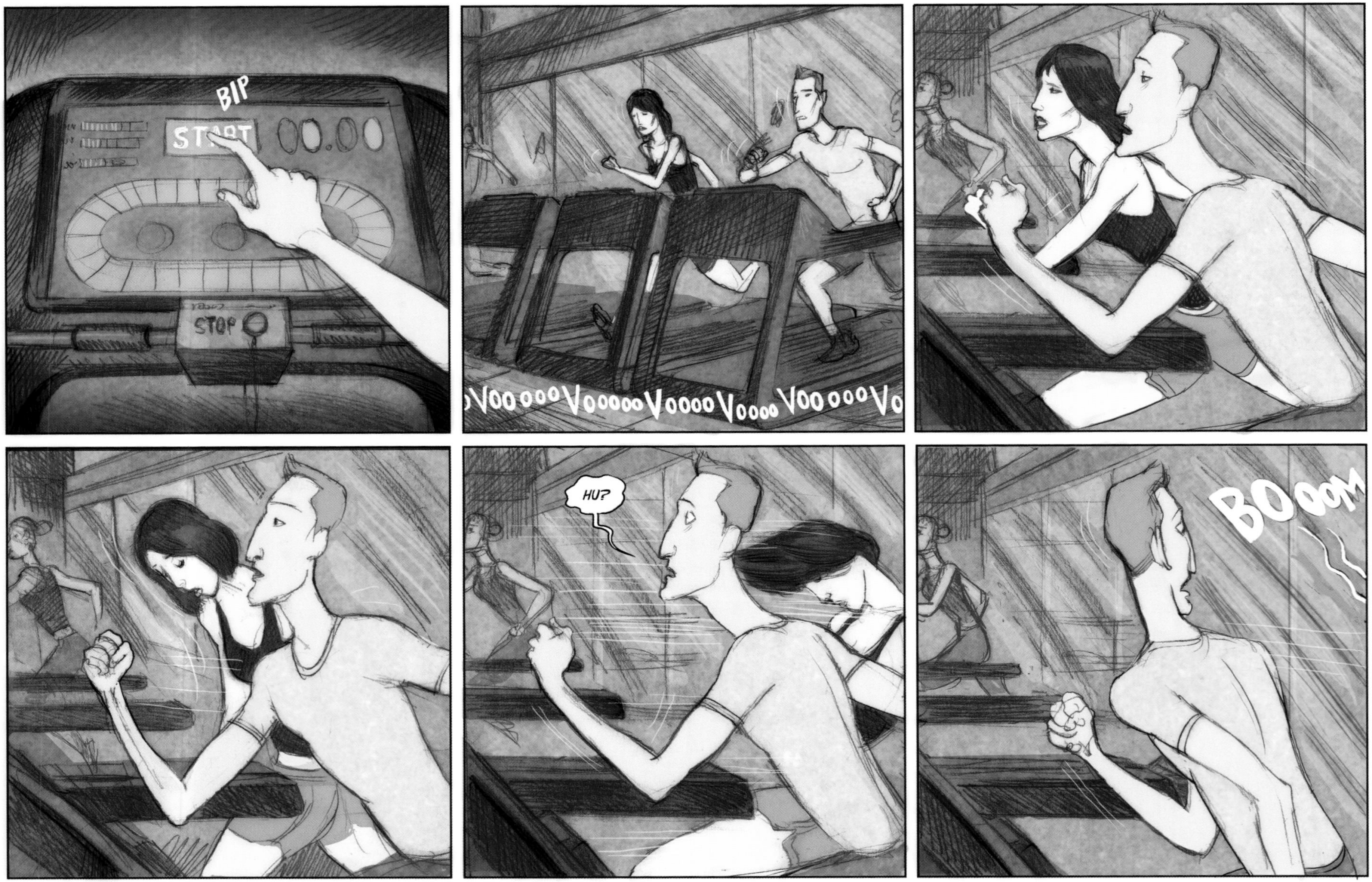
BIP
START
00.00
STOP
Voo ooo Vooooo Voooo Voooo Voo ooo Vo
HU?
BOOOM

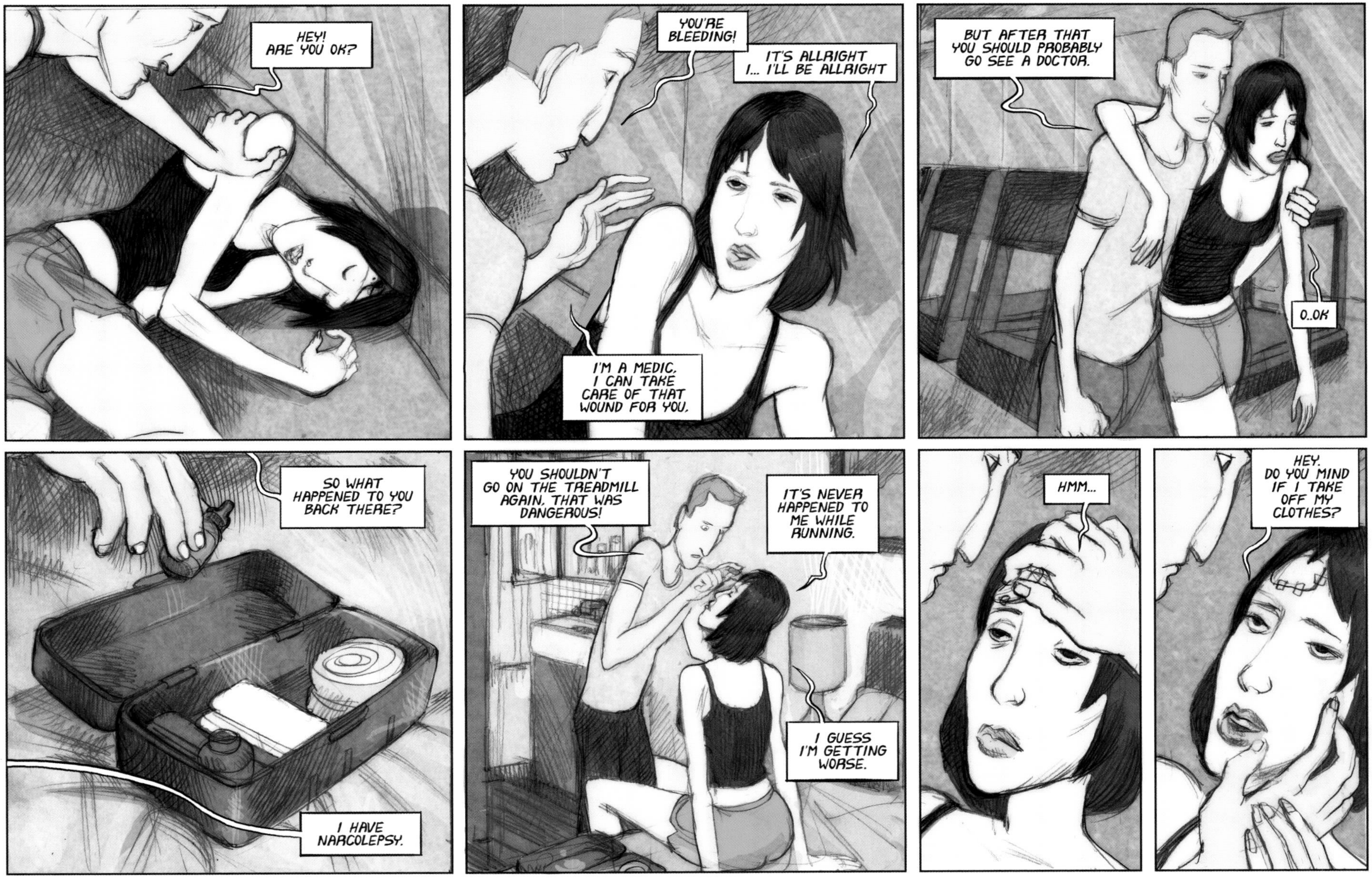
HEY! ARE YOU OK?
YOU'RE BLEEDING!
IT'S ALLRIGHT I... I'LL BE ALLRIGHT
I'M A MEDIC. I CAN TAKE CARE OF THAT WOUND FOR YOU.
BUT AFTER THAT YOU SHOULD PROBABLY GO SEE A DOCTOR.
O..OK
SO WHAT HAPPENED TO YOU BACK THERE?
I HAVE NARCOLEPSY.
YOU SHOULDN'T GO ON THE TREADMILL AGAIN. THAT WAS DANGEROUS!
IT'S NEVER HAPPENED TO ME WHILE RUNNING.
I GUESS I'M GETTING WORSE.
HMM...
HEY. DO YOU MIND IF I TAKE OFF MY CLOTHES?

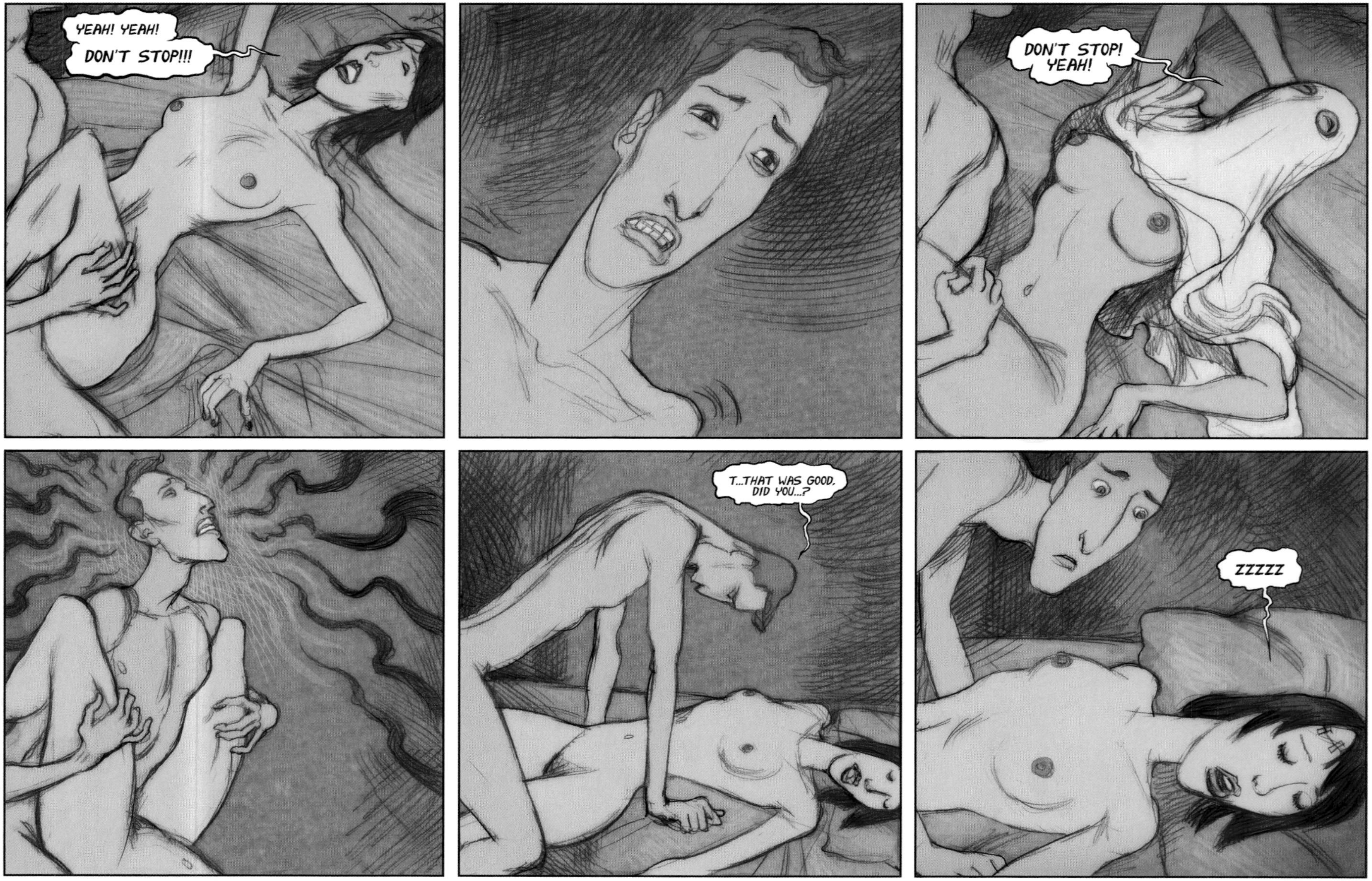
YEAH! YEAH!
DON'T STOP!!!
DON'T STOP! YEAH!
T...THAT WAS GOOD, DID YOU...?
ZZZZZ

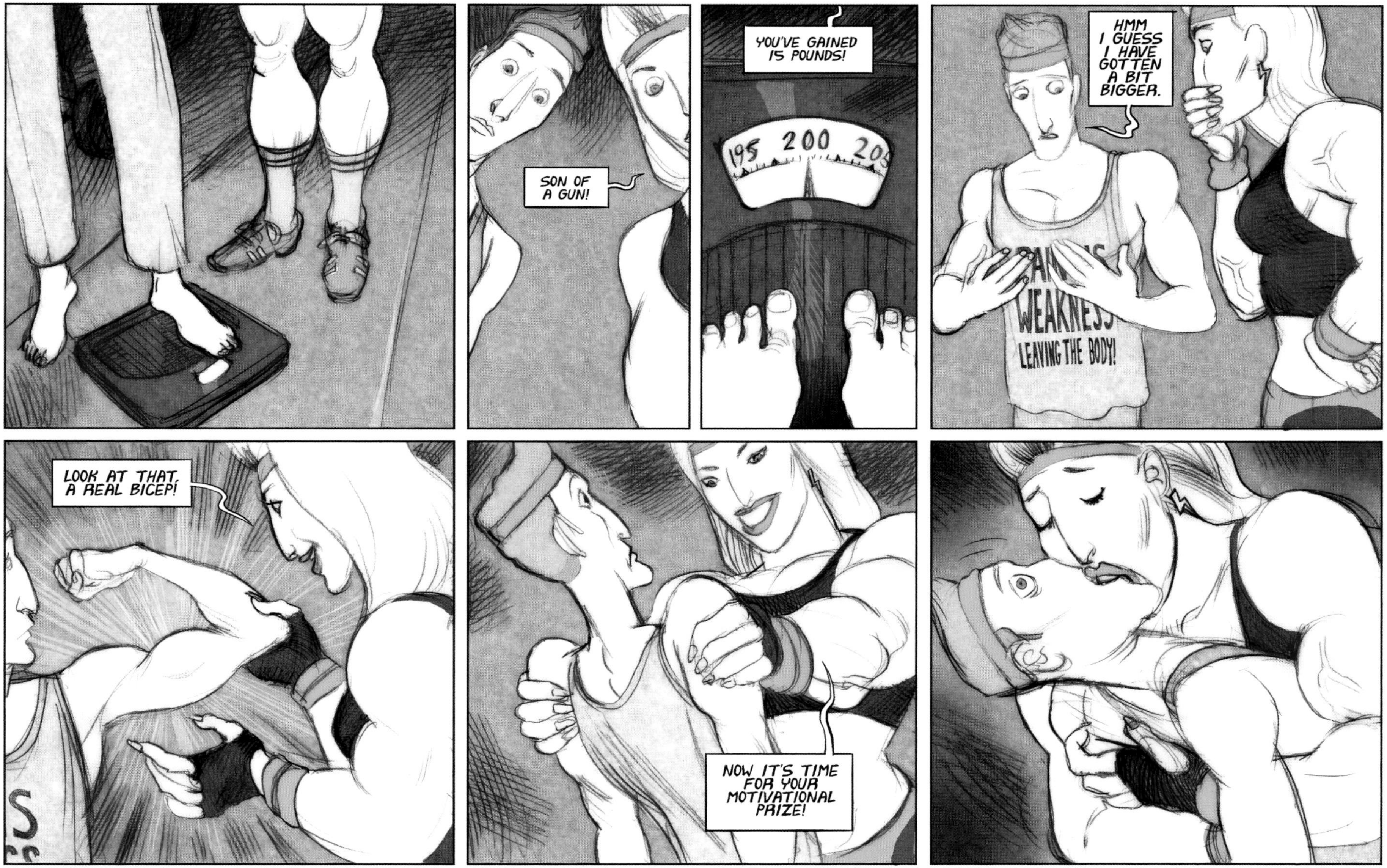
SON OF A GUN!
YOU'VE GAINED 15 POUNDS!
195 200 205
HMM I GUESS I HAVE GOTTEN A BIT BIGGER.
WEAKNESS LEAVING THE BODY!
LOOK AT THAT, A REAL BICEP!
NOW IT'S TIME FOR YOUR MOTIVATIONAL PRIZE!

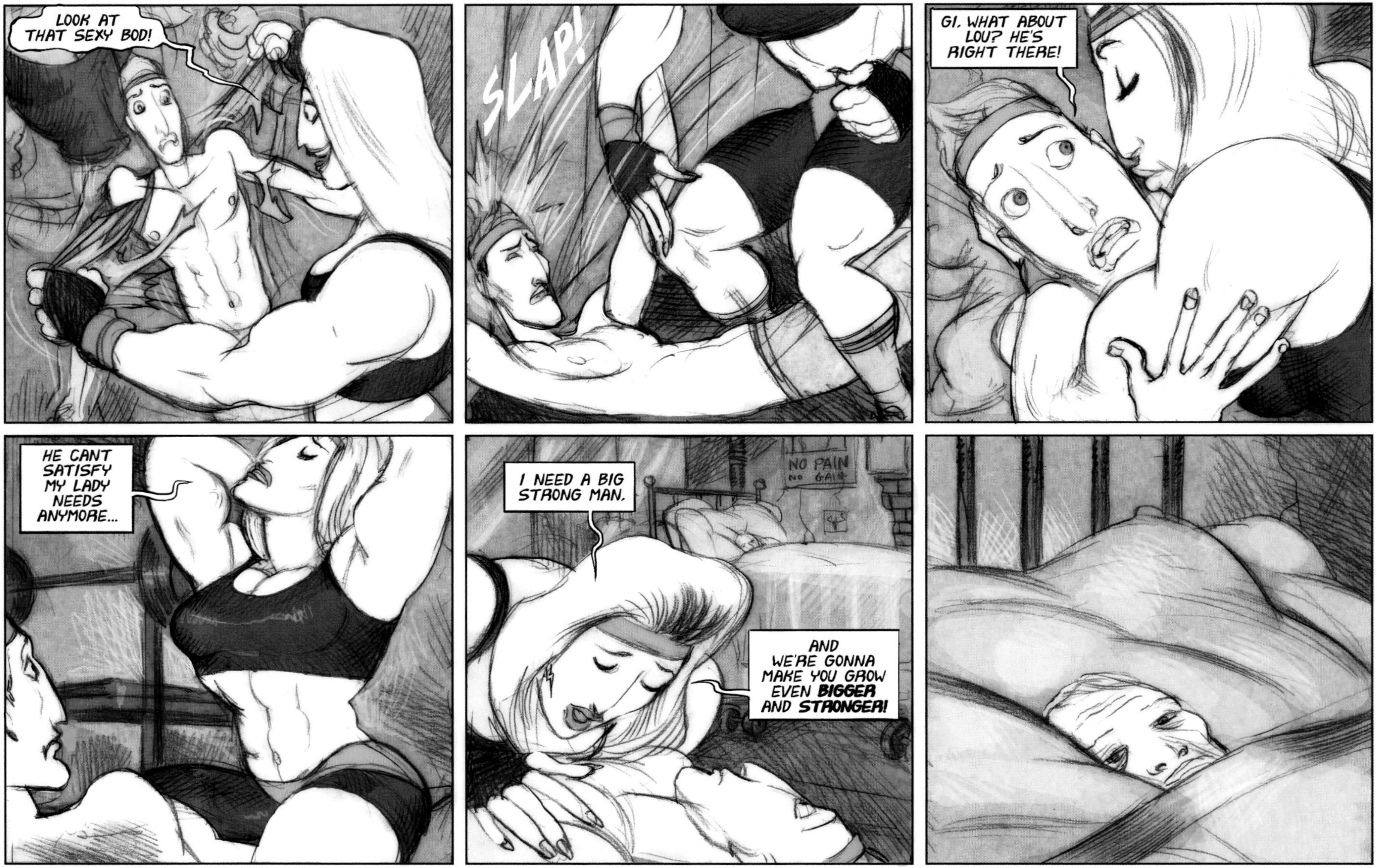
LOOK AT THAT SEXY BOD!
SLAP!
GI, WHAT ABOUT LOU? HE'S RIGHT THERE!
HE CANT SATISFY MY LADY NEEDS ANYMORE...
NO PAIN NO GAIN
I NEED A BIG STRONG MAN.
AND WE'RE GONNA MAKE YOU GROW EVEN **BIGGER** AND **STRONGER!**

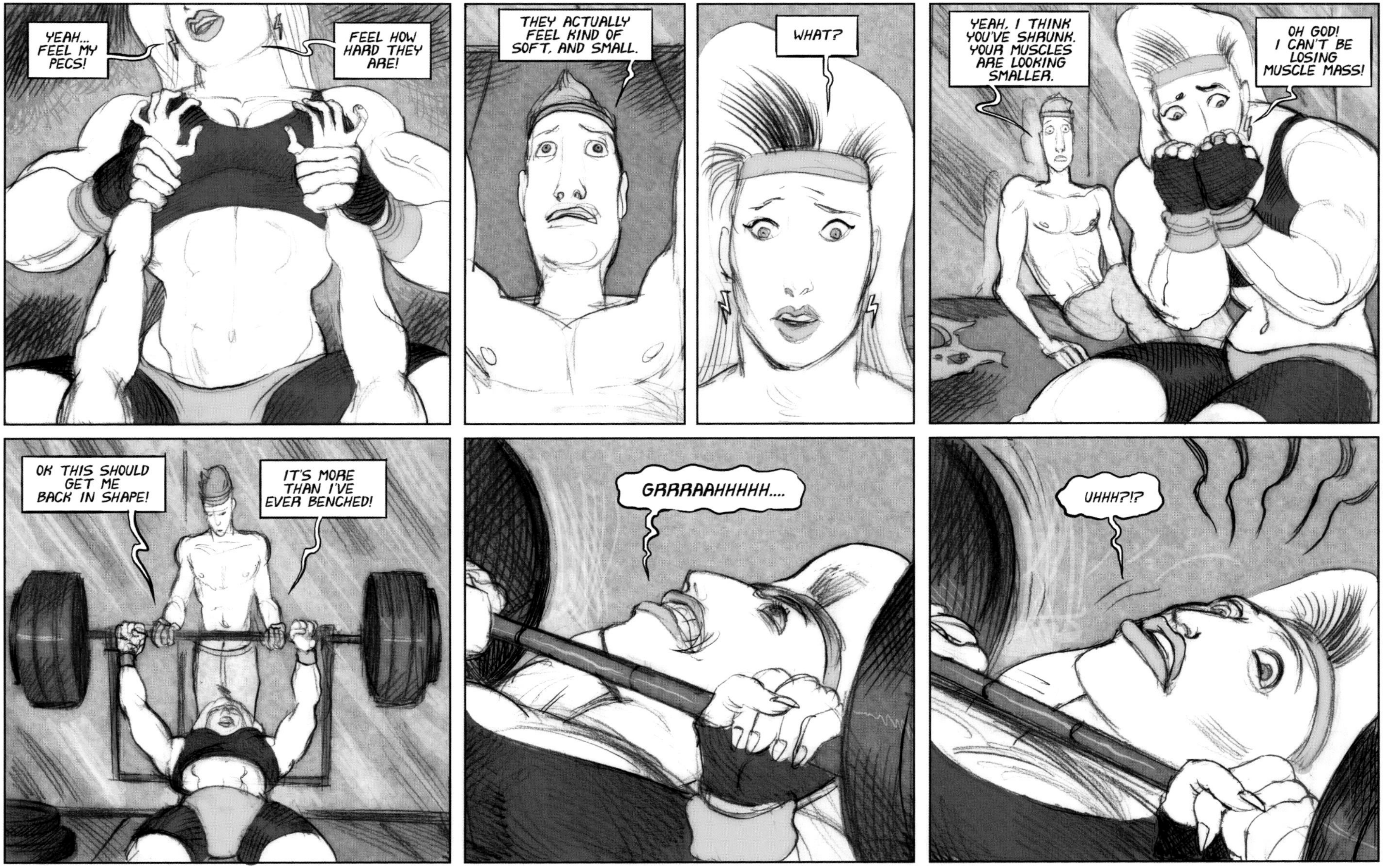
YEAH... FEEL MY PECS!
FEEL HOW HARD THEY ARE!
THEY ACTUALLY FEEL KIND OF SOFT, AND SMALL.
WHAT?
YEAH, I THINK YOU'VE SHRUNK. YOUR MUSCLES ARE LOOKING SMALLER.
OH GOD! I CAN'T BE LOSING MUSCLE MASS!
OK THIS SHOULD GET ME BACK IN SHAPE!
IT'S MORE THAN I'VE EVER BENCHED!
GRRRAAHHHHH....
UHHH?!?

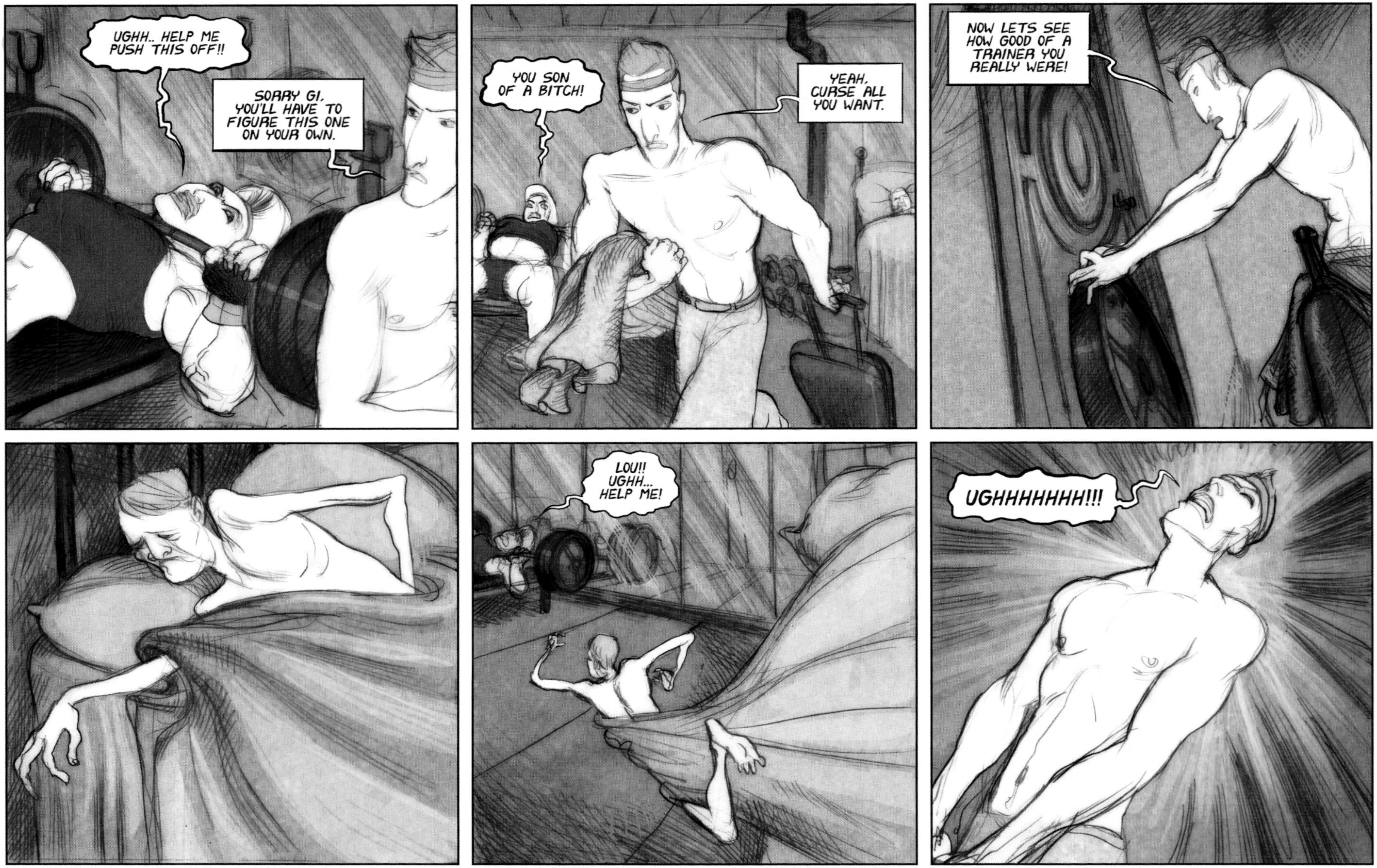
UGHH.. HELP ME PUSH THIS OFF!!
SORRY GI, YOU'LL HAVE TO FIGURE THIS ONE ON YOUR OWN.
YOU SON OF A BITCH!
YEAH, CURSE ALL YOU WANT.
NOW LETS SEE HOW GOOD OF A TRAINER YOU REALLY WERE!
LOU!! UGHH... HELP ME!
UGHHHHHHHH!!!

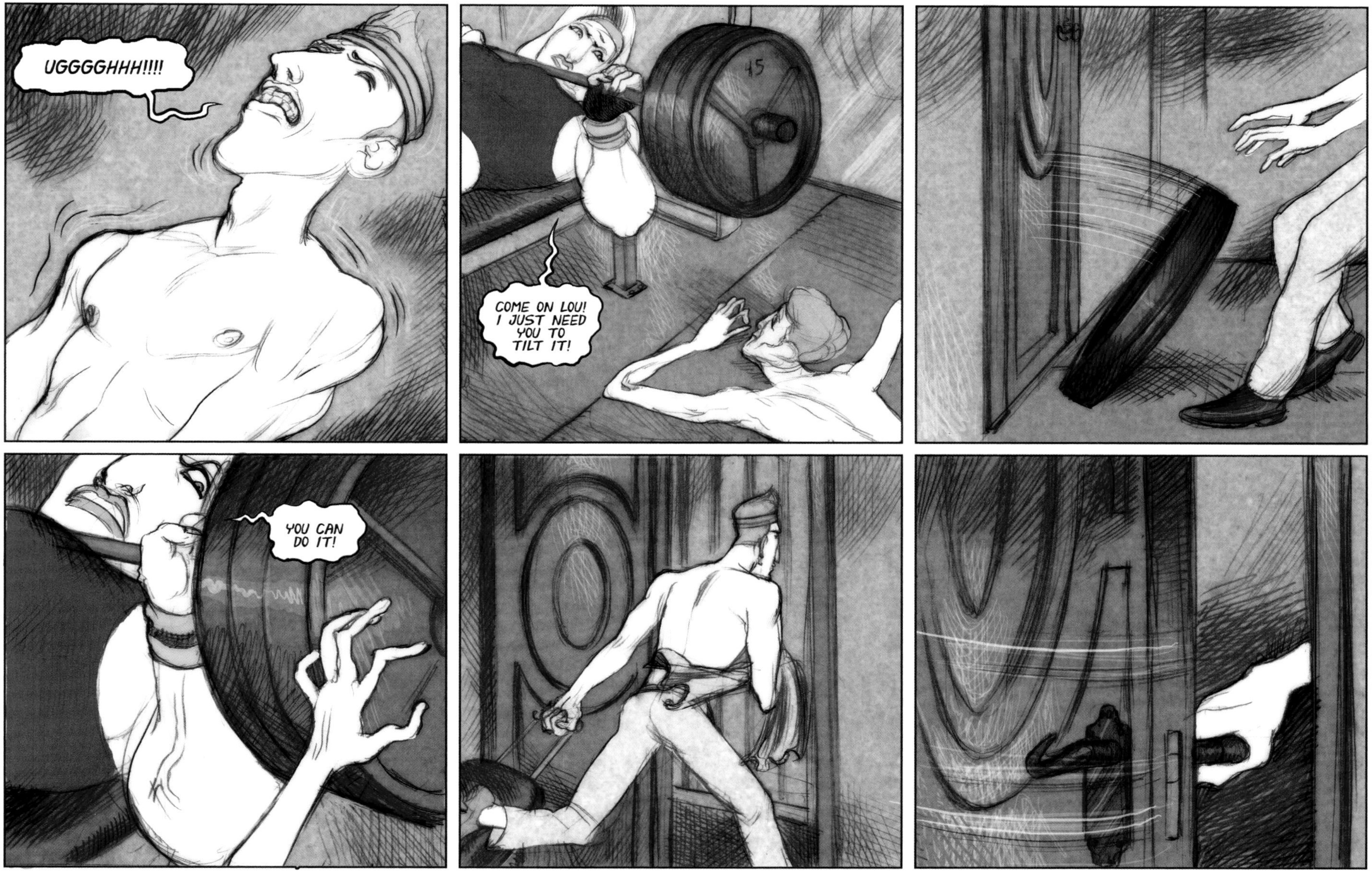
UGGGGHHH!!!!
COME ON LOU! I JUST NEED YOU TO TILT IT!
YOU CAN DO IT!

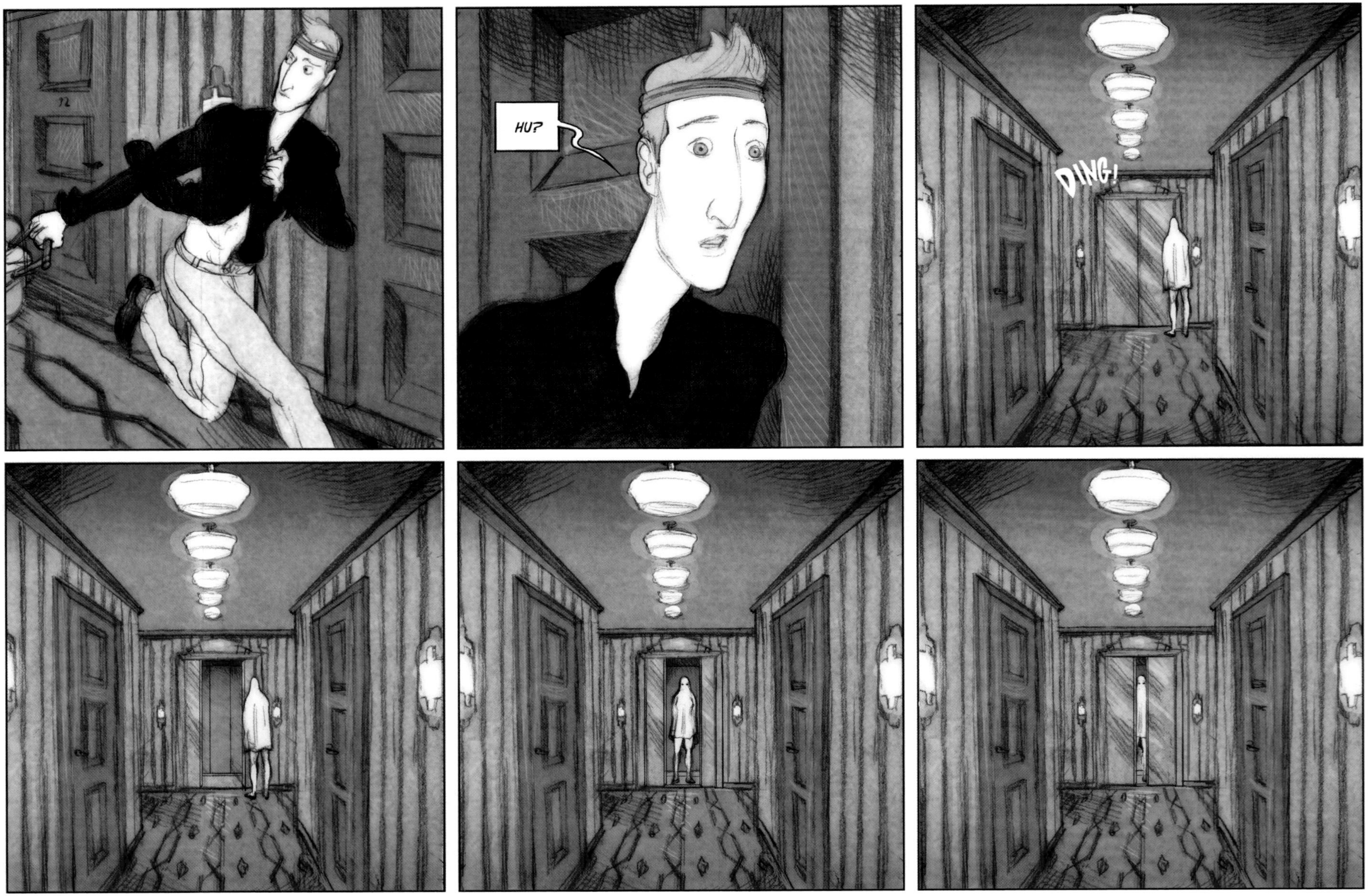
HU?
DING!

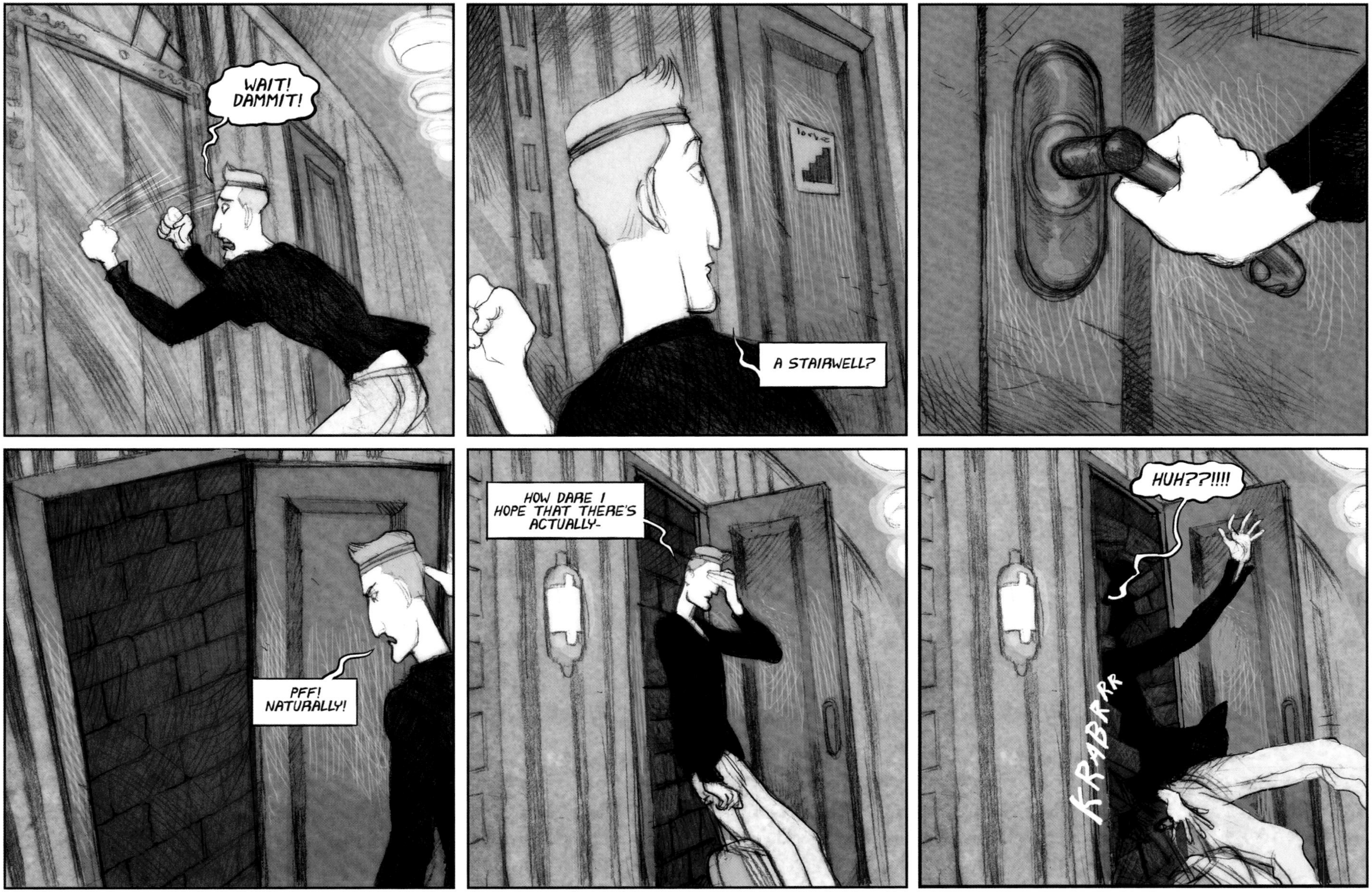
WAIT! DAMMIT!
A STAIRWELL?
PFF! NATURALLY!
HOW DARE I HOPE THAT THERE'S ACTUALLY-
HUH??!!!!
KRABRRR

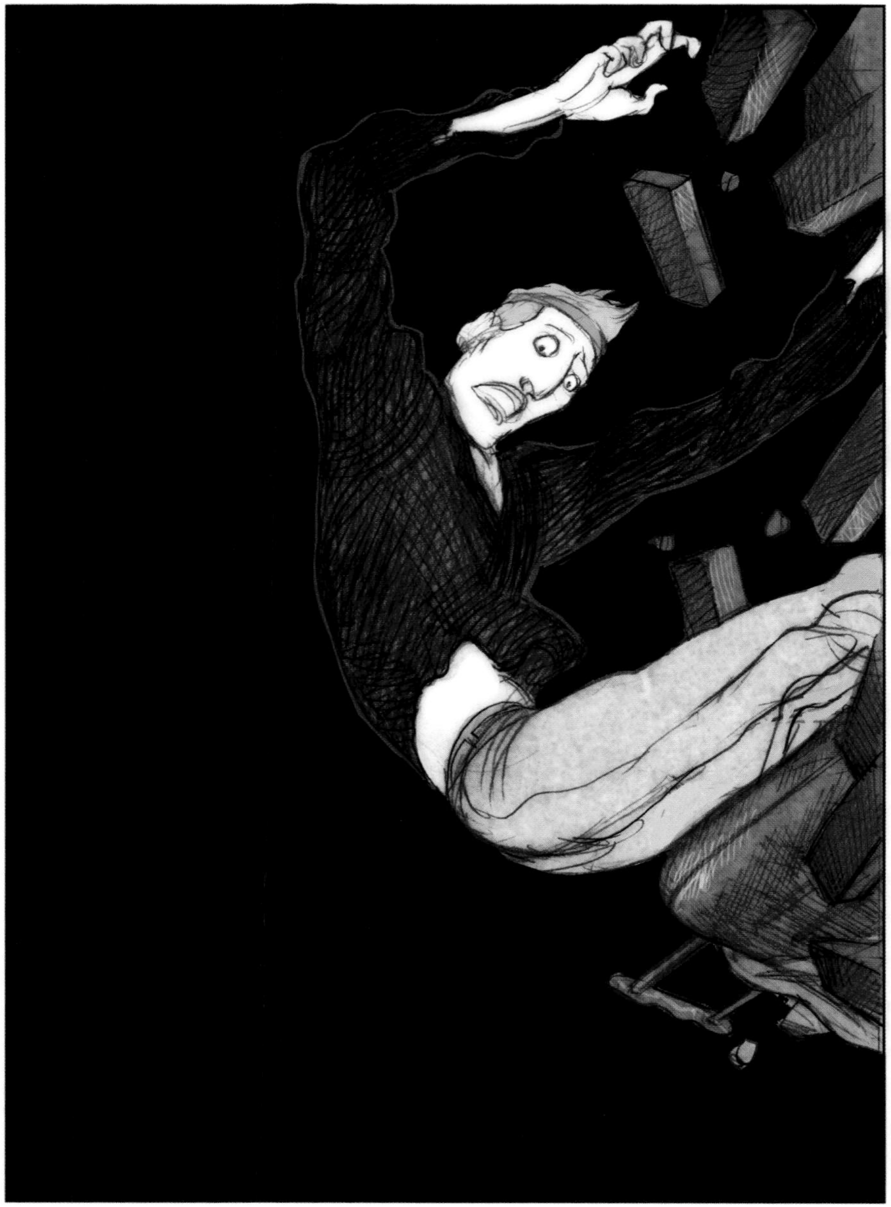

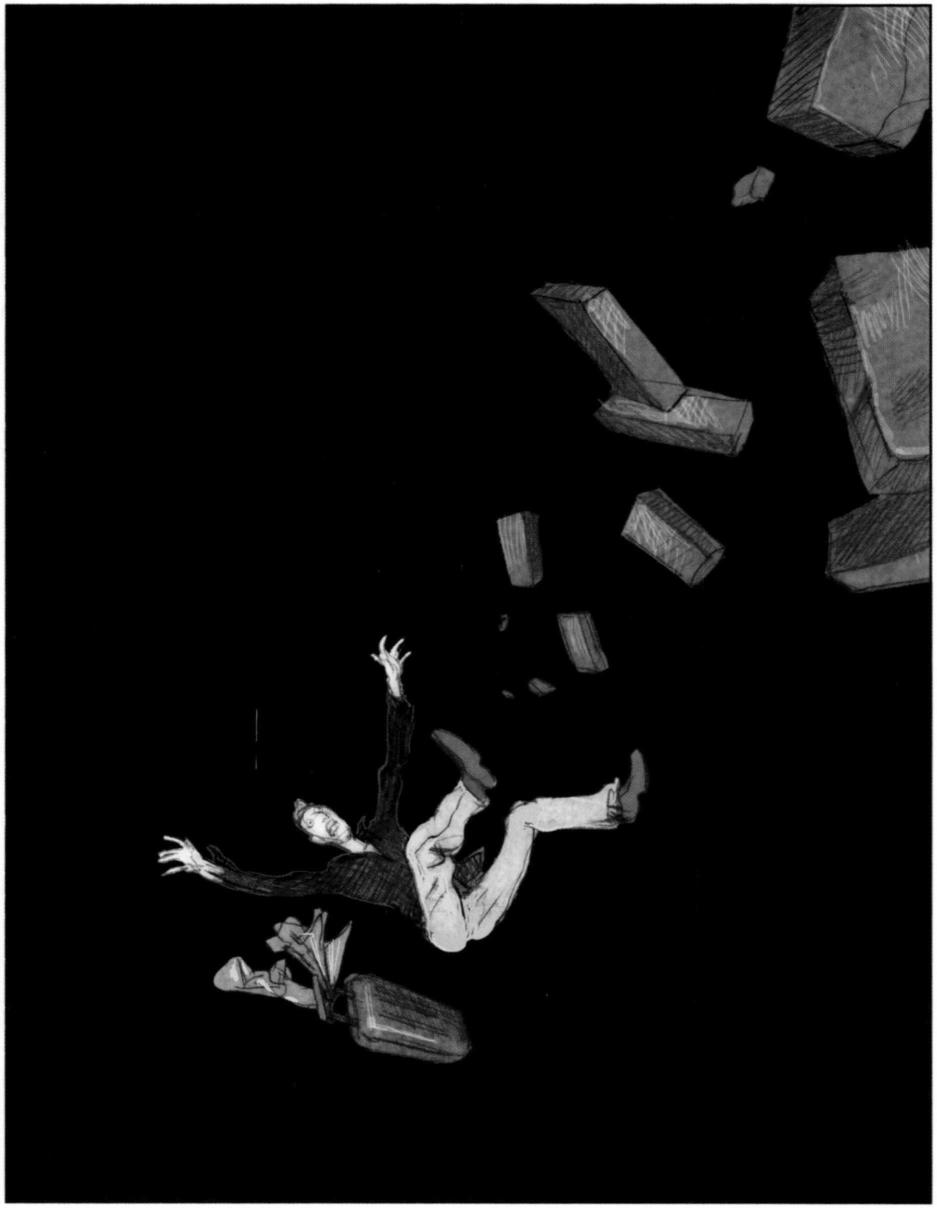

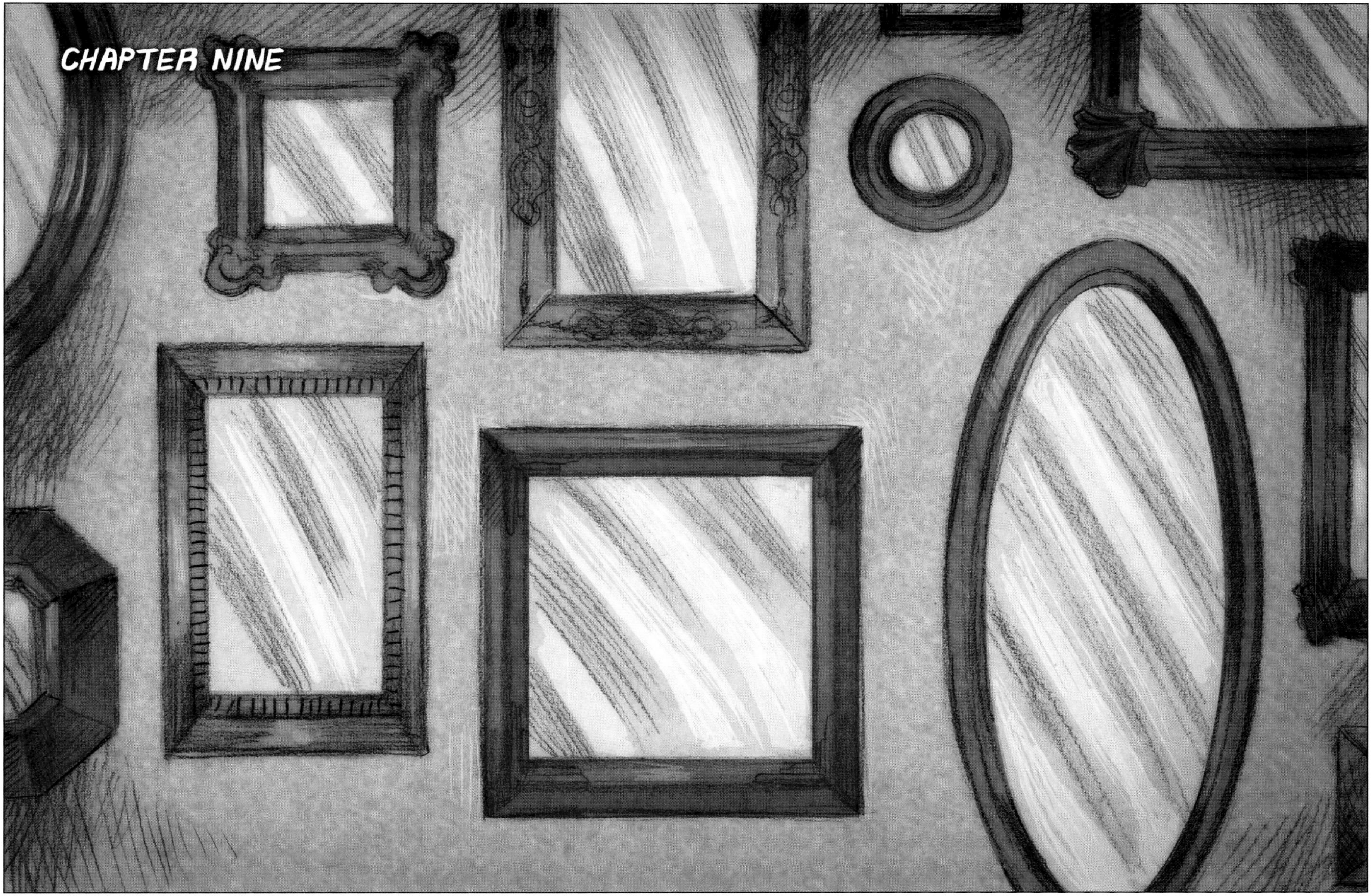
CHAPTER NINE

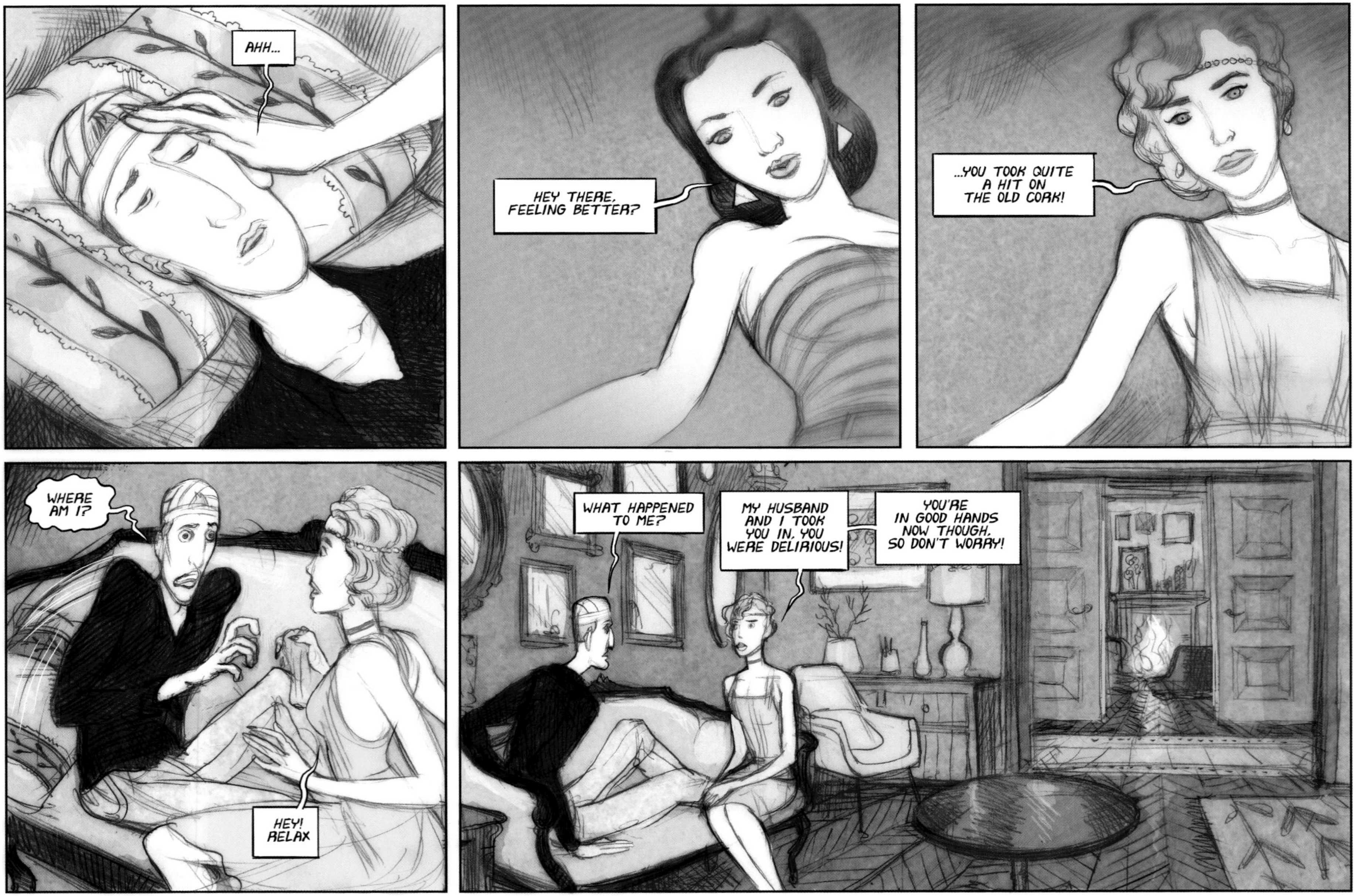
AHH...
HEY THERE, FEELING BETTER?
...YOU TOOK QUITE A HIT ON THE OLD CORK!
WHERE AM I?
HEY! RELAX
WHAT HAPPENED TO ME?
MY HUSBAND AND I TOOK YOU IN. YOU WERE DELIRIOUS!
YOU'RE IN GOOD HANDS NOW THOUGH, SO DON'T WORRY!

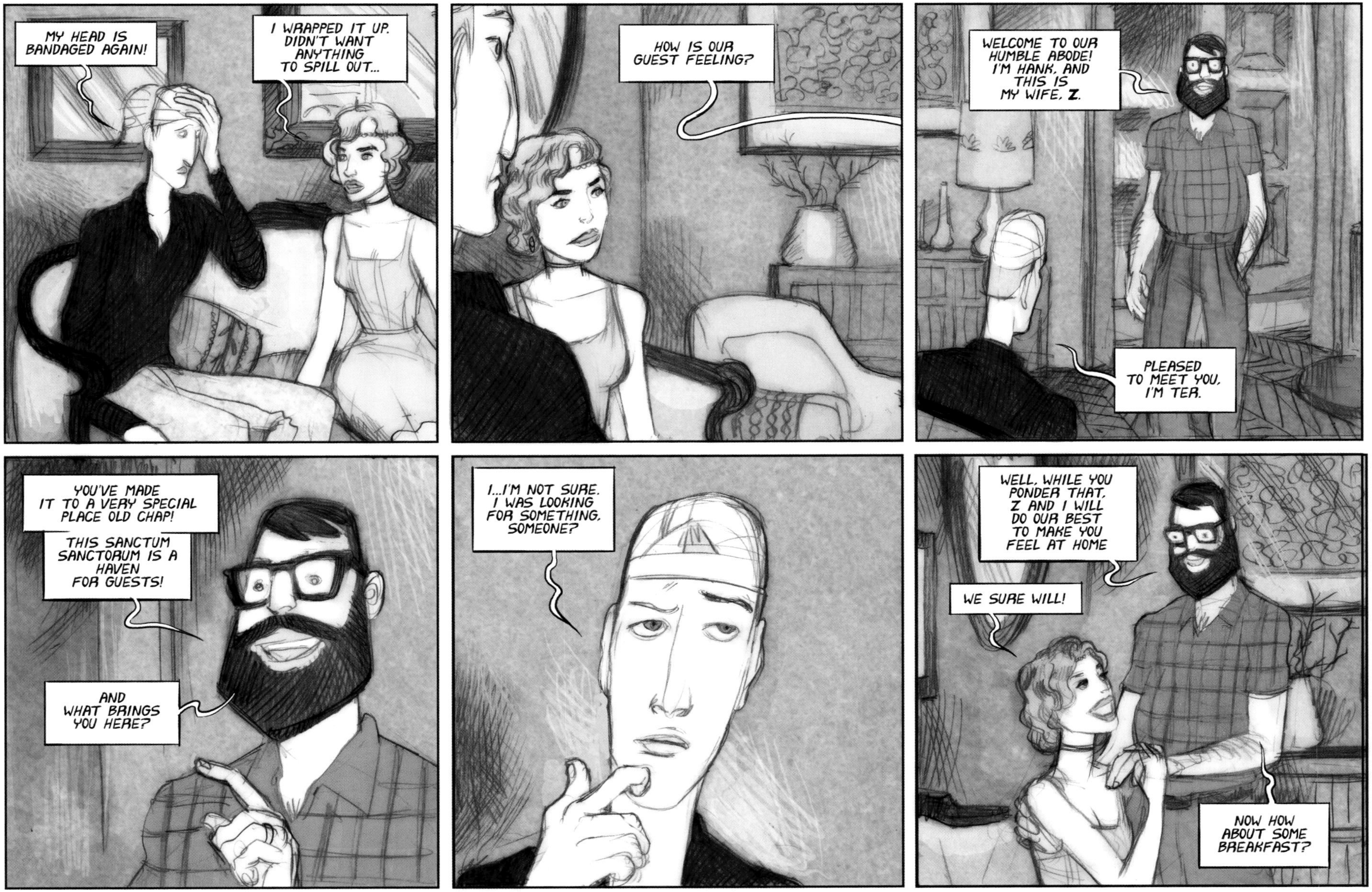
MY HEAD IS BANDAGED AGAIN!
I WRAPPED IT UP. DIDN'T WANT ANYTHING TO SPILL OUT...
HOW IS OUR GUEST FEELING?
WELCOME TO OUR HUMBLE ABODE! I'M HANK, AND THIS IS MY WIFE, Z.
PLEASED TO MEET YOU, I'M TER.
YOU'VE MADE IT TO A VERY SPECIAL PLACE OLD CHAP!
THIS SANCTUM SANCTORUM IS A HAVEN FOR GUESTS!
AND WHAT BRINGS YOU HERE?
I...I'M NOT SURE. I WAS LOOKING FOR SOMETHING, SOMEONE?
WELL, WHILE YOU PONDER THAT, Z AND I WILL DO OUR BEST TO MAKE YOU FEEL AT HOME
WE SURE WILL!
NOW HOW ABOUT SOME BREAKFAST?

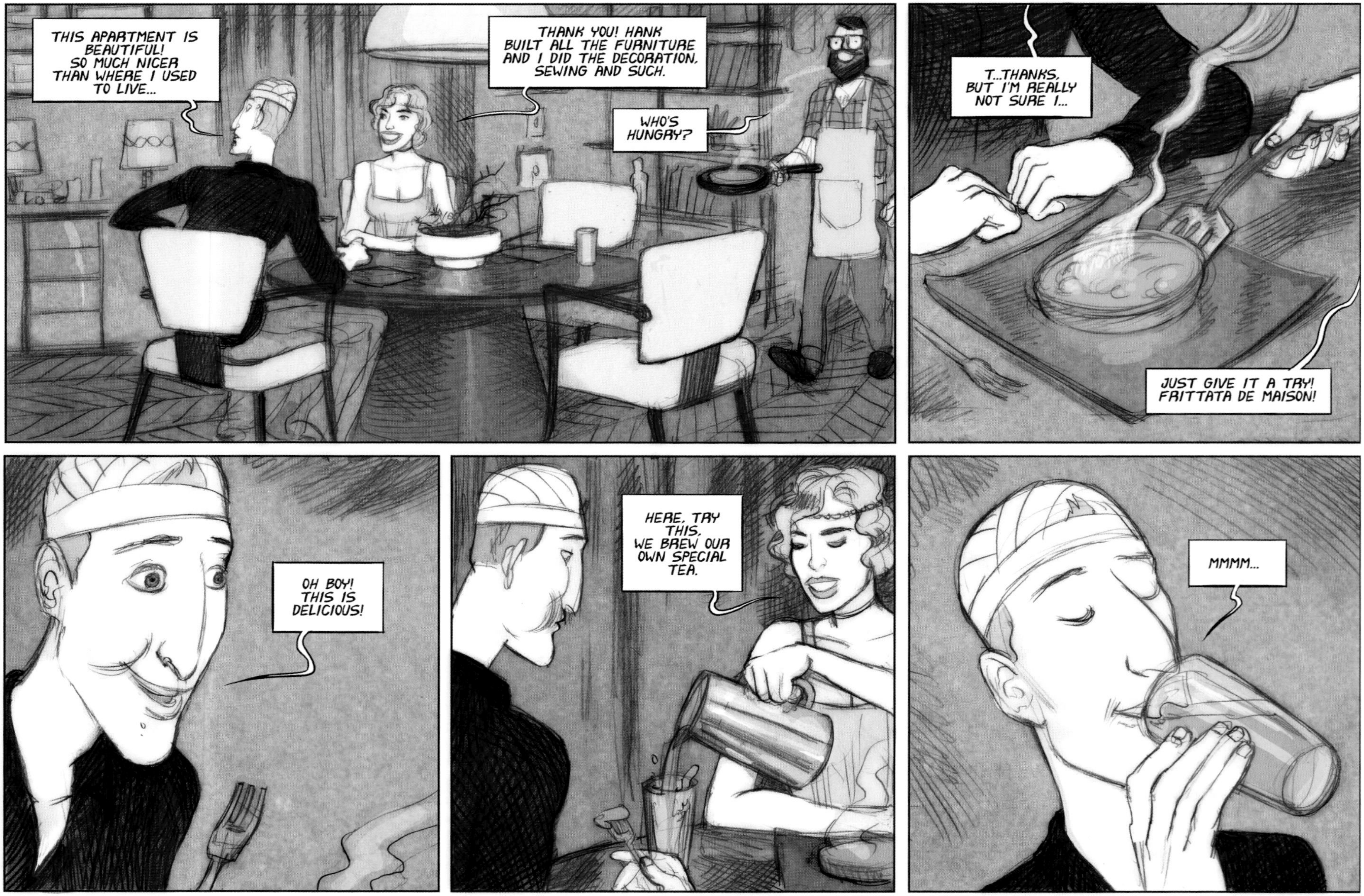
THIS APARTMENT IS BEAUTIFUL! SO MUCH NICER THAN WHERE I USED TO LIVE...
THANK YOU! HANK BUILT ALL THE FURNITURE AND I DID THE DECORATION, SEWING AND SUCH.
WHO'S HUNGRY?
T...THANKS, BUT I'M REALLY NOT SURE I...
JUST GIVE IT A TRY! FRITTATA DE MAISON!
OH BOY! THIS IS DELICIOUS!
HERE, TRY THIS, WE BREW OUR OWN SPECIAL TEA.
MMMM...

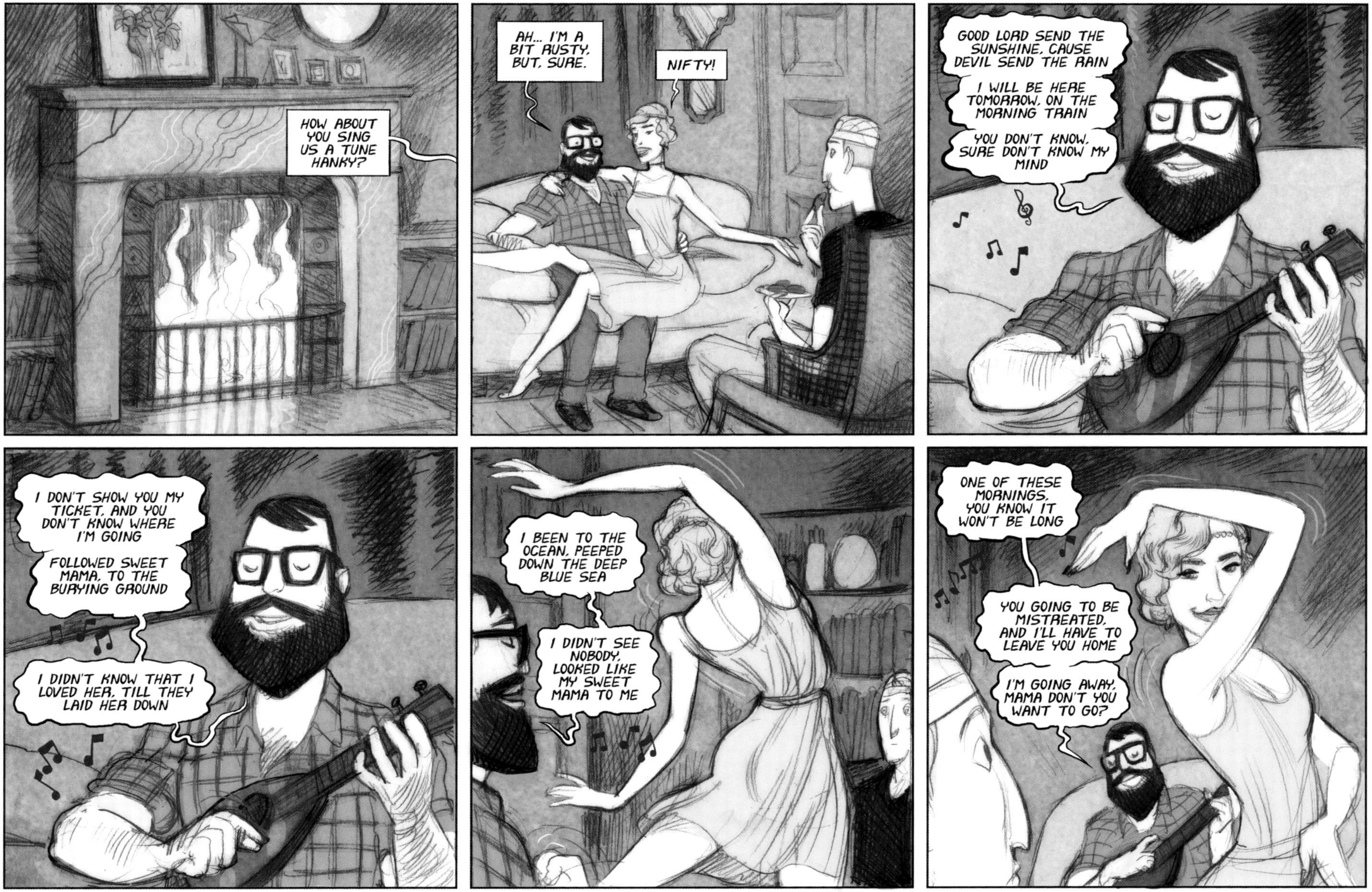
HOW ABOUT YOU SING US A TUNE HANKY?
AH... I'M A BIT RUSTY, BUT, SURE.
NIFTY!
GOOD LORD SEND THE SUNSHINE, CAUSE DEVIL SEND THE RAIN
I WILL BE HERE TOMORROW, ON THE MORNING TRAIN
YOU DON'T KNOW, SURE DON'T KNOW MY MIND
I DON'T SHOW YOU MY TICKET, AND YOU DON'T KNOW WHERE I'M GOING
FOLLOWED SWEET MAMA, TO THE BURYING GROUND
I DIDN'T KNOW THAT I LOVED HER, TILL THEY LAID HER DOWN
I BEEN TO THE OCEAN, PEEPED DOWN THE DEEP BLUE SEA
I DIDN'T SEE NOBODY, LOOKED LIKE MY SWEET MAMA TO ME
ONE OF THESE MORNINGS, YOU KNOW IT WON'T BE LONG
YOU GOING TO BE MISTREATED, AND I'LL HAVE TO LEAVE YOU HOME
I'M GOING AWAY, MAMA DON'T YOU WANT TO GO?

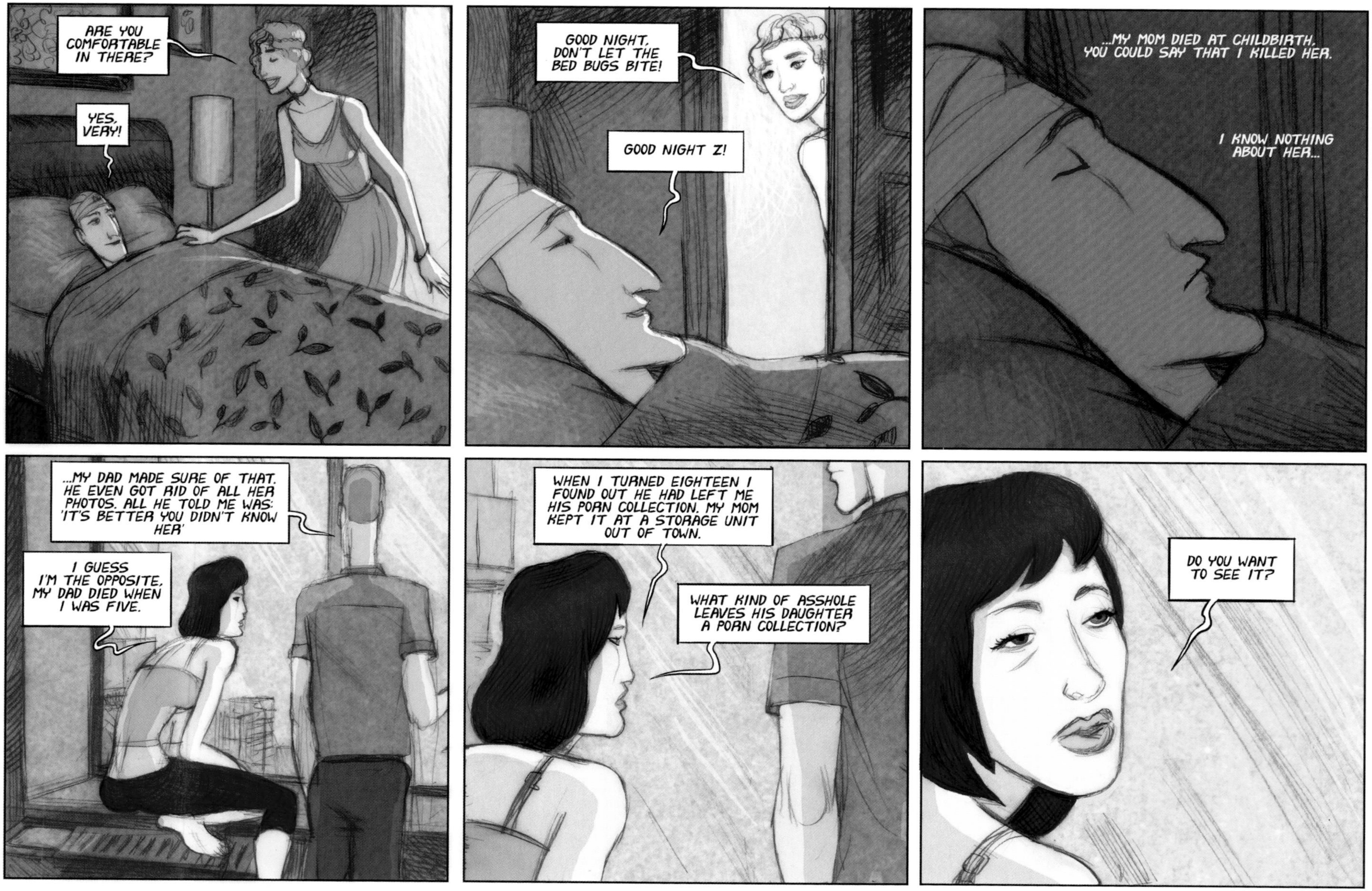

ARE YOU COMFORTABLE IN THERE?
YES, VERY!
GOOD NIGHT, DON'T LET THE BED BUGS BITE!
GOOD NIGHT Z!
...MY MOM DIED AT CHILDBIRTH. YOU COULD SAY THAT I KILLED HER.
I KNOW NOTHING ABOUT HER...
...MY DAD MADE SURE OF THAT. HE EVEN GOT RID OF ALL HER PHOTOS. ALL HE TOLD ME WAS: 'IT'S BETTER YOU DIDN'T KNOW HER'
I GUESS I'M THE OPPOSITE, MY DAD DIED WHEN I WAS FIVE.
WHEN I TURNED EIGHTEEN I FOUND OUT HE HAD LEFT ME HIS PORN COLLECTION. MY MOM KEPT IT AT A STORAGE UNIT OUT OF TOWN.
WHAT KIND OF ASSHOLE LEAVES HIS DAUGHTER A PORN COLLECTION?
DO YOU WANT TO SEE IT?

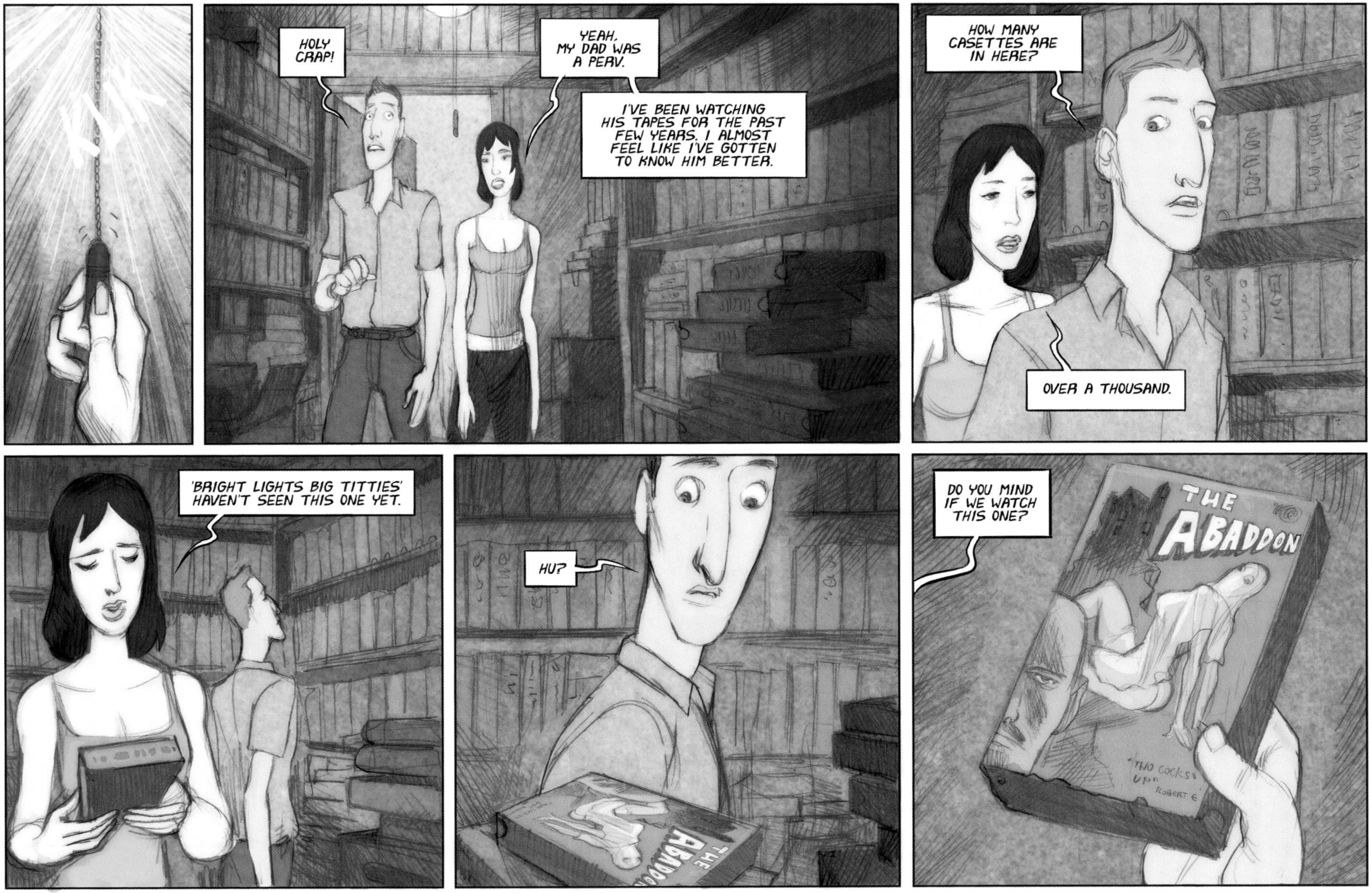
KLIK
HOLY CRAP!
YEAH, MY DAD WAS A PERV.
I'VE BEEN WATCHING HIS TAPES FOR THE PAST FEW YEARS. I ALMOST FEEL LIKE I'VE GOTTEN TO KNOW HIM BETTER.
HOW MANY CASETTES ARE IN HERE?
OVER A THOUSAND.
'BRIGHT LIGHTS BIG TITTIES' HAVEN'T SEEN THIS ONE YET.
HU?
THE ABADDON
DO YOU MIND IF WE WATCH THIS ONE?
THE ABADDON
"TWO COCKS UP" ROBERT E

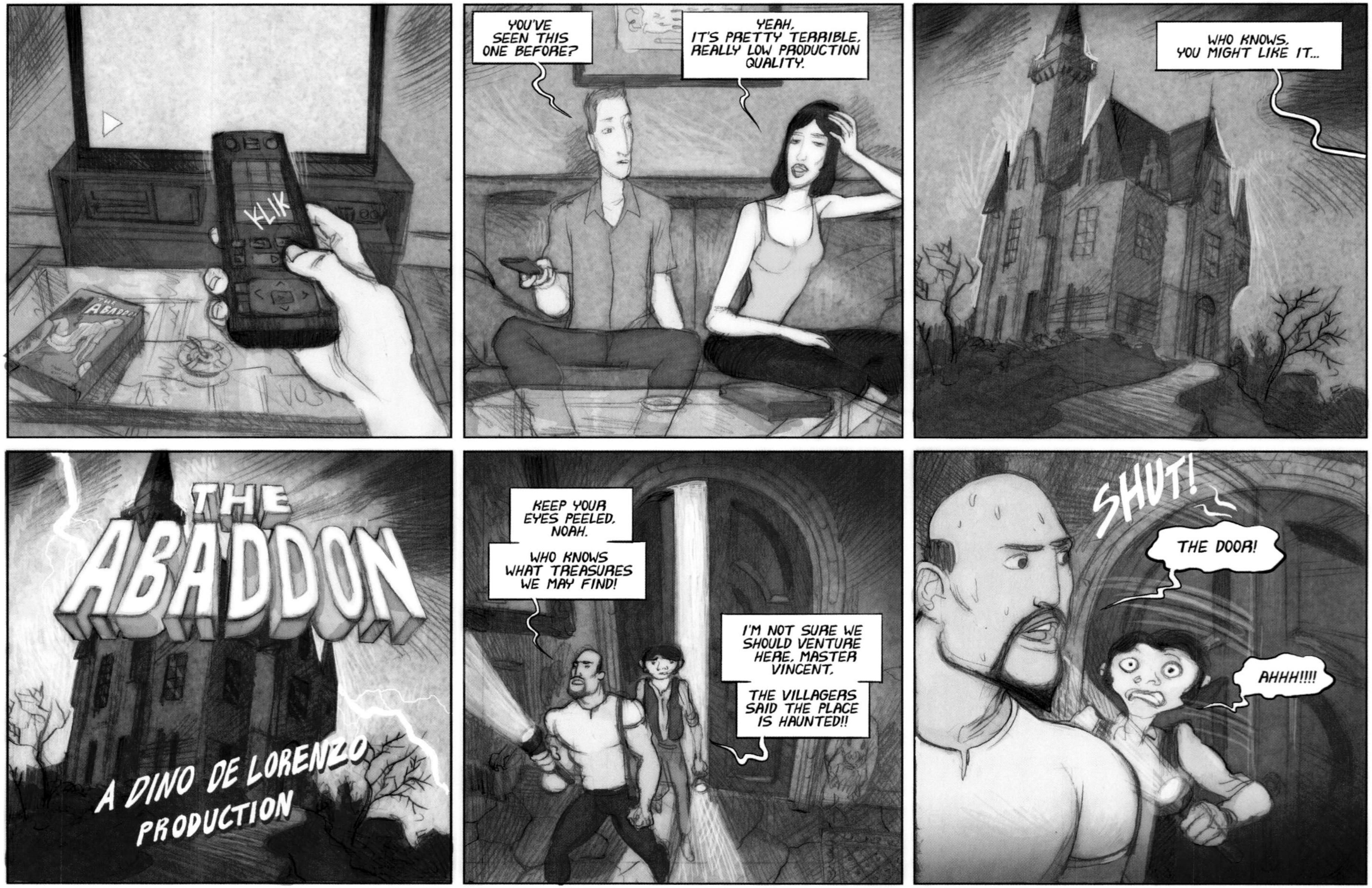
KLIK
YOU'VE SEEN THIS ONE BEFORE?
YEAH, IT'S PRETTY TERRIBLE, REALLY LOW PRODUCTION QUALITY.
WHO KNOWS, YOU MIGHT LIKE IT...
THE ABADDON
A DINO DE LORENZO PRODUCTION
KEEP YOUR EYES PEELED, NOAH.
WHO KNOWS WHAT TREASURES WE MAY FIND!
I'M NOT SURE WE SHOULD VENTURE HERE, MASTER VINCENT,
THE VILLAGERS SAID THE PLACE IS HAUNTED!!
SHUT!
THE DOOR!
AHHH!!!!

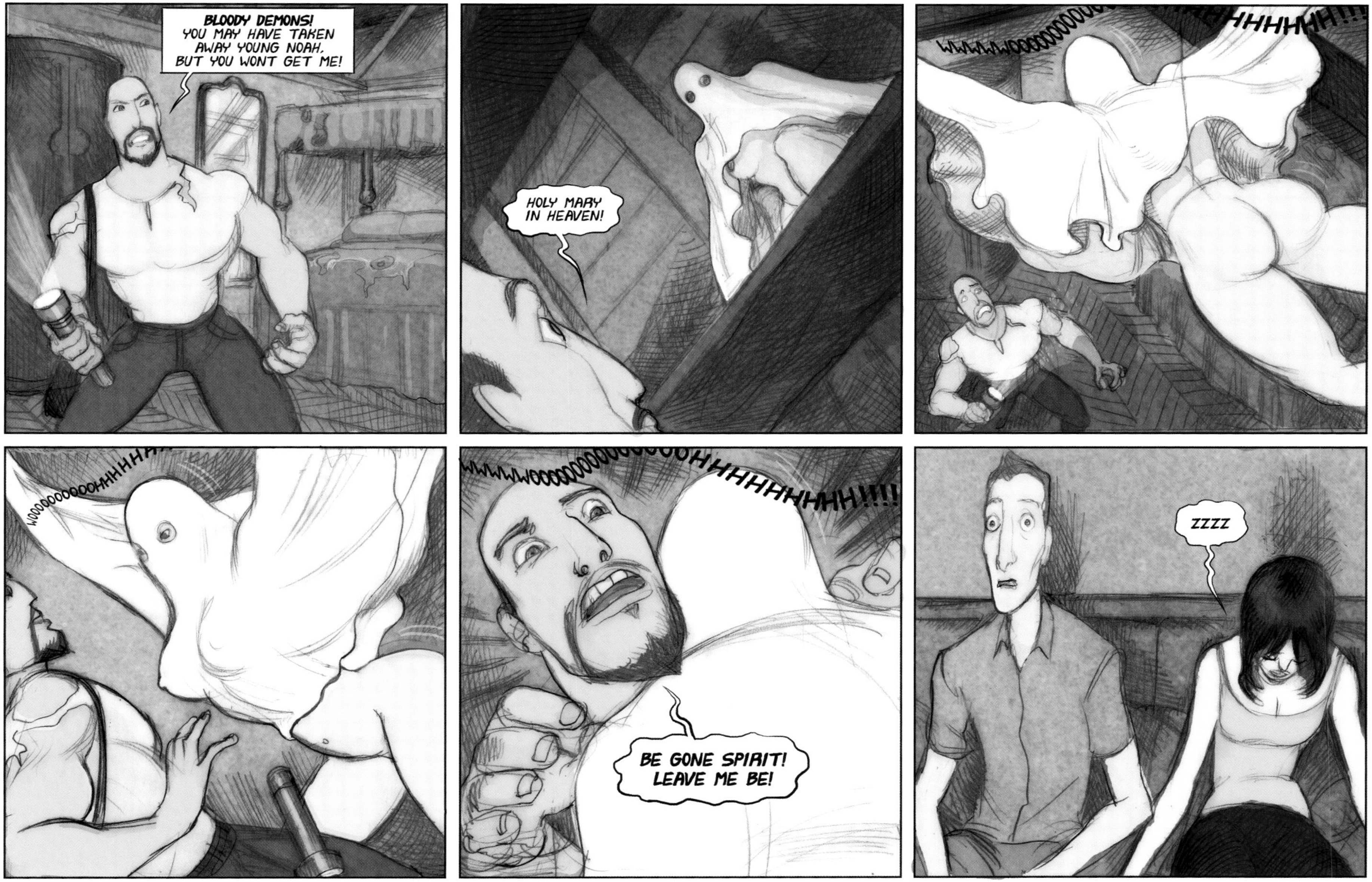
BLOODY DEMONS!
YOU MAY HAVE TAKEN AWAY YOUNG NOAH, BUT YOU WONT GET ME!
HOLY MARY IN HEAVEN!
WWWWWOOOOOOOOOOO
HHHHHHH!!!
WOOOOOOOOOOOHHHHH
WWWWWOOOOOOOOOOOOOOOOHHHHHHHHH!!!!
BE GONE SPIRIT! LEAVE ME BE!
ZZZZ

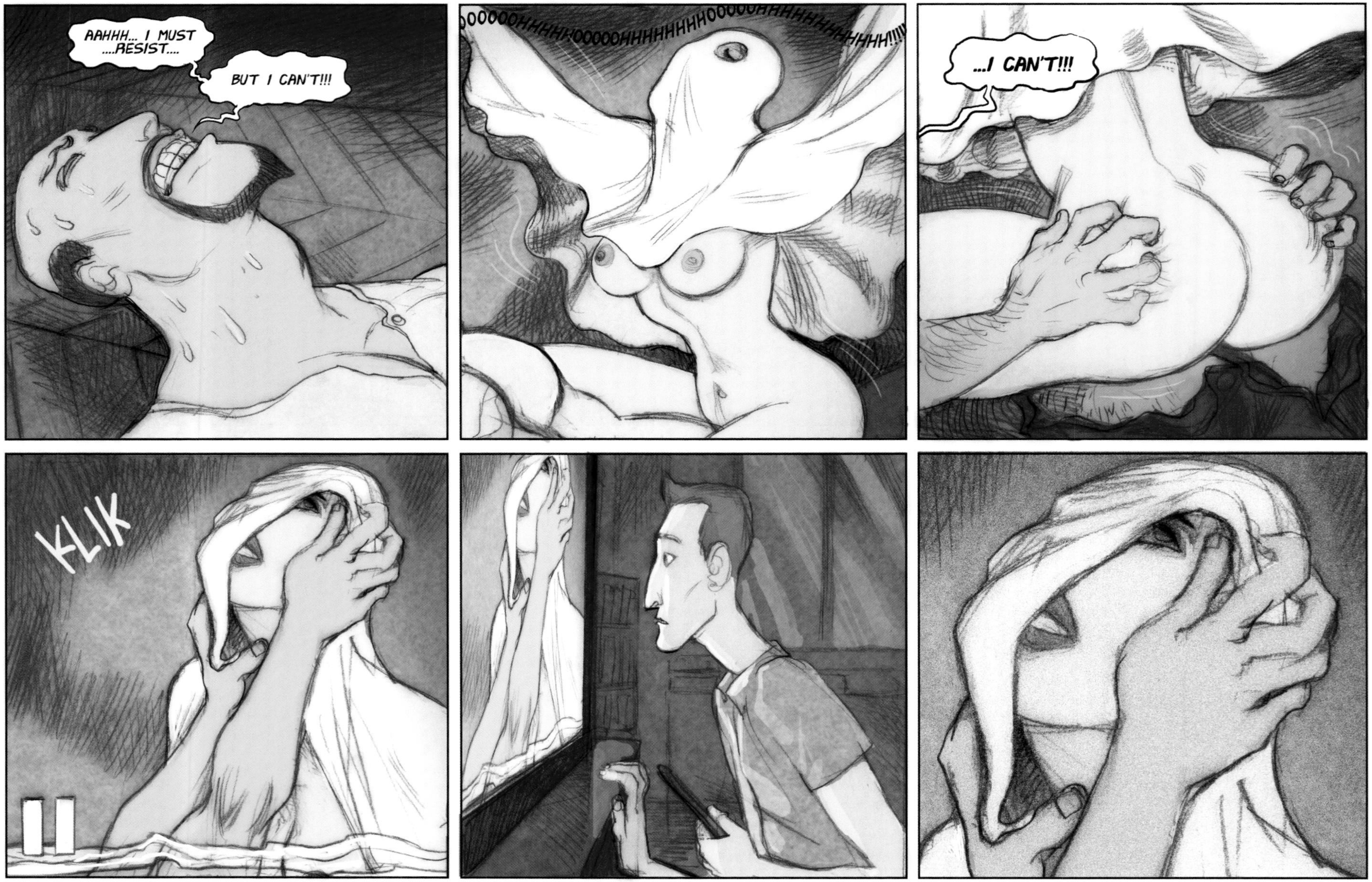
AAHHH... I MUST ....RESIST....
BUT I CAN'T!!!
OOOOOOHHHHHOOOOOOHHHHHHHHHHOOOOOOHHHHHHHHHHH!!!!
...I CAN'T!!!
KLIK

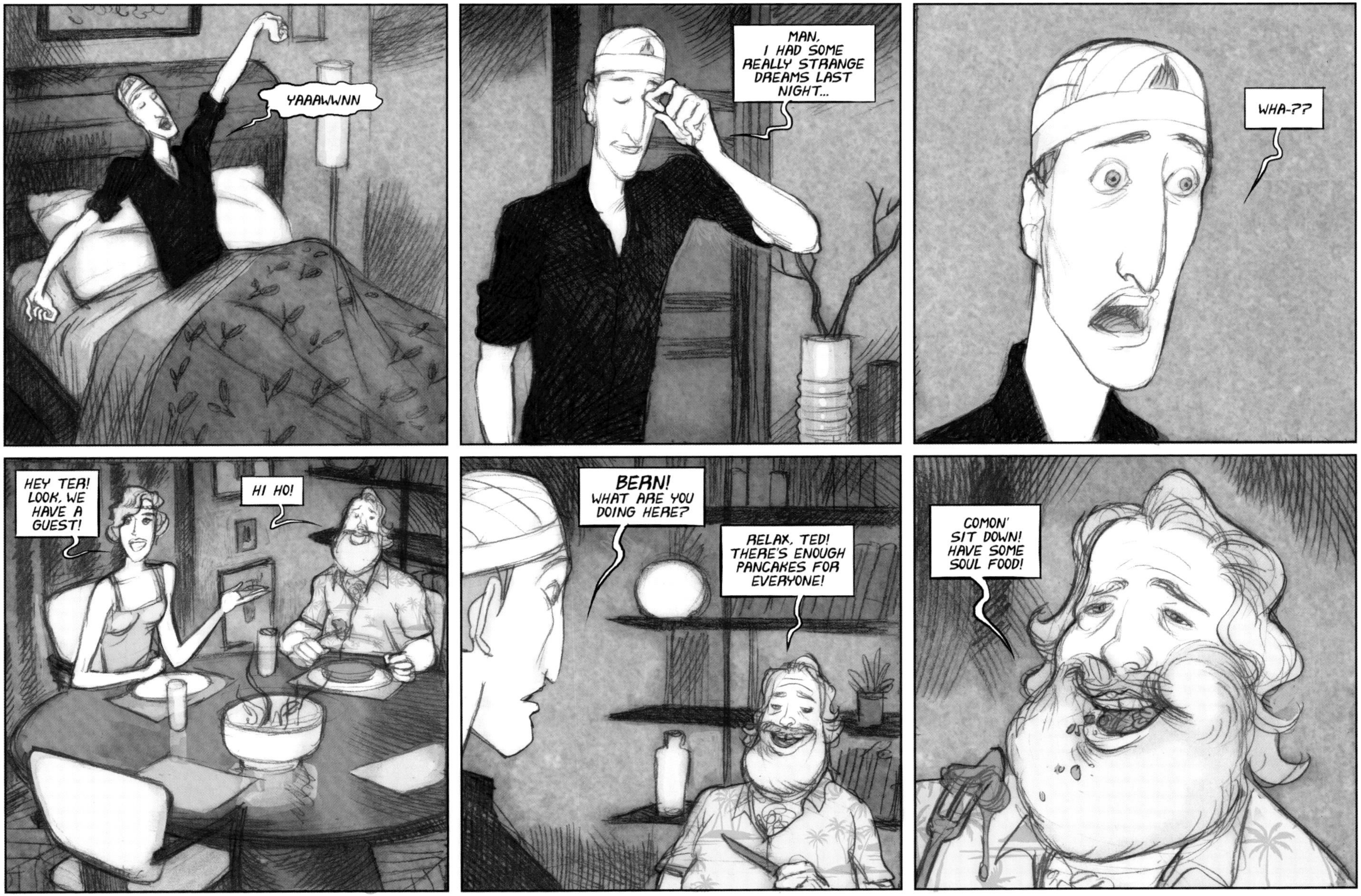
YAAAWWNN
MAN, I HAD SOME REALLY STRANGE DREAMS LAST NIGHT...
WHA-??
HEY TED! LOOK, WE HAVE A GUEST!
HI HO!
BERN! WHAT ARE YOU DOING HERE?
RELAX, TED! THERE'S ENOUGH PANCAKES FOR EVERYONE!
COMON' SIT DOWN! HAVE SOME SOUL FOOD!

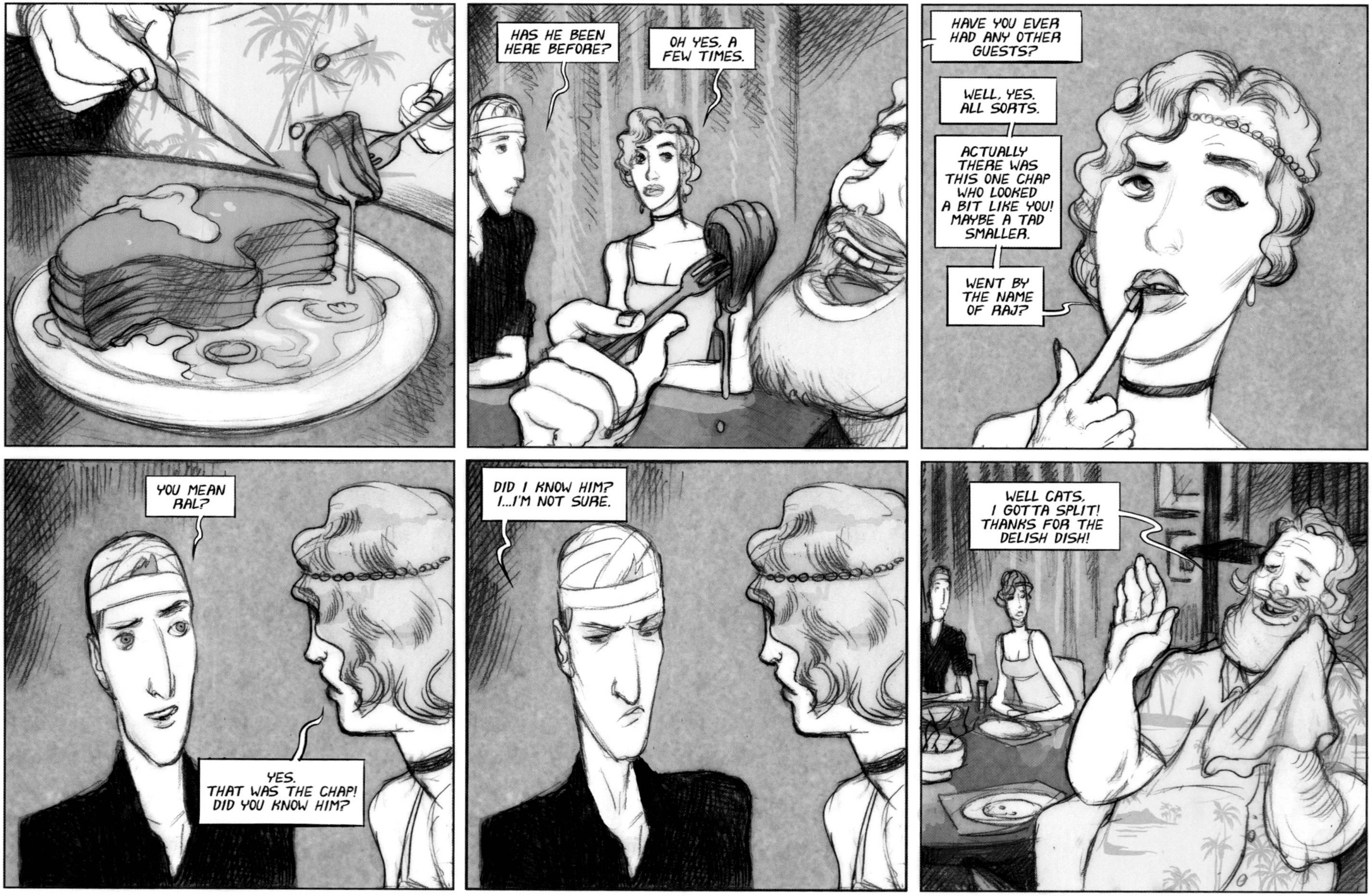
HAS HE BEEN HERE BEFORE?
OH YES, A FEW TIMES.
HAVE YOU EVER HAD ANY OTHER GUESTS?
WELL, YES. ALL SORTS.
ACTUALLY THERE WAS THIS ONE CHAP WHO LOOKED A BIT LIKE YOU! MAYBE A TAD SMALLER.
WENT BY THE NAME OF RAJ?
YOU MEAN RAJ?
YES. THAT WAS THE CHAP! DID YOU KNOW HIM?
DID I KNOW HIM? I...I'M NOT SURE.
WELL CATS, I GOTTA SPLIT! THANKS FOR THE DELISH DISH!

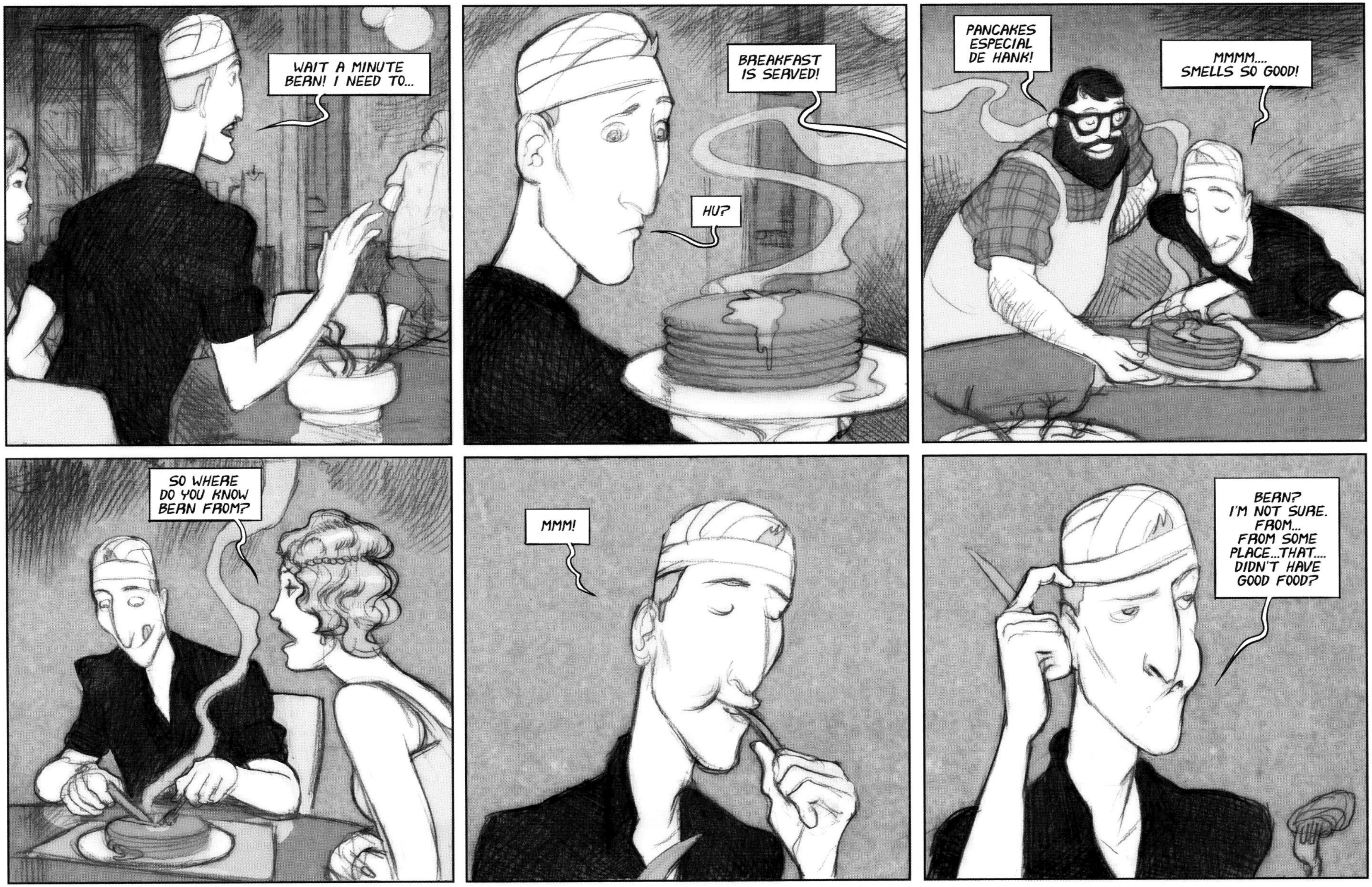
WAIT A MINUTE BERN! I NEED TO...
BREAKFAST IS SERVED!
HU?
PANCAKES ESPECIAL DE HANK!
MMMM.... SMELLS SO GOOD!
SO WHERE DO YOU KNOW BERN FROM?
MMM!
BERN? I'M NOT SURE. FROM... FROM SOME PLACE...THAT.... DIDN'T HAVE GOOD FOOD?

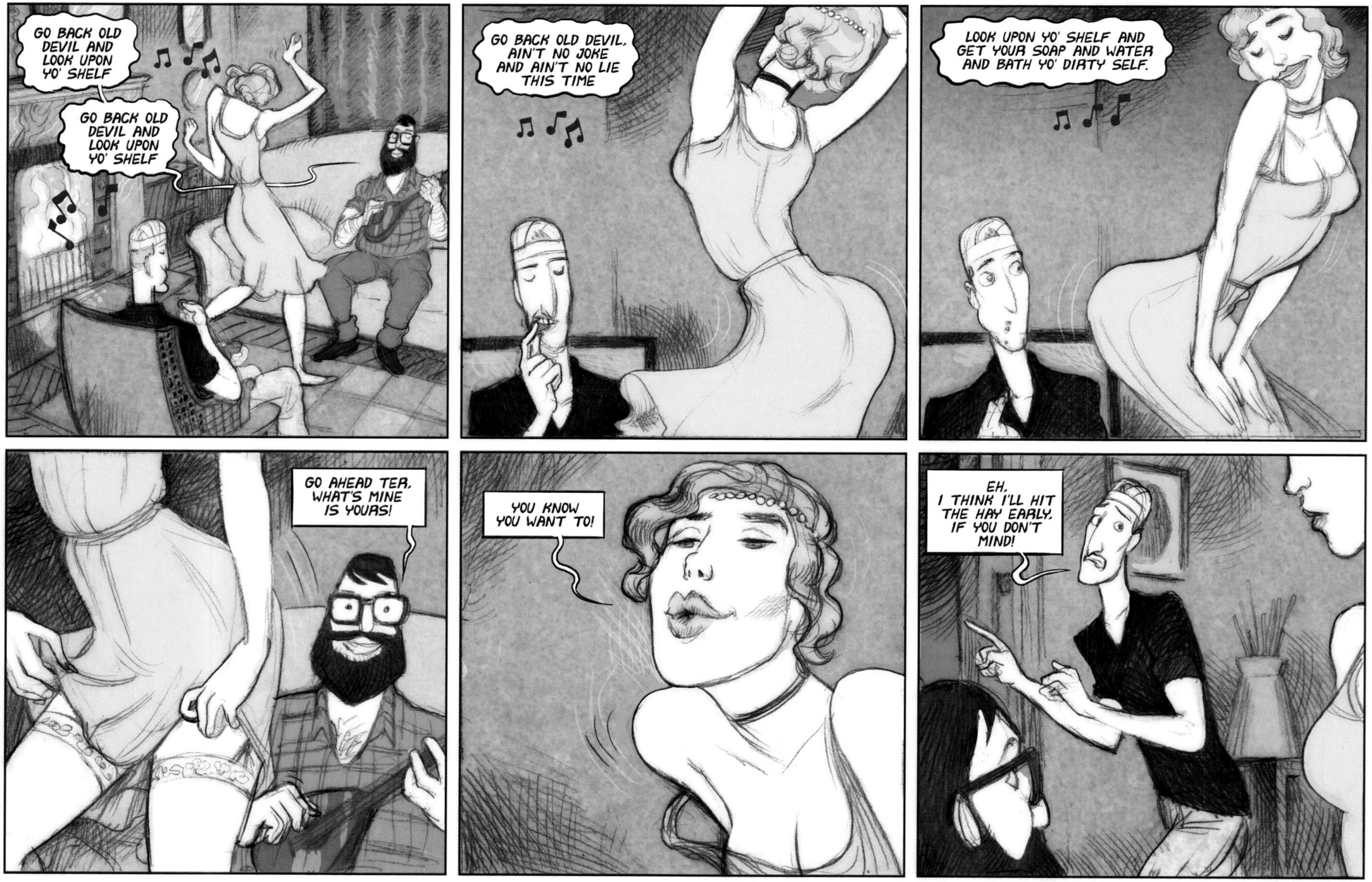
GO BACK OLD DEVIL AND LOOK UPON YO' SHELF
GO BACK OLD DEVIL AND LOOK UPON YO' SHELF
GO BACK OLD DEVIL, AIN'T NO JOKE AND AIN'T NO LIE THIS TIME
LOOK UPON YO' SHELF AND GET YOUR SOAP AND WATER AND BATH YO' DIRTY SELF.
GO AHEAD TER, WHAT'S MINE IS YOURS!
YOU KNOW YOU WANT TO!
EH, I THINK I'LL HIT THE HAY EARLY, IF YOU DON'T MIND!

AHHHHH!!!!
WHAT THE HELL?
AHHHHHHAA!!! AHHHHHH!

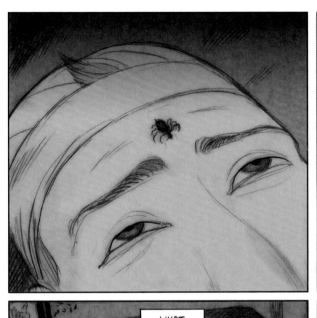

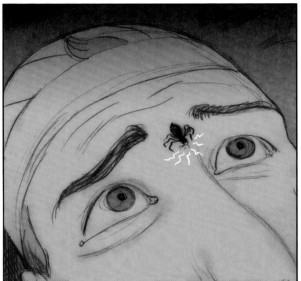

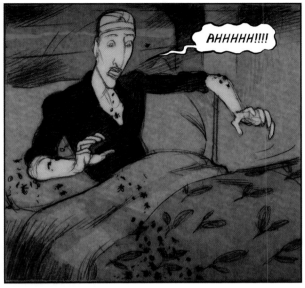

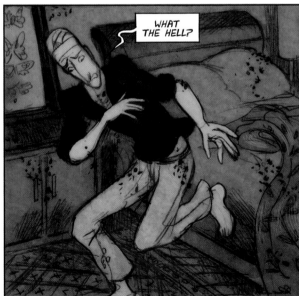

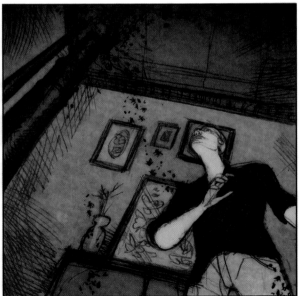

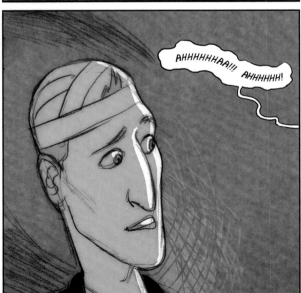

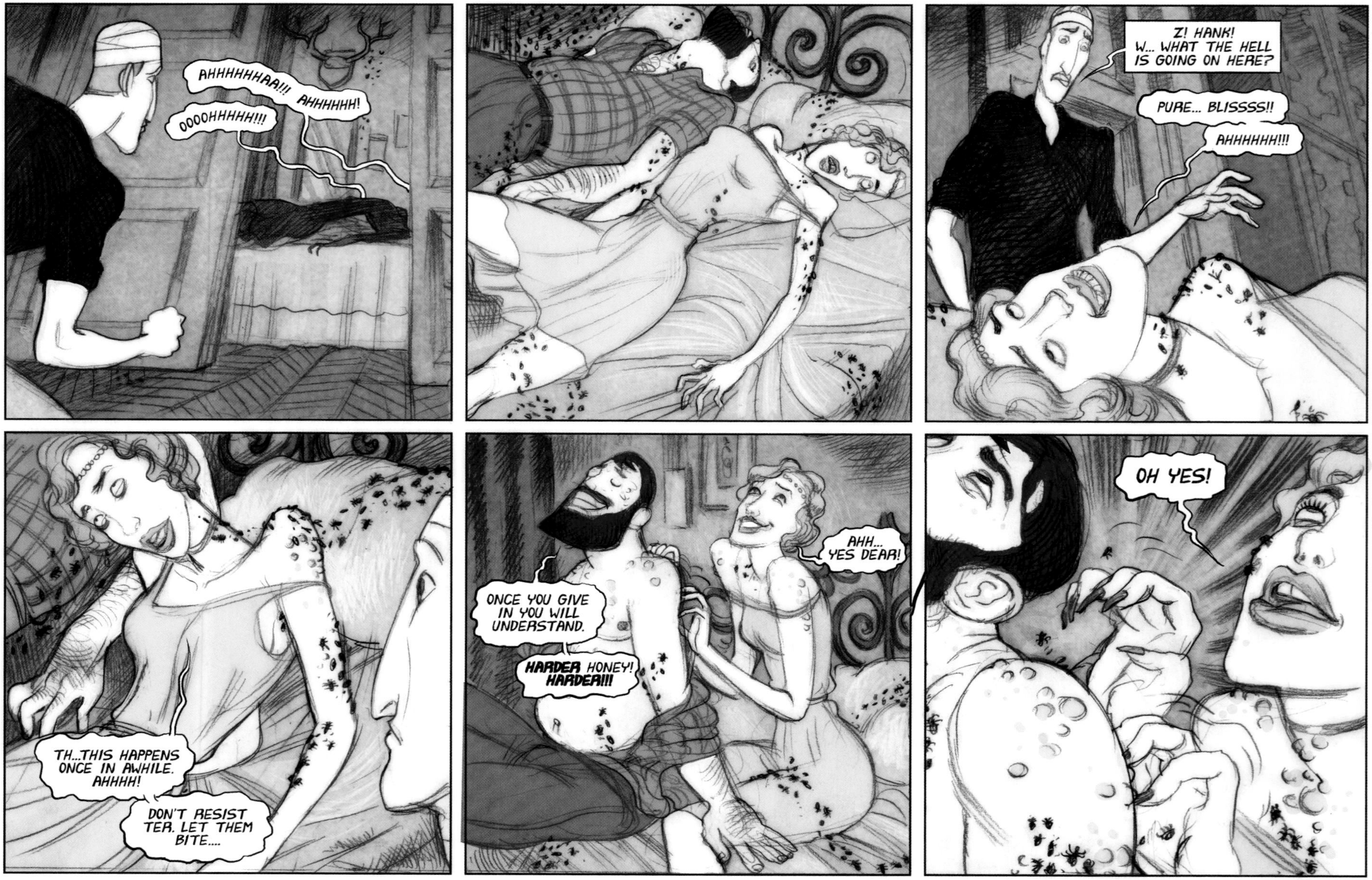
AHHHHHHAA!!! AHHHHHH!
OOOOHHHHH!!!
Z! HANK!
W... WHAT THE HELL
IS GOING ON HERE?
PURE... BLISSSS!!
AHHHHHH!!!
TH...THIS HAPPENS
ONCE IN AWHILE.
AHHHH!
DON'T RESIST
TER. LET THEM
BITE....
ONCE YOU GIVE
IN YOU WILL
UNDERSTAND.
HARDER HONEY!
HARDER!!!
AHH...
YES DEAR!
OH YES!

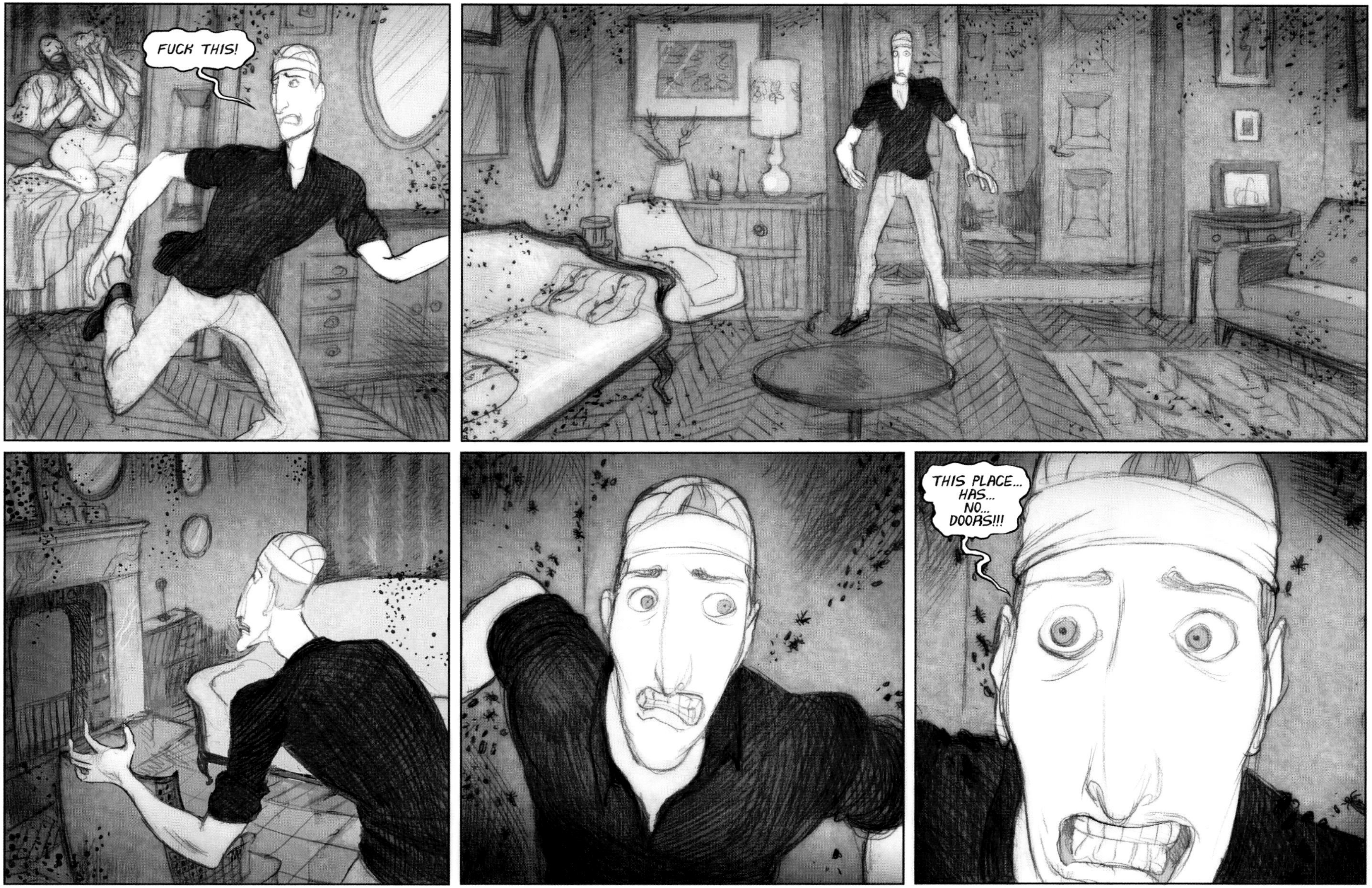
FUCK THIS!
THIS PLACE... HAS... NO... DOORS!!!

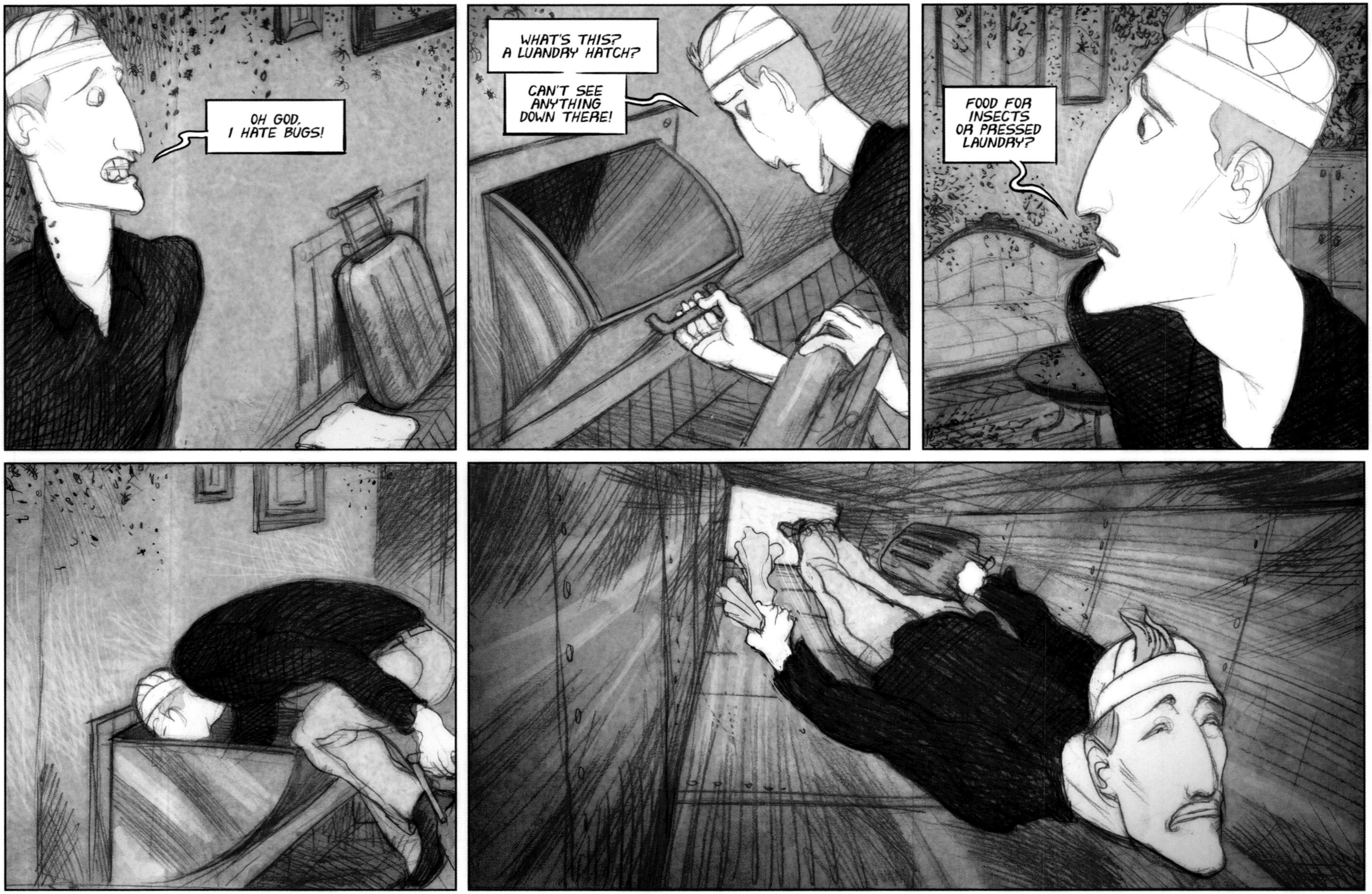
OH GOD, I HATE BUGS!
WHAT'S THIS? A LUANDRY HATCH?
CAN'T SEE ANYTHING DOWN THERE!
FOOD FOR INSECTS OR PRESSED LAUNDRY?

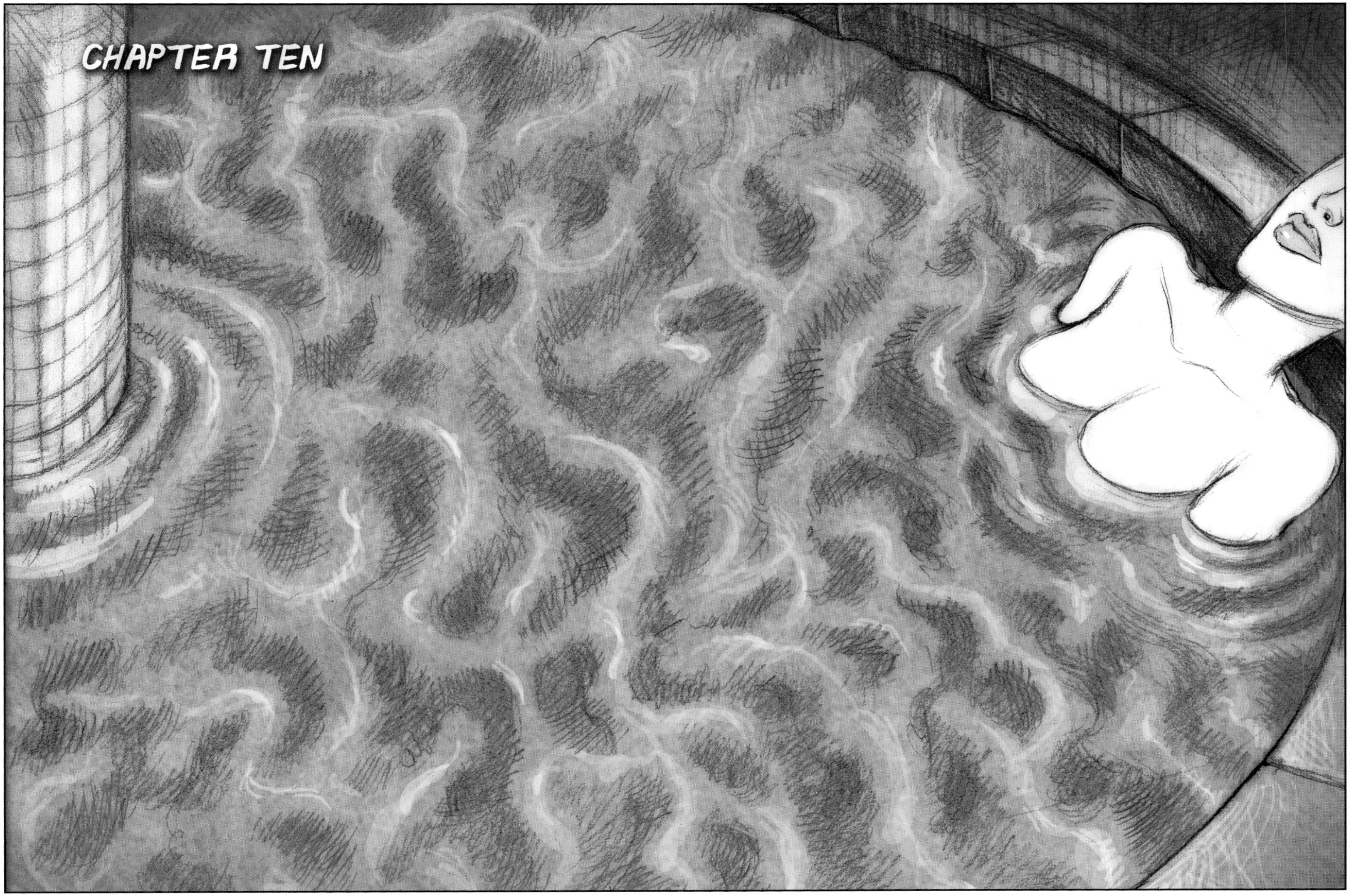
CHAPTER TEN

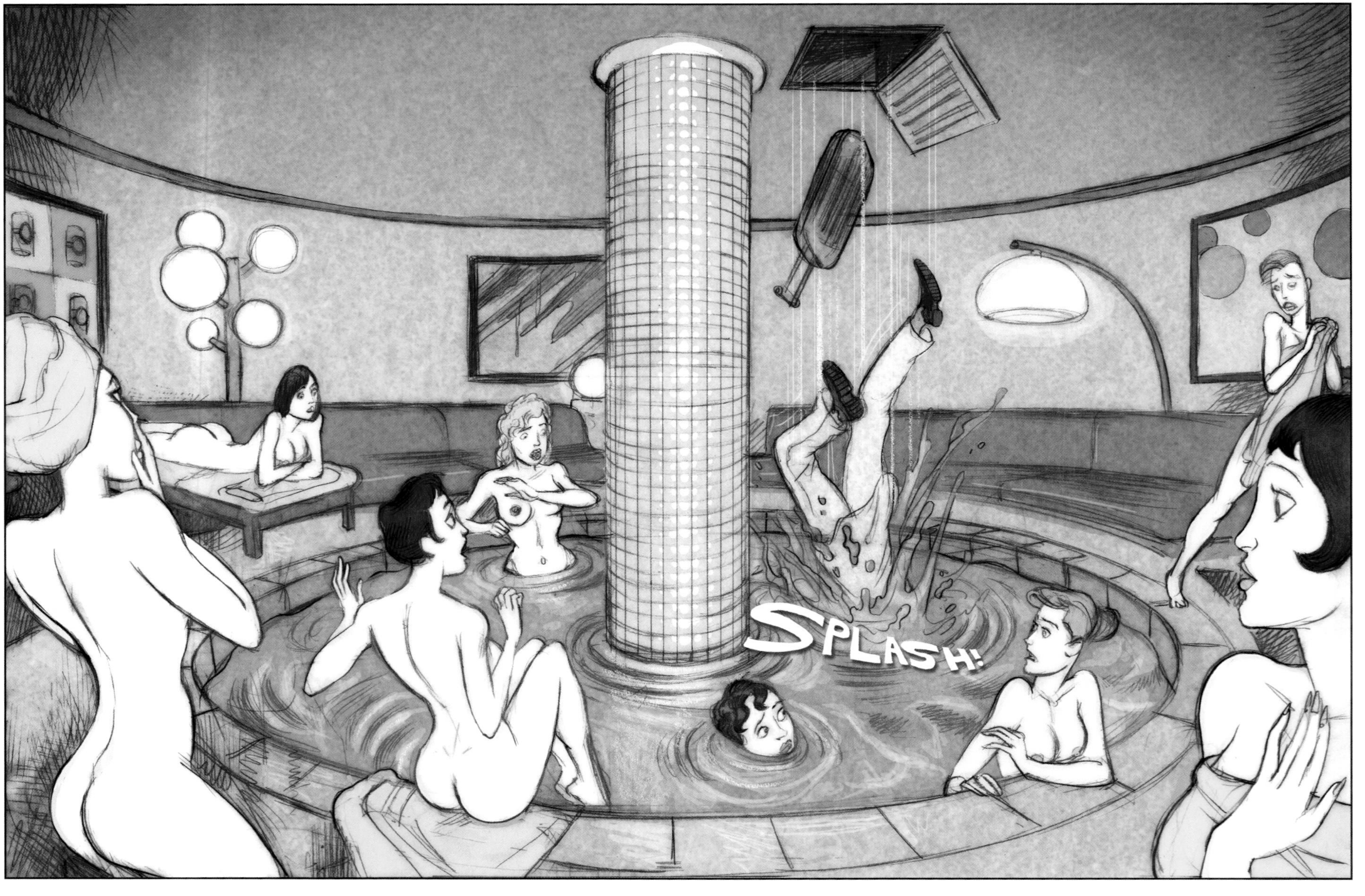
SPLASH!

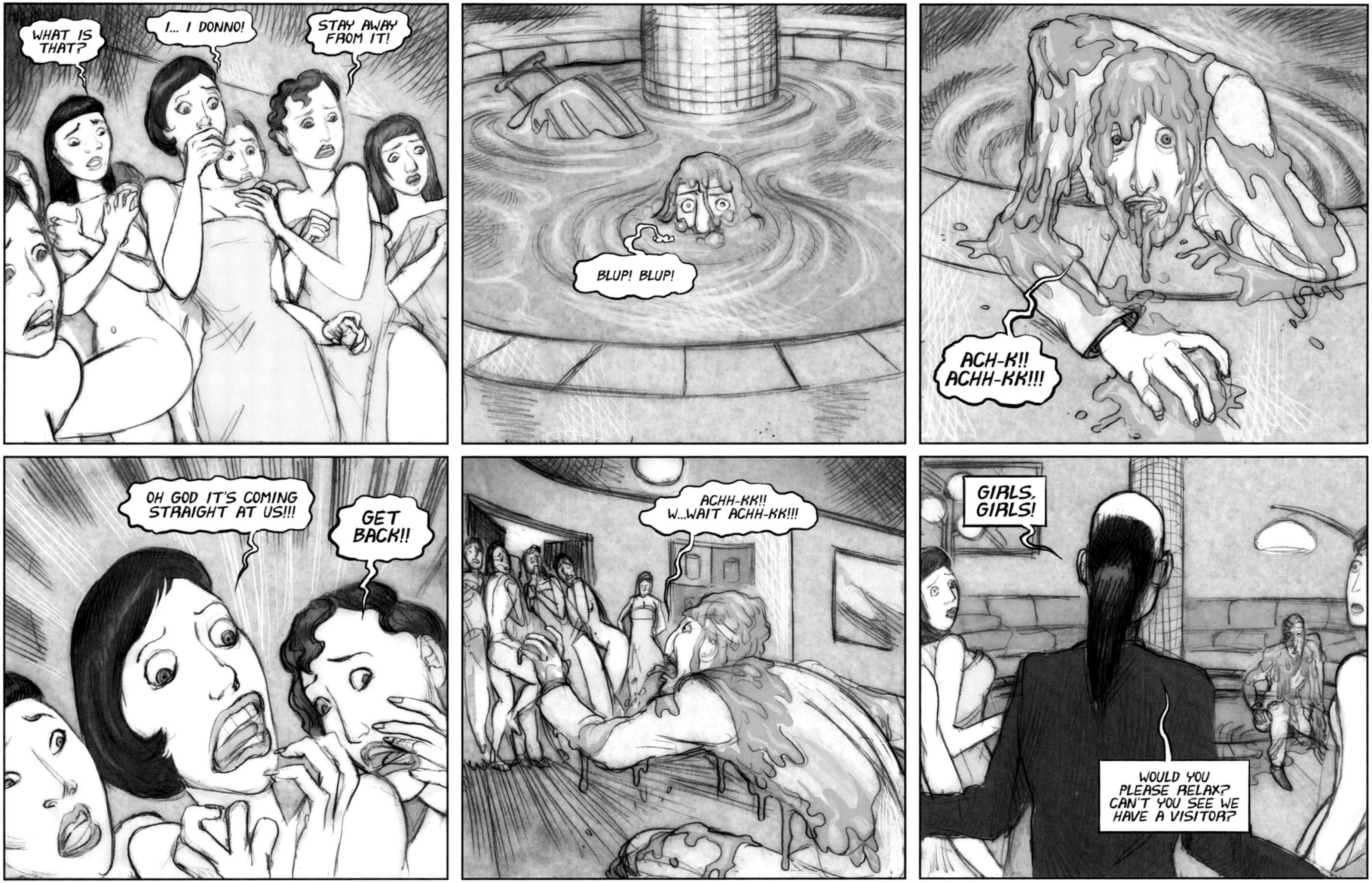
WHAT IS THAT?
I... I DONNO!
STAY AWAY FROM IT!
BLUP! BLUP!
ACH-K!! ACHH-KK!!!
OH GOD IT'S COMING STRAIGHT AT US!!!
GET BACK!!
ACHH-KK!! W...WAIT ACHH-KK!!!
GIRLS, GIRLS!
WOULD YOU PLEASE RELAX? CAN'T YOU SEE WE HAVE A VISITOR?

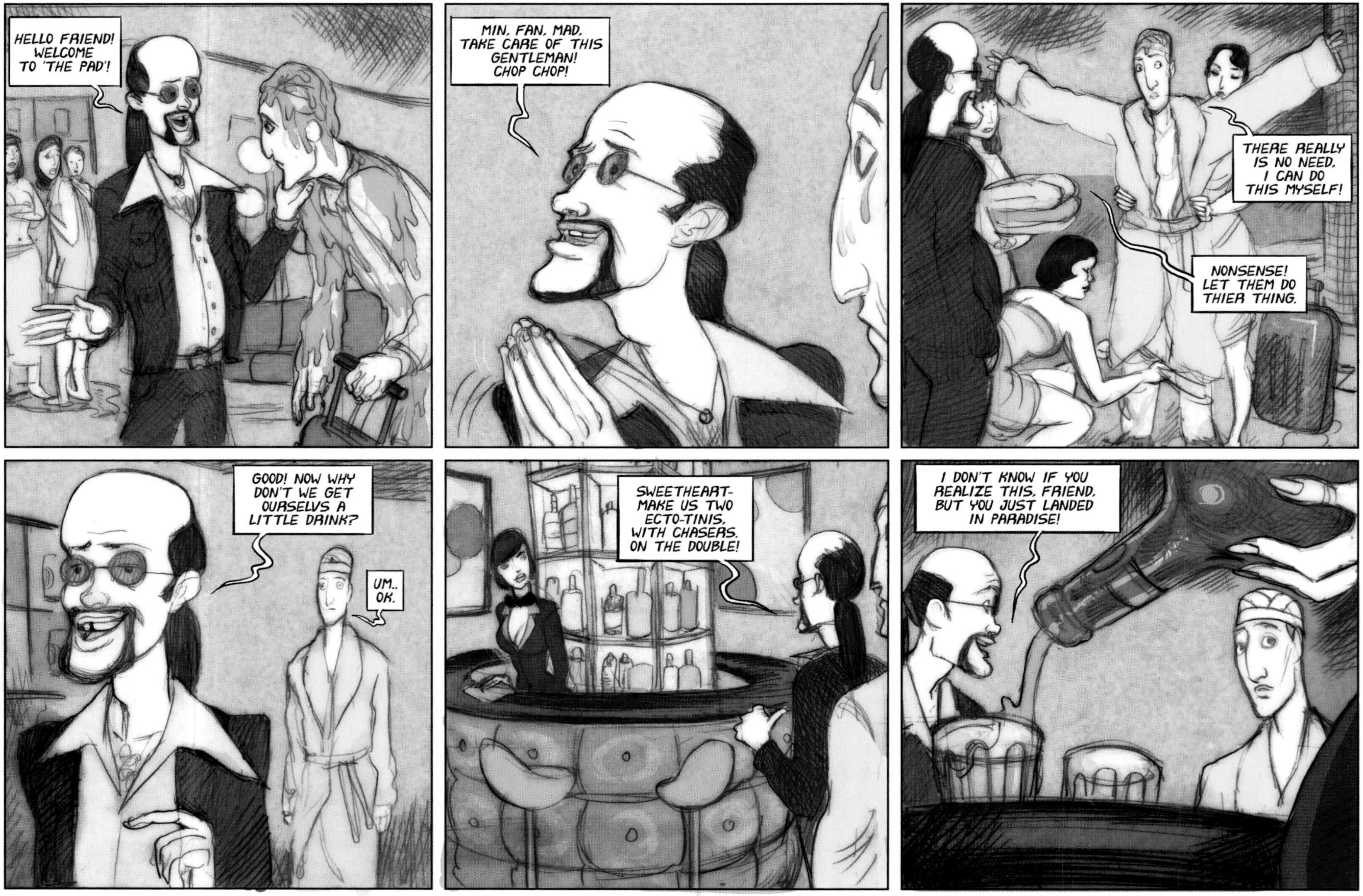
HELLO FRIEND! WELCOME TO 'THE PAD'!
MIN, FAN, MAD, TAKE CARE OF THIS GENTLEMAN! CHOP CHOP!
THERE REALLY IS NO NEED, I CAN DO THIS MYSELF!
NONSENSE! LET THEM DO THIER THING.
GOOD! NOW WHY DON'T WE GET OURSELVS A LITTLE DRINK?
UM.. OK.
SWEETHEART- MAKE US TWO ECTO-TINIS, WITH CHASERS. ON THE DOUBLE!
I DON'T KNOW IF YOU REALIZE THIS, FRIEND, BUT YOU JUST LANDED IN PARADISE!

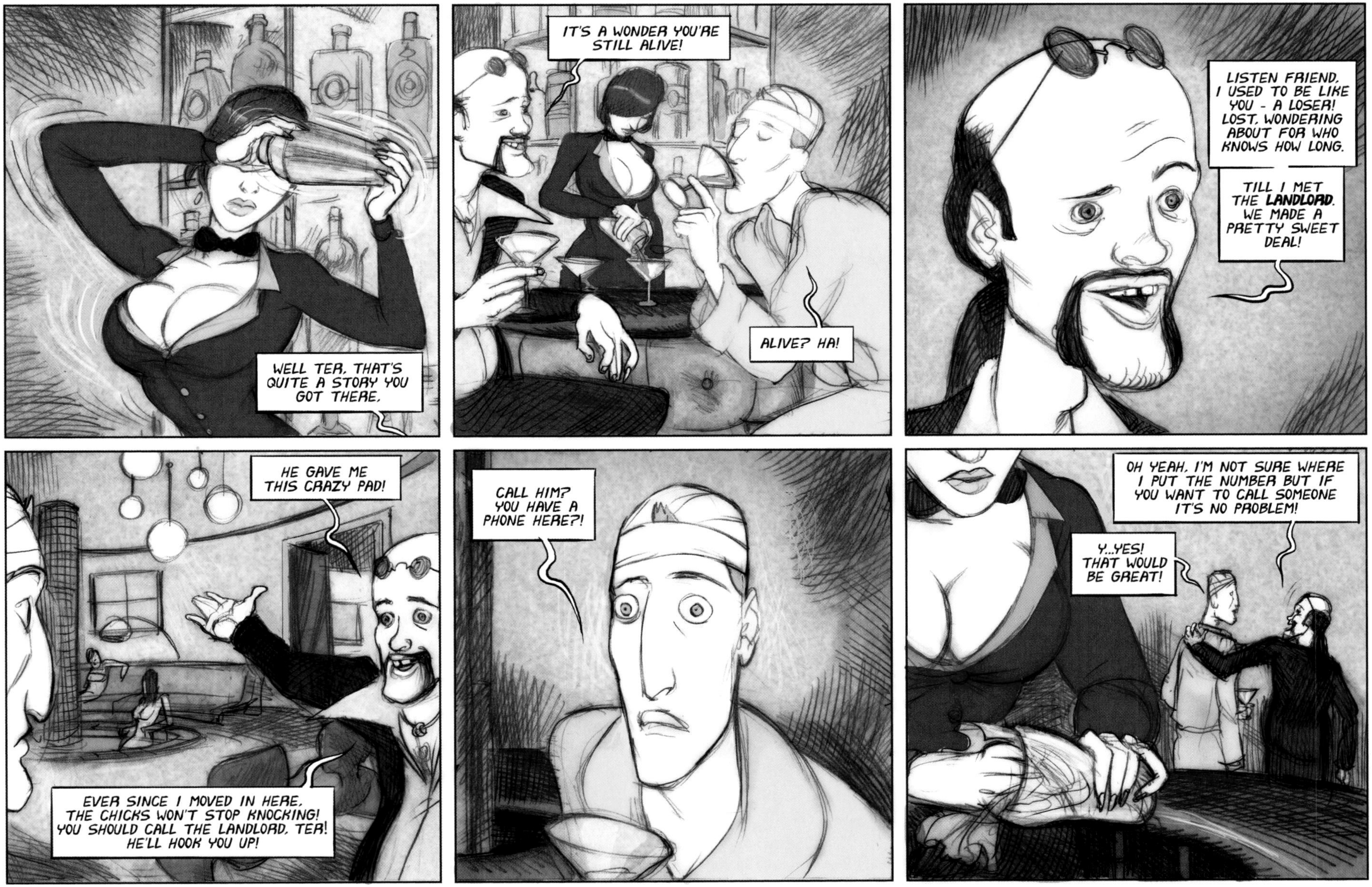
WELL TER, THAT'S QUITE A STORY YOU GOT THERE.
IT'S A WONDER YOU'RE STILL ALIVE!
ALIVE? HA!
LISTEN FRIEND, I USED TO BE LIKE YOU - A LOSER! LOST, WONDERING ABOUT FOR WHO KNOWS HOW LONG.
TILL I MET THE **LANDLORD**. WE MADE A PRETTY SWEET DEAL!
HE GAVE ME THIS CRAZY PAD!
EVER SINCE I MOVED IN HERE, THE CHICKS WON'T STOP KNOCKING! YOU SHOULD CALL THE LANDLORD, TER! HE'LL HOOK YOU UP!
CALL HIM? YOU HAVE A PHONE HERE?!
OH YEAH, I'M NOT SURE WHERE I PUT THE NUMBER BUT IF YOU WANT TO CALL SOMEONE IT'S NO PROBLEM!
Y...YES! THAT WOULD BE GREAT!

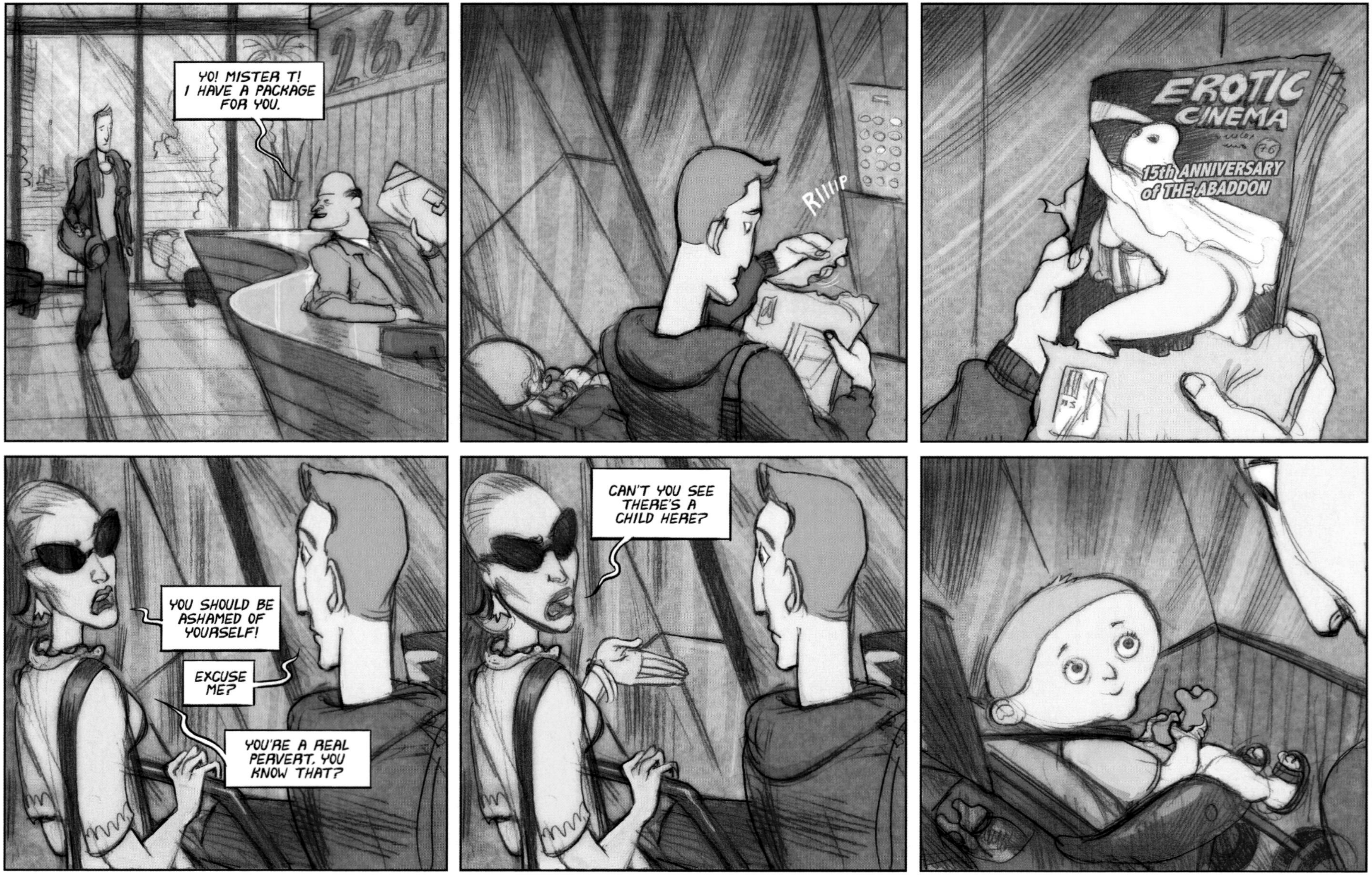
262
YO! MISTER T! I HAVE A PACKAGE FOR YOU.
RIIIIP
EROTIC CINEMA
15th ANNIVERSARY of THE ABADDON
YOU SHOULD BE ASHAMED OF YOURSELF!
EXCUSE ME?
YOU'RE A REAL PERVERT, YOU KNOW THAT?
CAN'T YOU SEE THERE'S A CHILD HERE?

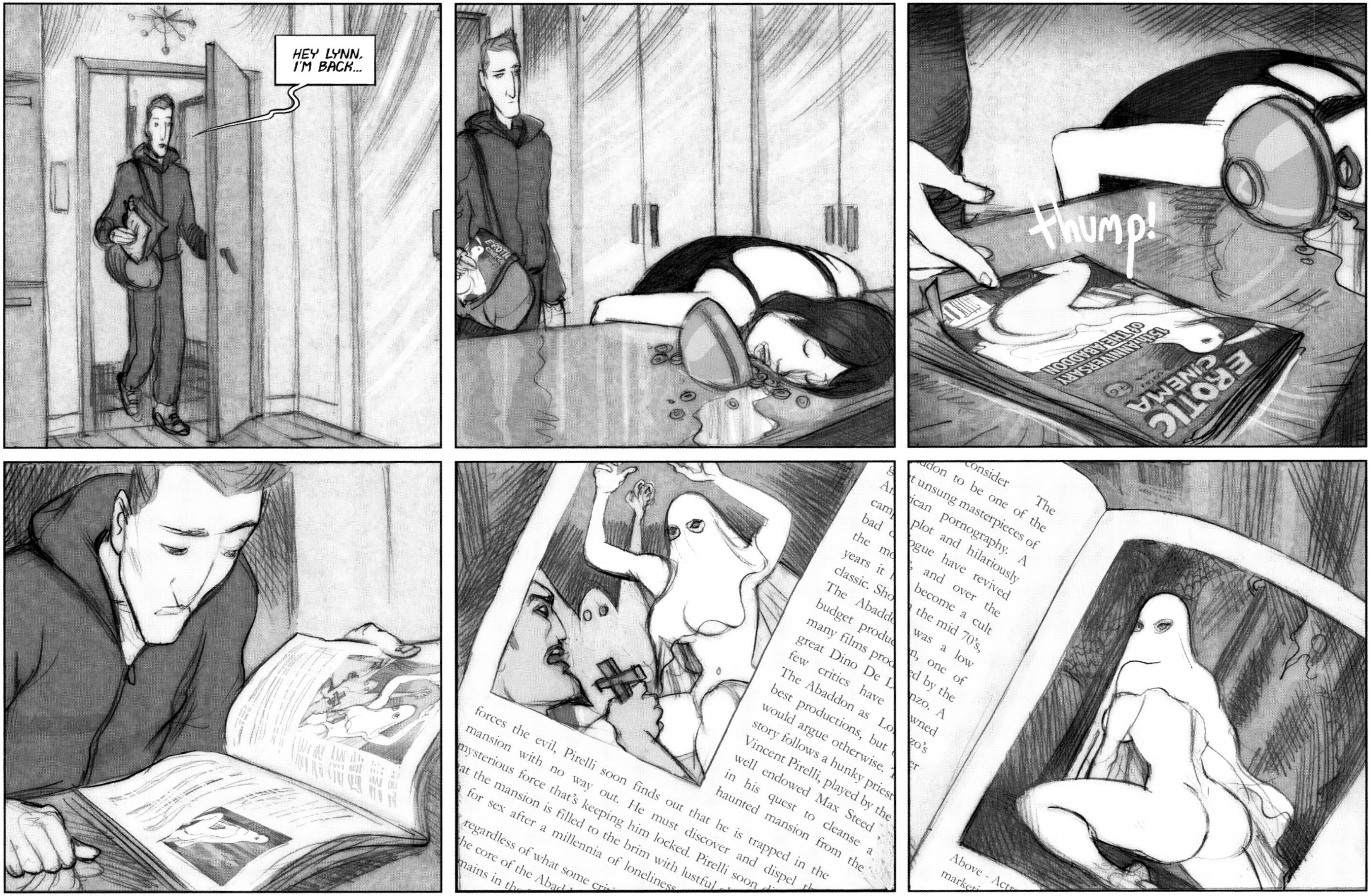
HEY LYNN. I'M BACK...
EROTIC CINEMA
thump!
EROTIC CINEMA
15th ANNIVERSARY OF THE ABADDON
forces the evil, Pirelli soon finds out that he is trapped in the
mansion with no way out. He must discover and dispel
mysterious force that's keeping him locked. Pirelli soon
at the mansion is filled to the brim with lustful
for sex after a millennia of loneliness
regardless of what some cri
the core of the Abad
The Abaddon as
few critics have
best productions, but
would argue otherwise,
story follows a hunky priest
Vincent Pirelli, played by the
well endowed Max Steed
in his quest to cleanse a
haunted mansion from the
consider
The
unsung masterpieces of the
pornography. A
plot and hilariously
have revived
and over the
become a cult
the mid 70's,
was a low
one of
by the
Above - Actr
marketi

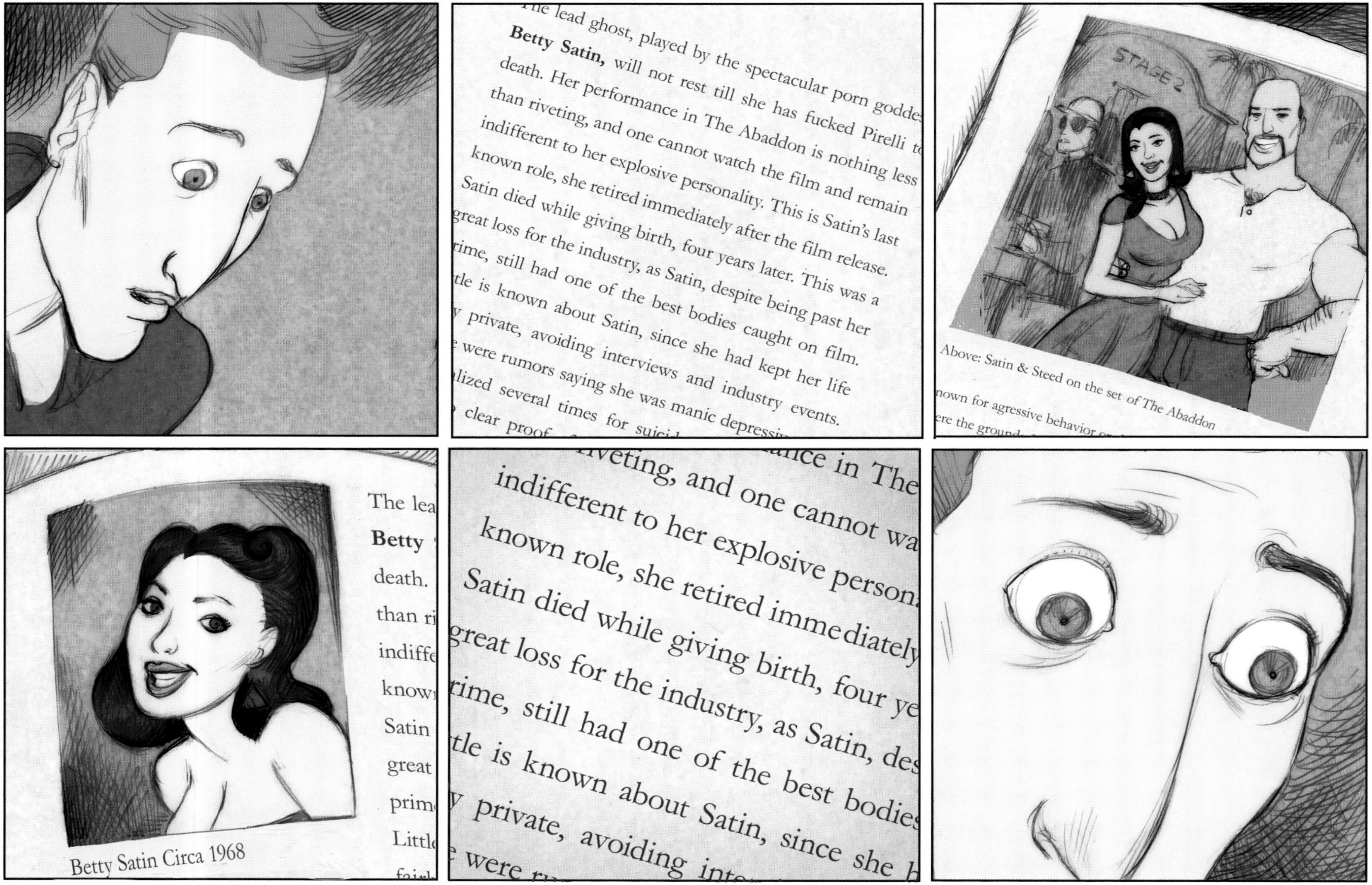
he lead ghost, played by the spectacular porn godde
Betty Satin, will not rest till she has fucked Pirelli t
death. Her performance in The Abaddon is nothing less
than riveting, and one cannot watch the film and remain
indifferent to her explosive personality. This is Satin's last
known role, she retired immediately after the film release.
Satin died while giving birth, four years later. This was a
great loss for the industry, as Satin, despite being past her
rime, still had one of the best bodies caught on film.
tle is known about Satin, since she had kept her life
private, avoiding interviews and industry events.
were rumors saying she was manic depress
lized several times for suici
clear proof
STAGE 2
Above: Satin & Steed on the set of The Abaddon
nown for agressive behavior o
ere the ground
The lea
Betty
death.
than ri
indiffe
know
Satin
great
prim
Littl
Betty Satin Circa 1968
iveting, and one cannot wa
indifferent to her explosive person
known role, she retired immediately
Satin died while giving birth, four ye
great loss for the industry, as Satin, des
rime, still had one of the best bodies
tle is known about Satin, since she h
private, avoiding inte
were

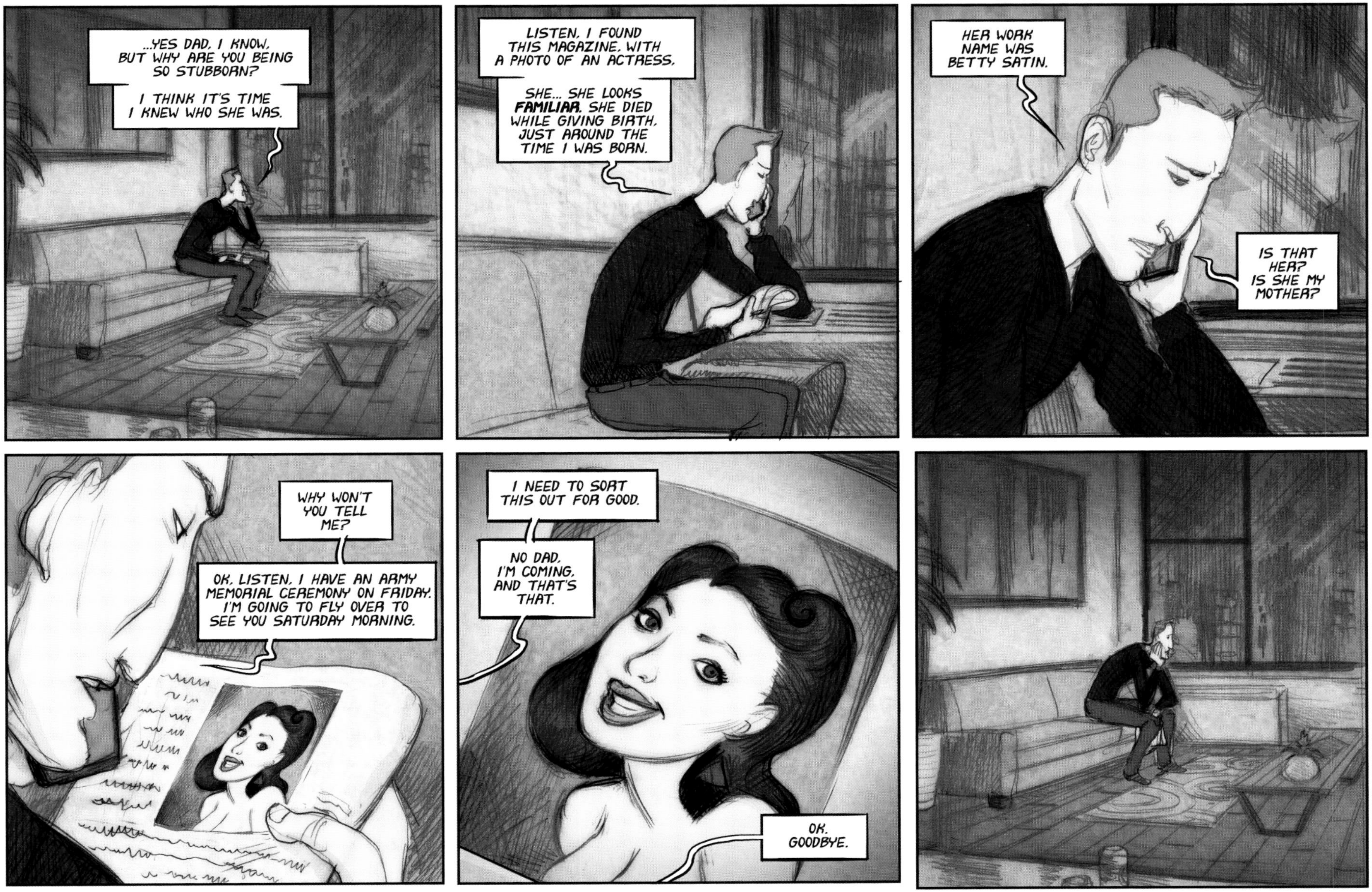
...YES DAD, I KNOW, BUT WHY ARE YOU BEING SO STUBBORN?
I THINK IT'S TIME I KNEW WHO SHE WAS.
LISTEN, I FOUND THIS MAGAZINE, WITH A PHOTO OF AN ACTRESS.
SHE... SHE LOOKS **FAMILIAR**. SHE DIED WHILE GIVING BIRTH, JUST AROUND THE TIME I WAS BORN.
HER WORK NAME WAS BETTY SATIN.
IS THAT HER? IS SHE MY MOTHER?
WHY WON'T YOU TELL ME?
OK, LISTEN, I HAVE AN ARMY MEMORIAL CEREMONY ON FRIDAY. I'M GOING TO FLY OVER TO SEE YOU SATURDAY MORNING.
I NEED TO SORT THIS OUT FOR GOOD.
NO DAD, I'M COMING, AND THAT'S THAT.
OK. GOODBYE.

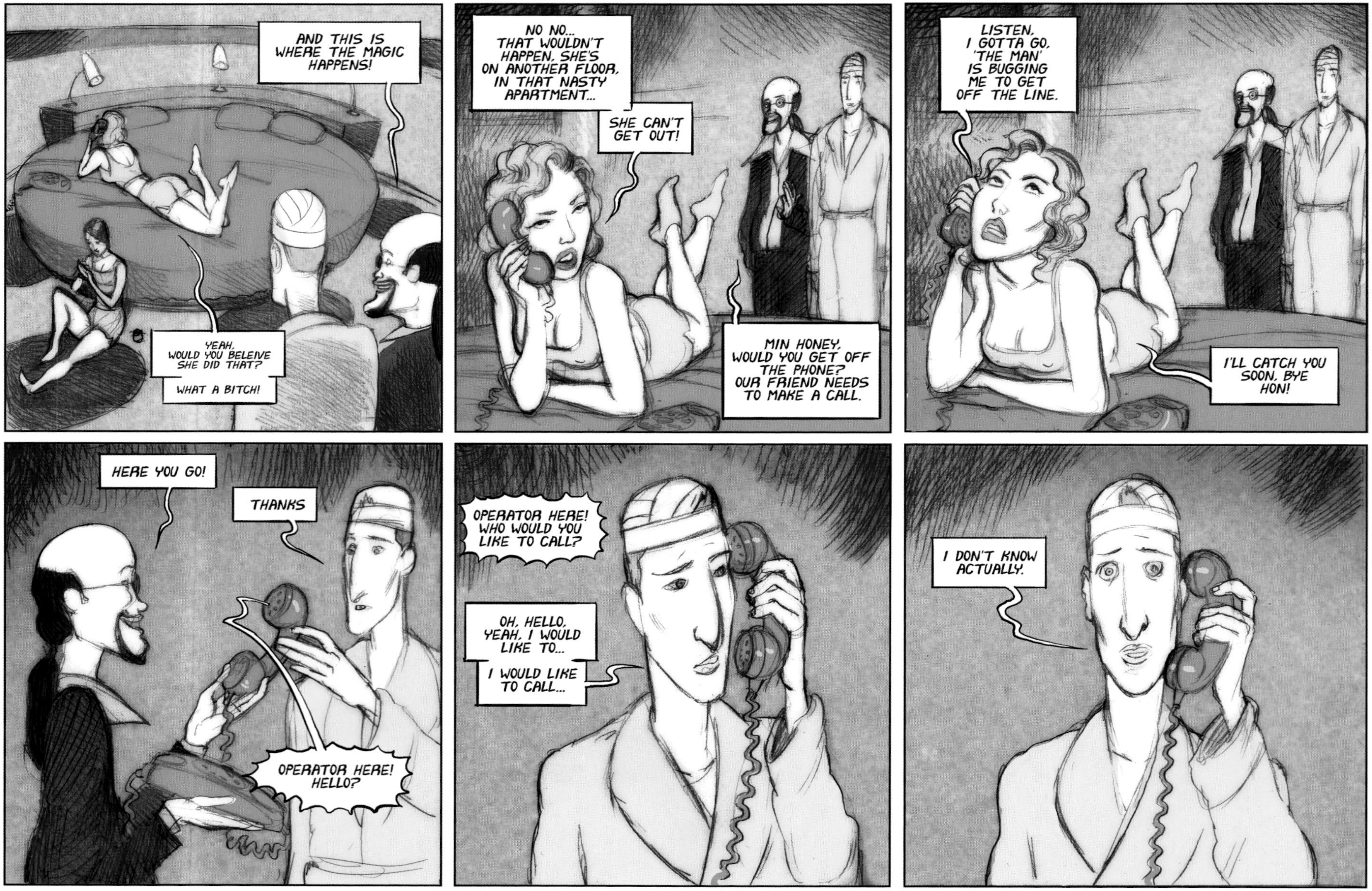
AND THIS IS WHERE THE MAGIC HAPPENS!
YEAH, WOULD YOU BELEIVE SHE DID THAT?
WHAT A BITCH!
NO NO... THAT WOULDN'T HAPPEN, SHE'S ON ANOTHER FLOOR, IN THAT NASTY APARTMENT...
SHE CAN'T GET OUT!
MIN HONEY, WOULD YOU GET OFF THE PHONE? OUR FRIEND NEEDS TO MAKE A CALL.
LISTEN, I GOTTA GO, 'THE MAN' IS BUGGING ME TO GET OFF THE LINE.
I'LL CATCH YOU SOON, BYE HON!
HERE YOU GO!
THANKS
OPERATOR HERE! HELLO?
OPERATOR HERE! WHO WOULD YOU LIKE TO CALL?
OH, HELLO, YEAH, I WOULD LIKE TO...
I WOULD LIKE TO CALL...
I DON'T KNOW ACTUALLY.

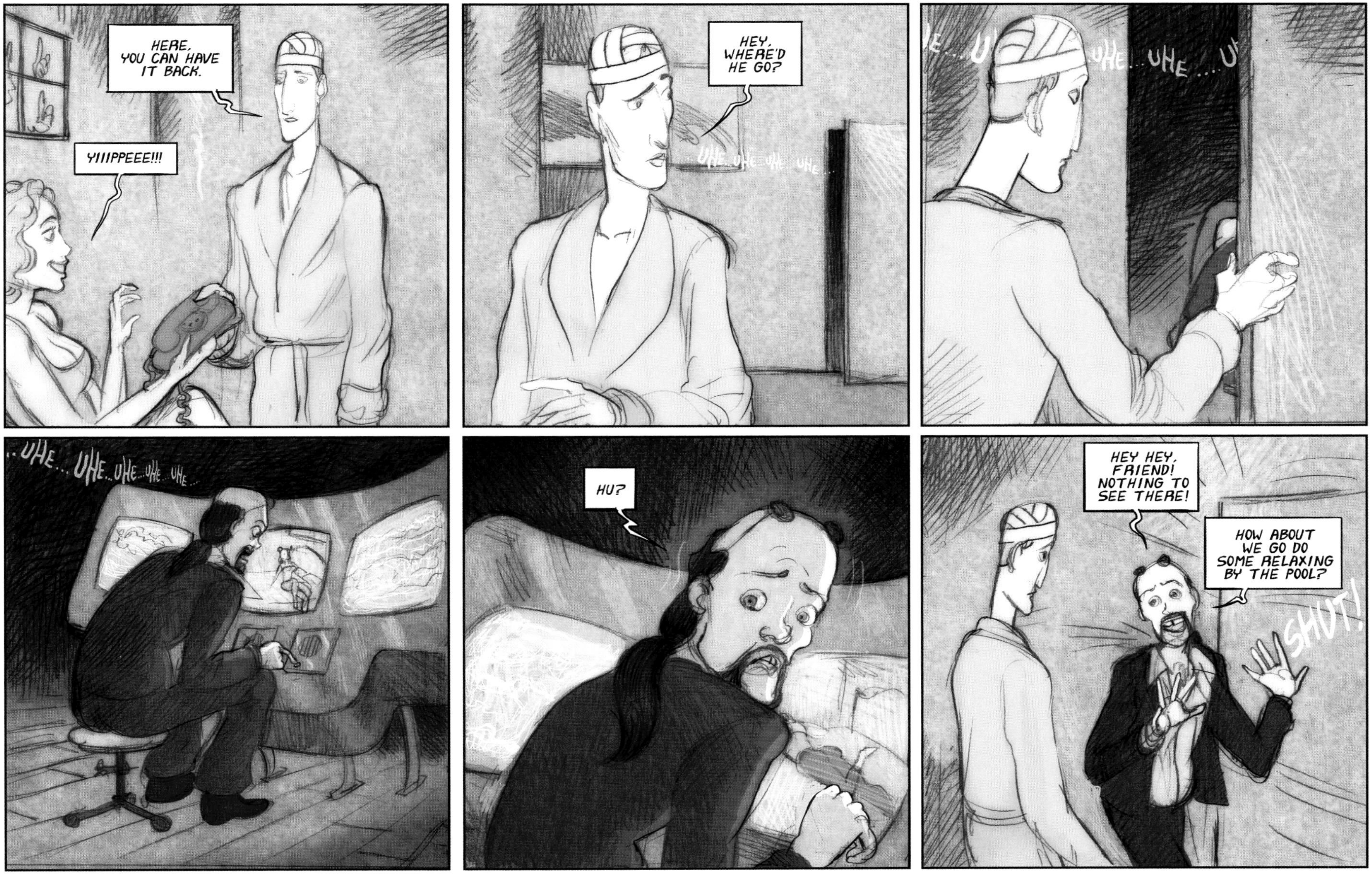
HERE, YOU CAN HAVE IT BACK.
YIIIPPEEE!!!
HEY, WHERE'D HE GO?
UHE... UHE... UHE... UHE...
HU?
HEY HEY, FRIEND! NOTHING TO SEE THERE!
HOW ABOUT WE GO DO SOME RELAXING BY THE POOL?
SHUT!

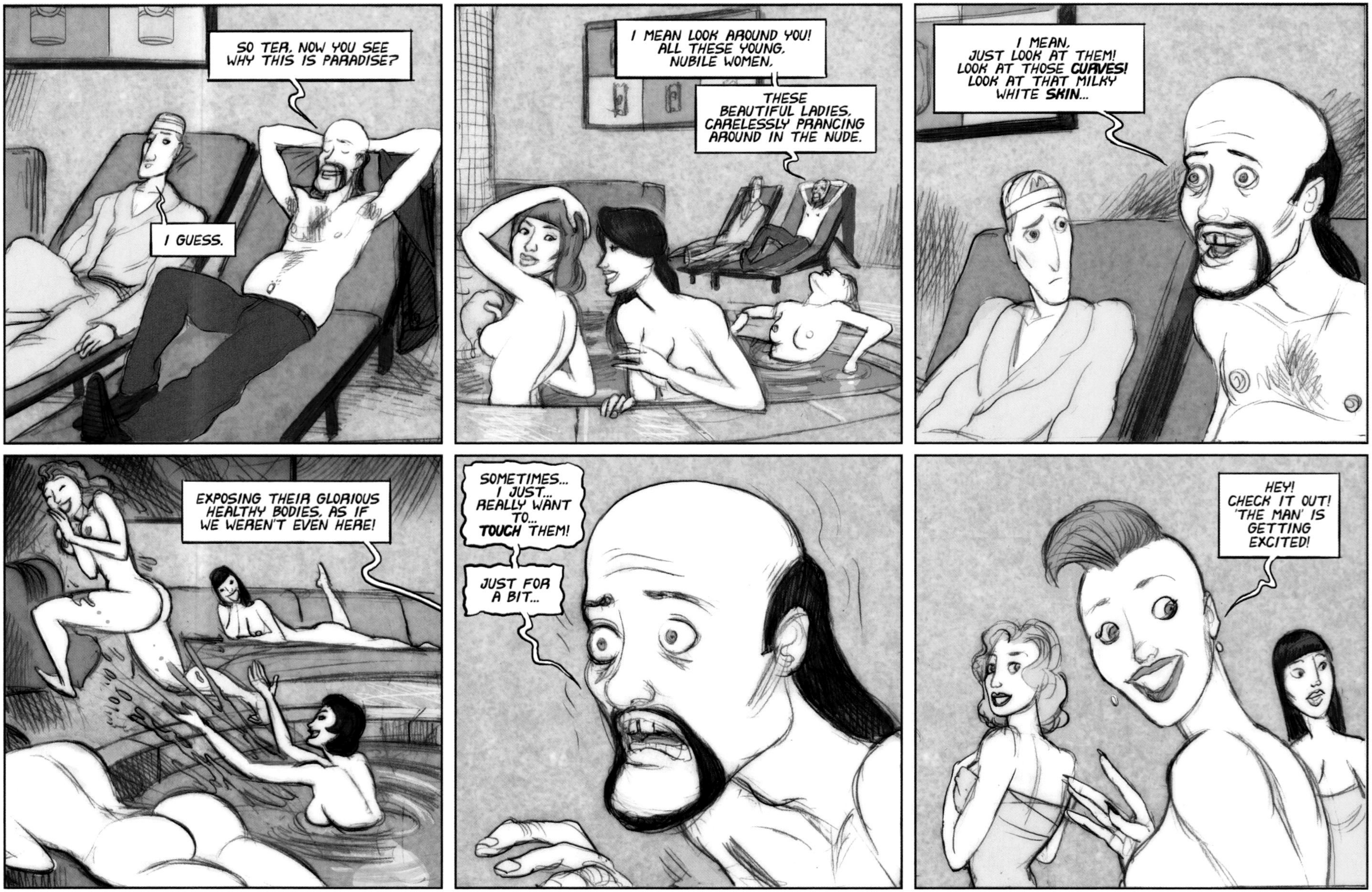
SO TEA, NOW YOU SEE WHY THIS IS PARADISE?
I GUESS.
I MEAN LOOK AROUND YOU! ALL THESE YOUNG, NUBILE WOMEN,
THESE BEAUTIFUL LADIES, CARELESSLY PRANCING AROUND IN THE NUDE.
I MEAN, JUST LOOK AT THEM! LOOK AT THOSE **CURVES!** LOOK AT THAT MILKY WHITE **SKIN**...
EXPOSING THEIR GLORIOUS HEALTHY BODIES, AS IF WE WEREN'T EVEN HERE!
SOMETIMES... I JUST... REALLY WANT TO... **TOUCH** THEM!
JUST FOR A BIT...
HEY! CHECK IT OUT! 'THE MAN' IS GETTING EXCITED!

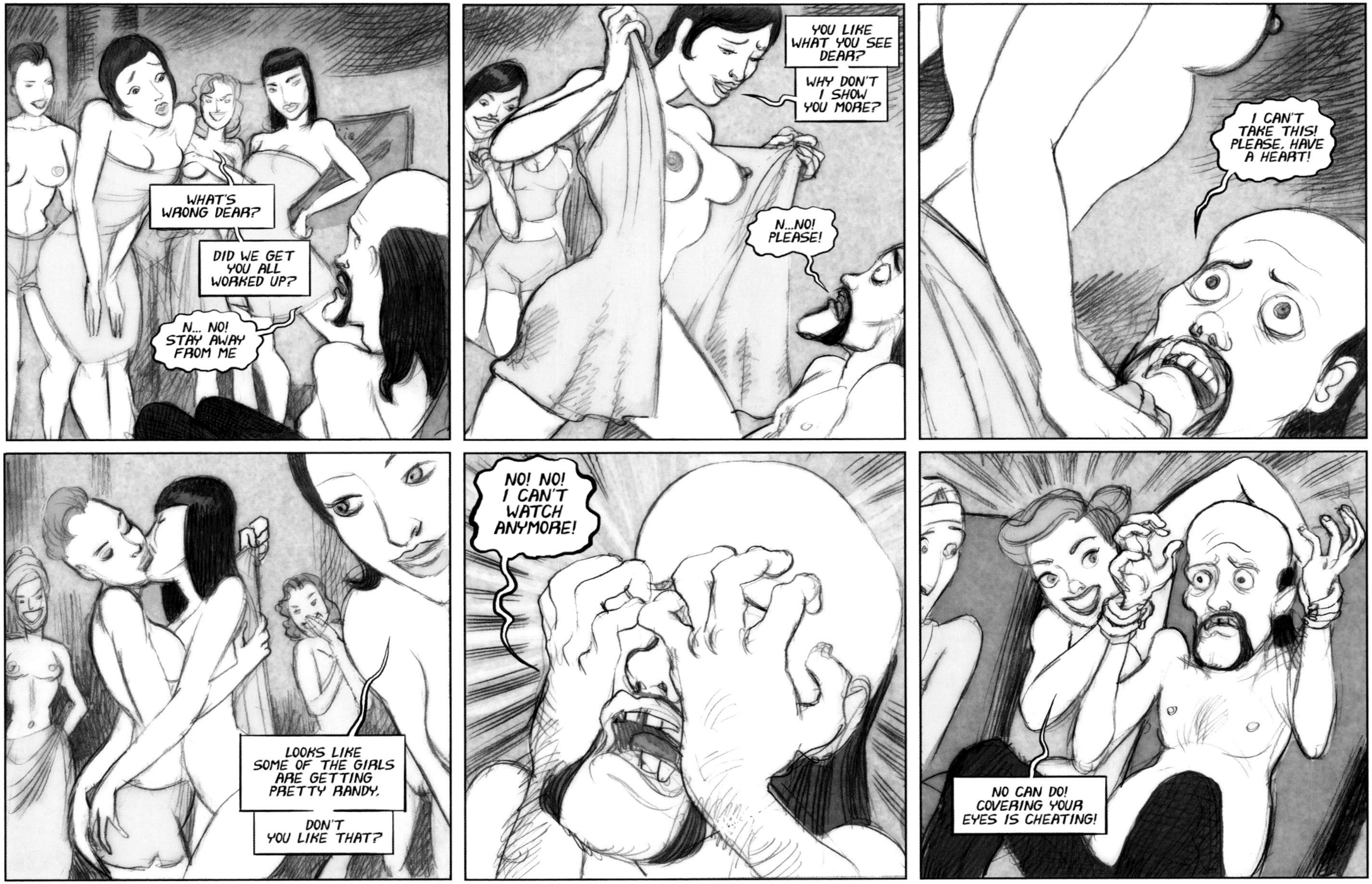
WHAT'S WRONG DEAR?
DID WE GET YOU ALL WORKED UP?
N... NO! STAY AWAY FROM ME
YOU LIKE WHAT YOU SEE DEAR?
WHY DON'T I SHOW YOU MORE?
N...NO! PLEASE!
I CAN'T TAKE THIS! PLEASE, HAVE A HEART!
LOOKS LIKE SOME OF THE GIRLS ARE GETTING PRETTY RANDY.
DON'T YOU LIKE THAT?
NO! NO! I CAN'T WATCH ANYMORE!
NO CAN DO! COVERING YOUR EYES IS CHEATING!

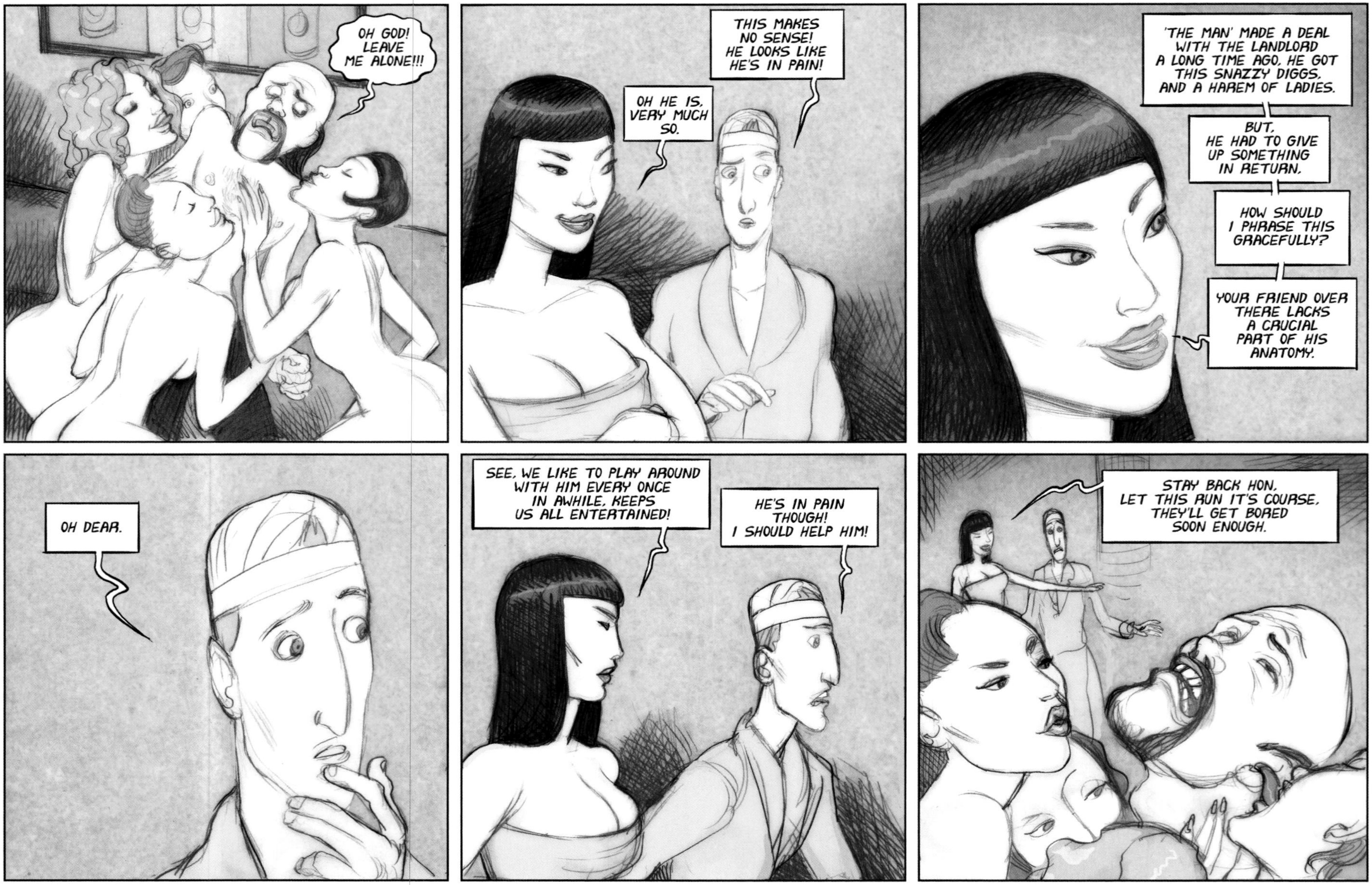
OH GOD! LEAVE ME ALONE!!!
THIS MAKES NO SENSE! HE LOOKS LIKE HE'S IN PAIN!
OH HE IS, VERY MUCH SO.
'THE MAN' MADE A DEAL WITH THE LANDLORD A LONG TIME AGO, HE GOT THIS SNAZZY DIGGS, AND A HAREM OF LADIES.
BUT, HE HAD TO GIVE UP SOMETHING IN RETURN,
HOW SHOULD I PHRASE THIS GRACEFULLY?
YOUR FRIEND OVER THERE LACKS A CRUCIAL PART OF HIS ANATOMY.
OH DEAR.
SEE, WE LIKE TO PLAY AROUND WITH HIM EVERY ONCE IN AWHILE, KEEPS US ALL ENTERTAINED!
HE'S IN PAIN THOUGH! I SHOULD HELP HIM!
STAY BACK HON, LET THIS RUN IT'S COURSE, THEY'LL GET BORED SOON ENOUGH.

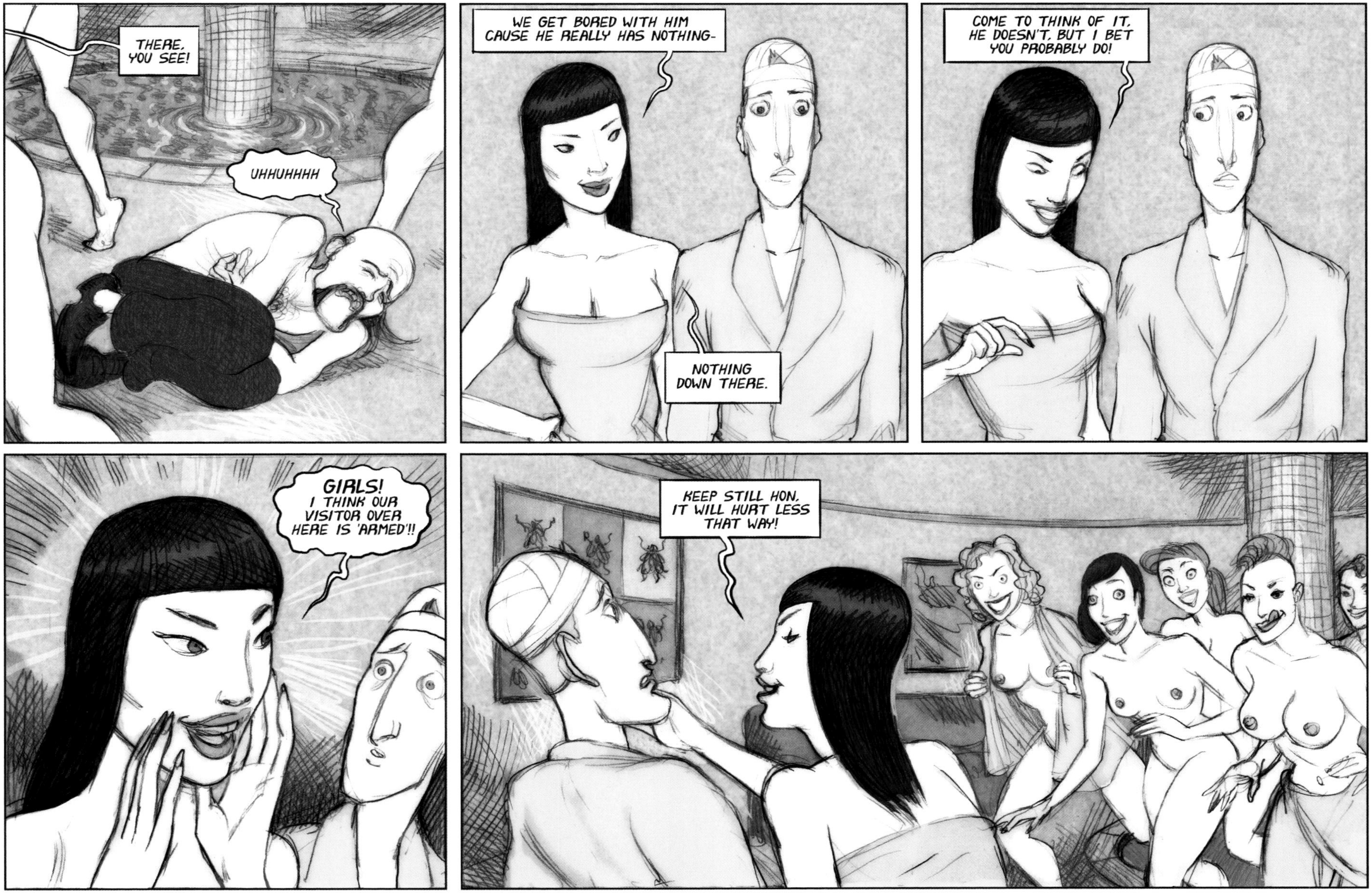
THERE, YOU SEE!
UHHUHHHH
WE GET BORED WITH HIM CAUSE HE REALLY HAS NOTHING-
NOTHING DOWN THERE.
COME TO THINK OF IT, HE DOESN'T, BUT I BET YOU PROBABLY DO!
GIRLS! I THINK OUR VISITOR OVER HERE IS 'ARMED'!!
KEEP STILL HON, IT WILL HURT LESS THAT WAY!

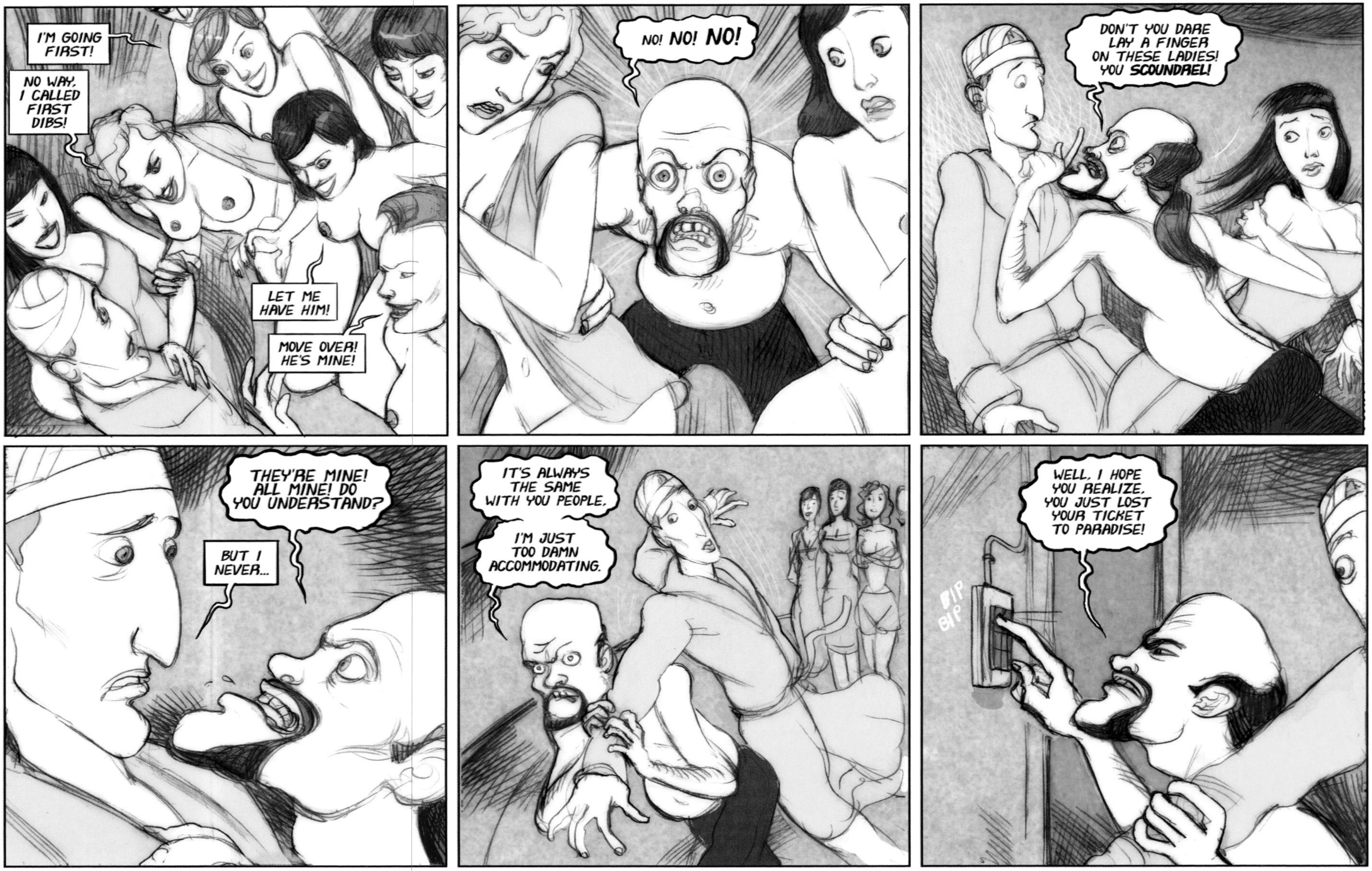

I'M GOING FIRST!
NO WAY, I CALLED FIRST DIBS!
LET ME HAVE HIM!
MOVE OVER! HE'S MINE!
NO! NO! NO!
DON'T YOU DARE LAY A FINGER ON THESE LADIES! YOU SCOUNDREL!
THEY'RE MINE! ALL MINE! DO YOU UNDERSTAND?
BUT I NEVER...
IT'S ALWAYS THE SAME WITH YOU PEOPLE,
I'M JUST TOO DAMN ACCOMMODATING.
BIP BIP
WELL, I HOPE YOU REALIZE, YOU JUST LOST YOUR TICKET TO PARADISE!

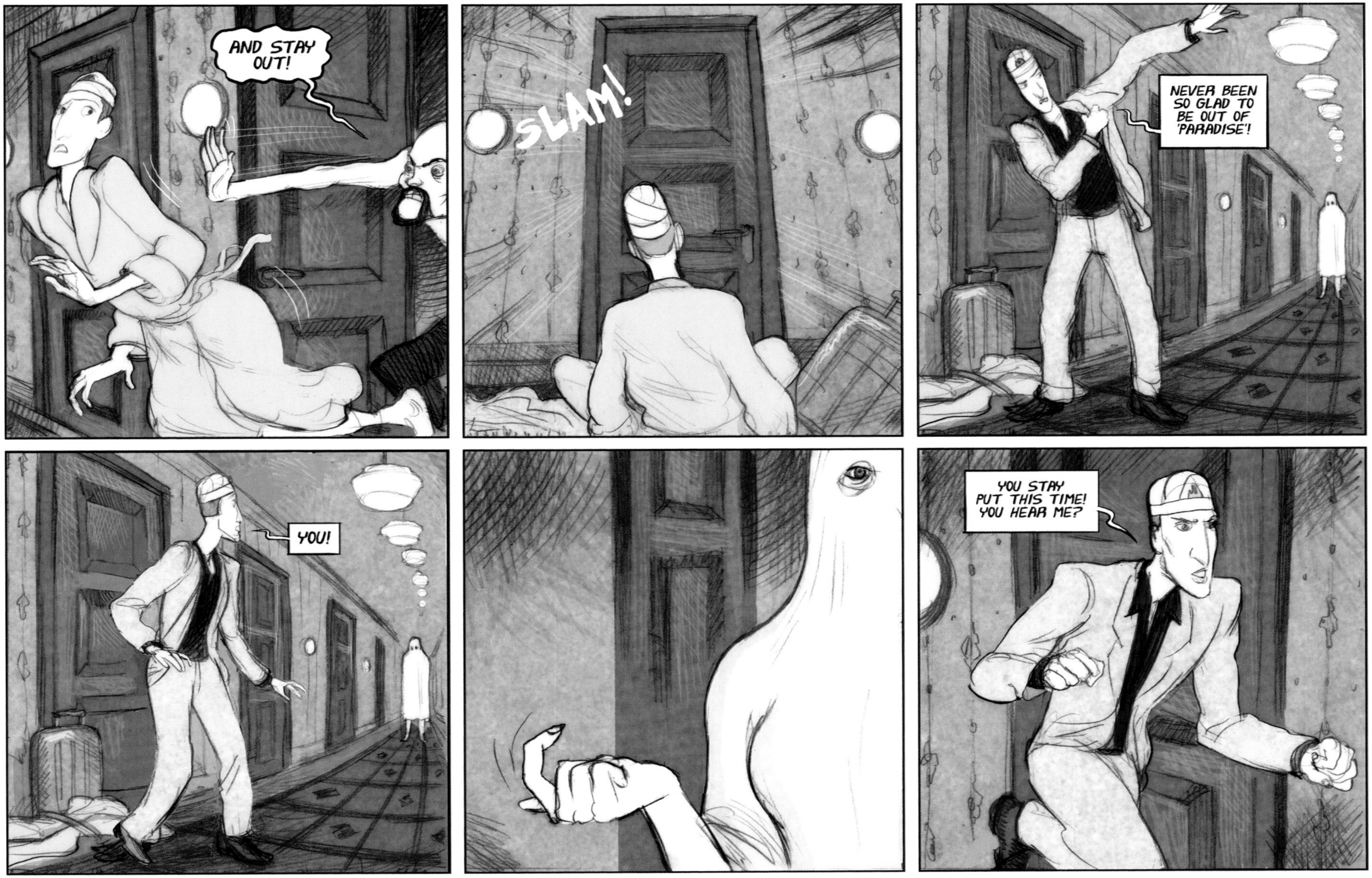
AND STAY OUT!
SLAM!
NEVER BEEN SO GLAD TO BE OUT OF 'PARADISE'!
YOU!
YOU STAY PUT THIS TIME! YOU HEAR ME?

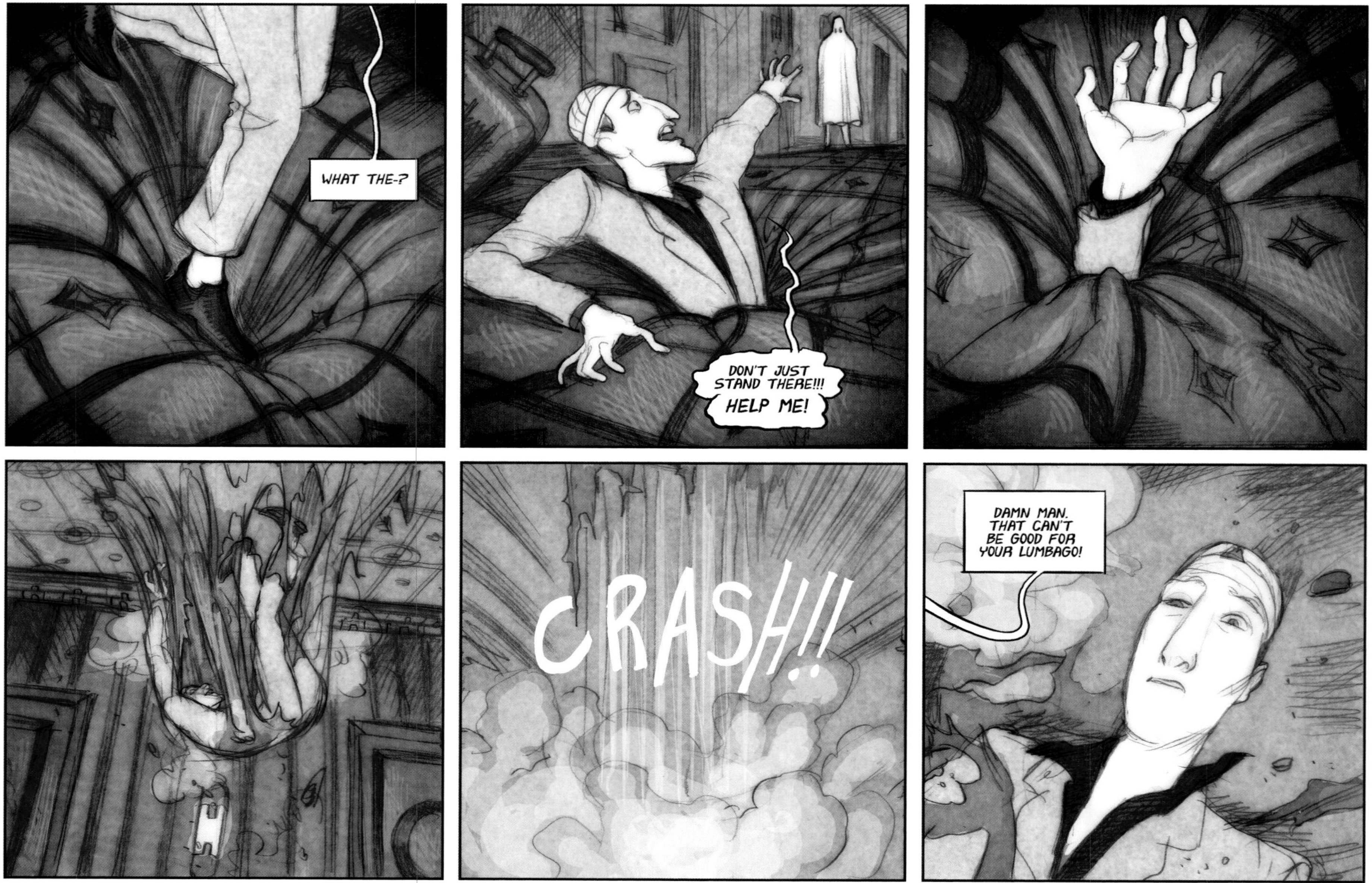
WHAT THE-?
DON'T JUST STAND THERE!!! HELP ME!
CRASH!!!
DAMN MAN. THAT CAN'T BE GOOD FOR YOUR LUMBAGO!

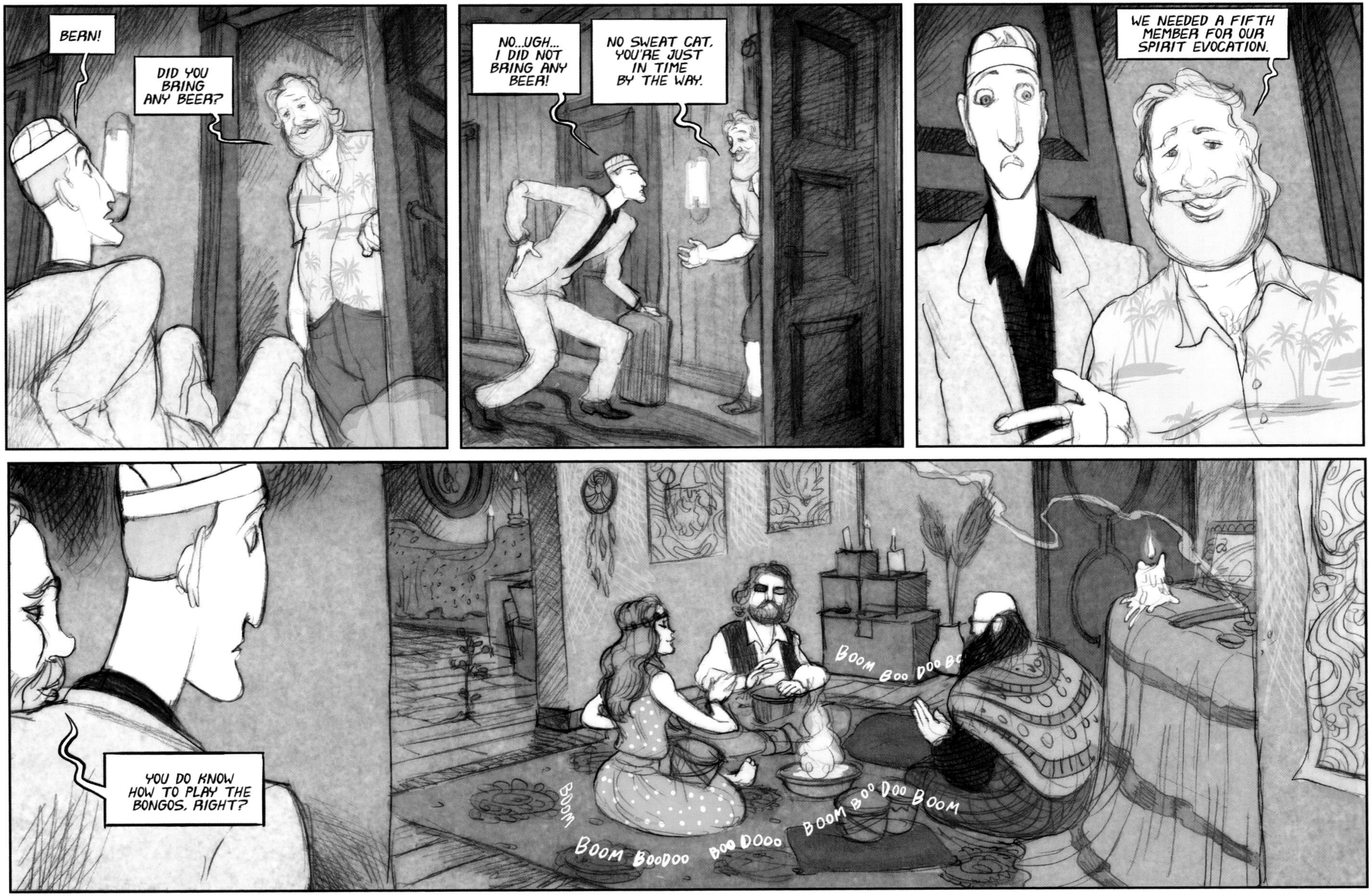
BERN!
DID YOU BRING ANY BEER?
NO...UGH... I DID NOT BRING ANY BEER!
NO SWEAT CAT, YOU'RE JUST IN TIME BY THE WAY.
WE NEEDED A FIFTH MEMBER FOR OUR SPIRIT EVOCATION.
YOU DO KNOW HOW TO PLAY THE BONGOS, RIGHT?
BOOM BOO DOO BO
BOOM
BOOM BOODOO
BOO DOOO
BOOM BOO DOO BOOM

BOOM
BOOM

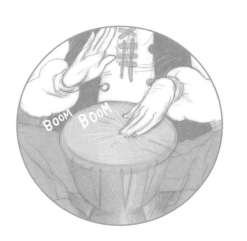

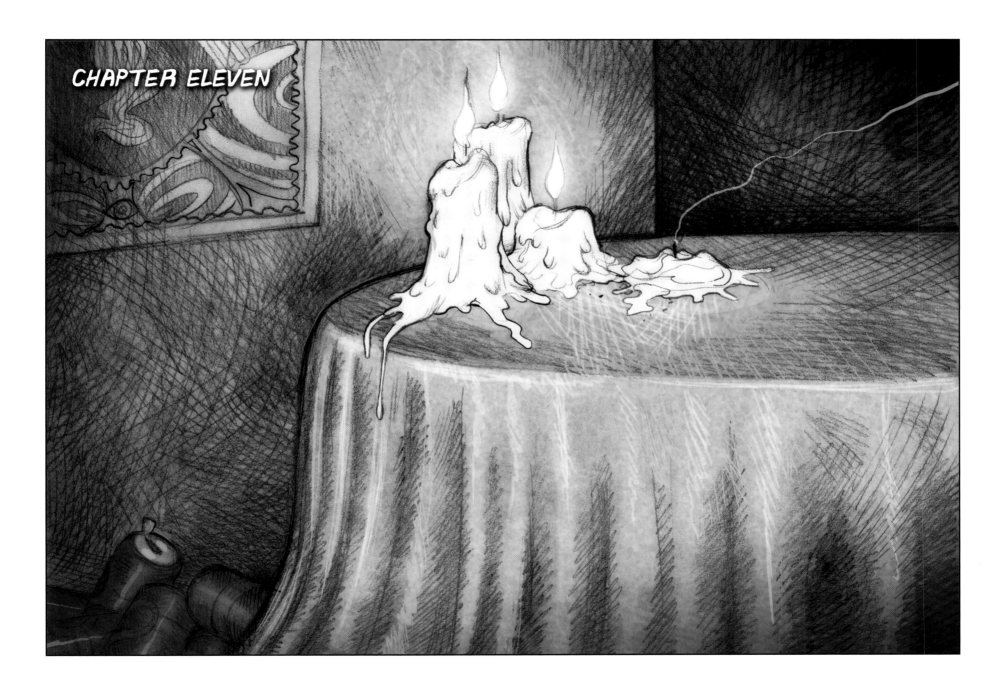

CHAPTER ELEVEN

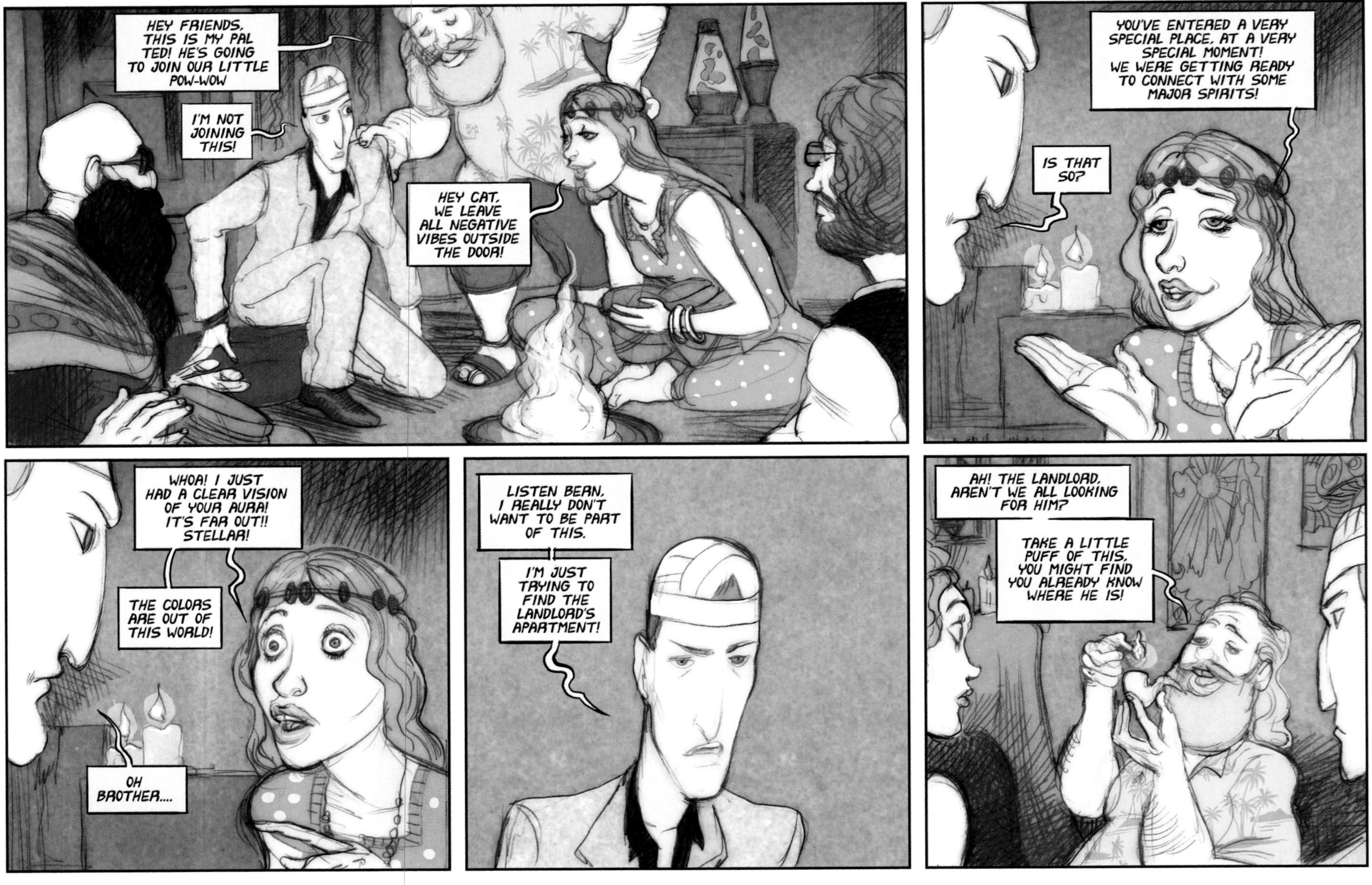
HEY FRIENDS, THIS IS MY PAL TED! HE'S GOING TO JOIN OUR LITTLE POW-WOW
I'M NOT JOINING THIS!
HEY CAT, WE LEAVE ALL NEGATIVE VIBES OUTSIDE THE DOOR!
YOU'VE ENTERED A VERY SPECIAL PLACE, AT A VERY SPECIAL MOMENT! WE WERE GETTING READY TO CONNECT WITH SOME MAJOR SPIRITS!
IS THAT SO?
WHOA! I JUST HAD A CLEAR VISION OF YOUR AURA! IT'S FAR OUT!! STELLAR!
THE COLORS ARE OUT OF THIS WORLD!
OH BROTHER....
LISTEN BERN, I REALLY DON'T WANT TO BE PART OF THIS.
I'M JUST TRYING TO FIND THE LANDLORD'S APARTMENT!
AH! THE LANDLORD, AREN'T WE ALL LOOKING FOR HIM?
TAKE A LITTLE PUFF OF THIS, YOU MIGHT FIND YOU ALREADY KNOW WHERE HE IS!

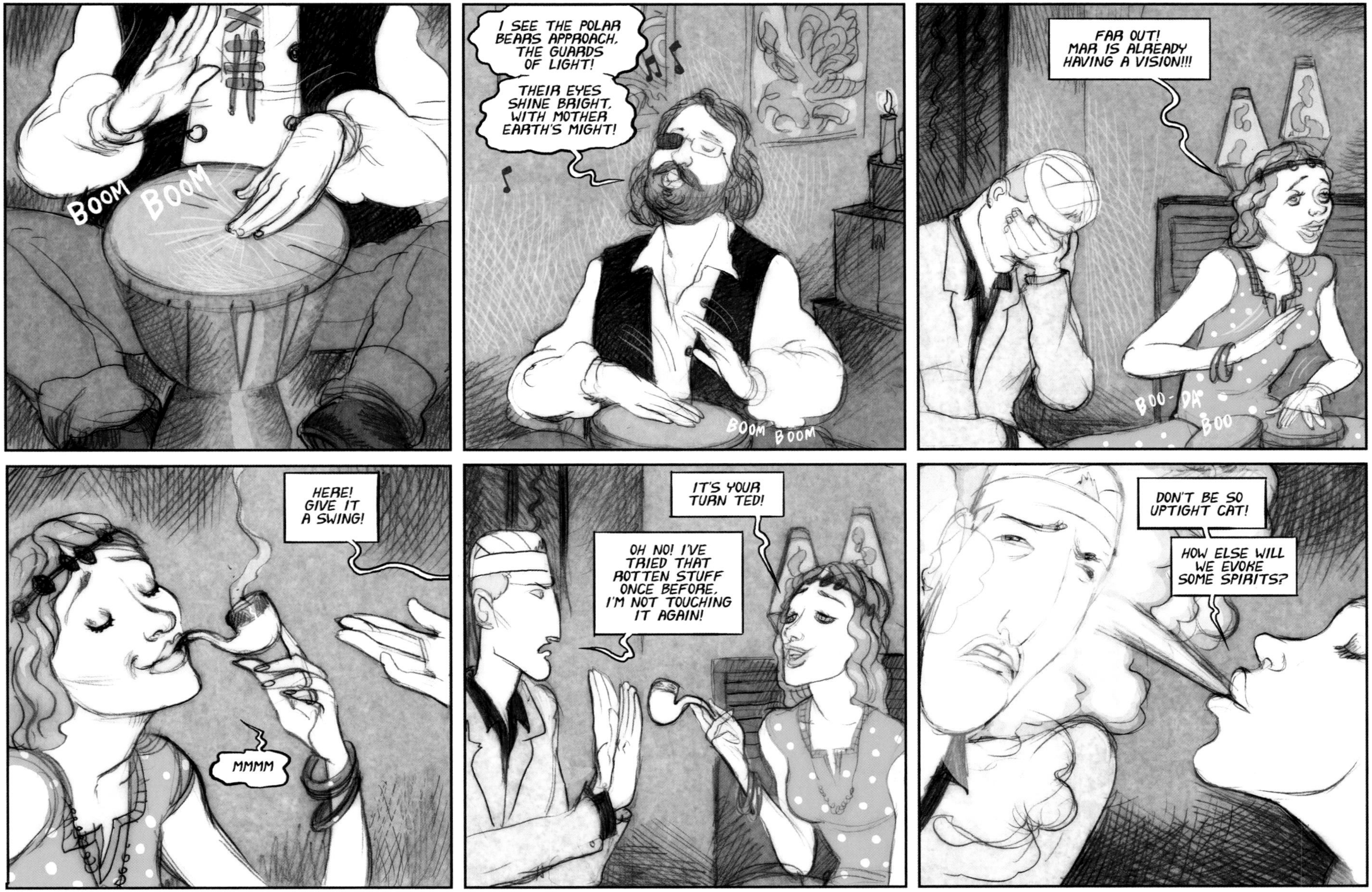
BOOM
BOOM
I SEE THE POLAR BEARS APPROACH, THE GUARDS OF LIGHT!
THEIR EYES SHINE BRIGHT, WITH MOTHER EARTH'S MIGHT!
BOOM BOOM
FAR OUT! MAR IS ALREADY HAVING A VISION!!!
BOO- DA BOO
HERE! GIVE IT A SWING!
MMMM
IT'S YOUR TURN TED!
OH NO! I'VE TRIED THAT ROTTEN STUFF ONCE BEFORE, I'M NOT TOUCHING IT AGAIN!
DON'T BE SO UPTIGHT CAT!
HOW ELSE WILL WE EVOKE SOME SPIRITS?

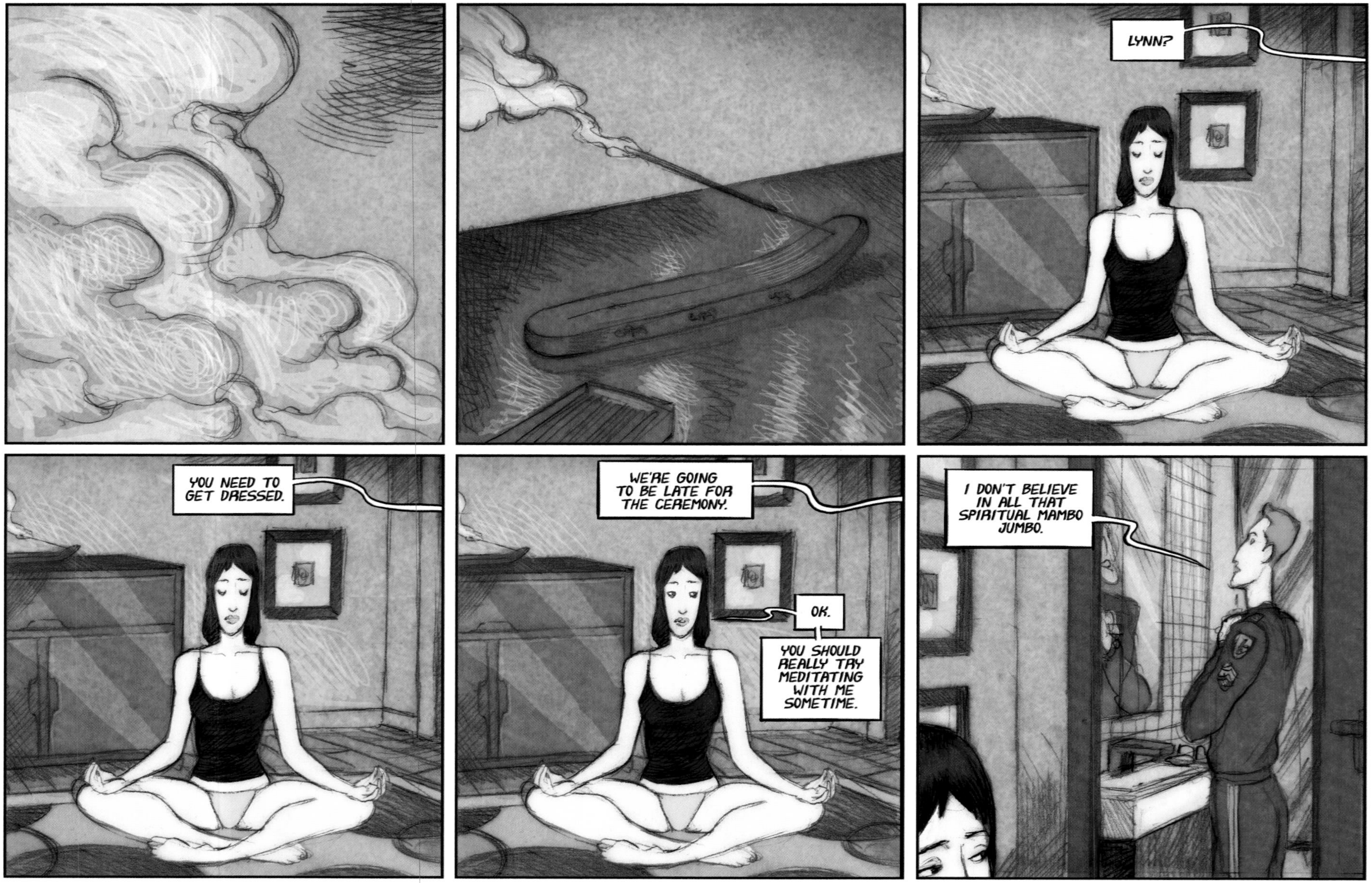
LYNN?
YOU NEED TO GET DRESSED.
WE'RE GOING TO BE LATE FOR THE CEREMONY.
OK.
YOU SHOULD REALLY TRY MEDITATING WITH ME SOMETIME.
I DON'T BELIEVE IN ALL THAT SPIRITUAL MAMBO JUMBO.

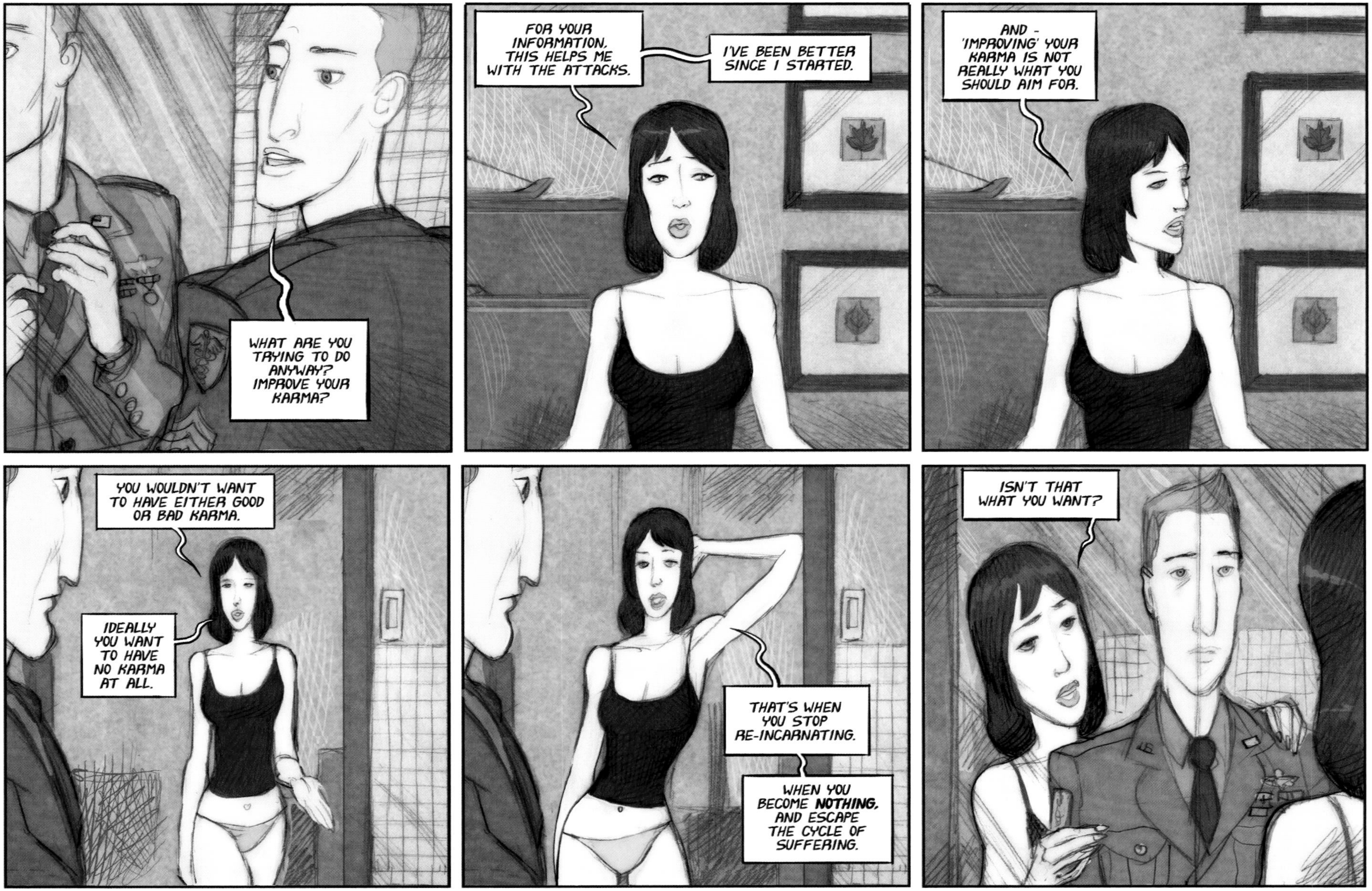
WHAT ARE YOU TRYING TO DO ANYWAY? IMPROVE YOUR KARMA?
FOR YOUR INFORMATION, THIS HELPS ME WITH THE ATTACKS.
I'VE BEEN BETTER SINCE I STARTED.
AND - 'IMPROVING' YOUR KARMA IS NOT REALLY WHAT YOU SHOULD AIM FOR.
YOU WOULDN'T WANT TO HAVE EITHER GOOD OR BAD KARMA.
IDEALLY YOU WANT TO HAVE NO KARMA AT ALL.
THAT'S WHEN YOU STOP RE-INCARNATING.
WHEN YOU BECOME **NOTHING**, AND ESCAPE THE CYCLE OF SUFFERING.
ISN'T THAT WHAT YOU WANT?

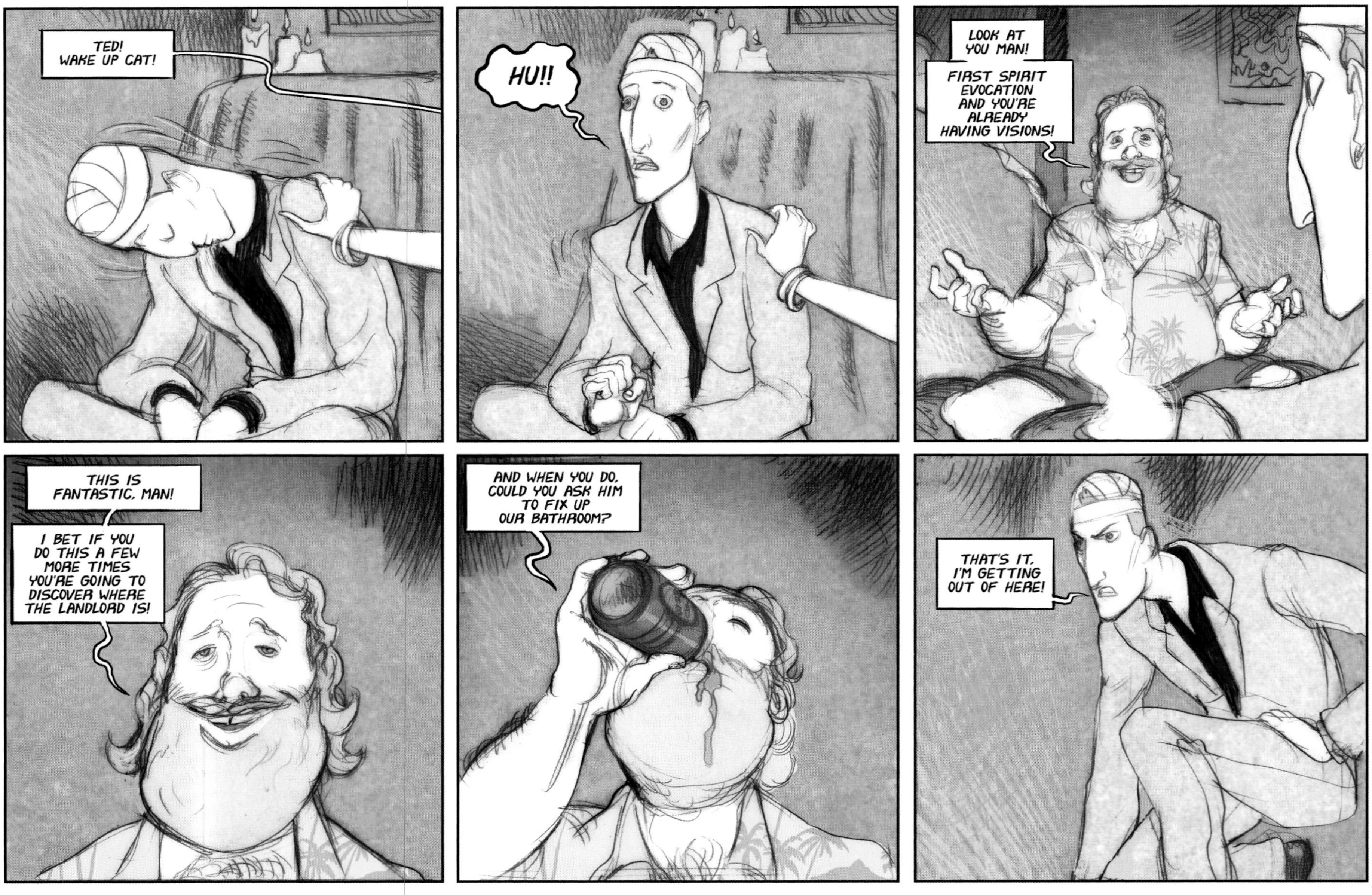
TED! WAKE UP CAT!
HU!!
LOOK AT YOU MAN!
FIRST SPIRIT EVOCATION AND YOU'RE ALREADY HAVING VISIONS!
THIS IS FANTASTIC, MAN!
I BET IF YOU DO THIS A FEW MORE TIMES YOU'RE GOING TO DISCOVER WHERE THE LANDLORD IS!
AND WHEN YOU DO, COULD YOU ASK HIM TO FIX UP OUR BATHROOM?
THAT'S IT, I'M GETTING OUT OF HERE!

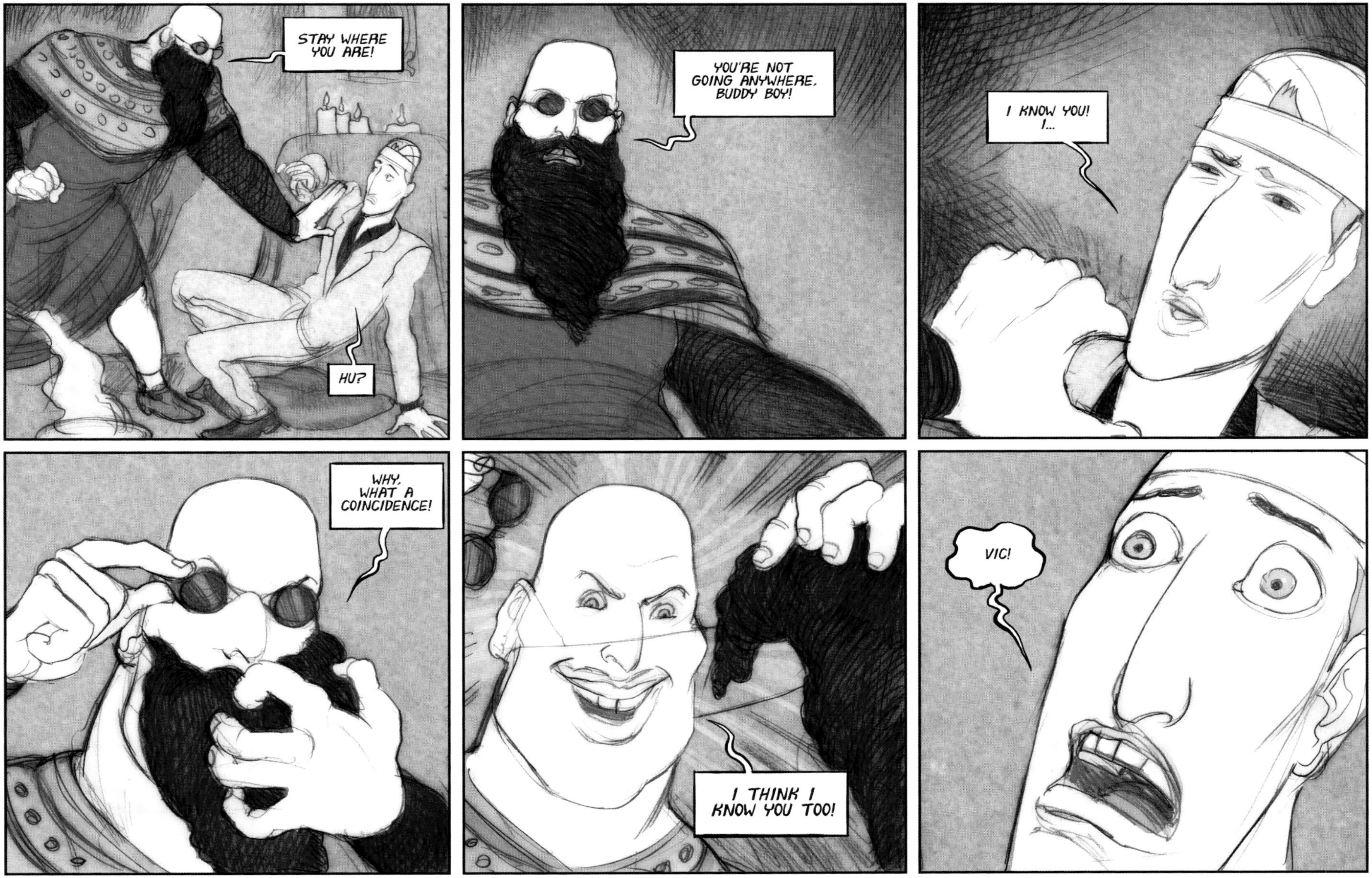
STAY WHERE YOU ARE!
HU?
YOU'RE NOT GOING ANYWHERE, BUDDY BOY!
I KNOW YOU! I...
WHY, WHAT A COINCIDENCE!
I THINK I KNOW YOU TOO!
VIC!

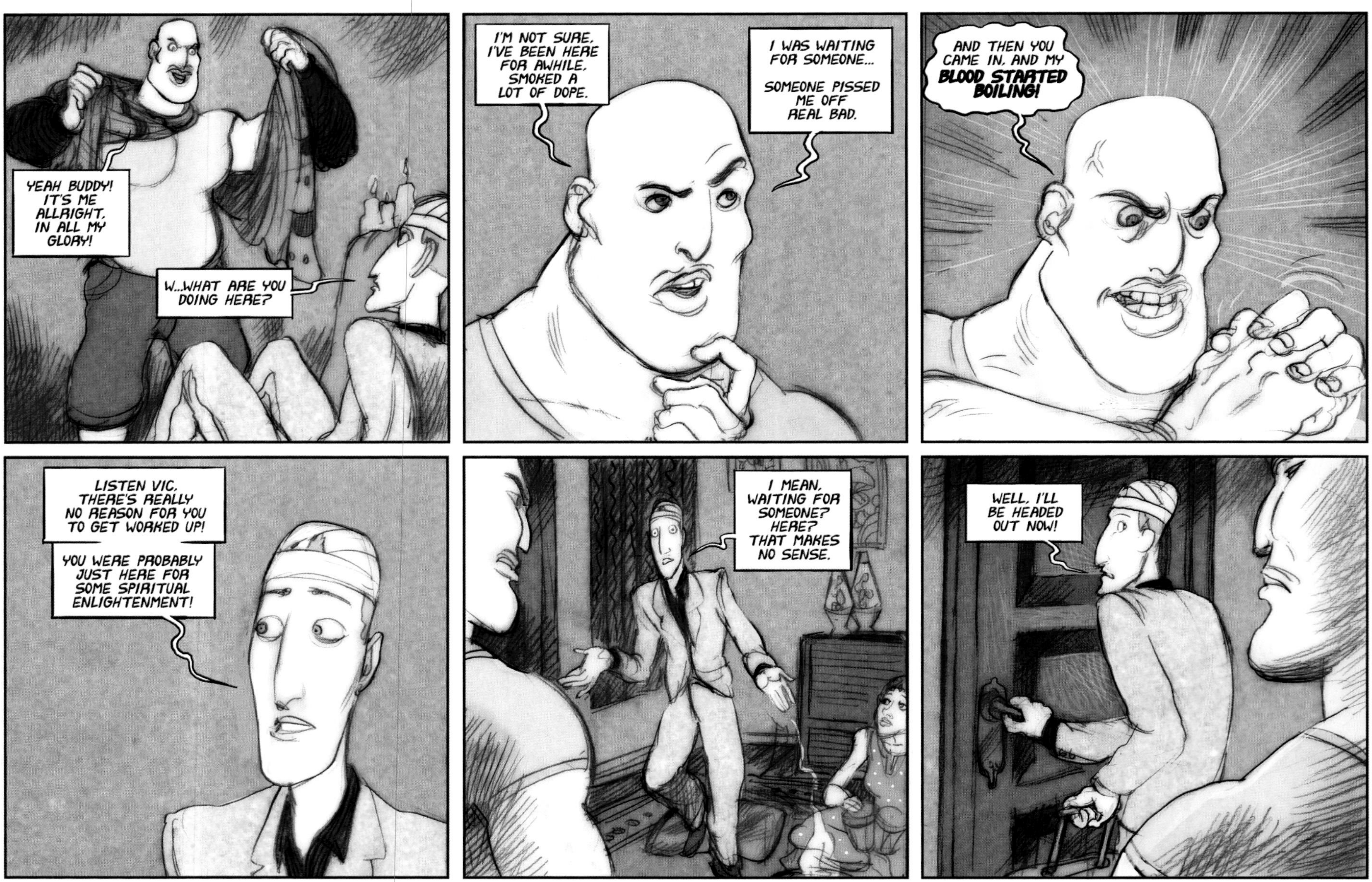
YEAH BUDDY! IT'S ME ALLRIGHT, IN ALL MY GLORY!
W...WHAT ARE YOU DOING HERE?
I'M NOT SURE, I'VE BEEN HERE FOR AWHILE, SMOKED A LOT OF DOPE.
I WAS WAITING FOR SOMEONE...
SOMEONE PISSED ME OFF REAL BAD.
AND THEN YOU CAME IN, AND MY BLOOD STARTED BOILING!
LISTEN VIC, THERE'S REALLY NO REASON FOR YOU TO GET WORKED UP!
YOU WERE PROBABLY JUST HERE FOR SOME SPIRITUAL ENLIGHTENMENT!
I MEAN, WAITING FOR SOMEONE? HERE? THAT MAKES NO SENSE.
WELL, I'LL BE HEADED OUT NOW!

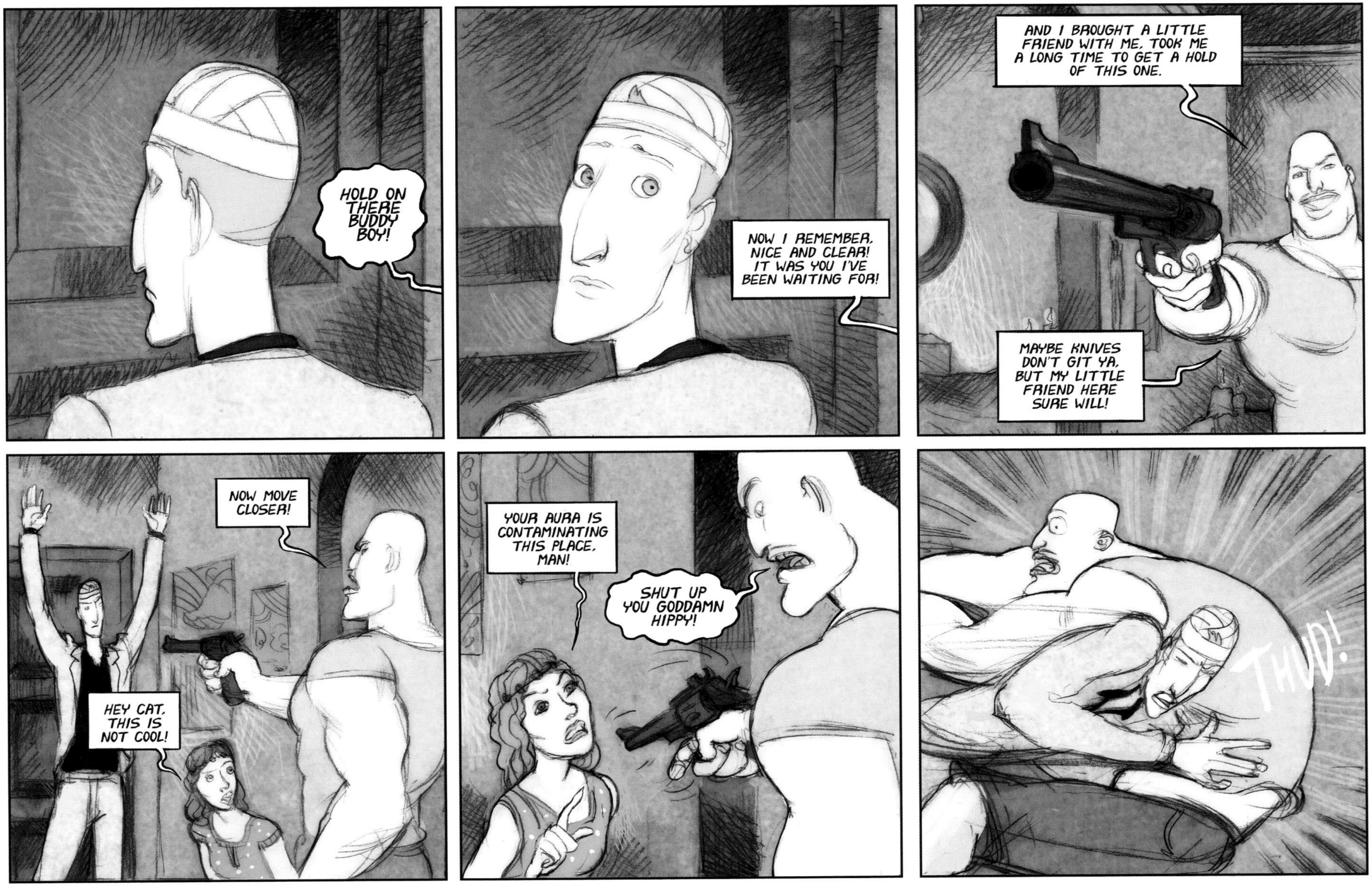
HOLD ON THERE BUDDY BOY!
NOW I REMEMBER, NICE AND CLEAR! IT WAS YOU I'VE BEEN WAITING FOR!
AND I BROUGHT A LITTLE FRIEND WITH ME, TOOK ME A LONG TIME TO GET A HOLD OF THIS ONE.
MAYBE KNIVES DON'T GIT YA, BUT MY LITTLE FRIEND HERE SURE WILL!
NOW MOVE CLOSER!
HEY CAT, THIS IS NOT COOL!
YOUR AURA IS CONTAMINATING THIS PLACE, MAN!
SHUT UP YOU GODDAMN HIPPY!
THUD!

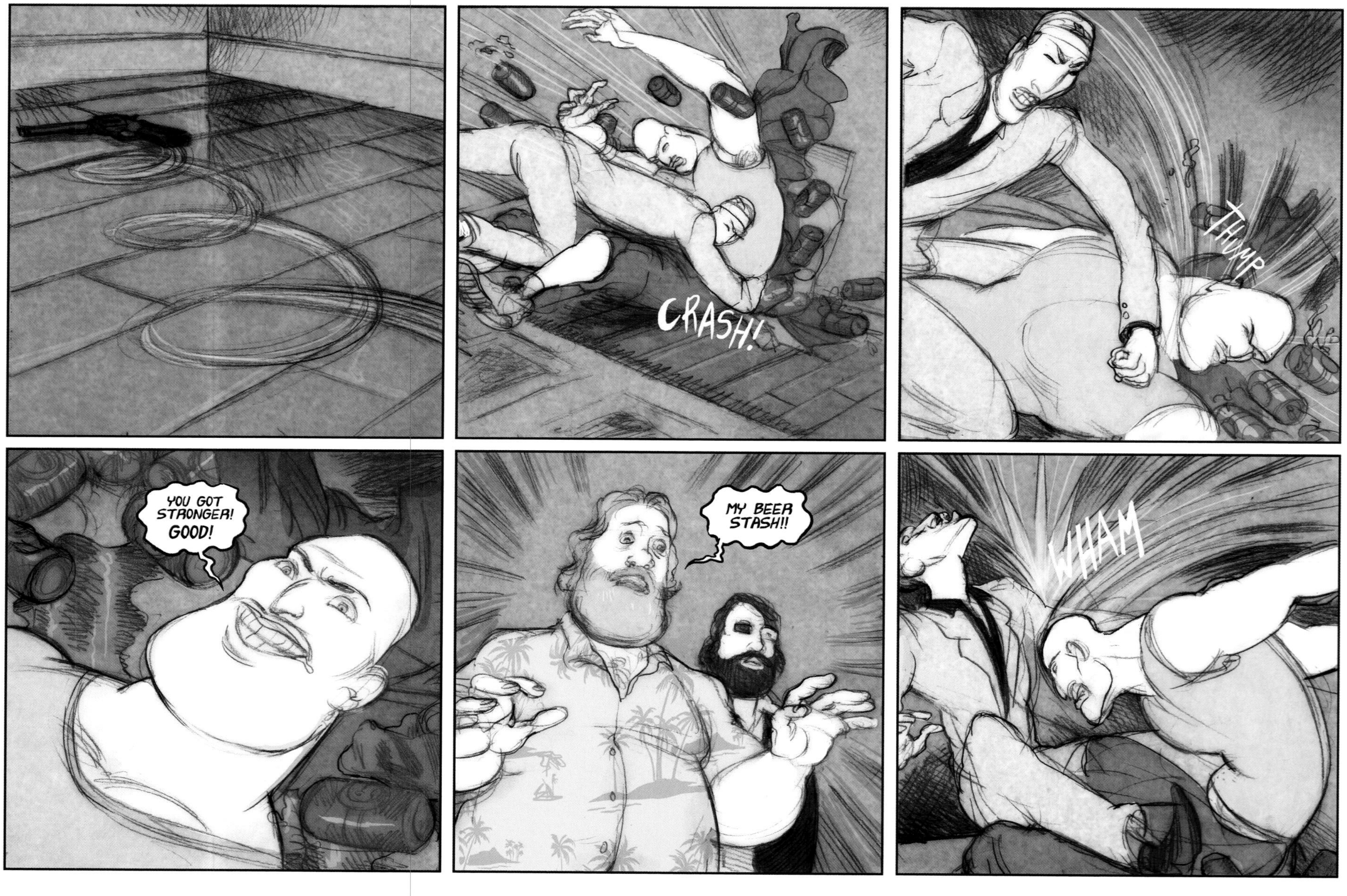
CRASH!
THUMP
YOU GOT STRONGER! GOOD!
MY BEER STASH!!
WHAM

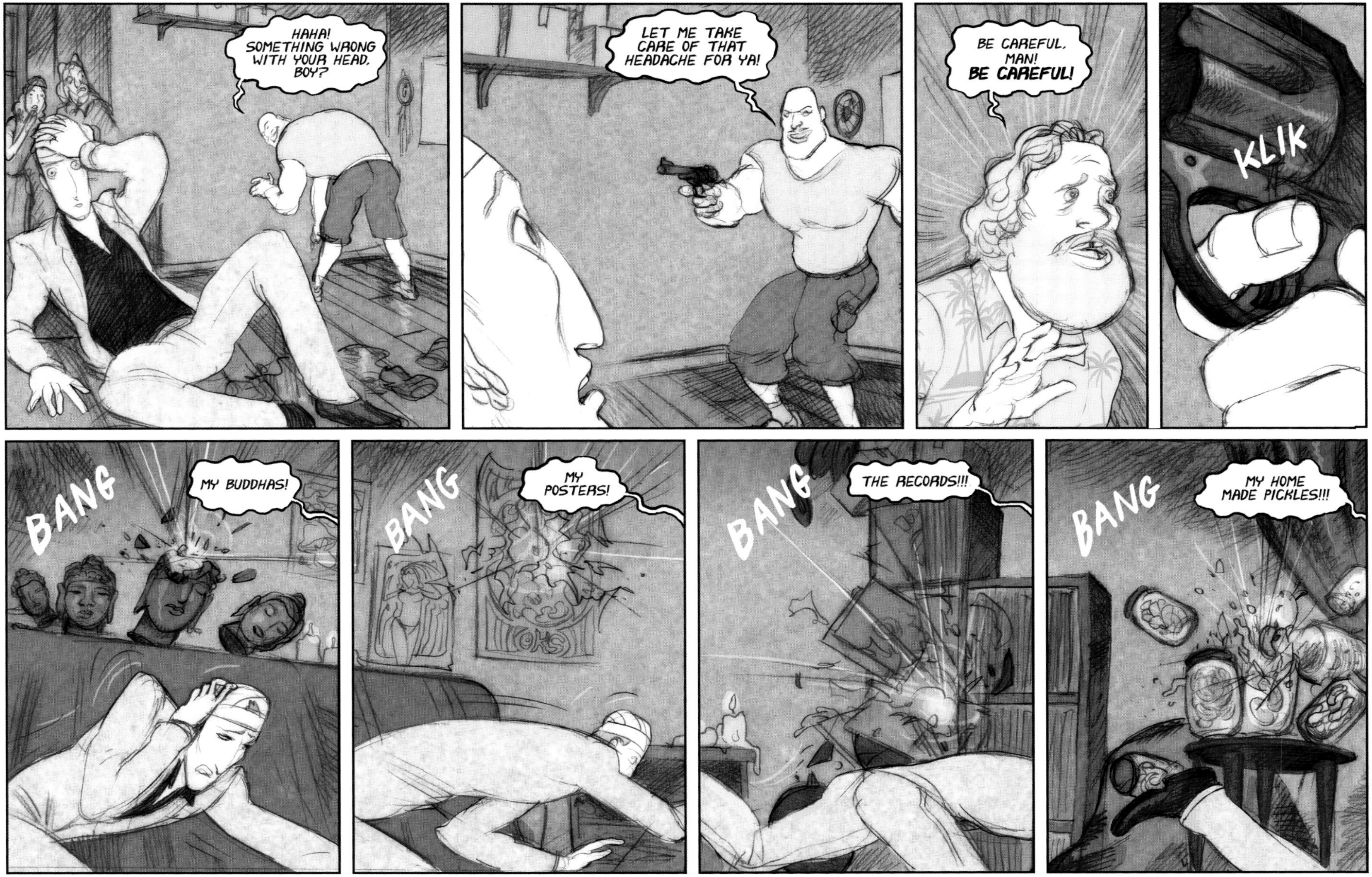
HAHA! SOMETHING WRONG WITH YOUR HEAD, BOY?
LET ME TAKE CARE OF THAT HEADACHE FOR YA!
BE CAREFUL, MAN! **BE CAREFUL!**
KLIK
BANG
MY BUDDHAS!
BANG
MY POSTERS!
BANG
THE RECORDS!!!
BANG
MY HOME MADE PICKLES!!!

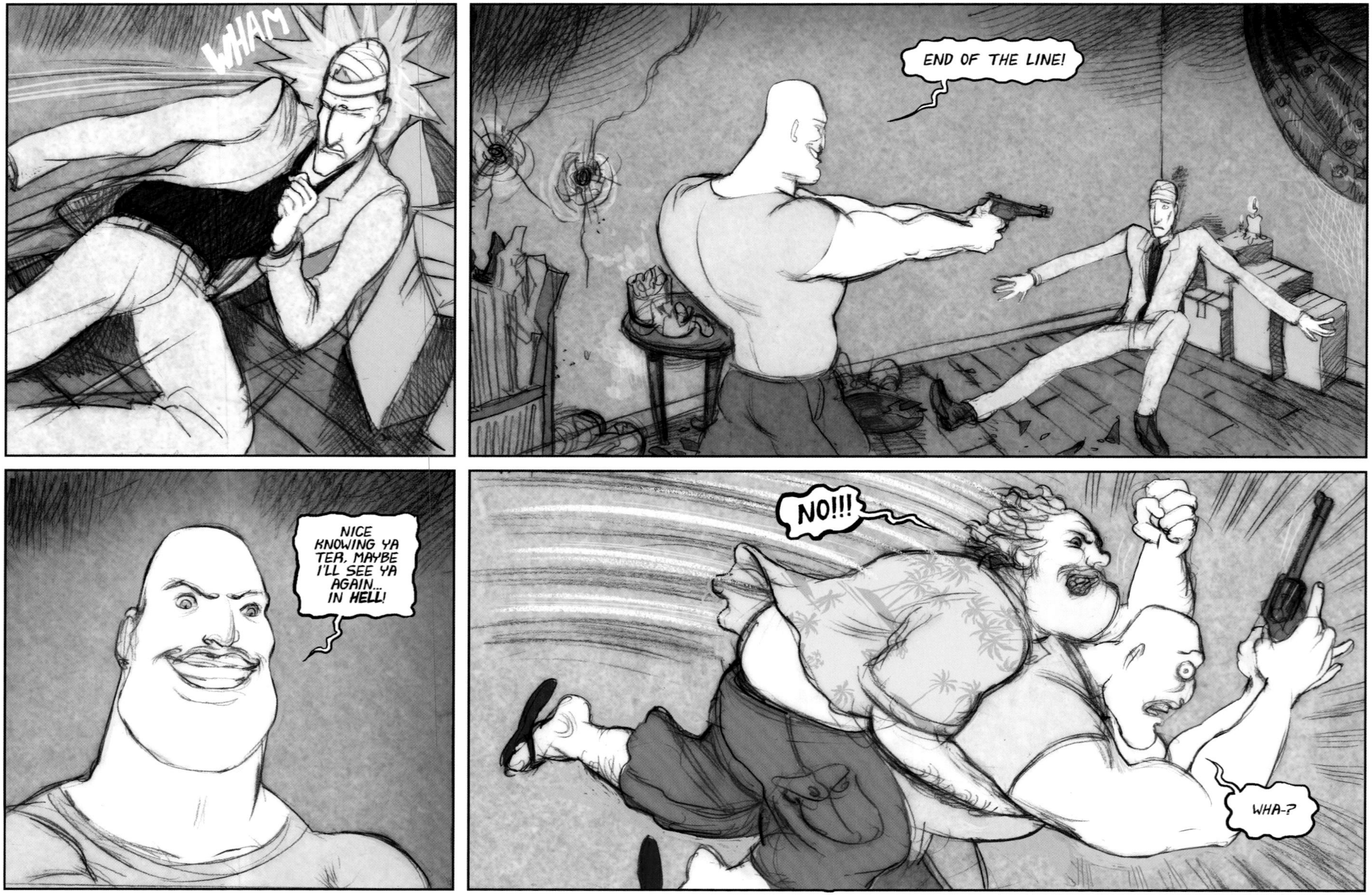
WHAM
END OF THE LINE!
NICE KNOWING YA TER, MAYBE I'LL SEE YA AGAIN... IN **HELL**!
NO!!!
WHA-?

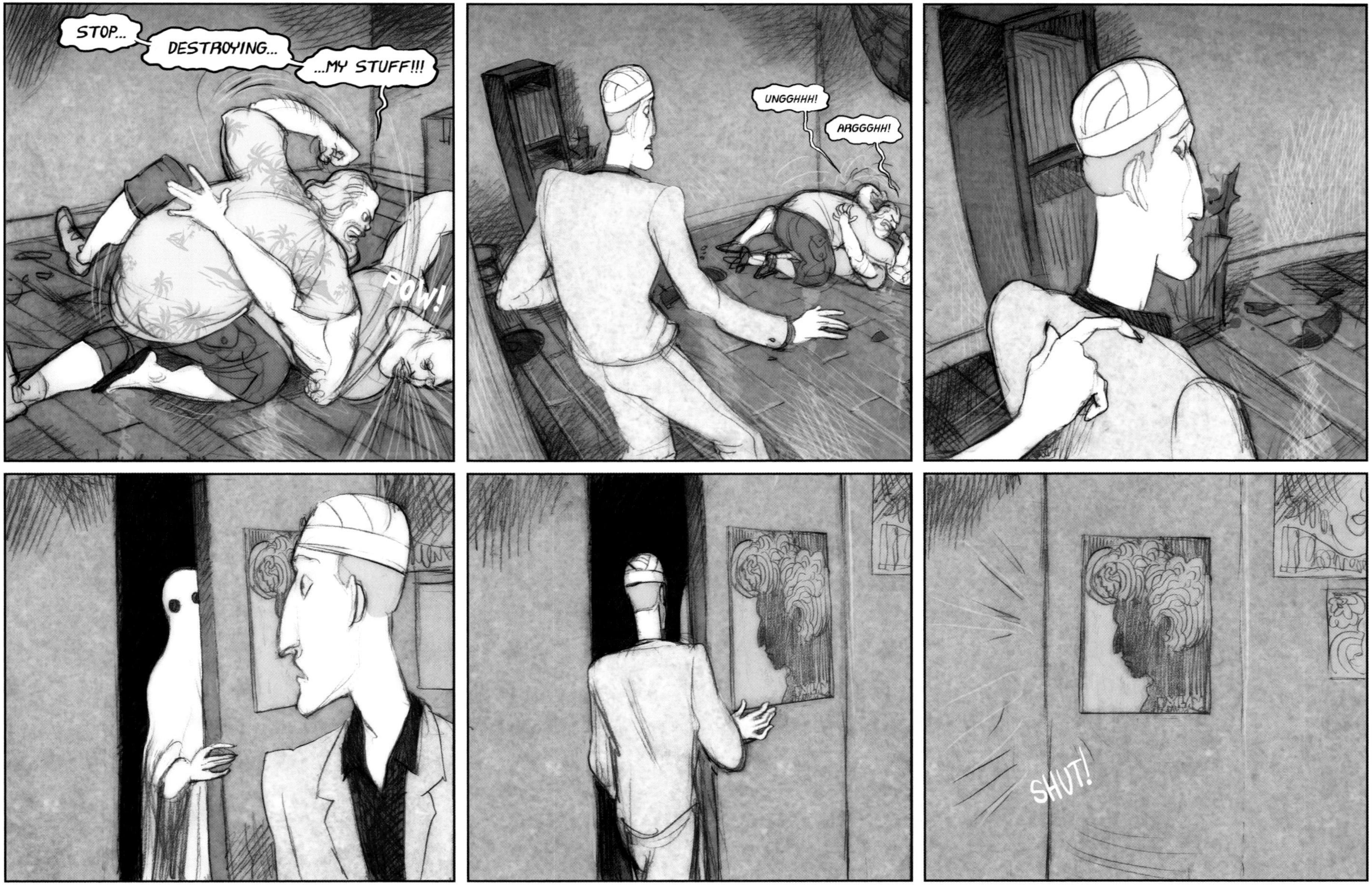
STOP...
DESTROYING...
...MY STUFF!!!
POW!
UNGGHHH!
ARGGGHH!
SHUT!

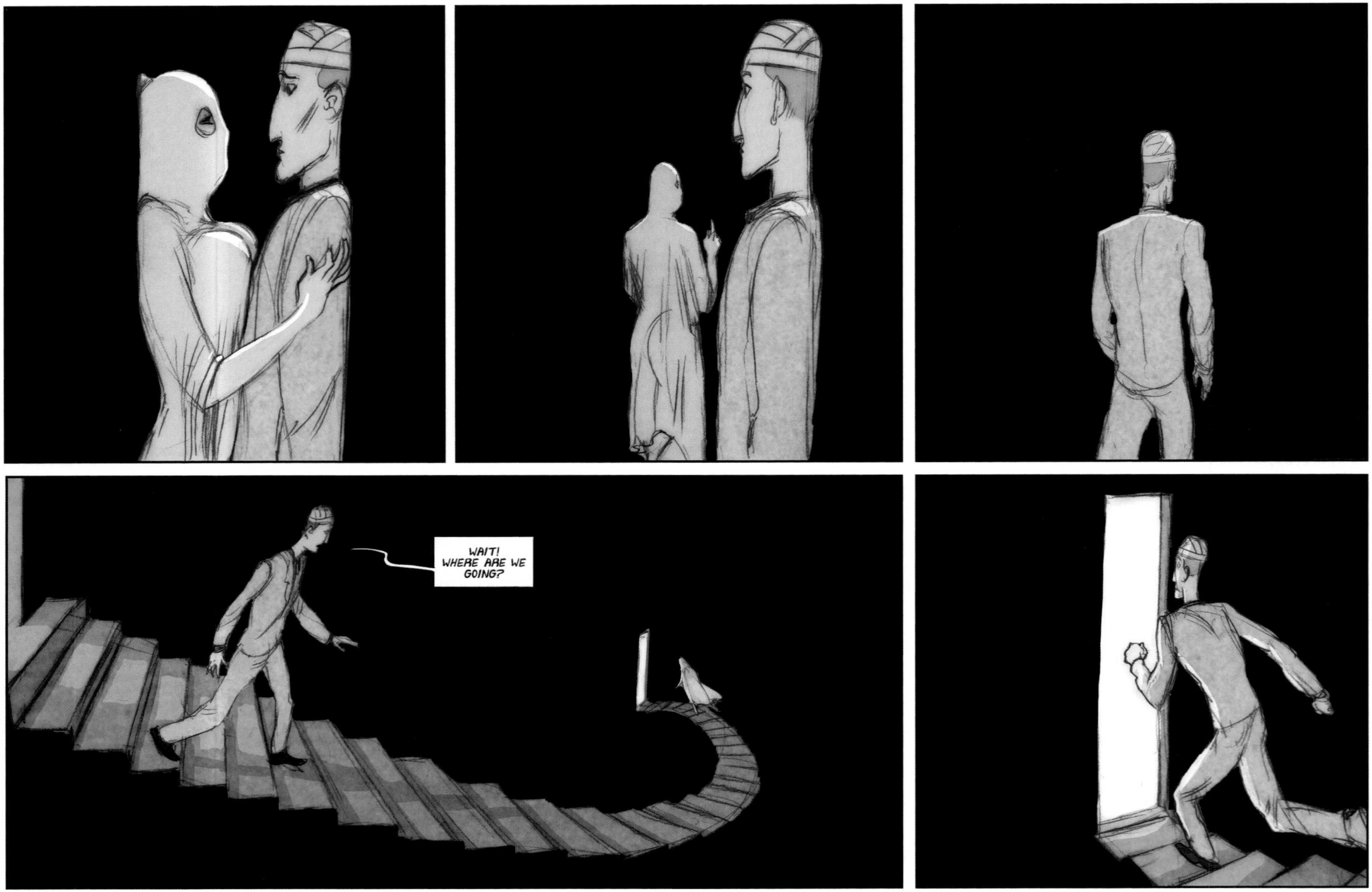
WAIT! WHERE ARE WE GOING?

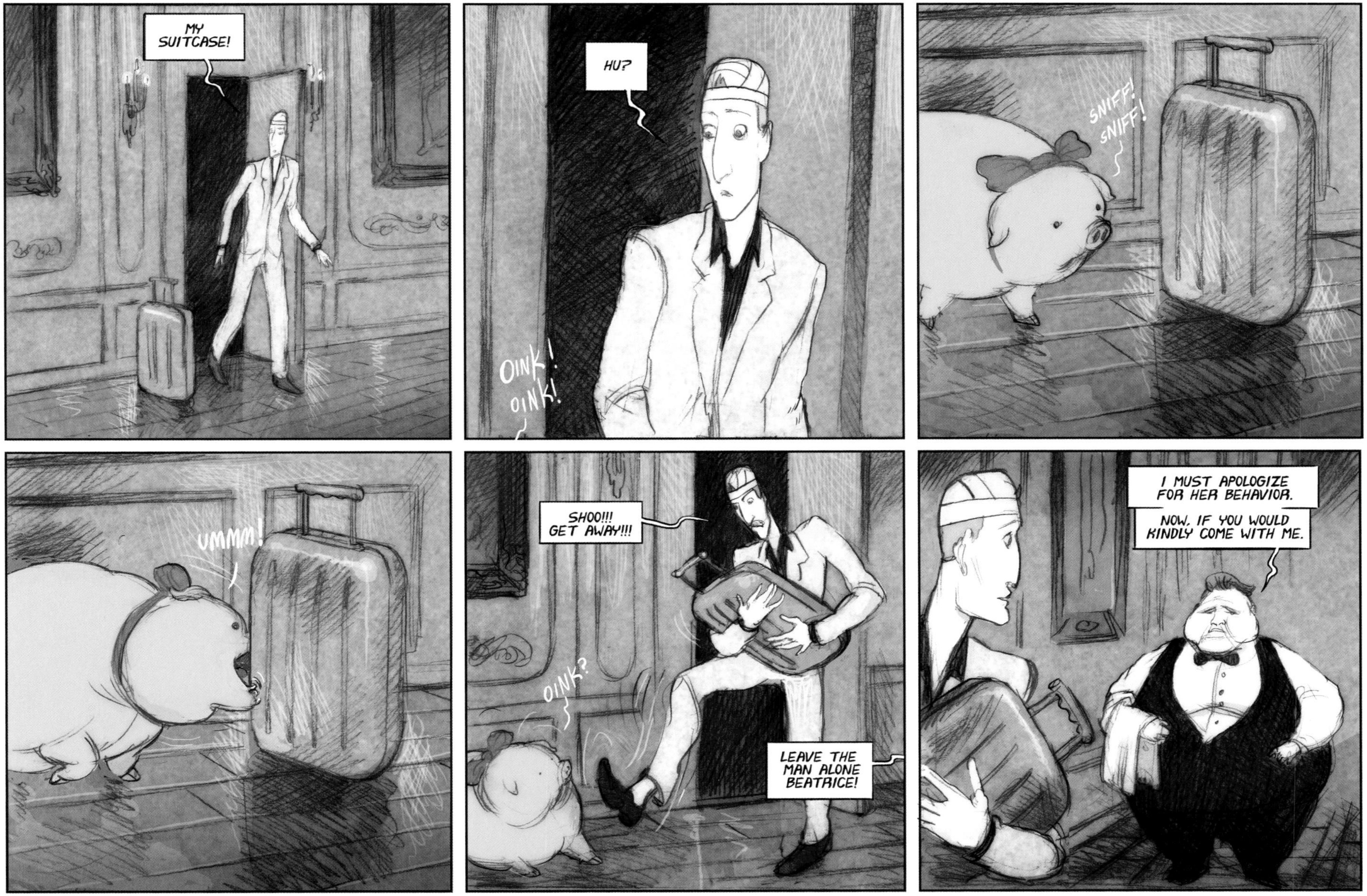

MY SUITCASE!
HU?
OINK! OINK!
SNIFF! SNIFF!
UMMM!
SHOO!!! GET AWAY!!!
OINK?
LEAVE THE MAN ALONE BEATRICE!
I MUST APOLOGIZE FOR HER BEHAVIOR.
NOW, IF YOU WOULD KINDLY COME WITH ME.

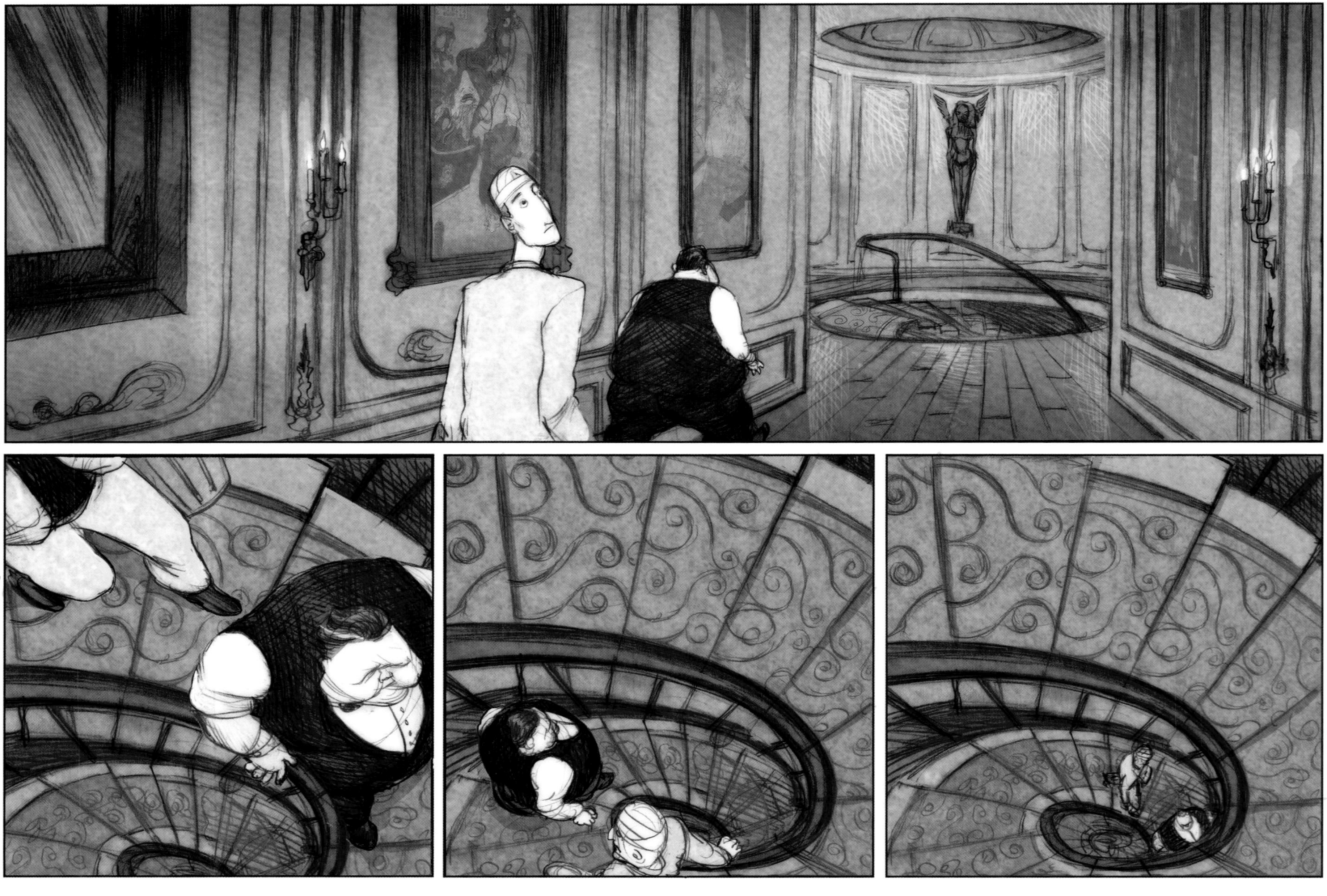

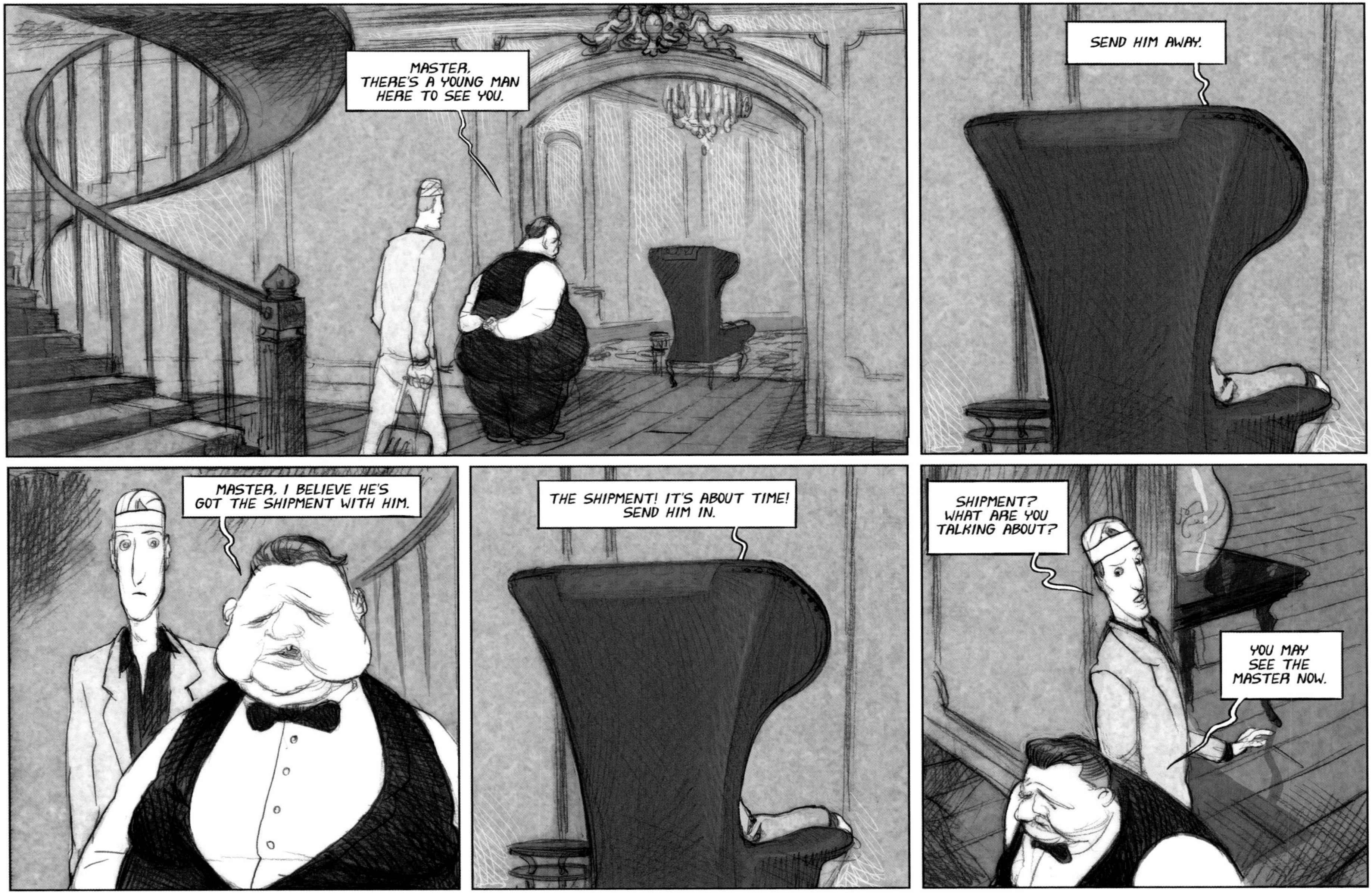
MASTER, THERE'S A YOUNG MAN HERE TO SEE YOU.
SEND HIM AWAY.
MASTER, I BELIEVE HE'S GOT THE SHIPMENT WITH HIM.
THE SHIPMENT! IT'S ABOUT TIME! SEND HIM IN.
SHIPMENT? WHAT ARE YOU TALKING ABOUT?
YOU MAY SEE THE MASTER NOW.

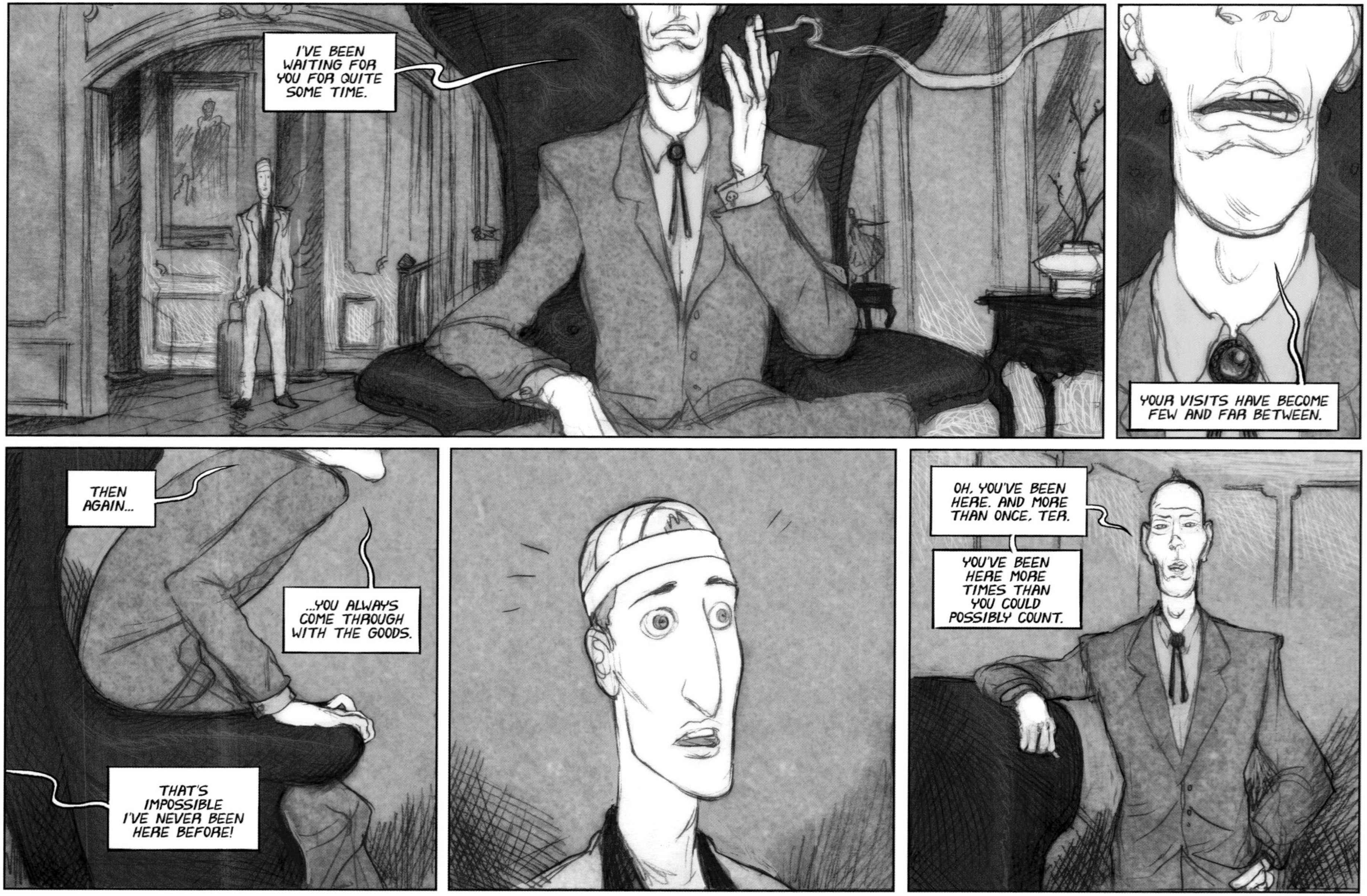
I'VE BEEN WAITING FOR YOU FOR QUITE SOME TIME.
YOUR VISITS HAVE BECOME FEW AND FAR BETWEEN.
THEN AGAIN...
...YOU ALWAYS COME THROUGH WITH THE GOODS.
THAT'S IMPOSSIBLE I'VE NEVER BEEN HERE BEFORE!
OH, YOU'VE BEEN HERE. AND MORE THAN ONCE, TER.
YOU'VE BEEN HERE MORE TIMES THAN YOU COULD POSSIBLY COUNT.

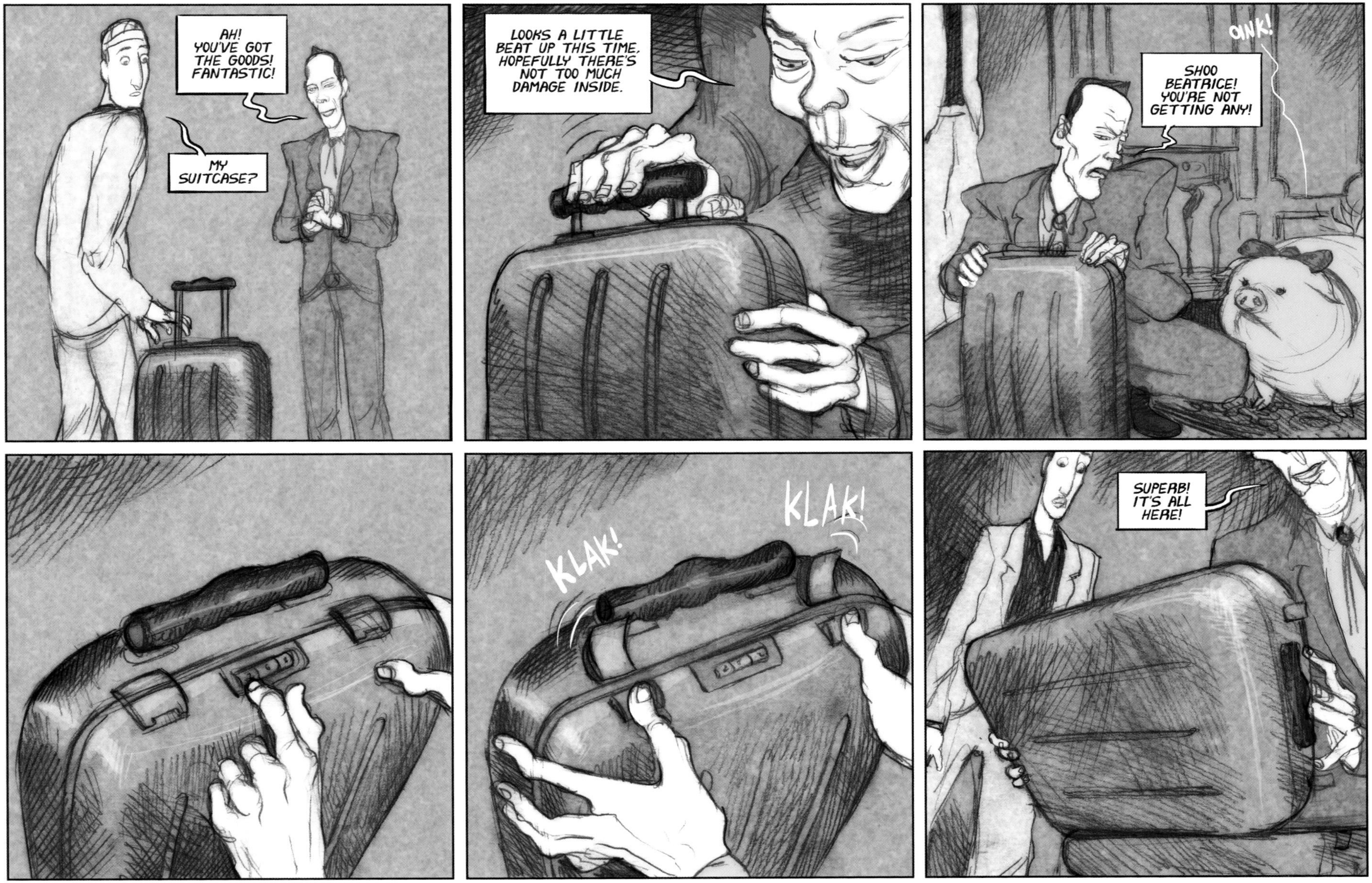
AH! YOU'VE GOT THE GOODS! FANTASTIC!
MY SUITCASE?
LOOKS A LITTLE BEAT UP THIS TIME, HOPEFULLY THERE'S NOT TOO MUCH DAMAGE INSIDE.
OINK!
SHOO BEATRICE! YOU'RE NOT GETTING ANY!
KLAK!
KLAK!
SUPERB! IT'S ALL HERE!

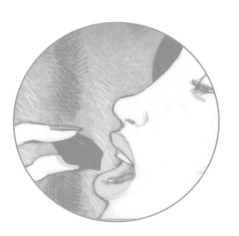

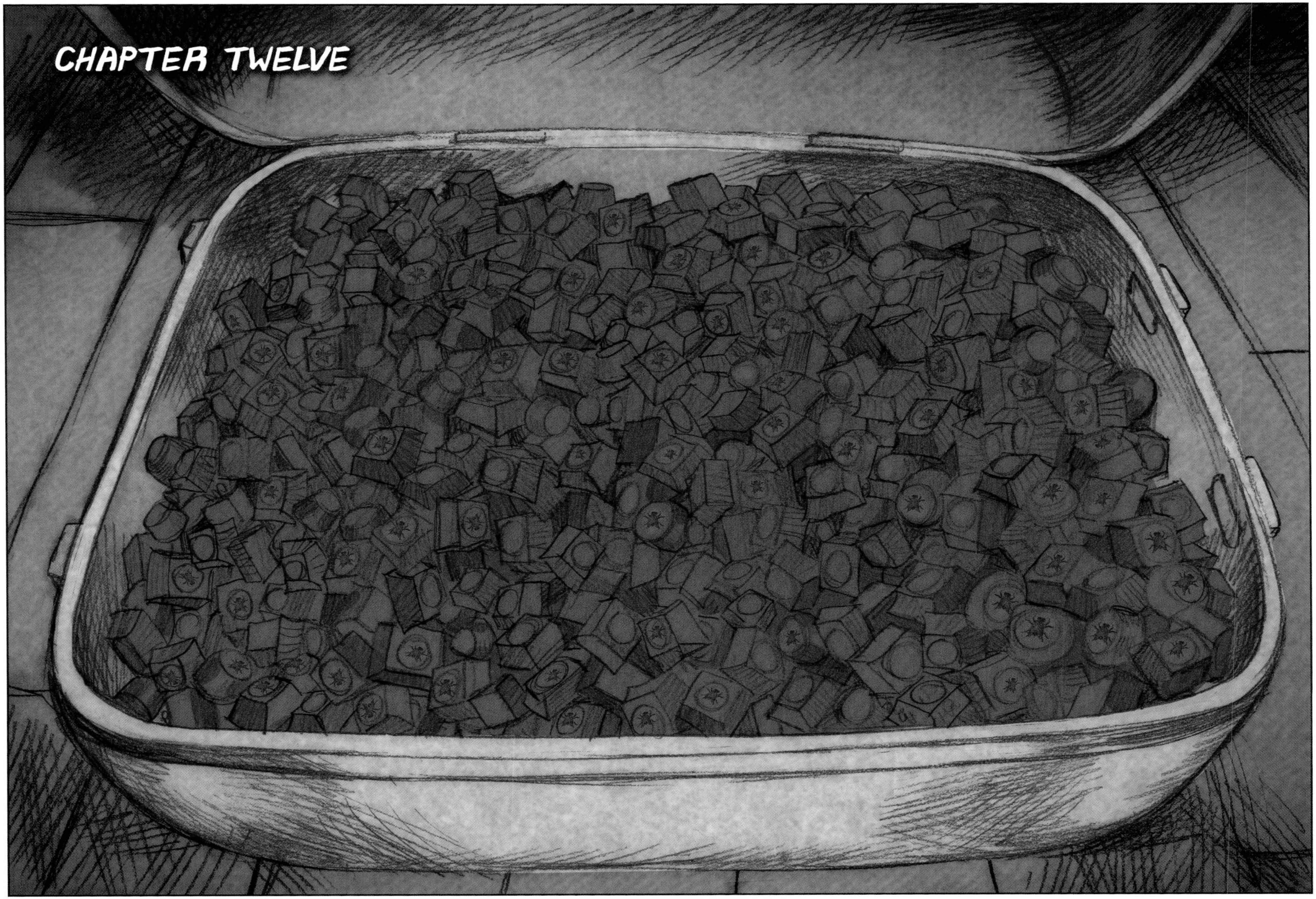
CHAPTER TWELVE

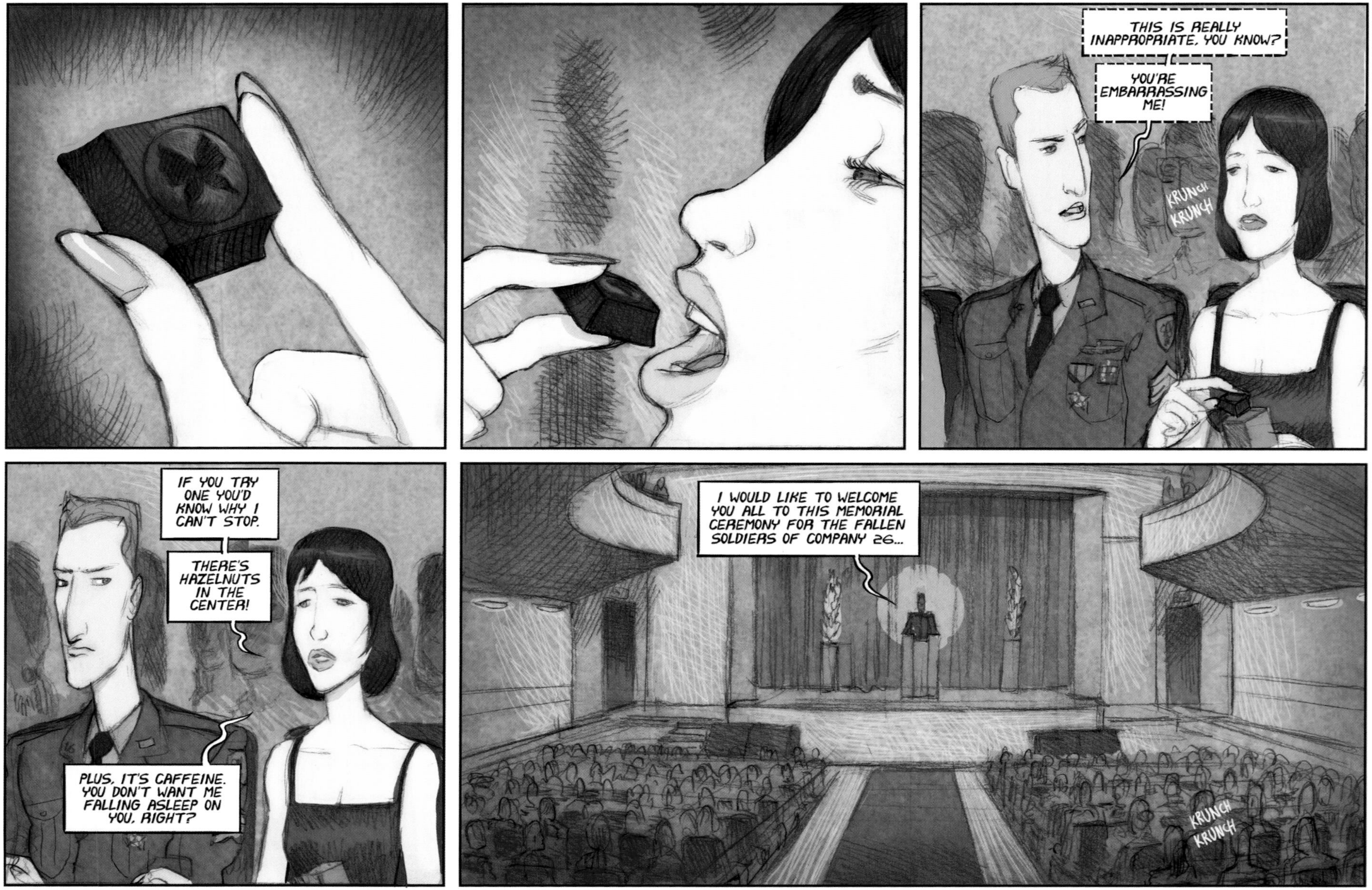
THIS IS REALLY INAPPROPRIATE, YOU KNOW?
YOU'RE EMBARRASSING ME!
KRUNCH KRUNCH
IF YOU TRY ONE YOU'D KNOW WHY I CAN'T STOP.
THERE'S HAZELNUTS IN THE CENTER!
PLUS, IT'S CAFFEINE. YOU DON'T WANT ME FALLING ASLEEP ON YOU, RIGHT?
I WOULD LIKE TO WELCOME YOU ALL TO THIS MEMORIAL CEREMONY FOR THE FALLEN SOLDIERS OF COMPANY 26...
KRUNCH KRUNCH

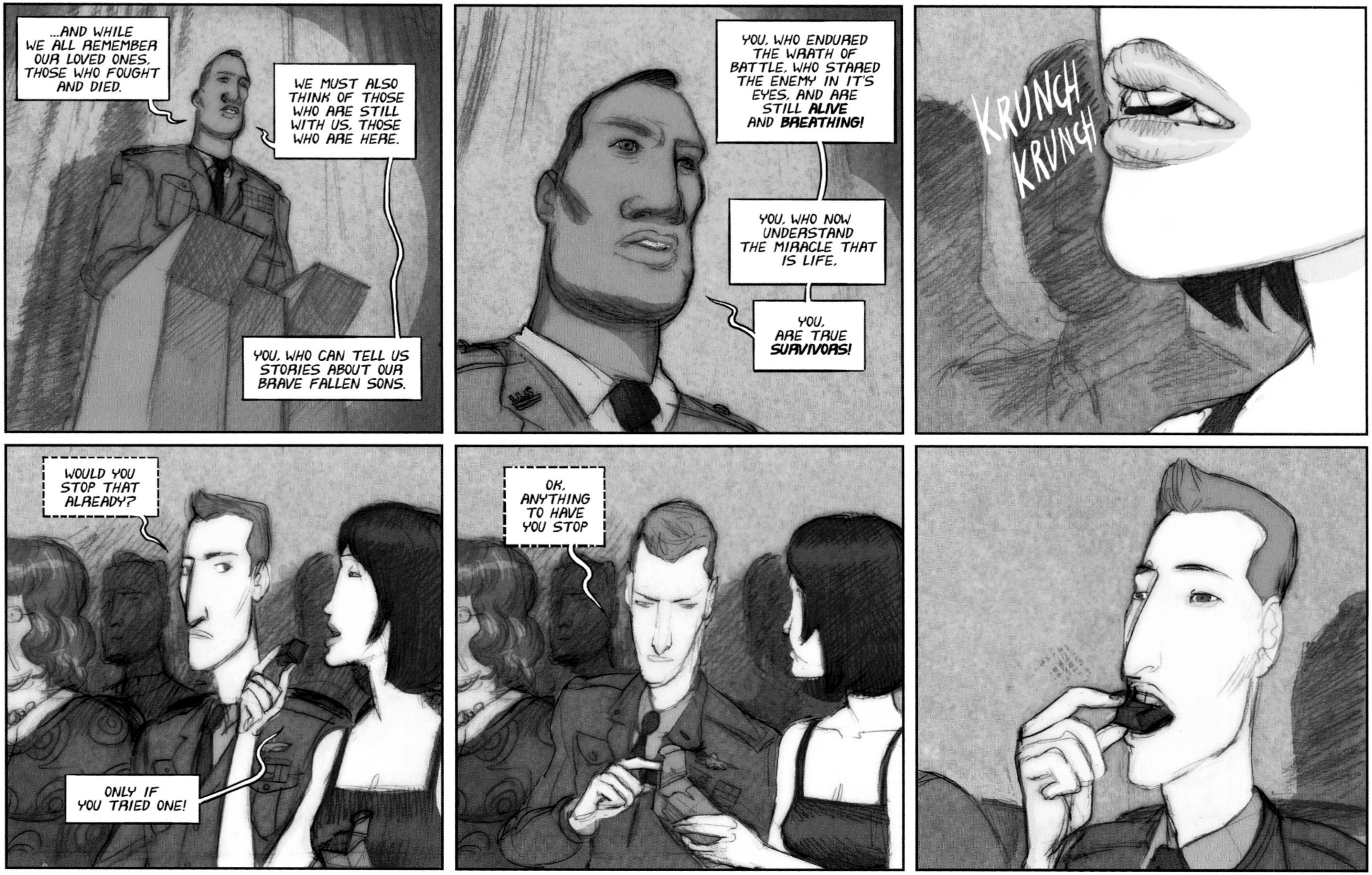
...AND WHILE WE ALL REMEMBER OUR LOVED ONES, THOSE WHO FOUGHT AND DIED.
WE MUST ALSO THINK OF THOSE WHO ARE STILL WITH US, THOSE WHO ARE HERE.
YOU, WHO CAN TELL US STORIES ABOUT OUR BRAVE FALLEN SONS.
YOU, WHO ENDURED THE WRATH OF BATTLE, WHO STARED THE ENEMY IN IT'S EYES, AND ARE STILL ALIVE AND BREATHING!
YOU, WHO NOW UNDERSTAND THE MIRACLE THAT IS LIFE,
YOU, ARE TRUE SURVIVORS!
KRUNCH KRUNCH
WOULD YOU STOP THAT ALREADY?
ONLY IF YOU TRIED ONE!
OK, ANYTHING TO HAVE YOU STOP

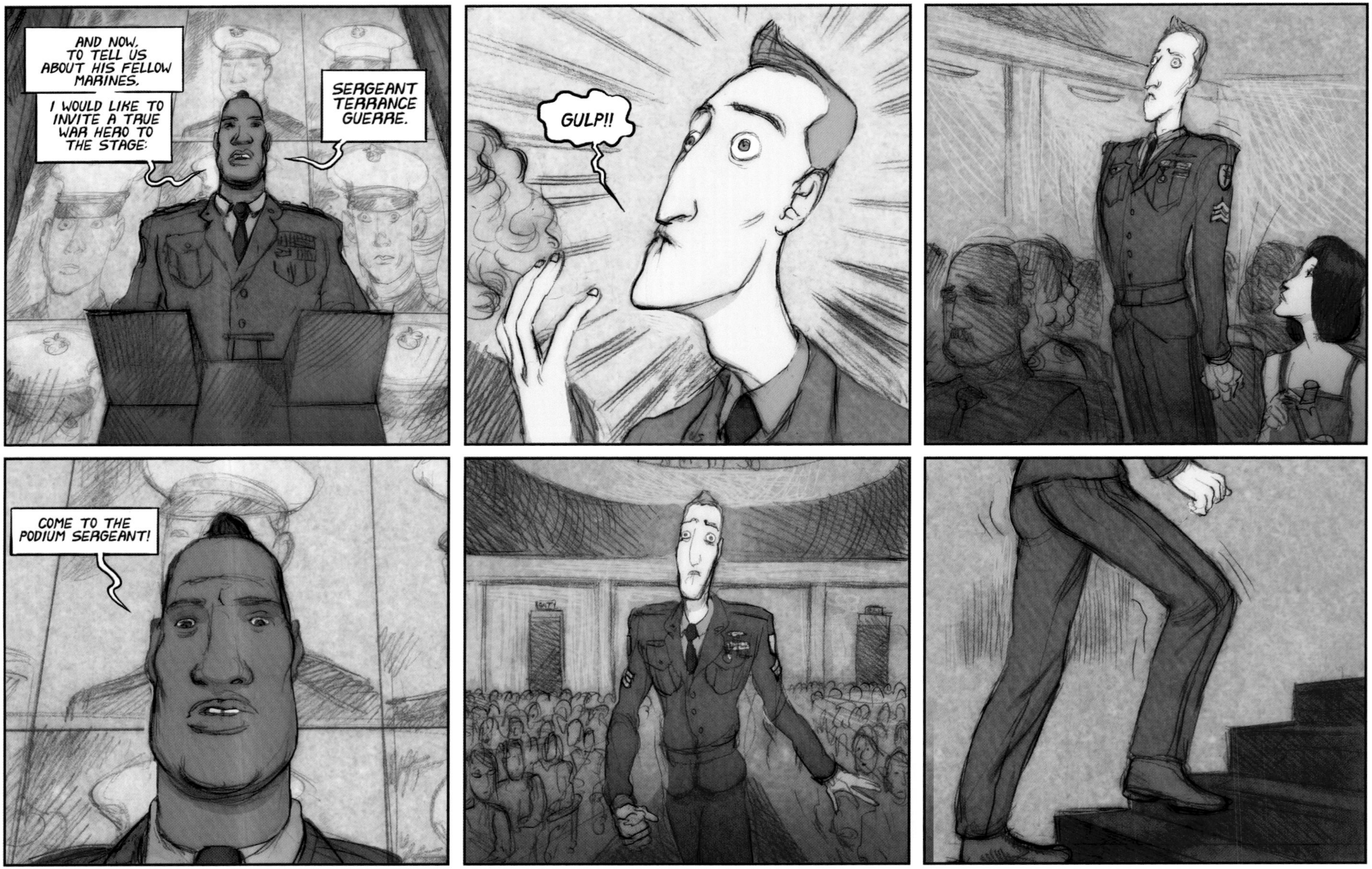
AND NOW, TO TELL US ABOUT HIS FELLOW MARINES,
I WOULD LIKE TO INVITE A TRUE WAR HERO TO THE STAGE:
SERGEANT TERRANCE GUERRE.
GULP!!
COME TO THE PODIUM SERGEANT!

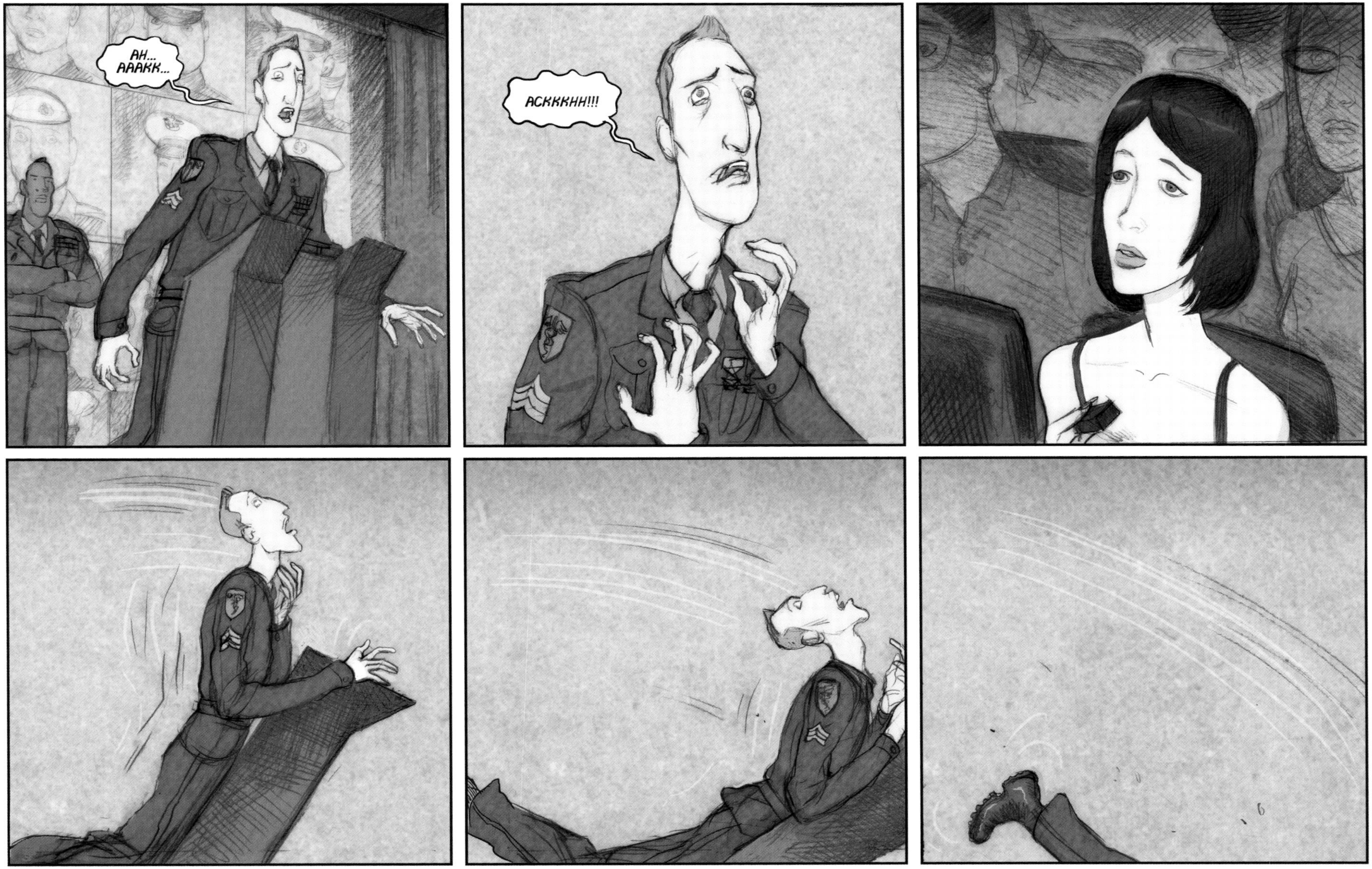
AH... AAAKK...
ACKKKHH!!!

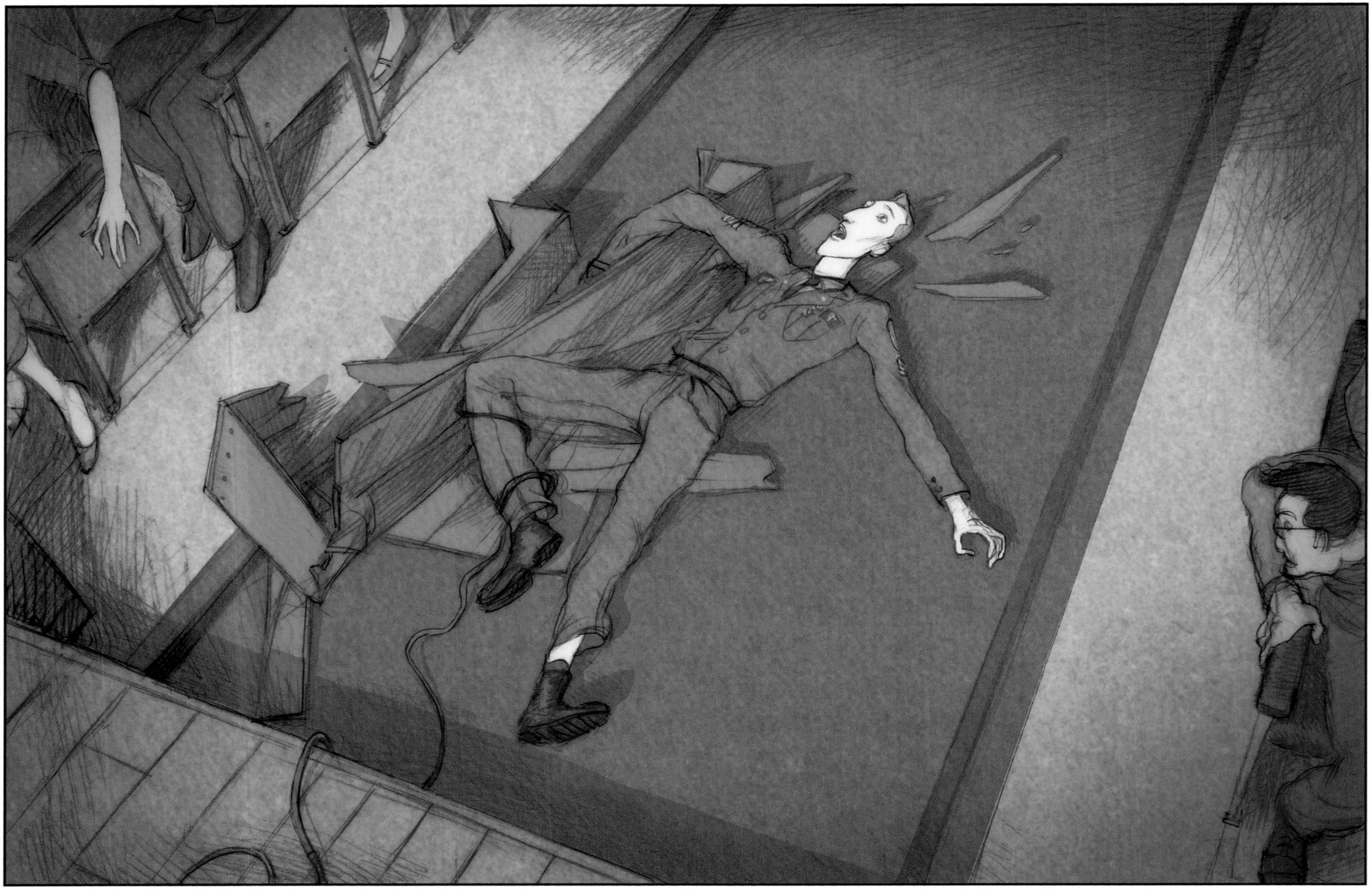

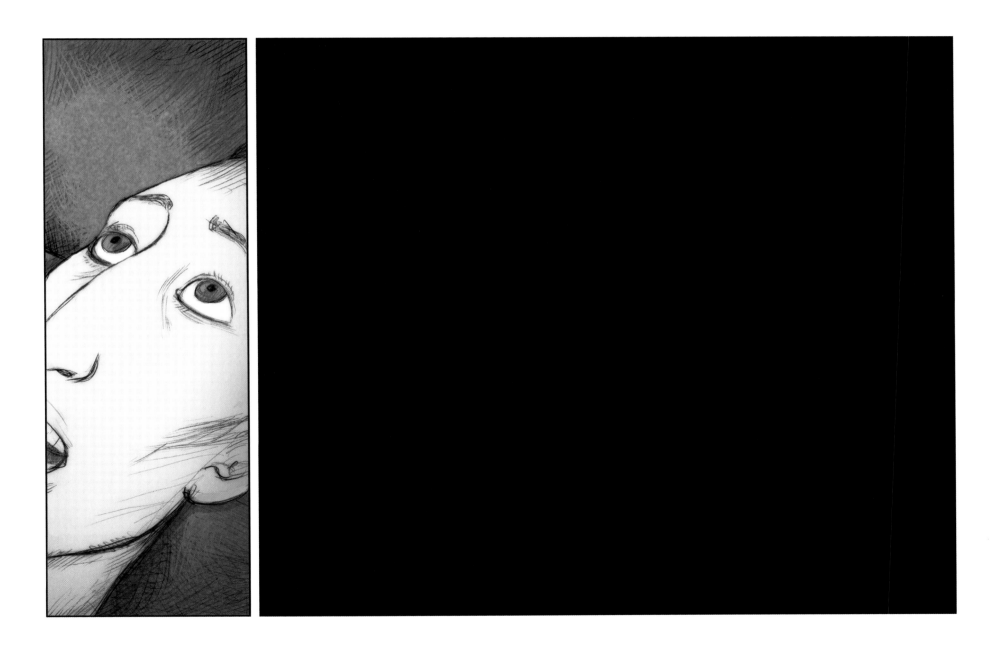

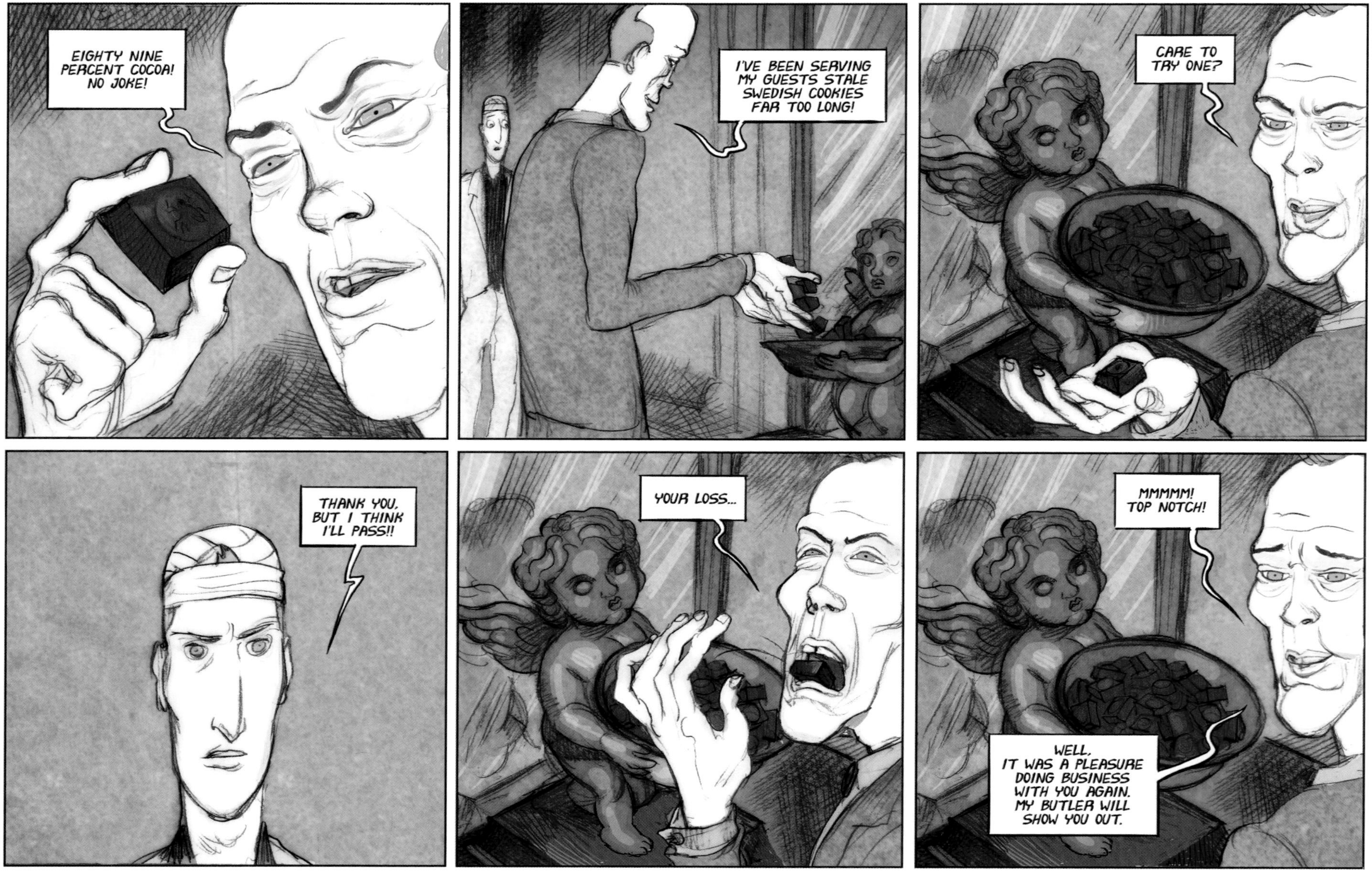
EIGHTY NINE PERCENT COCOA! NO JOKE!
I'VE BEEN SERVING MY GUESTS STALE SWEDISH COOKIES FAR TOO LONG!
CARE TO TRY ONE?
THANK YOU, BUT I THINK I'LL PASS!!
YOUR LOSS...
MMMMM! TOP NOTCH!
WELL, IT WAS A PLEASURE DOING BUSINESS WITH YOU AGAIN. MY BUTLER WILL SHOW YOU OUT.

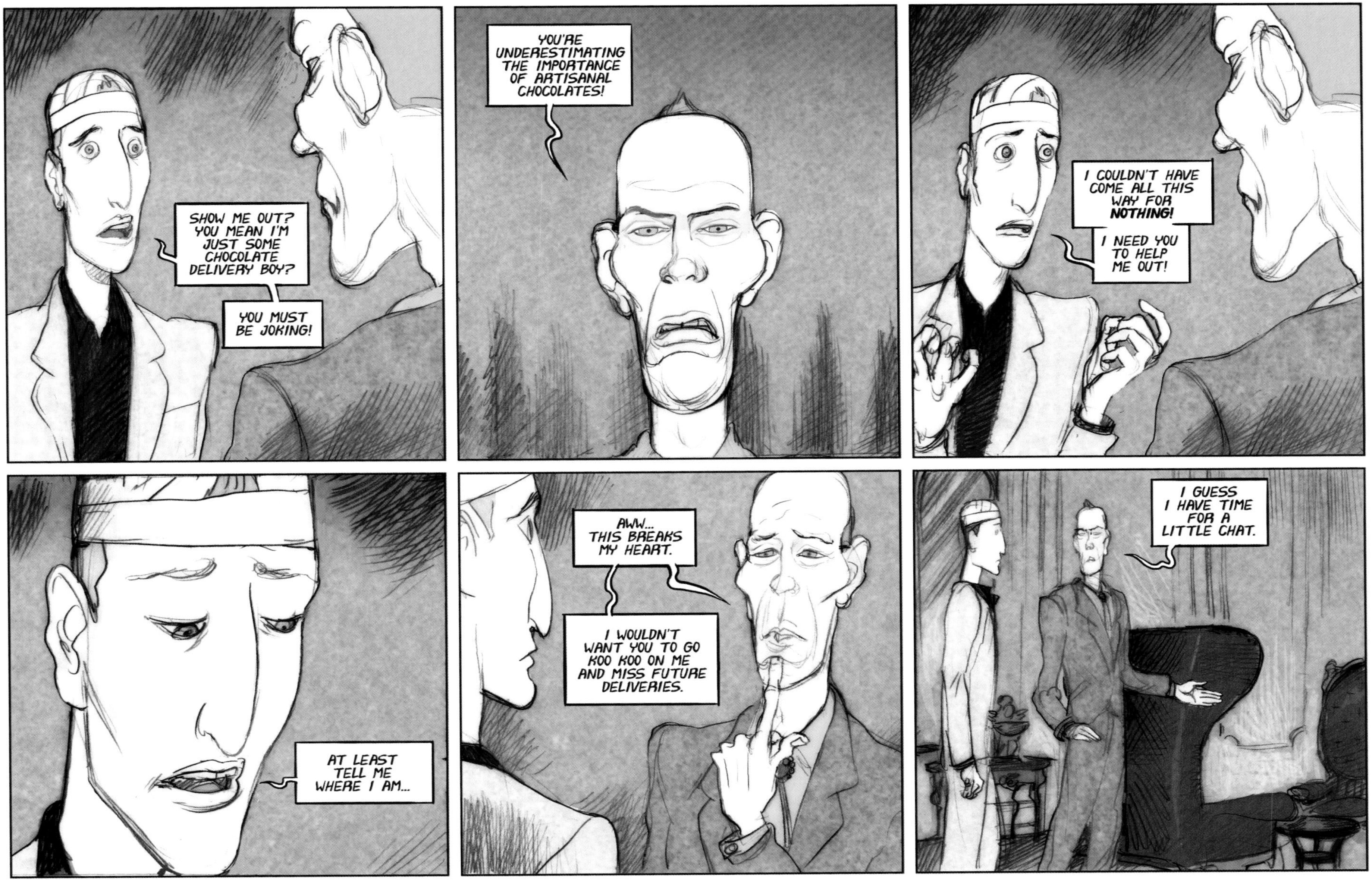
SHOW ME OUT? YOU MEAN I'M JUST SOME CHOCOLATE DELIVERY BOY?
YOU MUST BE JOKING!
YOU'RE UNDERESTIMATING THE IMPORTANCE OF ARTISANAL CHOCOLATES!
I COULDN'T HAVE COME ALL THIS WAY FOR **NOTHING!**
I NEED YOU TO HELP ME OUT!
AT LEAST TELL ME WHERE I AM...
AWW... THIS BREAKS MY HEART.
I WOULDN'T WANT YOU TO GO KOO KOO ON ME AND MISS FUTURE DELIVERIES.
I GUESS I HAVE TIME FOR A LITTLE CHAT.

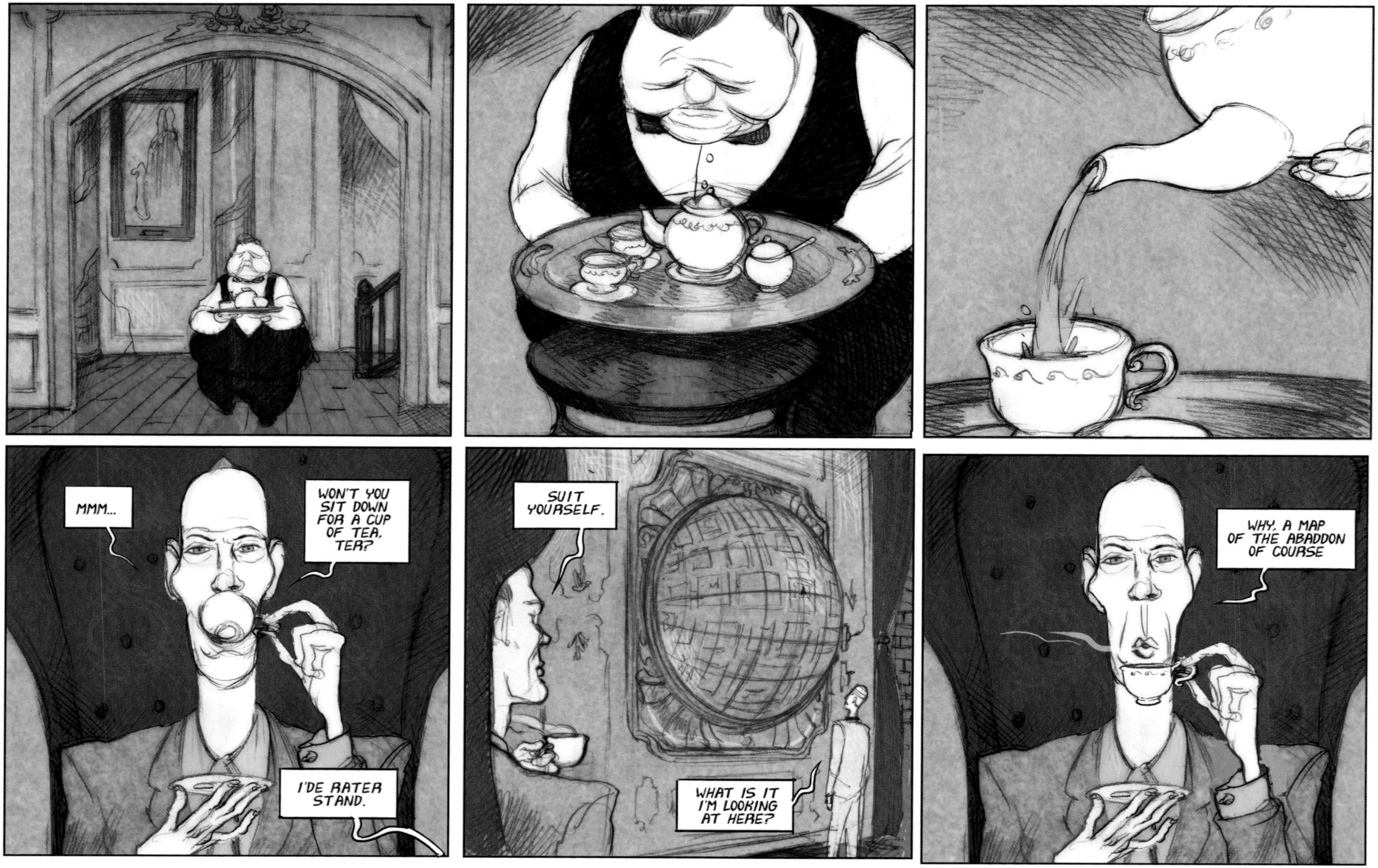
MMM...
WON'T YOU SIT DOWN FOR A CUP OF TEA, TER?
I'DE RATER STAND.
SUIT YOURSELF.
WHAT IS IT I'M LOOKING AT HERE?
WHY, A MAP OF THE ABADDON OF COURSE

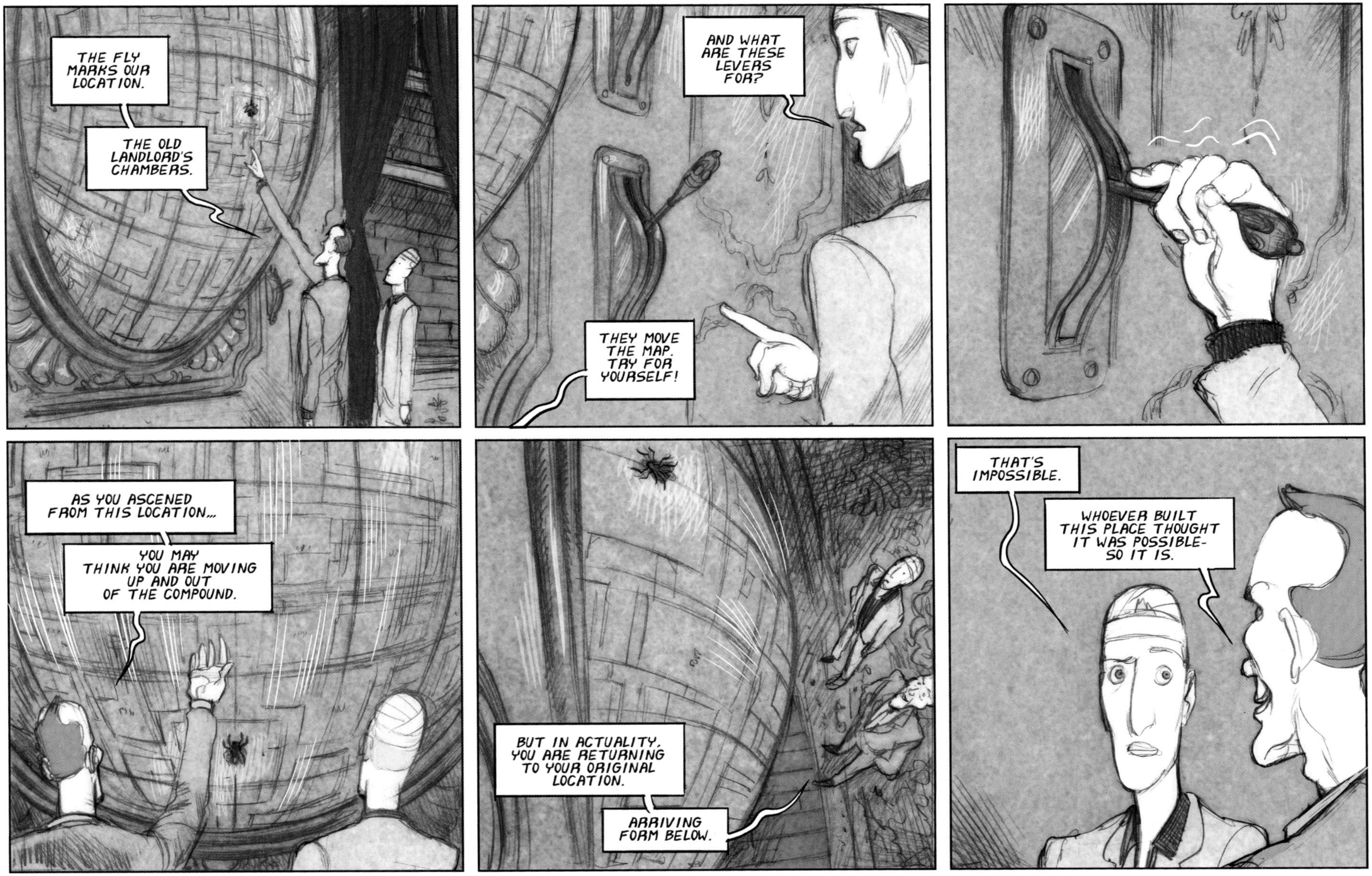
THE FLY MARKS OUR LOCATION.
THE OLD LANDLORD'S CHAMBERS.
AND WHAT ARE THESE LEVERS FOR?
THEY MOVE THE MAP. TRY FOR YOURSELF!
AS YOU ASCENED FROM THIS LOCATION...
YOU MAY THINK YOU ARE MOVING UP AND OUT OF THE COMPOUND.
BUT IN ACTUALITY, YOU ARE RETURNING TO YOUR ORIGINAL LOCATION.
ARRIVING FORM BELOW.
THAT'S IMPOSSIBLE.
WHOEVER BUILT THIS PLACE THOUGHT IT WAS POSSIBLE- SO IT IS.

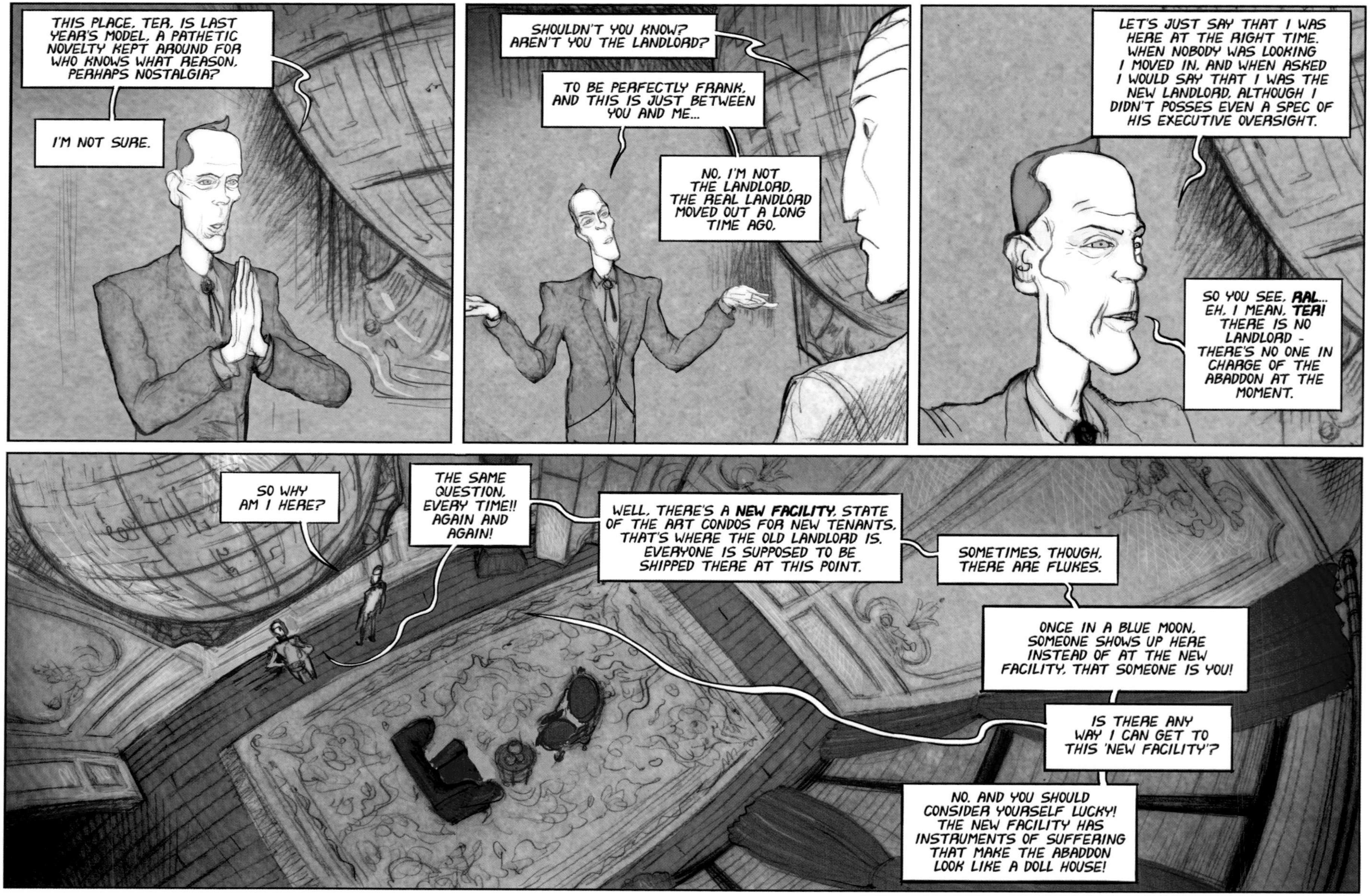

THIS PLACE, TER, IS LAST YEAR'S MODEL, A PATHETIC NOVELTY KEPT AROUND FOR WHO KNOWS WHAT REASON, PERHAPS NOSTALGIA?
I'M NOT SURE.
SHOULDN'T YOU KNOW? AREN'T YOU THE LANDLORD?
TO BE PERFECTLY FRANK, AND THIS IS JUST BETWEEN YOU AND ME...
NO, I'M NOT THE LANDLORD, THE REAL LANDLORD MOVED OUT A LONG TIME AGO,
LET'S JUST SAY THAT I WAS HERE AT THE RIGHT TIME. WHEN NOBODY WAS LOOKING I MOVED IN, AND WHEN ASKED I WOULD SAY THAT I WAS THE NEW LANDLORD, ALTHOUGH I DIDN'T POSSES EVEN A SPEC OF HIS EXECUTIVE OVERSIGHT.
SO YOU SEE, **RAL**... EH, I MEAN, **TER**! THERE IS NO LANDLORD - THERE'S NO ONE IN CHARGE OF THE ABADDON AT THE MOMENT.
SO WHY AM I HERE?
THE SAME QUESTION, EVERY TIME!! AGAIN AND AGAIN!
WELL, THERE'S A **NEW FACILITY**, STATE OF THE ART CONDOS FOR NEW TENANTS, THAT'S WHERE THE OLD LANDLORD IS. EVERYONE IS SUPPOSED TO BE SHIPPED THERE AT THIS POINT.
SOMETIMES, THOUGH, THERE ARE FLUKES.
ONCE IN A BLUE MOON, SOMEONE SHOWS UP HERE INSTEAD OF AT THE NEW FACILITY, THAT SOMEONE IS YOU!
IS THERE ANY WAY I CAN GET TO THIS 'NEW FACILITY'?
NO. AND YOU SHOULD CONSIDER YOURSELF LUCKY! THE NEW FACILITY HAS INSTRUMENTS OF SUFFERING THAT MAKE THE ABADDON LOOK LIKE A DOLL HOUSE!

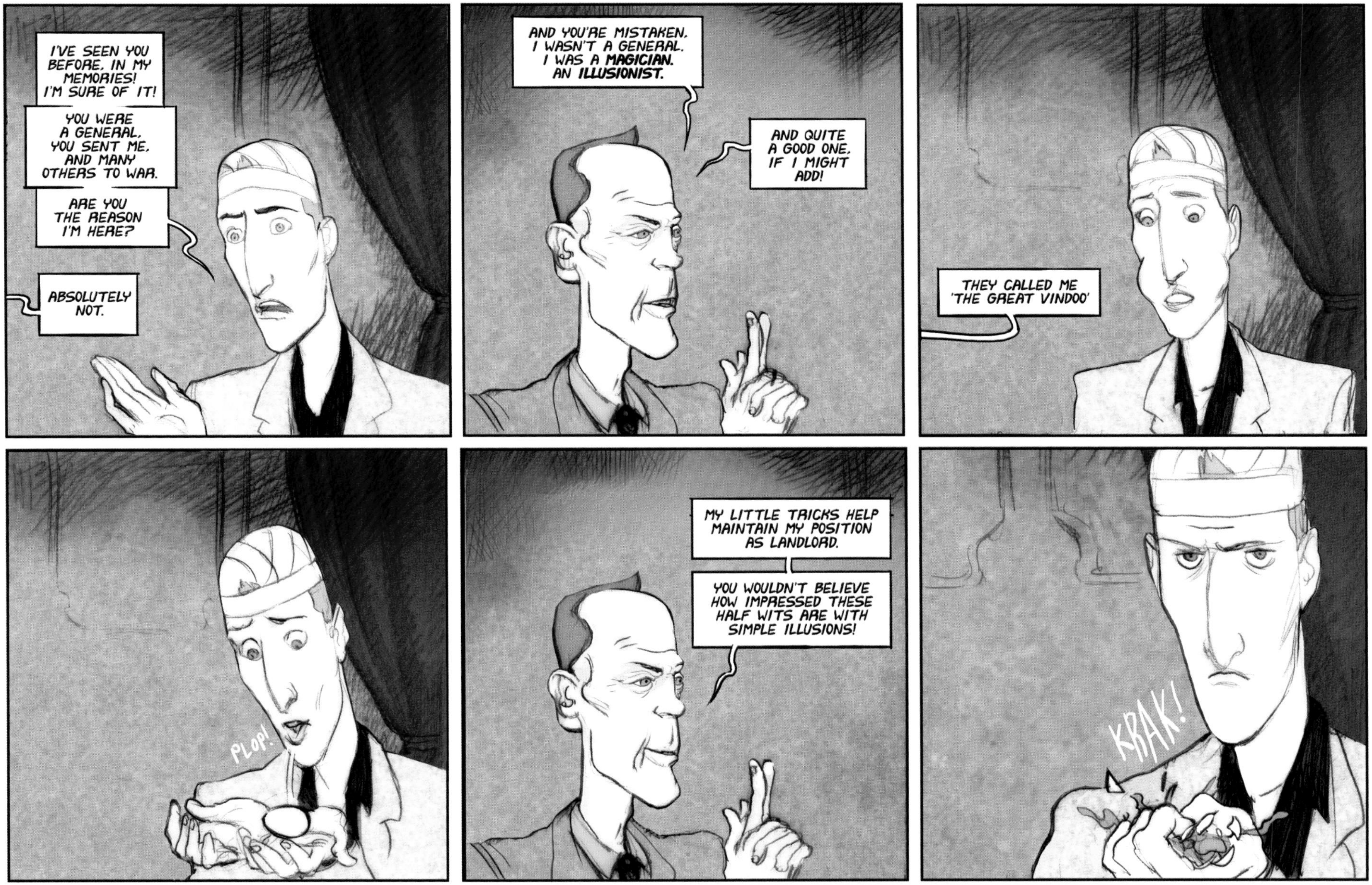
I'VE SEEN YOU BEFORE, IN MY MEMORIES! I'M SURE OF IT!
YOU WERE A GENERAL, YOU SENT ME, AND MANY OTHERS TO WAR.
ARE YOU THE REASON I'M HERE?
ABSOLUTELY NOT.
AND YOU'RE MISTAKEN. I WASN'T A GENERAL. I WAS A **MAGICIAN.** AN **ILLUSIONIST.**
AND QUITE A GOOD ONE, IF I MIGHT ADD!
THEY CALLED ME 'THE GREAT VINDOO'
PLOP!
MY LITTLE TRICKS HELP MAINTAIN MY POSITION AS LANDLORD.
YOU WOULDN'T BELIEVE HOW IMPRESSED THESE HALF WITS ARE WITH SIMPLE ILLUSIONS!
KRAK!

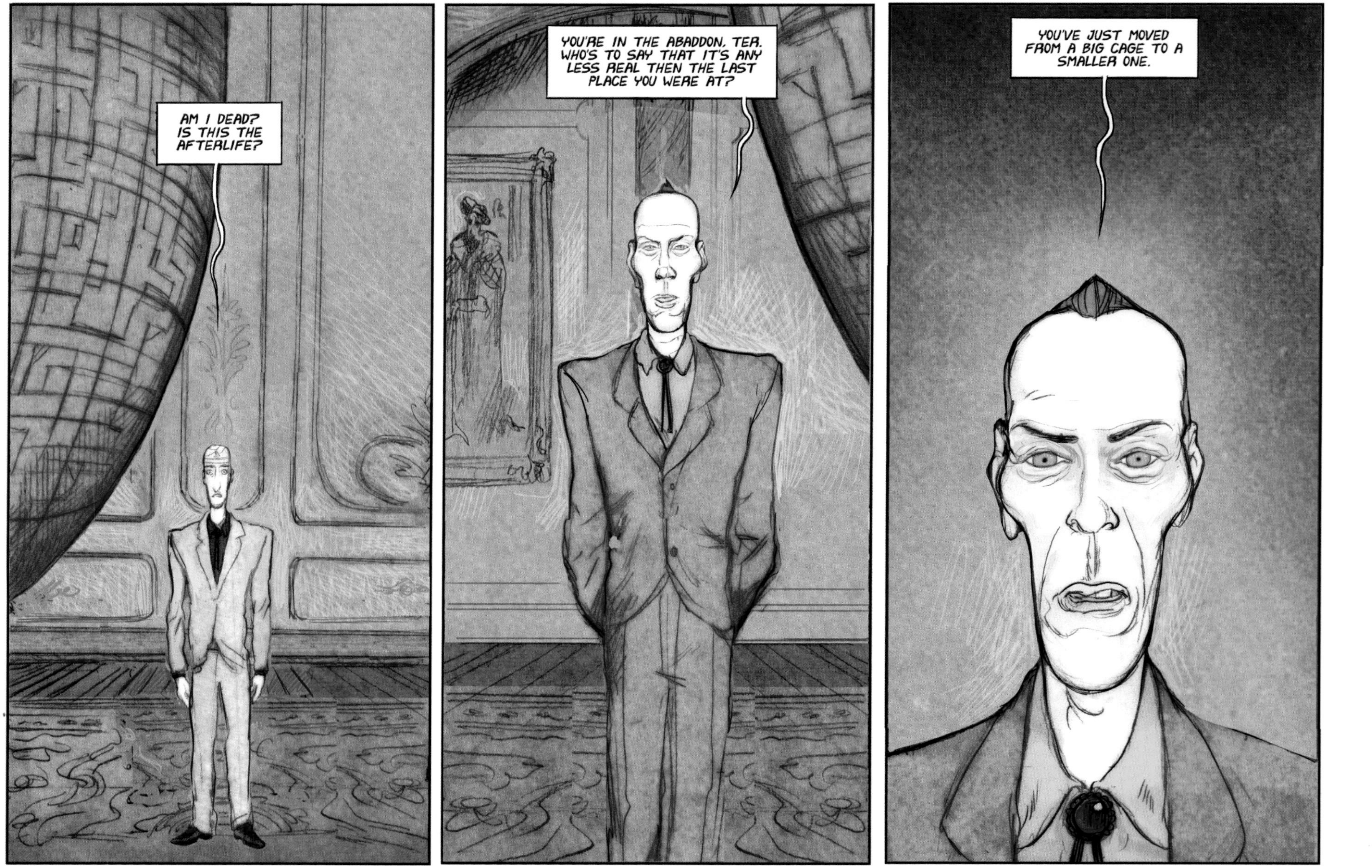
AM I DEAD? IS THIS THE AFTERLIFE?
YOU'RE IN THE ABADDON, TER. WHO'S TO SAY THAT IT'S ANY LESS REAL THEN THE LAST PLACE YOU WERE AT?
YOU'VE JUST MOVED FROM A BIG CAGE TO A SMALLER ONE.

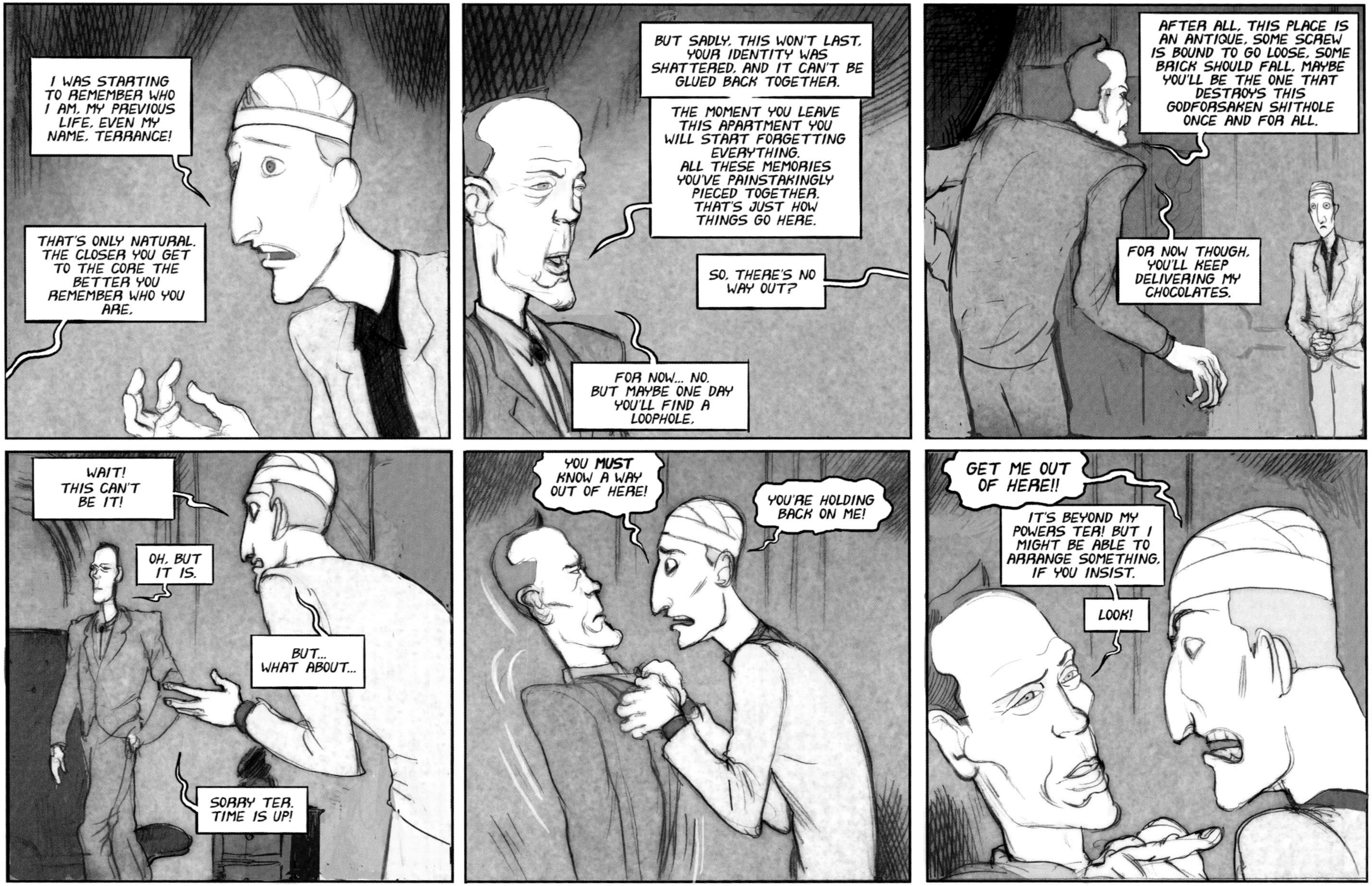
I WAS STARTING TO REMEMBER WHO I AM. MY PREVIOUS LIFE. EVEN MY NAME. TERRANCE!
THAT'S ONLY NATURAL. THE CLOSER YOU GET TO THE CORE THE BETTER YOU REMEMBER WHO YOU ARE.
BUT SADLY, THIS WON'T LAST. YOUR IDENTITY WAS SHATTERED, AND IT CAN'T BE GLUED BACK TOGETHER.
THE MOMENT YOU LEAVE THIS APARTMENT YOU WILL START FORGETTING EVERYTHING. ALL THESE MEMORIES YOU'VE PAINSTAKINGLY PIECED TOGETHER. THAT'S JUST HOW THINGS GO HERE.
SO, THERE'S NO WAY OUT?
FOR NOW... NO. BUT MAYBE ONE DAY YOU'LL FIND A LOOPHOLE.
AFTER ALL, THIS PLACE IS AN ANTIQUE. SOME SCREW IS BOUND TO GO LOOSE, SOME BRICK SHOULD FALL. MAYBE YOU'LL BE THE ONE THAT DESTROYS THIS GODFORSAKEN SHITHOLE ONCE AND FOR ALL.
FOR NOW THOUGH, YOU'LL KEEP DELIVERING MY CHOCOLATES.
WAIT! THIS CAN'T BE IT!
OH, BUT IT IS.
BUT... WHAT ABOUT...
SORRY TER. TIME IS UP!
YOU **MUST** KNOW A WAY OUT OF HERE!
YOU'RE HOLDING BACK ON ME!
GET ME OUT OF HERE!!
IT'S BEYOND MY POWERS TER! BUT I MIGHT BE ABLE TO ARRANGE SOMETHING, IF YOU INSIST.
LOOK!

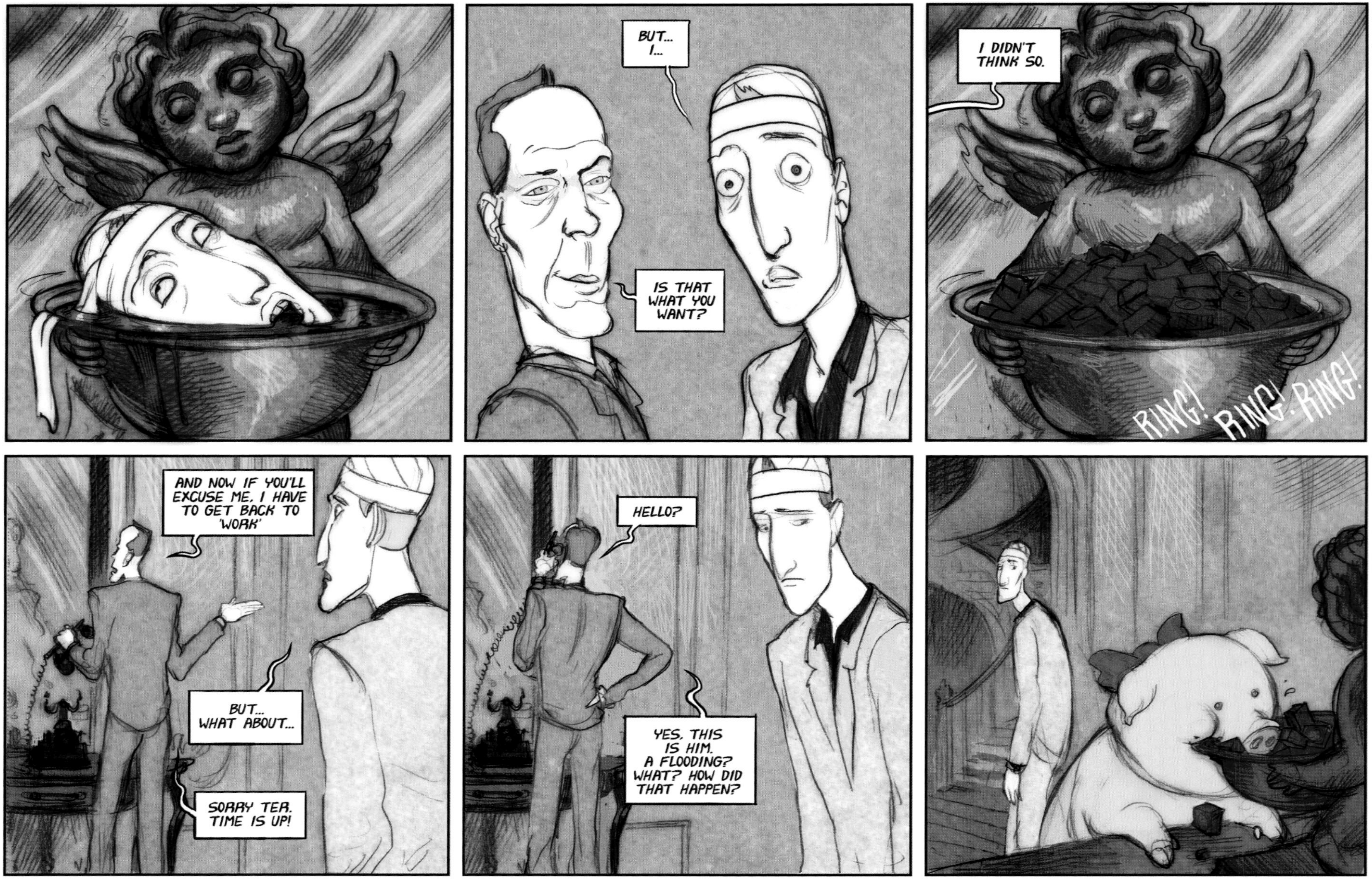
BUT... I...
IS THAT WHAT YOU WANT?
I DIDN'T THINK SO.
RING! RING! RING!
AND NOW IF YOU'LL EXCUSE ME, I HAVE TO GET BACK TO 'WORK'
BUT... WHAT ABOUT...
SORRY TEB. TIME IS UP!
HELLO?
YES, THIS IS HIM. A FLOODING? WHAT? HOW DID THAT HAPPEN?

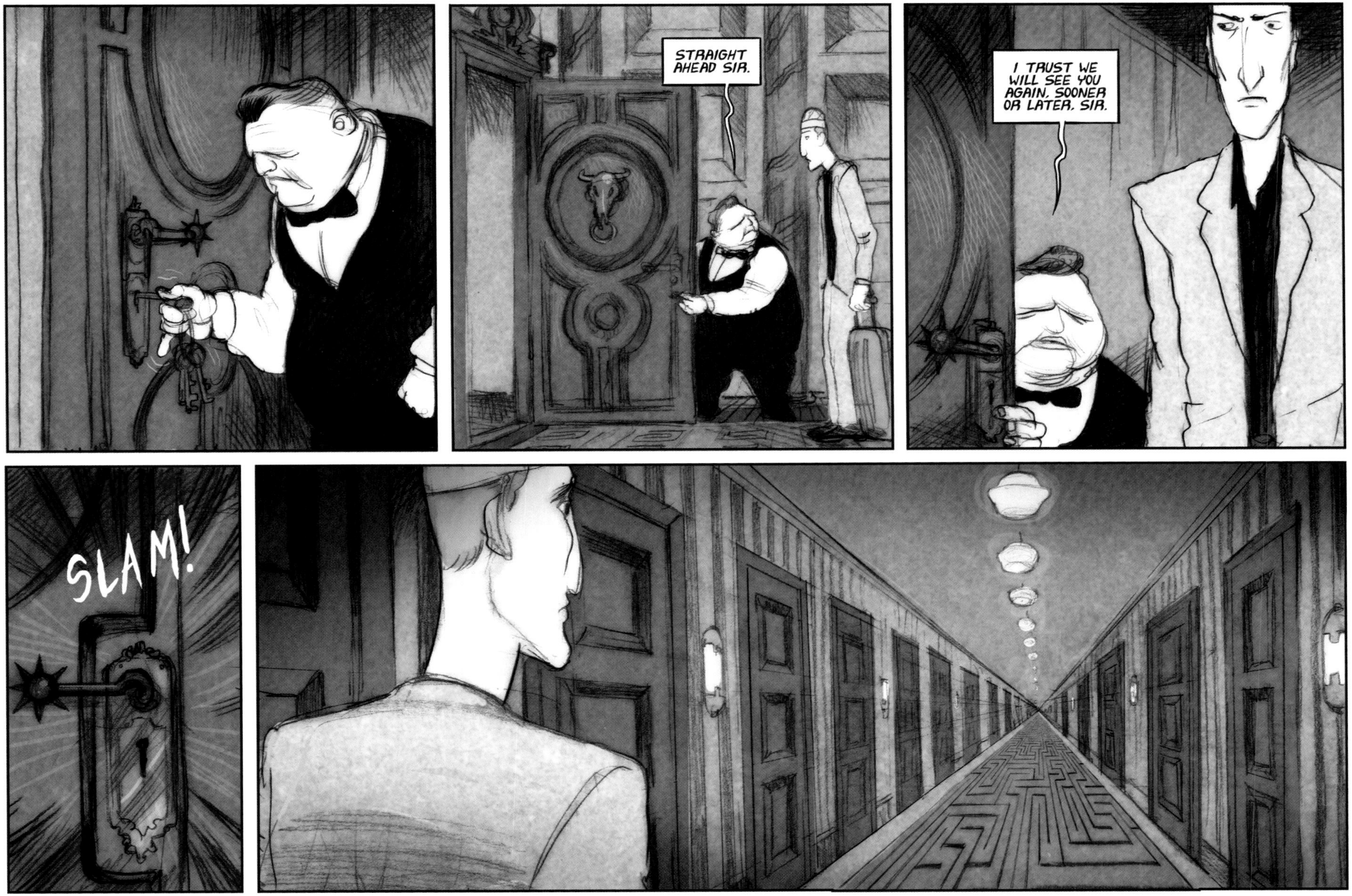
STRAIGHT AHEAD SIR.
I TRUST WE WILL SEE YOU AGAIN, SOONER OR LATER, SIR.
SLAM!

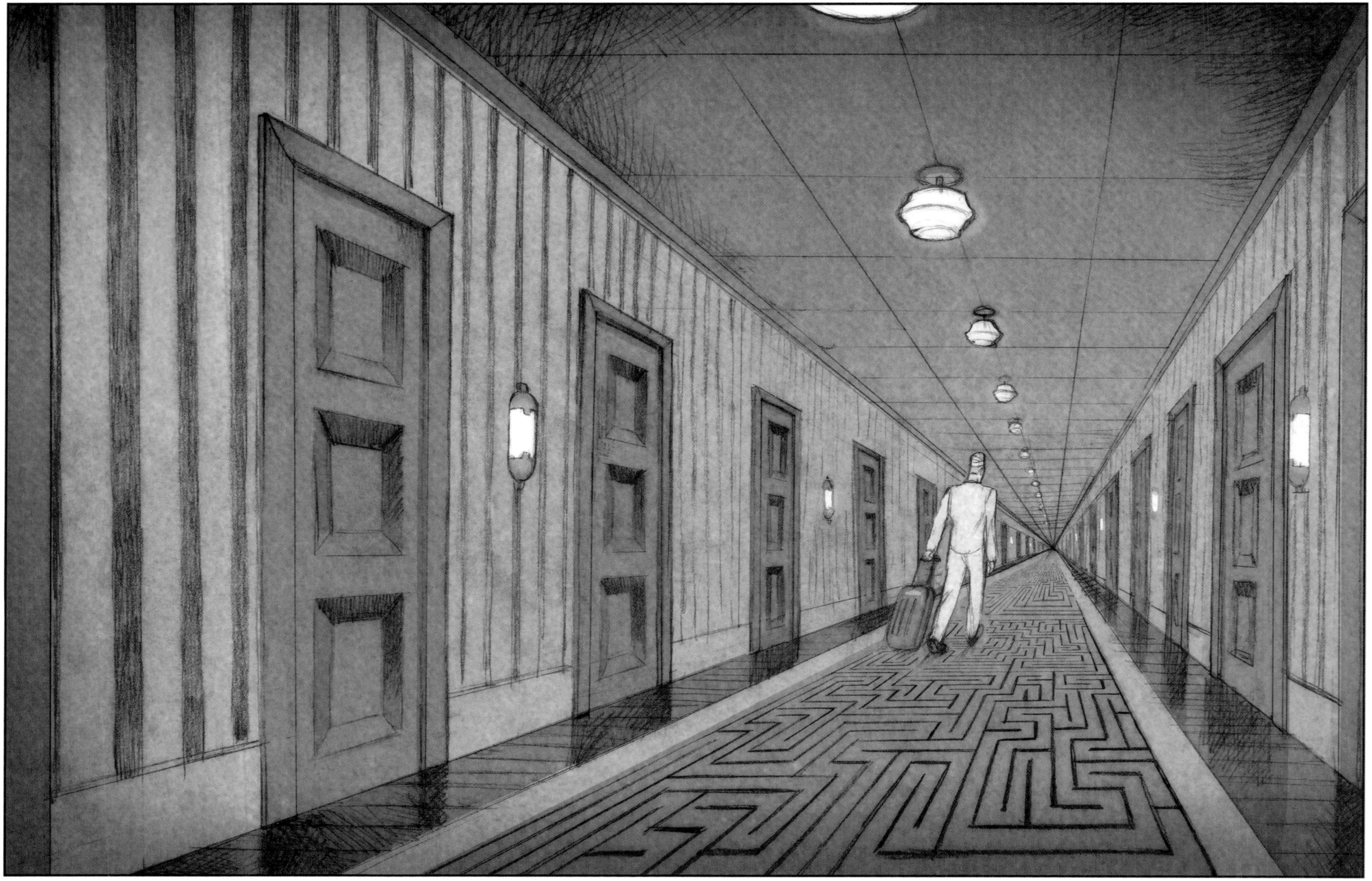

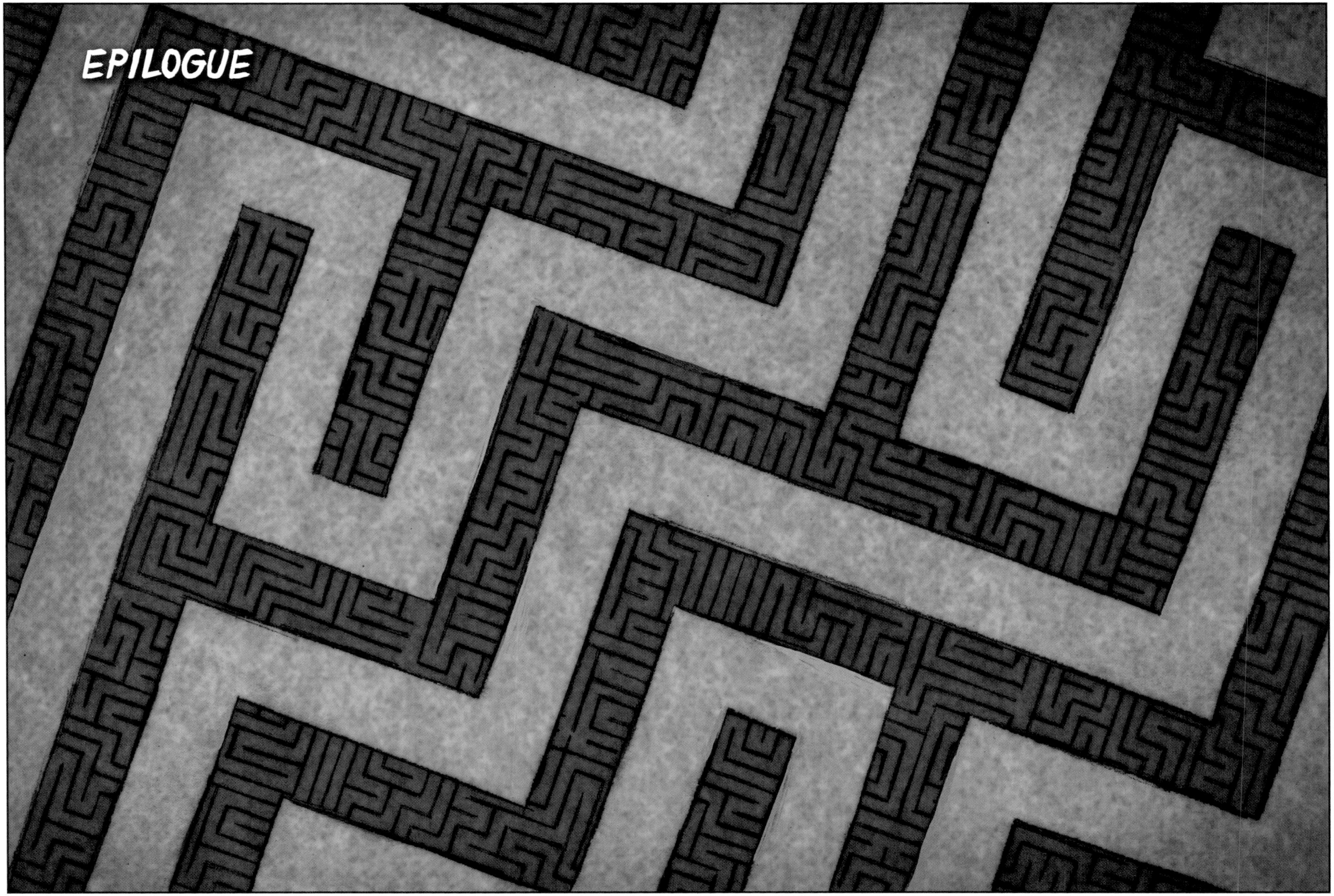
EPILOGUE

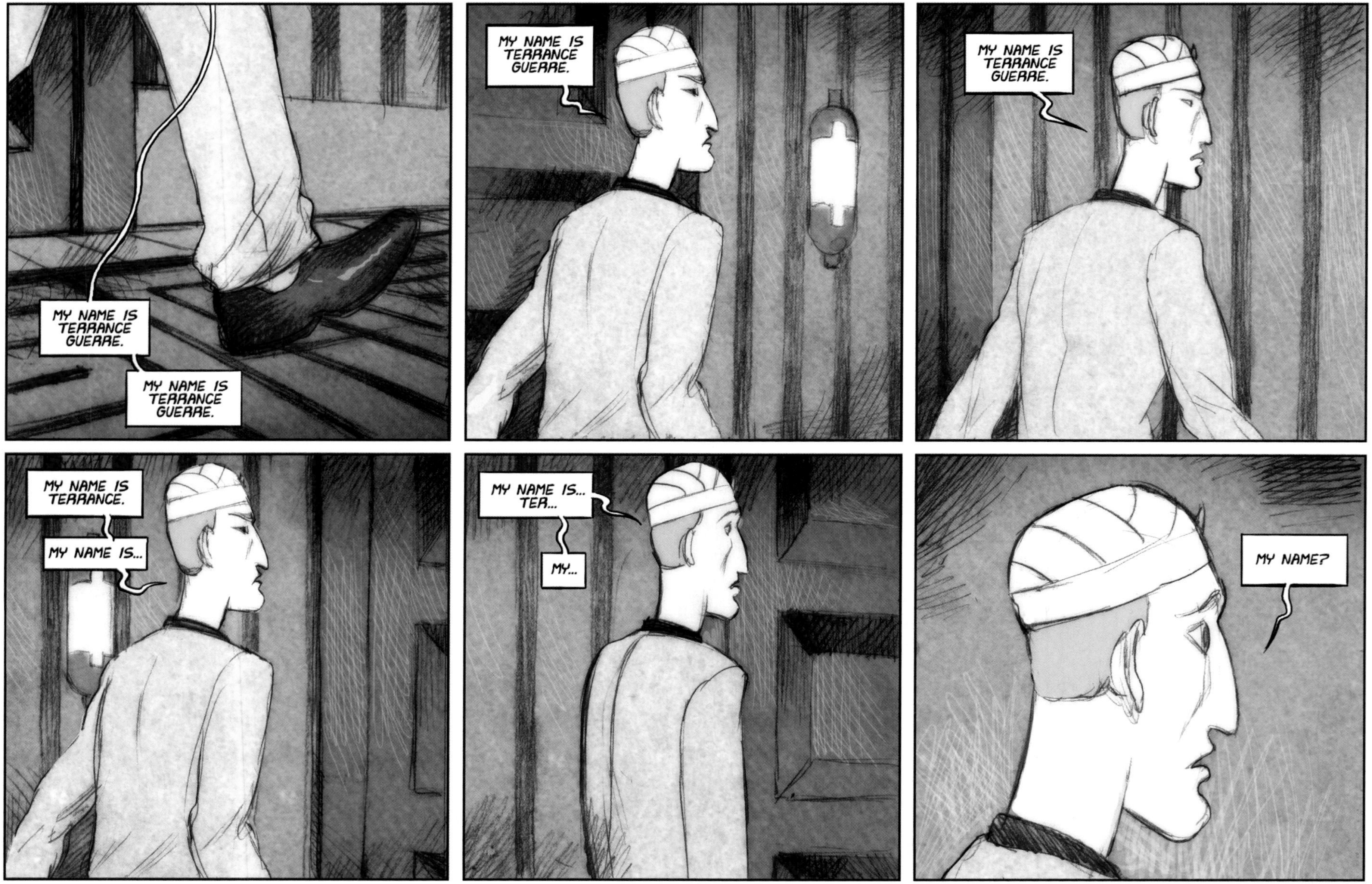
MY NAME IS TERRANCE GUERRE.
MY NAME IS TERRANCE GUERRE.
MY NAME IS TERRANCE GUERRE.
MY NAME IS TERRANCE GUERRE.
MY NAME IS TERRANCE.
MY NAME IS...
MY NAME IS... TER...
MY...
MY NAME?

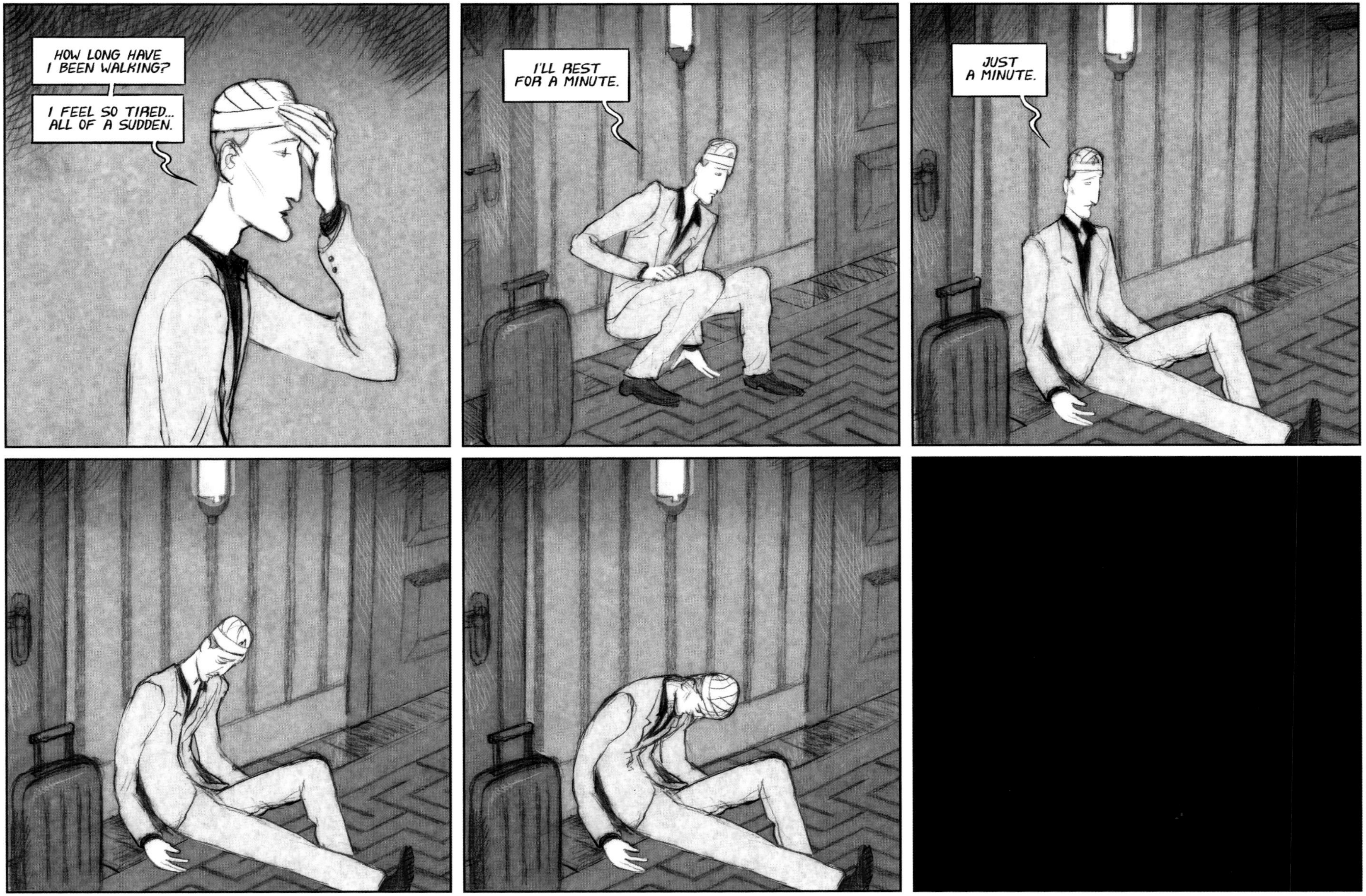
HOW LONG HAVE I BEEN WALKING?
I FEEL SO TIRED... ALL OF A SUDDEN.
I'LL REST FOR A MINUTE.
JUST A MINUTE.

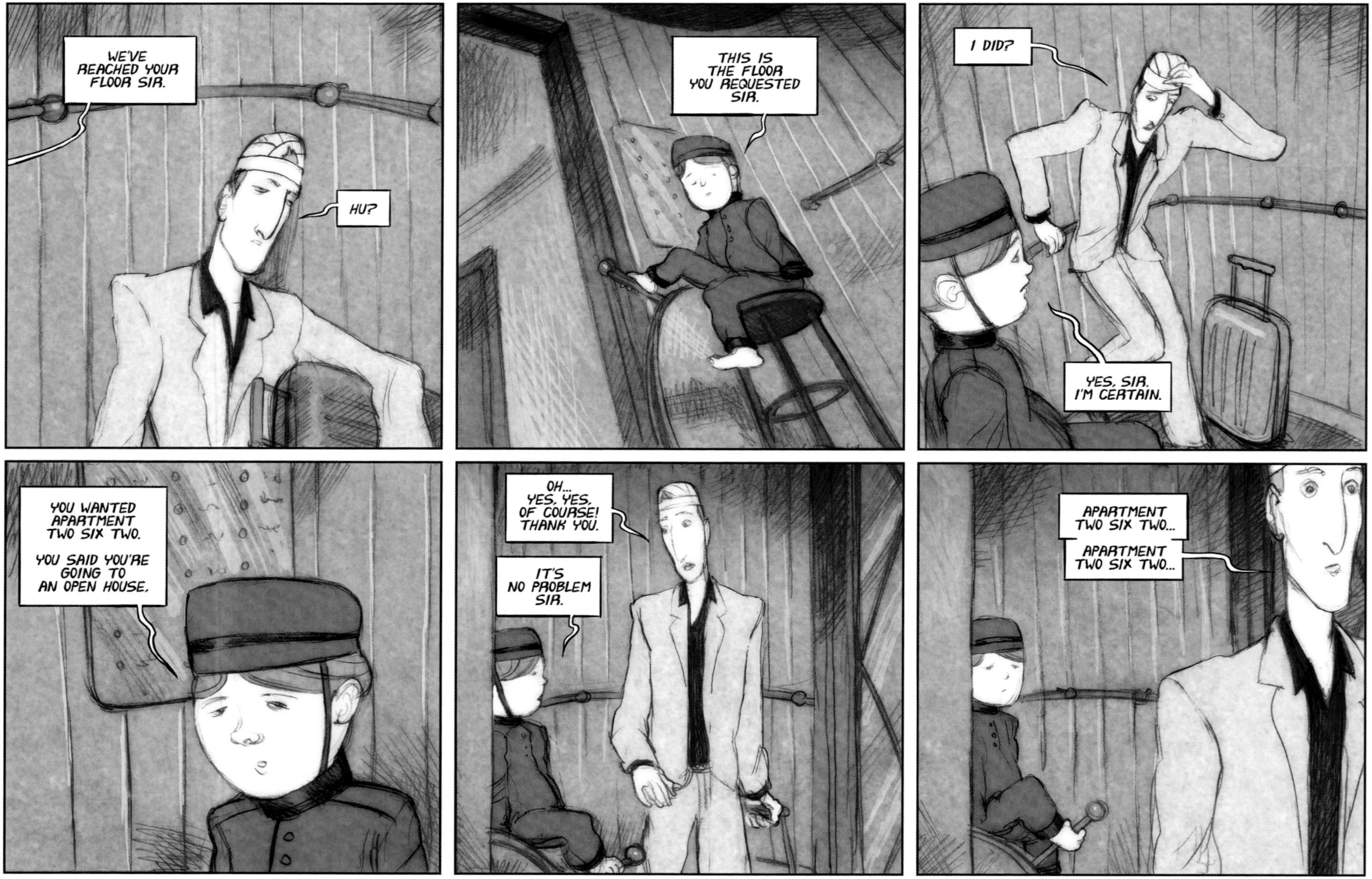
WE'VE REACHED YOUR FLOOR SIR.
HU?
THIS IS THE FLOOR YOU REQUESTED SIR.
I DID?
YES, SIR. I'M CERTAIN.
YOU WANTED APARTMENT TWO SIX TWO.
YOU SAID YOU'RE GOING TO AN OPEN HOUSE.
OH... YES, YES, OF COURSE! THANK YOU.
IT'S NO PROBLEM SIR.
APARTMENT TWO SIX TWO...
APARTMENT TWO SIX TWO...

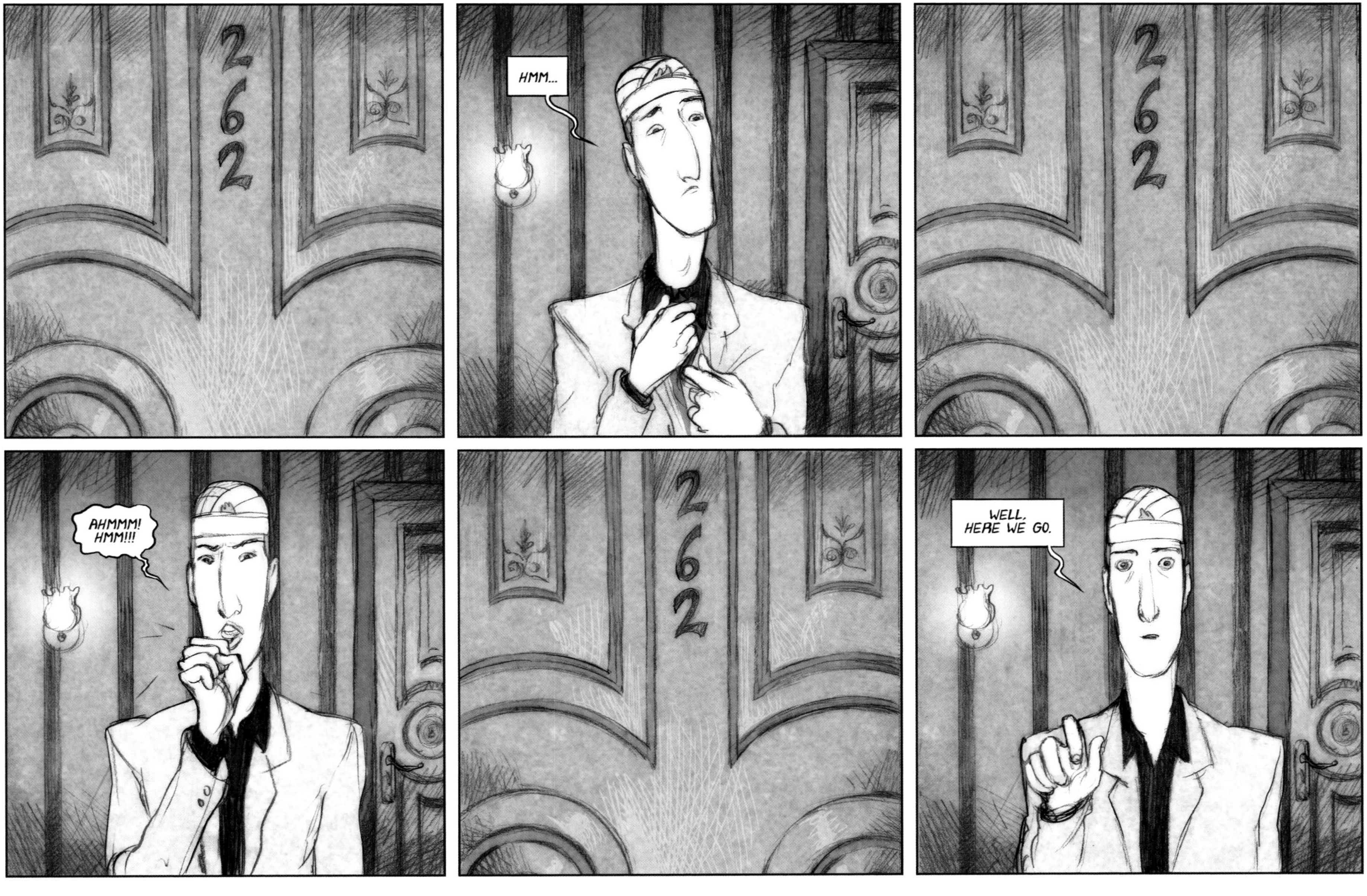
262
HMM...
262
AHMMM! HMM!!!
262
WELL, HERE WE GO.

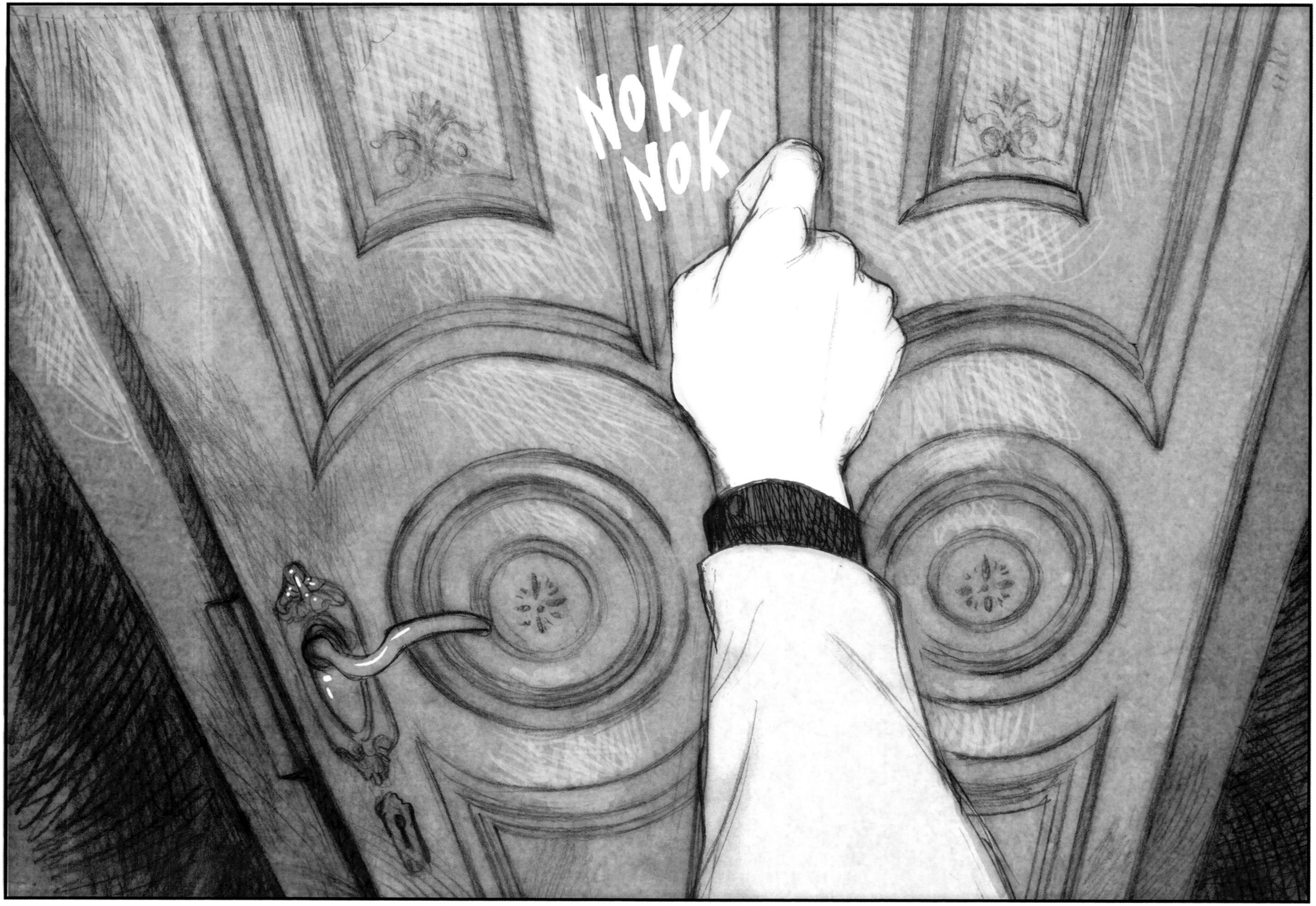
NOK NOK

END

The author would like to thank:

Raymond Sohn, Victor Cayro, Aaron Cansler, Agaton Strom, Sarah Namias,
Andrew Lucido, Austin English, Lizz Hickey, Bill Kartalopoulos,
Mary Abramson, Nicolas Grivel, Niko Henrichon, George Moore, Sean Bloch,
Bérengère Orieux, Fano Loco,
and everyone who participated in The Abaddon Kickstarter.